Study Skills for Science, Engineering and Technology Students

PEARSON

Education

We work with leading authors to develop the
strongest educational materials in study skills,
bringing cutting-edge thinking and best
learning practice to a global market.

Under a range of well-known imprints, including
Longman, we craft high quality print and
electronic publications which help readers to understand
and apply their content, whether studying or at work.

To find out more about the complete range of our
publishing, please visit us on the World Wide Web at:
www.pearsoned.co.uk

Study Skills for Science, Engineering and Technology Students

Pat Maier, Anna Barney and Geraldine Price

PEARSON
Longman

Harlow, England • London • New York • Boston • San Francisco • Toronto • Sydney • Singapore • Hong Kong
Tokyo • Seoul • Taipei • New Delhi • Cape Town • Madrid • Mexico City • Amsterdam • Munich • Paris • Milan

Pearson Education Limited
Edinburgh Gate
Harlow
Essex CM20 2JE
England

and Associated Companies throughout the world

Visit us on the World Wide Web at:
www.pearsoned.co.uk

First published 2009

ISBN: 978-0-273-72073-7

British Library Cataloguing-in-Publication Data
A catalogue record for this book is available from the British Library

Library of Congress Cataloging-in-Publication Data
A catalog record for this book is available from the Library of Congress

10 9 8 7 6 5 4 3 2 1
13 12 11 10 09

Typeset in 10/12 Helvetica by 30
Printed in Great Britain by Henry Ling Ltd., at the Dorset Press, Dorchester, Dorset.

The publisher's policy is to use paper manufactured from sustainable forests.

Contents

THIS BOOK WILL HELP YOU:

1 Manage yourself

2 Improve your work

3 Apply your skills

4 Develop your technical writing

Contents

Foreword

The authors of this study skills book would like to congratulate you on deciding to go on to further study; you will find it a true 'rite of passage' for your own personal development both socially and professionally.

Your time in Higher Education should be seen as an opportunity to develop yourself through study. The authors have designed the chapters to enable you to get the most out of your science, engineering or technical subjects. There are plenty of activities in the book to help you focus on key intellectual skills to improve not only your studies, but also your approach to being a professional in later life. If you can develop a self-reflective and 'can do' approach, this will mark you out as an independent lifelong learner, a vital attribute for anyone today.

Don't forget to update your personal development planners (PDPs) as you go through the book, as this will help you make your learning explicit and become a good aide-memoire when you come to that important interview.

Finally, we would like to wish you all the best with your studies and beyond.

Pat Maier
Anna Barney
Geraldine Price

How to use this book

Why this book?

Academic study skills are a set of skills that set you up as a lifelong learner within and beyond your official study period. The tone of the book is one of personal development, encouraging you to reflect on your skills, develop a 'can do' attitude and identify what you need to do to improve.

The book can be used by individual students or tutors wishing to embed these skills in the curriculum and link into personal development planners. We are living through a period of rapid change where our knowledge needs updating regularly throughout our lives in order to remain current. Lifelong learning skills therefore become important and enable us to improve and keep up to date throughout our working life.

For you – the student

This book explores the challenges of university life showing how you can move from a novice to an experienced learner in your field. The challenges for you are at many levels: your engagement with the subject, your ability to manage your time and your motivation to take responsibility for your own learning. Those of you who take up the challenges and develop a deeper understanding of your subject are more likely to succeed and do well. The book helps you to take control of your own learning, with self-management being an overarching skill underlying in each of the chapters. Self-knowledge and reflection will improve your grades and give you the qualities employers seek. It is an interactive book which prompts and guides you to more effective and efficient working habits.

To help you do this, each chapter provides *activities* which enable you to develop your skills. The activities in the book are not a once-and-for-all activity and should be revisited throughout your stay at university as your skills develop. It is important, therefore, that you reflect on your stages of learning by completing the *personal development planner* (PDP) section at the end of each chapter. These mini PDPs can be used with your tutor, or linked into your department's own PDP to encourage you to move ever forward and onward.

It is advisable to start with the first chapter as this will give you that broad-brush view on getting started in Higher Education. If you are already in later years, you will also gain from the focus in this chapter.

For you – the tutor

Tutors wanting to use this book may be working centrally as learning advisers or with a department as a subject tutor. As a learning adviser you may be working individually with students, outside their curriculum or collaboratively with subject tutors. Whichever role you have, this activity-focused book could be adapted to your own circumstances and slot in easily with other material.

The authors, as subject and skills tutors themselves, have developed this material from their own practice and tested the material with their students. Some suggestions for using the book are as follows:

- *Induction for first years*. It is useful to include information from. 'Learning in Higher Education' which gives a broad-brush view on moving into Higher Education. The chapters on stress and time management are also useful for adaptation in induction sessions, at undergraduate and postgraduate level.

- *Personal development planners*. Every chapter encourages students to reflect on the skills they are developing. You may expect students to carry out some of the activities in this book for initial proof of their reflective ability.

- *Skills application*. For science, engineering and technology students this has been addressed through a discussion of why we have laboratory work and how we can conduct ourselves safely and effectively in this environment. In addition, they are given a framework for approaching mathematical and creative problem-solving activities that enhances their ability to apply their developing knowledge.

- *Presentation skills*. The chapters on teamwork and presenting their work have proved very useful for giving students guidance on poster preparation, oral presentations and working in real teams.

- *Learning outcomes.* Each of the chapters conforms to academic practice and includes learning outcomes. There is no assessment, but informal reflective exercises at the beginning and the end could serve to 'assess' increased awareness.

Getting the most out of the book

Each chapter opens with a *navigation page* giving a brief overview of the sections within the chapter along with the learning outcomes. This means that you can easily dip into the section and activities you want. Each chapter begins and ends with your own reflection on how you feel your skills are developing. It is valuable to reflect on your skills prior to reading the chapter and then see how you have increased your awareness as a result of working through the activities. These mini PDPs are intended to be used as part of your institution's own system.

Some of the *activities* require you to take stock of your own skills while others give you valuable practice, i.e. putting into operation what you have read. Towards the end of each chapter you will find a *summary map* combining all the parts of the chapter into a visible whole. Finally, each chapter also gives you advice on where you might go for further help, if you still feel unsure of your performance.

Unlock your potential

You have the potential to do well, obtain good grades and be employed in an area that interests you. So, use this book as part of your strategy for personal development and realise your potential.

> *In times of change, learners inherit the Earth, while the learned find themselves beautifully equipped to deal with a world that no longer exists.*
>
> Eric Hoffer, an important social thinker/writer of the twentieth century

Additional student support is available at: **www.smartstudyskills.com**

Learning in Higher Education

Learning in Higher Education is, and should be, challenging. The challenges for you are at many levels: your engagement with the subject, your ability to manage your time and your motivation to take responsibility for your own learning. Those who take up the challenges and develop a deep understanding of their subject are more likely to succeed and do well. Those of you who do the minimum work and take a 'surface' approach to learning are more likely to fail or drop out. Although your tutors and advisers are there to give you the support you need, the decision to take this responsibility, to reflect and act on your development, is yours and yours alone. Take it and succeed.

> *We don't receive wisdom; we must discover it for ourselves after a journey that no one can take for us or spare us.*
> Marcel Proust (1871–1922), French novelist

In this chapter you will learn how to:

1. recognise what makes you a proficient learner
2. understand what plagiarism is and how to avoid it
3. identify the key documents that describe your programme and units
4. know how to start thinking about your own employability.

USING THIS CHAPTER

Estimate your current levels of confidence. At the end of the chapter you will have the chance to reassess these levels and incorporate this into your personal development planner (PDP). Mark between 1 (poor) and 5 (good) for the following:

I understand what I can do to become a proficient learner.	I know what plagiarism is.	I understand the key documents describing my course.	I know why I should consider employability throughout my studies.

Date: _____

1 Become a proficient learner

You may not think this, but being a good learner is a skill. It is not just about sitting in front of your book and reading and hoping something will 'stick', or about completing yet another problem sheet or exam. Of course, you can go through your studies just doing this. However, your learning will be fairly shallow and often crammed in before the next exam. In order to become interested and proficient in the topic you are studying, you will need to go a bit deeper and your ability to do this makes you a skilled and lifelong learner, a learner that not only knows 'what', but also 'how' and 'why'.

Knowing 'how' and 'why' is increasingly important as knowledge has a shelf life, like so many other things. This is referred to as the **half-life of knowledge** and, to give you a flavour of this, 95% of the drugs in use in 1978 were unheard of in 1950 (Smith, 1978, p. 914). Environmental Science for example probably has a half-life of 1 to 3 years, especially in relation to environmental law and aspects of climate change. Since knowledge is an economic resource in a knowledge economy, having up-to-date knowledge is vital for a company. Employers therefore will want employees that are prepared to be lifelong learners. Having the skills to do this, with study skills being a prime example, becomes an important employability skill.

Your degree of motivation for your subject will determine how you study and how much effort you put in. If you are not very motivated you will more than likely be someone who will memorise enough facts to get you through the coursework and exams; you will be what is called a 'surface learner', take little time to reflect on your learning, have a 'make-do' attitude to your studies and have difficulty managing your commitments. As you can imagine, this is not the ideal student, or the ideal employee. This lack of motivation is very evident both to your tutors and to potential employers.

Therefore, learning is something that is not restricted to your time at university. It is more than likely going to be part of you for the rest of your life. In order to do this you need to:

- be responsible for your own learning
- know yourself as a learner
- reflect on your learning.

Be responsible for your own learning

The first thing you must do is to get to know yourself as a learner. It is important you are honest with yourself and your mode of learning in the past may have served you well, but now you need to make a step change in order to get the most out of your studies. Activity 1, below, indicates some of the features that characterise dependent and independent learning. As you can see, the 'independent learner' shows a greater responsibility for his or her own learning.

ACTIVITY 1 Your motivation to learn

At this point in time where would you place yourself?

Your learning	A	B	Generally me (A or B)
Motivation to learn	I am motivated to get my degree and as long as it is a respectable grade I don't mind. I expect my tutors to provide me with interesting material to keep me on track. I will only do work if I am going to get assessed. If I get a bad degree grade it is probably due to a bad course.	You expect a well-organised course and good teaching, but you know this is a two-way process and you have to find out information yourself in order to complete assignments as well as seek support from various people. You know your final degree will reflect not only the course organisation and teaching, but also the amount of work you have put in yourself.	
Learning resources	The content and resources are determined by my tutors and I limit myself to what is provided for me. I think exams are passed by memorising facts and I have a good memory.	Although my tutors have given me guidance on the resources I need, I generally seek out my own resources. I really want to understand the principles and concepts of my subject, not just a load of facts.	

▶

Your learning	A	B	Generally me (A or B)
Time	Tutors tend to set coursework deadlines too close together, so when I try to get the work done I am having to cram everything in at the same time to meet these deadlines. I prefer working to tight deadlines and this means I leave all my work to the last minute. It would be better if tutors spread out the deadlines as that would suit me better.	Although we get coursework deadlines set close together, we are told in advance and I try where possible to set my own staggered deadlines so that I am not working on all coursework at the same time.	
Reflection on learning	I find little opportunity in my studies to do this and we are generally not encouraged to do it either, so why bother? I had to do this in school and feel that it should be left there.	I am keen to reflect on what and how I learn. Tutorials and seminars are good for this as discussion helps me see what I understand and don't understand. I always want to know how I can improve.	

Are you predominantly A or B? You may have guessed that A represents a dependent learner while B an independent learner.

How independent and responsible do you feel you are with regard to your learning? What might you do to improve this? Write three things below. Read the remainder of this chapter and identify the later chapters you think could be relevant to you.

1.

2.

3.

NOTE Your tutors can only do so much. It is up to you to be prepared to take full advantage of what is on offer.

Know yourself as a learner

At this stage of your studies you are really preparing yourself for work and part of that, as indicated earlier, is about being a lifelong, independent learner. Increasingly employers will expect you to learn on the job, take further study or follow a continuing professional development programme. Being able therefore to reflect on how best you learn, on the skills you are acquiring and on improvements you need to make will be vital as you progress your career. Take a look at some of the relevant later chapters in areas you feel you could do with checking.

What kind of learner are you?

In Chapter 5, 'Working in a real team', you are asked to identify the kind of learner you feel you are based on the learning styles proposed by two psychologists, Peter Honey and Alan Mumford (1992):

An activist: you like to learn by doing things. You are happier with project work, and all kinds of active learning. You are less happy reading long papers, analysing data and sitting in lectures.	*A reflector:* you are more cautious and like to weigh up all the issues before acting. When you make a decision, it is thought through. You are probably happy to work on a project, if you are given time to digest all the facts before making a decision. You dislike having work dumped on you and get worried by tight deadlines.
A pragmatist: you like taking theories and putting them into practice and you need to see the benefit and relevance of what you are doing. If you are learning something you feel has no practical value, you lose interest. You may want to ask your tutor 'why are we learning this?' If you are a student who says 'I don't like this course as it is all theory' then your learning preference is probably 'pragmatist' or 'activist'.	*A theorist:* you like to understand what is behind certain actions and enjoy working through issues theoretically and in a well-structured way and whether you apply it or not doesn't interest you so much. You may be the one to ask questions as to why and how something occurs. You dislike unstructured sessions and dislike it when you are asked to reflect on some activity or say what you felt about it.

Each of these learning styles represents a point on our learning cycle proposed by David Kolb in 1975 (Figure A1.1). The cycle illustrates that when we learn something we need concrete experience, time to observe and reflect on abstract concepts and theories before we apply these ideas in new situations. We can start this learning cycle at any point, and as a learner we are happier in some of the stages than others; it is this that gives us our learning preferences.

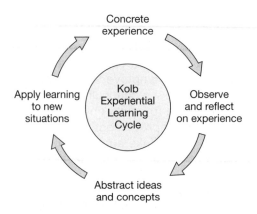

Figure A1.1 Kolb's experiential learning cycle
Adapted from Smith (2001)

Which part of the learning cycle do you feel more comfortable with and how might this affect your learning? Can you find ways of working around other aspects of the learning cycle that you don't feel so comfortable with? To be a successful learner you will need to be able at least to function on all points of the learning cycle, even though you may be happier in one area.

Move from novice to expert

Knowing how novices see things and how experts see things is a helpful shorthand in understanding how we learn. No one is expecting you to become an expert overnight, but you will see your tutors as experts and wonder why you can't understand things that appear so simple to them, and, vice versa, they may be puzzled why you can't understand something. But just remember: you are probably much better on mobile phone technology than any of your lecturers!

How often have you felt that you just don't know what your brain can do with yet another piece of information? These pieces seem to be all unconnected. You feel frustrated as you panic trying to remember it all. This is because you haven't yet been able to process this information into chunks and store it away ready for retrieval when you want it. The more you learn, reflect on and revise a subject, the more you will start to see patterns in the information and you can start to group things. At that point, these chunks of information become knowledge and you can then start applying it.

One of the major things that experts do that you won't do as a novice is find order and patterns in information and they do this by chunking pieces of information together; they know how to make these chunks and identify the patterns. This means that, unlike novices, they are not working with discrete pieces of information, they already know how it fits into a larger jigsaw. Experts therefore have that bigger picture.

One way to help you integrate these pieces of information, and start to build the bigger picture, is to draw a concept map (see Activity 2). This technique was developed by Joseph Novak in the 1960s and is a visual method of showing linkages between ideas, concepts or topics. Each topic is linked by a line that indicates the nature of that relationship. See the example below.

Concept maps can be drawn as hierarchies, flow charts or networks (as below). If you prefer a more linear approach, use an indented list that indicates at least a hierarchical relationship. However, a list on its own is less useful as you need to see the relationships between things.

Concept maps enable you to see the relationship between concepts and how chunks of things belong together. You may find this difficult at the beginning of a topic but if you persist it will pay off and you will develop an integrated view of your topic and start to mimic the experts. Also, for each topic you are revising for an exam, finalise your revision with a concept map or a list. Then use this for quick revision prior to the exam.

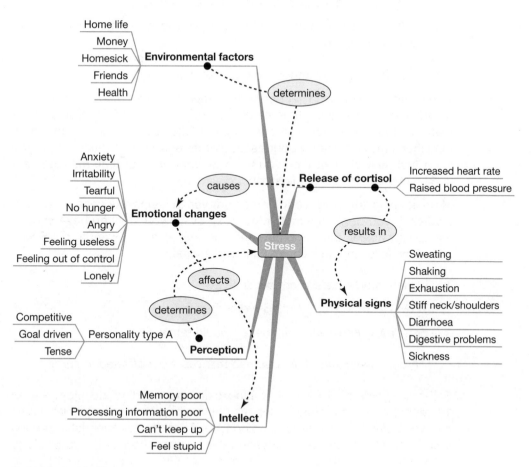

Produced using MindManager

ACTIVITY 2 Create a concept map

Look at Chapter 2, 'Managing your time', and develop a concept map for your current approach to time management using the concepts in that chapter. How well can you piece information together into a set of related topics? Try using this technique when you are note-taking. You may first have to take a set of linear notes as you read through a text, but then afterwards, after your lectures, and reading more, you can link it together through a concept map. If you really don't like creating concept maps write out a hierarchical list or flow chart.

Get organised

In order to be an effective learner you need to understand how you learn and how you manage yourself in order to learn. Sue Drew from Sheffield Hallam University carried out a piece of research in 2001 asking students what helped or hindered their academic achievement (Drew, 2001). She reported that students came up with four main areas:

- self-management, including taking responsibility for their own learning
- motivation to study
- understanding and reflection of their learning experience
- support from their tutors and the institution.

These findings were also supported by a report on the first-year experience of UK Higher Education students (Yorke and Longden, 2007). Some of the features that first-year students do not like are: workload and time management, confusion about assessments and lack of feedback. If you are a first-year student then you need to work on your time management and be prepared to ask for feedback.

Motivation to study is your primary driver in being successful in your studies. If you don't feel motivated to study, or you feel you have chosen the wrong subject, then stop now and consider what you want to do. Select one of the following questions to answer privately:

1. I want to study this subject because …

2. I know I want to study, but I'd prefer to study …

3. I don't really know why I am here, I would rather do …

From now on, it will be assumed that you are motivated to study.

Self-management is an overarching skill you need to develop. As an 18-year-old first-year student this may be the first time you have left home and you have to sort out accommodation, finance, new friendship groups and understand all the documentation associated with your study programme as well as start to learn something. If you are a mature or international student you will have additional issues to contend with. So, being able to manage all these aspects of your 'new life' can be daunting.

You need to quickly identify where you can get support for your needs. The Students Union is an excellent place to start. It will have an overview of all the services available to you at your institution. Your teaching department will probably have a student office where you can sort out specific things relating to your study. Get familiar with what is available and build a rapport with key people.

If you feel that self-management is an issue for you, take a look at the chapters on stress and time management and develop your own strategies.

Develop an attitude

The greatest discovery of my generation is that a human being can alter his life by altering his attitudes of mind.

William James (1842–1910), US pragmatist philosopher and psychologist

Developing a 'can do' attitude is going to help you enormously. This will enable you to manage yourself and feel in control of events around you. Your confidence will develop and you will easily be able to manage your time and stress. Chapter 1, 'Managing your stress', will help you work through the concept of self-belief or 'self-efficacy', a term that was first coined by the psychologist Albert Bandura. For self-belief to gain a hold you need to:

- be motivated in what you do
- believe in yourself
- recognise and deal with things that stress you so you can control your anxiety
- look for solutions not obstacles
- organise your time so you feel on top of things and in control
- reflect and recognise your strengths and weaknesses in order to make informed choices.

If you feel this is an issue for you, you may want to look now at Chapter 1 on managing stress.

Reflect on your learning

If someone said to you 'Just reflect on what you have just said for a moment', you know that you would be expected to think about what you have just said, and then reconsider the implications of it and what you've learned from it. What you are actually doing is: (a) recapping on what you said (replay), (b) taking a more objective look at the implications of what you said (reframing your actions) and (c) learning from it (reassessing your actions and future actions). Activity 3 helps you reflect on your learning.

ACTIVITY 3 How do you feel about reflecting on your progress?

What I feel ...	Usually me	Think again ...
I find reflection difficult because I can't see what I am learning.		Work with a friend. Sometimes it is difficult when you first start to be objective about your own skills, especially when we are encouraged to be modest most of the time.
I find it a waste of time.		So, don't call it reflecting, but make a list of the things you can do well, OK, or poorly and work out how you can improve. If someone asked you in an interview if you were a good team player how would you answer? And if they asked what makes a good team player, what would you say?
I can't see where I'm developing skills in my courses.		Each course/unit should have a description of what you'll be expected to learn along with the assessment. Check the assessments and the learning outcomes (these should also include a list of skills you're learning) and from this you can see what skills and knowledge you are developing.
I don't know what to do with my personal development planner when I complete it.		Your PDP should be part of every year in your degree. In some degrees it is built into the first year and then vaguely mentioned in years after that. Try to keep it up to date; this is for you and you can use it to adjust your CV and keep you prepared for those interviews and even for part-time work.

Sum up your own feelings about reflecting on your own skills and knowledge.

Reflection is important if you are to develop your understanding of your skills, yourself and your knowledge. You will be expected to work in teams, write essays and give presentations, etc., and through reflection you will be able to recap, reframe and reassess your learning. Many students dislike the reflection aspect, but once they get used to doing it, they see the value.

For most of the time we go about our business, interacting with people, developing skills and gaining knowledge without really being aware that we are doing this. A lot of what we learn is 'implicit', which means we are not aware that we are learning. Sometimes it takes another person to say what you have been learning in order to realise how you are developing. Implicit learning therefore comprises the skills and knowledge you have, but you don't know you have. However, if you reflect on what you have been doing and you are able to 'stand back' objectively and think about it, you start to see the skills and knowledge you have and these then become 'explicit', i.e. you are conscious of them. Once these are explicit you are able to refer to them in your CV, talk about them at an interview and plan to use them again. On the other hand, while our skills and knowledge remain implicit, we can only react to our environment and when someone asks us what we can do, we tend to look a bit vague and trot out the usual 'I don't know'. Good reflection therefore enables us to be more strategic and create opportunities to improve ourselves, while having a better understanding of how we will perform in a similar event. This is the hallmark of a good graduate.

Reflection is not just thinking about what happened at the end of some event; it occurs at various stages. For an assignment it is:

- at the beginning when you reflect on what you have to do
- during the assignment where you adjust your plans in light of your experience
- afterwards, and it is this reflection that you may resent doing. However, post-reflection provides you with the strategic information you need to take forward to the next assignment and it also makes you articulate what you have learnt.

Students in clinical practice for example will be familiar (if not now, then later) with 'reflection in action' and 'reflection on action'. This is a term coined by Donald Schön (1930–1997), an American philosopher whose work has been adopted by many in the health professions in order to develop the 'reflective practitioner'.

When studying, reflection can take many forms, such as:

Personal development planner	This is a record of your own assessment of your developing skills, which should include any part-time or volunteering work you do.
Reflective aspects of coursework, e.g. working in groups	Sometimes a formal part of your coursework assessment.
Tutor feedback	Feedback from your tutors is important for your learning. Most students complain they don't have enough feedback. Try asking for specific feedback when you hand in your coursework if you feel you are not getting the feedback you want. Remember: good feedback enables you to make an action plan for improvement.
Peer feedback	Sometimes you may be asked to assess your peers, e.g. on an oral presentation, part of a report or their ability to work in a group. Once again, be objective and act fairly. Don't give marks on your likes or dislikes for that person. Be professional.

End-of-unit evaluation	This allows you to reflect on the whole unit, how coherent it was, how much you've learned, the organisation and how well you've been taught. Think about this objectively and professionally and reflect fairly. Don't give your tutor a low score because you simply don't like him or her or because you got some low marks.
Tutorials and seminars	An opportunity to go over difficult topics and discuss.
A student representative on a department committee	A chance to represent fellow students and reflect on your educational provision constructively.
Study groups with friends	Informal opportunity.

The PDP is the key document for recording your reflections. Ensure you keep this up to date, whether your tutors ask you to or not. This is primarily *for you* and the more explicit you can be with what you know and can do, the easier it is to talk about it to a potential employer. All the chapters in this book have been designed to incorporate reflective aspects; try using these activities to get you in the habit of reflecting. Activity 4 asks you to consider what you know about reflection.

2 Academic integrity – plagiarism

A Times Higher Education UK survey (March 2006) found that one in six students admitted to copying from friends, one in ten to looking for essays online and four in ten said they knew someone who had passed off work of someone else as their own. This is now recognised as an international problem and universities across the world are starting to tackle it. The main problem with academic cheating, particularly if it escalates, is that it is unfair to those students who don't cheat and eventually will undermine the value of your degree, as its standard cannot then be guaranteed. Would you like to be treated by a doctor or a nurse who you knew cheated throughout their degree? Would you like to walk over a bridge where the structural calculations were checked by the structural engineer who cheated through his or her degree? We are sure the answer is a resounding 'no'.

Violating academic integrity can take several forms:

1. No referencing

■ You must have read some authors' work, even if it is in a textbook, to give you ideas for your paper. Make sure you have the correct reference at the back of your paper. Ensure you use the correct referencing style for your subject. If you are not sure, ask your tutor or a librarian in your institution.

2. **No in-text referencing** (citations)

- If you report a fact, or some information from an author, you need to put that person's name as close to the statement as possible and use the following convention:
  - Barlow (2001) discovered that ...
  - The term 'flight or fight' was first used by Cannon (1920) when he ...
  - Innis and Shaw (1997) surveyed students' study habits and found ...
  - Barlow [1] claimed that ...[1]

  You still need to put the full reference in at the end of your paper.

3. **Taking chunks of text without attributing it to the original author**

- This happens quite frequently. You may find a really good website and just copy and paste chunks of information into your text. You can take chunks of text from another author if you put it in quotes and make an in-text reference next to it.

4. **Buying an essay online or from a friend**

- This is quite simply cheating and unethical.

5. **Taking part of your work from a friend (colluding)**

- It is easy for your tutors to see if you and your friend have handed in essentially the same work, even if it is only in parts. You are both liable, and could be accused of colluding. Similarly, if a friend asks to see your work, you may not know if he or she is copying it or not, so it is better not to share your work before you hand it in.

6. **Feeling your English is not good enough**

- Sometimes if you are not a confident writer you feel that you just cannot write out that idea better than the author. No one is expecting you to write better than the author and it is important that you put ideas down in your own words and then attribute the idea to the original author. If you feel your writing is very poor, you should consult your institution and get support.

Are you at risk of plagiarising?

The first two instances, in particular, are very often due to the fact that you don't fully realise what plagiarism is. In your first year, you should be given a talk by your tutor or someone from the library explaining what plagiarism is and what happens if you are accused of it. If you aren't given any advice, then carry out a web search; there's plenty of information to select from. The other violations of academic integrity are more associated with

---

[1] This style is used in scientific/engineering papers and is the IEEE format.

cheating and the most serious one relates to buying essays which you then pass off as your own.

If you find that you can't meet all your deadlines, due to part-time work, family, parents, sickness, lectures or coursework load, then you are at risk of cutting corners somewhere. If it is your coursework, and you feel tempted to buy an essay, or copy chunks from a website or your friend, then beware, as your institution may have some strong penalties against this. Poor referencing is a lesser offence than buying an essay, but once you have been given a warning, you will also be subject to penalties relating to plagiarism. If managing time and stress is a problem, then check later chapters in this book. Activity 4 helps you to consider why some people plagiarise.

NOTE If you feel your writing is a problem, check out Part 4 of this book.

ACTIVITY 4 Why do some people plagiarise?

Look at the following scenarios and identify why plagiarism could occur: (a) poor writing skills, (b) poor time management, (c) poor note-taking skills. Once you have done that, consider how that student could improve the situation to avoid falling into the trap of plagiarism.

Scenario	What would you recommend?
1. Sam is a first-year student. He is having difficulty organising himself and suddenly finds that several pieces of coursework are due. Time is not on his side so he asks a close friend if he can just look over his work so that he has some ideas. When the work was marked the tutor found these two pieces of work very similar and called both students in. They were both given an official warning.	Reason: a b c
2. Sally has been reading for her assignment for a few weeks and put a lot of work in. The work is due on Monday and it is now Friday. She has taken lots of notes and now wants to start writing, but she realises she has a lot of information, but no references as to where she got it from. She has a vague idea of what the references are and decides to take a guess at the references; she is sure the marker won't notice.	Reason: a b c
3. Jamal feels that he doesn't write very well and whenever he reads anything he feels he can't put it better himself so tends to take chunks of information from books or a good website. The more he reads, the more inadequate he feels his writing ability is. This next coursework is an essay and he has decided to put in bits of text he has found on the Web without putting it in quotes or making an in-text reference.	Reason: a b c

NOTE When you take chunks of text and place them in your own work, it is obvious as the style changes dramatically. You don't have to be a forensic linguist to notice it.

In all of the scenarios above, there was no malicious attempt to cheat, but it has resulted from the various pressures and lack of awareness. Be careful: plagiarism is on the rise and institutions are under pressure to crack down. Some tutors are using anti-plagiarism software, and the most well-known one for UK universities is 'Turnitin' which highlights potentially copied work (see **www.plagiarism.org/**).

For more information on plagiarism, or academic integrity as it is sometimes called, see Chapter 13.

3 Understand your programme or course

Your institution and lecturers would have spent a surprisingly large amount of time preparing programme and course information for you. You might just see it as a heap of information that you may get round to reading one day, and then when you do get around to reading some of it, you don't understand all that educational mumbo-jumbo. So let's try and dissect some of the things that go into these documents for the UK.

The programme specification

The programme refers to the degree you are studying for, whether it is a BSc in Textiles, a BA in History or an MEng in Engineering. The programme specification tells you the aim of the programme as a whole, across the three or four years of your study. It also gives you some idea of what you will learn through a list of learning outcomes. The learning outcomes indicate what you should know and be able to do at the end of your studies. If you read nothing else, read the learning outcomes. There will also be information on how you get support while at the institution.

This document should be available to you either on request or on your department's website. Ideally you should look at this before you sign up for your degree, but not many students realise that this document exists.

Module/unit/course description

Every programme will be supported by units, modules or courses (each department seems to have different names for these). The unit is where the learning and teaching takes place. You may find you have core units and elective units. Each of these units also has a description outlining the aims of the unit, the learning outcomes and the assessments.

It is important to read the unit description, as your assessment will be based on the learning outcomes stated there.

About credits

In the UK, institutions of Higher Education use a Credit Accumulation and Transfer Scheme (CATS), sometime written as credits. This system allows us to value and measure the size of a unit. A three-year honours degree will accumulate 360 credits (120 each year). Each institution will package the number of credits you have to do in different ways.

NOTE It is a good idea to ask your tutors how many hours of learning (this includes face-to-face teaching and private study time) a credit is worth. This will give you some idea of the credit value of the unit. For example, if 1 credit equates to 10 hours of learning, then you are looking at 100 hours of learning for a 10-credit unit. Check how many face-to-face hours you have and then you can see the amount of work expected of you as private study for this unit.

As the European Higher Education systems become more aligned, we shall be moving to a European Credit Transfer and Accumulation System (ECTS), and currently 10 UK credits are worth approximately 5 ECTS. If you go on an exchange visit with the Erasmus/Socrates scheme and have to collect credits for your course, make sure you check out how many you have to do.

4 Your employability

If you are in your first few years of study, you may wonder why you should be thinking of employability now. Well, you should be. Employability is about you consciously developing your knowledge and a wide range of skills even if you still don't know what you want to do later. You record your developing skills in your PDP, which will enable you to see your progress across the years. You should take advantage of what is on offer now, be that sponsorship schemes, volunteering, work placements, career talks, talks from past students, career sessions or full career management courses (with or without credits), as this will help you develop yourself and focus on what you really want. It will also help you with part-time work.

If you are in your final year of studies, you may still not know what you want to do, you may want to take a gap year or you may have found the job you want. Make sure you complete your PDP as this will enable you to articulate what you know and can do, as well as remind you where the evidence is to support this. You should visit your Careers Service for advice – most institutions allow you to use this service for several years after graduation.

What is the difference between employability and employment?

Employability refers to your personal qualities, your attitude to work, the knowledge you have and the skills, both practical and intellectual, that you have developed. This refers therefore to your ability to find a job, stay in that job and progress to the next step. Employment on the other hand refers to simply 'getting a job'. One of the aims of Higher Education is to make you more employable and by doing that also develop your interests in a particular topic.

What do employers want?

Your degree is only the first tick in the box. For the graduate jobs that you will be expecting to do once you have finished, your degree will just enable you to apply, not necessarily get the job. A recent UK government report (Leitch Review, 2007) stated that 40% of the adult population should have a first degree by 2020. So if you want to get noticed, you will have to develop some aspect of yourself that marks you out individually.

Some employers want graduates with discipline-specific knowledge while others are interested in the graduate quality regardless of discipline. The graduateness qualities that employers refer to are: knowledge of a subject area, analytical skills, interpersonal skills, communication skills, time management skills, personal belief in yourself, taking responsibility for your own learning, and the ability to reflect and improve yourself. You will have the opportunity to work on all of these areas while at university, if you take the opportunities available.

What's the knowledge economy – and why should it concern me?

We are living through a knowledge explosion. New communications technologies enable research and new knowledge to be exchanged much faster than ever before. Knowledge becomes a valuable resource and since it is moving so fast the life span of knowledge, especially technologies, is ever shortened. We are all in a vicious circle of trying to 'keep up' with the latest knowledge.

During your studies, therefore, you will learn knowledge that could be out of date in five years, and sometimes less. It is important, therefore, that you learn a set of skills that enable you to update your knowledge and make you a proficient lifelong learner. The whole purpose of this book hinges on this. This book aims to help with personal development where you can enhance your skills rather than immediate quick-fix tips. It is valuable, therefore, to understand the current thrust of Higher Education worldwide.

Look at the map below and see if you can add any more aspects of employability that applies to you.

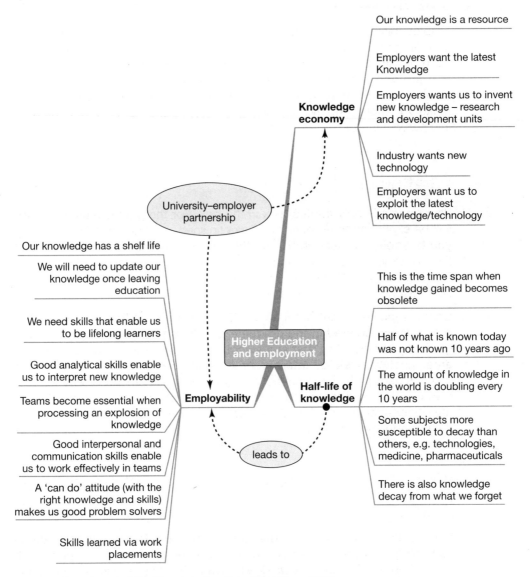

Our knowledge is a resource

Employers want the latest Knowledge

Employers wants us to invent new knowledge – research and development units

Industry wants new technology

Employers want us to exploit the latest knowledge/technology

Knowledge economy

University–employer partnership

Our knowledge has a shelf life

We will need to update our knowledge once leaving education

We need skills that enable us to be lifelong learners

Good analytical skills enable us to interpret new knowledge

Teams become essential when processing an explosion of knowledge

Good interpersonal and communication skills enable us to work effectively in teams

A 'can do' attitude (with the right knowledge and skills) makes us good problem solvers

Skills learned via work placements

Higher Education and employment

Employability

Half-life of knowledge

leads to

This is the time span when knowledge gained becomes obsolete

Half of what is known today was not known 10 years ago

The amount of knowledge in the world is doubling every 10 years

Some subjects more susceptible to decay than others, e.g. technologies, medicine, pharmaceuticals

There is also knowledge decay from what we forget

Source of information on half-life of knowledge from Peter Knight-Moore (1997)

What should I be doing now?

You will probably have been given a PDP by your department. Some departments will fully develop this with you, while others will have it very much on the side. The PDP is for *you* and regardless of how your tutors feel about this, it is in your interest to keep it as up to date as you can. This really is your evidence of how you are developing, within and outside your studies.

Use your part-time job to your advantage and include what you are learning in your PDP. If you are alert to what you are learning, you will be able to articulate it. Even sitting at a checkout in a supermarket will mean that you have to learn to deal with difficult customers. Take note on how you do this and how effective (or not!) you are. How have you improved this skill?

Take advantage of volunteering and other similar schemes, career management sessions or courses, talks and visits from employers.

Once you have left your university, you will find that most offer access to the Careers Service for a few years after graduation.

5 Going forward

This chapter has set the scene for the remainder of the book, and from working through it you may know now which section to dip into next. Before you do that take time to assess how prepared you are to take full advantage of learning in Higher Education. How does your current assessment compare with your assessment at the beginning of the chapter?

Activity 5 Update your personal development planner

Grade your confidence on a scale of 1–5 where 1 = poor and 5 = good.

Moving into Higher Education – my plan	Confidence level 1–5	Plans to improve
I understand what I can do to become a proficient learner, e.g. be responsible for my own learning, understand myself as a learner, get organised, see the value of reflection (via PDPs).		
I understand the principles of plagiarism and realise why it has to be controlled.		
I understand the key documents relating to my programme and courses.		
I understand why employability is something I should consider throughout my studies and what to do about it.		

Getting extra help

- Your local Students Union as well as the National Students Union at: **www.nusonline.co.uk**.
- If you have any kind of condition that you feel could interfere with your studies, check out your own institution. There are usually places within student services that are available for all kinds of help.
- If you feel you aren't coping, first check with your personal tutor (or someone in your department), and then go and get help from one of the specialist units in your institution.
- There is always someone in student services, or the Students Union, to show you where to get help with finances.
- If you feel you are on the wrong course, talk to your personal tutor and see if you can change. Do this early in your first year if possible.
- If you want to do some volunteering, first go to your Students Union; it will know of schemes within your institution.
- Don't forget the library. Staff are usually very friendly and more than happy to help you. Libraries can appear daunting, but don't be afraid to ask.

References

- Drew, S. (2001) 'Student perceptions of what helps them learn and develop in High Education', *Teaching in Higher Education*, 6(3), 309–331.
- Honey, P. and Mumford, A. (1992) *The Manual of Learning Styles*. Maidenhead, Peter Honey.
- Knight-Moore, P. T. (1997) 'The half-life of knowledge and structural reform of the education sector for the global knowledge-based economy', Paper prepared for the Forum on Education in the Information Age organized by the Inter-American Development Bank and the Global Information Infrastructure Commission and hosted by the Universidad de los Andes Cartagena, Colombia, 9–11 July 1997, available at: **www.knight-moore.com/pubs/halflife.html** [last accessed March 2007].
- Kolb, D. A. and Fry, R. (1975) 'Toward an applied theory of experiential learning', in C. Cooper (ed.) *Theories of Group Process*. London, John Wiley.
- Leitch Review (2007) *Prosperity for all in the Global Economy: World Class Skills*, HM Treasury, UK Government, available at: **www.hm-treasury.gov.uk/leitch** [last accessed March 2007].
- Schön, D. A. at Informal Education (Infed), available at: **www.infed.org/thinkers/et-schon.htm** [last accessed March 2007].
- Smith, E. P. (1978) 'Measuring professional obsolescence: a half life model for the physician', *The Academy of Management Review*, available online at Jstor, pp. 914–917. Available from: **www.jstor.org/search/ArticleLocatorSearch** [last accessed March 2007].

- Smith, M. K. (2001) 'David A. Kolb on experiential learning', *The Encyclopedia of Informal Education*, available at: **www.infed.org/b-explrn.htm** [last accessed March 2007].

- Yorke, M. and Longden, B. (2007) *The First-year Experience in Higher Education in the UK*, Higher Education Academy, available at: **www.heacademy.ac.uk/research/FirstYearExperience.pdf** [last accessed March 2007].

1 Manage yourself

We all have a multitude of things to do at work, at home, with friends and for our studies. We are all juggling these aspects of our lives and we may find at times that one of these areas starts demanding more of us. At this point we feel the pressure and we start to feel we are 'running out of time' or are 'stressed out'. Two of the chapters in this part refer to time management and stress management; however, in reality it is about you managing yourself and about your relationship with time and stress.

If you are dealing with a busy course full of lectures and coursework deadlines, you will need to look at the whole of your life commitments during this period and discover how *you* react to these pressures and then find ways of dealing with them. If you don't do this, you will compromise your ability to do well.

As a part-time student, you will have particular pressures from the demands made on you. You may also be learning apart from your fellow students, which increases your need to develop a virtual learning community that can sustain you through difficult times. Knowing what motivates you, and dealing with your time and stress issues will be vital. Much of the information in Chapter 3 will also be of interest to all students.

The following chapters will help you focus on developing these key skills that will enable you to juggle your busy life and come out on top.

1 Managing your stress

Most of your time at university will be a happy and enjoyable one. There may be times, however, when you feel things are getting out of control and you feel uncomfortably stressed. This can be related to your studies, your personal life, or both. Knowing what stress does to our bodies, our own tendencies towards being stressed, and the approaches we use to handle stressful events is an important life skill.

In this chapter you will learn how to:

1. identify signs of stress in yourself and others
2. develop proactive strategies to dealing with stress
3. recognise a personal tendency to be more stressed
4. recognise what your stressors are and how to manage them.

USING THIS CHAPTER

Estimate your current levels of confidence. At the end of the chapter you will have the chance to reassess these levels and incorporate this into your personal development planner (PDP). Mark between 1 (poor) and 5 (good) for the following:

I can recognise my own signs of stress.	I can recognise what stresses me.	I can apply proactive strategies to combat stress.

Date: _____

1 Introduction

Of students surveyed for the Student Experience Report in 2006, 98% said that university life is a happy one. You may well be one of those and may look at the title of this chapter and feel that you are not particularly stressed and that, if you were, you could cope with it. However, 56% of those students also said that since being at university they were under a lot more stress than before.

If you are thinking of not reading this chapter because you currently don't feel stressed, **stop now** and consider the following: I know what happens to my body when I am stressed; I can recognise the symptoms and I fully understand what stresses me. I have also reflected on my attitude to things in my life and realise this plays a role in how stressed I feel and I have enough belief in myself to solve any issues that cause anxiety. If you are happy with all these statements, move on. If not, and you wish to develop or hone this life skill, read on.

2 What happens to our bodies under stress?

Richard Lazarus, an eminent psychologist who won the prestigious award of 'American Psychologist' in 2002, claimed that stress and anxiety mainly occur when we believe we can't cope with the problem we perceive as stressful (Lazarus and Folkman, 1984). When we see this problem as overwhelming and feel we have no way of escaping or solving it, we experience anxiety or stress. However, we don't all see the same events as stressful. We have different perceptions of what is stressful, we have different levels of confidence in dealing with it and different ways of coping with it. There is therefore no one solution, but in general it is the feeling of being out of control that makes us anxious and stressed.

How do our bodies respond to stress?

When we perceive an event as stressful, our bodies react physiologically to it. The Harvard physiologist Walter Cannon coined the term 'fight or flight' in the 1920s and it refers to our body's physiological response to a threatening situation, be this physical or emotional. When we feel threatened our heart rate speeds up, our blood pressure rises and our muscles tighten. At the same time our body releases the hormone cortisol that increases the flow of energy to our muscles. This makes us ready for action; we either stay and fight or run. Once we have dealt with the threat our body returns to normal. However, if our perceived threat doesn't result in action, then cortisol takes longer to disappear. If we 'run away' from a piece of coursework, for example, it isn't going to help very much. We may find ourselves even more stressed. 'Running away' from many of our stressors often means making excuses, and this can make things worse in the long run, making us feel even more stressed. If this continues over a long period of time, it attacks our immune system, our cardiovascular system, digestive system and musculoskeletal system until we are exhausted and eventually become ill.

Excess cortisol also affects the part of the brain that is central to learning and memory by interfering with how our brain cells communicate with one another. In a crisis, we often don't remember what went on exactly; it is as if our 'lines are down' and we only react to that which is vital. So, not handling stress well, or being under constant stress, will affect our ability to learn.

Being alert to what creates stress in our lives, and developing techniques that can enable us to cope with this, and reduce excess flow of cortisol, is therefore an essential life skill.

NOTE   Although stressors increase the amount of cortisol in our bloodstream, we also have 'daily shots' of cortisol throughout our daily cycle (circadian rhythm). This helps to keep us alert, by maintaining our blood pressure and enabling us to react to our environment.

3 What are the symptoms of stress?

When we feel stressed we notice changes in our emotions and our behaviour. Activities 1 and 2 help you to identify stress in yourself and others.

ACTIVITY 1 Identifying signs of stress

Look at the scenarios below and complete the table.

Carlos is a very outgoing and confident person and has decided to study abroad. He is now reaching the end of his first semester. He is very gregarious and has a good friendship group. However, his friends are noticing that he is becoming increasingly withdrawn, is not eating properly and appears 'on edge' a lot of the time. When they try to talk to him he becomes irritable and no one feels they should pry any further.

Lucy is a third-year student and has always had a very full social life. Her tutors have spoken to her many times for handing work in late and missing classes. However, she always seemed to pull things together at the last minute. Just recently, however, you have noticed that she has started drinking more and when you pointed this out to her she said she wasn't sleeping well and needed some alcohol to help. You have also noticed that your fun-loving friend has little interest in the things you used to do together. She is also getting into difficulties with her third-year project group who are complaining of her forgetfulness and lack of interest in the project.

	Signs of stress	What he/she might be feeling	What he/she should do
Carlos			
Lucy			

Check the feedback section for more information.

ACTIVITY 2 Recognising your own symptoms of stress

When **you** feel stressed what symptoms do you have? List them under how you **feel** – including physical characteristics (e.g. heart pounding, feeling sick, tired) and how you **act** (e.g. irritable, lack of interest, get emotional).

How do you feel? (Include physical and emotional characteristics)	How do you act and behave?

Check the feedback section for more information.

Let's keep things in proportion. We all get stressed at times. Most of the time symptoms are uncomfortable but short-lived and manageable. Sometimes we aren't even aware of feeling stressed until someone points out how irritable we are. However, we can get chronic stress symptoms and this needs to be dealt with.

Is all stress bad?

Stress can be both positive and negative. Positive stress is having just about enough stress to motivate and challenge us. It can give us a buzz. However, generally, when we hear the word 'stress' we associate it as a negative state, as our symptoms above show. So, for some, a group project, an essay or a presentation may be seen as positive and challenging while for others it could be seen as negative and worrying.

Also, we need some stress in our lives to keep us alert and ready for that challenge. We have probably all experienced a rise in our heart rate just as we are about to do something we feel challenging or stressful, but often that is what we need to get us up and running – a healthy dose of cortisol that dissipates quite soon afterwards. How many of us have put off a task because the deadline is just too far away? As the deadline approaches, we get the 'rush' and this stimulates us into activity. The trick is knowing when this can flip over from being the kick-start you need to being stressful.

Reflect on how you deal with deadlines: are you generally operating too close for comfort or just about right? You will probably find you have a particular tendency (see Chapter 2, 'Managing your time'). You need to identify this so you can tackle it, if you need to.

Some symptoms of positive stress are:

- I feel excited
- I get motivated
- it gives me a buzz
- it stretches me intellectually or physically
- it enables me to learn.

4 Personal development in handling stress

Broadly speaking, our attitudes will affect how we relate to others, how we cast blame when things don't work out, how we go about our tasks and the degree of control we feel over our lives. We need to develop our self-awareness in identifying stress and stressful events as well as confidence (self-belief) in being able to regain control over our lives.

Making personal changes – developing emotional intelligence

Daniel Goleman, author of the popular book *Emotional Intelligence* (1995), claims that intellectual IQ alone does not give us all the skills needed to be successful in everyday life. We need to develop self-awareness and recognise what others are feeling (empathy), know how to handle our emotions and to have self-discipline. This, Goleman claims, is emotional intelligence or emotional quotient (EQ). Group work projects, for example, if taken seriously, develop our interpersonal skills (emotional literacy). Similarly, effective use of the personal development planner (PDP) enables us to reflect on our progress and personal development. These aspects of the curriculum therefore have good reasons for being there.

Activities 1 and 2 have been included so that you can see the importance of being aware of your own and your friends' behaviour as an initial step in dealing with stress.

Emotional intelligence comprises, in essence, three areas: know yourself, choose yourself, give yourself. These are summarised in the next table.

By developing your emotional intelligence, you have the grounding to develop your self-belief and self-confidence, which gives you confidence to become more in control of your life. You also become aware of your own behaviour and how this can limit you as well as increasing your empathy towards your friends' troubles.

Emotional intelligence categories	Questions	Application to your studies
Know yourself	• What makes you think and feel the way you do? • What parts of your reactions are habitual or consciously thought through? • What are you afraid/anxious of?	Being honest with yourself enables you to reflect on your qualities and faults. You learn from your experiences. Reflect on this through your studies, part-time work, etc., and make notes in your PDP. This reflection should alert you to habitual actions – possibly fear of exams, particular course work, etc. When you become aware of this you can then try to prevent yourself being a hostage to previously learned negative reactions.
Choose yourself	• How do you know what's right for you? • If you were not afraid or anxious what would you do? • Can you increase your awareness of your actions?	Manage your feelings. If something starts to stress you, identify exactly what it is and objectively assess why this is a stressor for you. Can you manage it yourself or do you need help?
Give yourself	• Am I helping or hurting people? • Am I working interdependently with others? • Have I developed empathy? • Do I work by a set of personal standards?	Be aware of your fellow students. When working together be alert to their needs as well as yours (be empathic).

Adapted from the Emotional Intelligence Network, **http://6seconds.org/index.php**.

Making personal changes – developing self-belief

As we have mentioned, an important aspect of dealing with stress is this ability to feel you can control your life. The modern-day reaction to 'flight or fight' is our ability to change things that stress us, and to do that we need to have confidence in ourselves (see Activity 3).

Albert Bandura, a famous Canadian professor of Psychology, began to see personality as an interaction between psychological processes, the environment and our behaviour. He noticed that those who felt more in control of their lives (had high self-efficacy) behaved differently and personally achieved more (Bandura, 1997).

ACTIVITY 3 Is it all down to fate?

Look at the following statements – do you agree with them or not?

	Agree	Disagree
When things go wrong for me, it is just bad luck.		
It doesn't matter how well I plan, what's going to be, will be.		
Friendships are a result of chemistry – they work or they don't.		
Some people have all the luck.		
When things go wrong, I can usually find out who is to blame.		

As you probably realised, these are statements that reflect someone who has little self-belief in their own ability to make changes. Make a note of where your tendency lies. Check the feedback section for comments on these statements.

Write a new list of statements below that reflects someone who has self-belief.

	Generally me	Generally not me

Check the feedback section for some more examples once you have written your own.

Strategies for improving self-belief

1. Select a specific task/activity you want to improve and feel confident about. Think of a specific task.

2. This activity needs to be important to you as this will give you the motivation to work on it.

3. Has your previous experience of doing this activity been negative? If so, identify the specific negative aspects so you can work on them (don't generalise because you can't work with generalisations).

4. Develop a picture of yourself, or someone, doing this activity well. What makes it good? Make sure you 'see' this performed well. Keep that picture in mind.

5. Set yourself specific and short-term goals to deal with aspects of the activity you have identified. See the section below on approaches to dealing with stressful events.

6. Seek feedback and work with it positively. If you feel you 'can't do something' always say 'I can't do that *yet*.' It has a powerfully confident feel about it.

7. Verbalise (write out) your strategy for achieving your short-term goals. This way you have articulated your success and you can 'hear' it, and it primes you for action.

8. Small successes breed overall success.

NOTE Being 'in control' of events in your life is not about being a 'control freak'. It is about feeling that you can *do* something to help. The higher your emotional intelligence, the better you will be at trusting others in order to give and receive help. Recognise when you need support and be proactive in seeking it out.

Checklist for signs of stress

Take the list of symptoms here as a warning signal. If these symptoms become chronic you must seek help.

Physical

Headaches, backache, exhaustion, insomnia, pounding heart, diarrhoea or constipation, stiff neck and shoulders, rashes, nausea.

Emotional

Feeling useless, worthless, not confident of abilities, not recognising your strengths, talking yourself down, feeling lonely, feeling 'out of control', feeling irritable and angry.

Intellectual

Feeling you can't learn another thing, you can't remember things, you don't process information very well in class, you have to keep going over something to make it 'stick'.

As a result of some of these symptoms you may find that you have negative reactions, such as: withdrawal from friends, mood swings, angry outbursts, inability to make decisions, weepy, not hungry or eating too much, feeling sick when you open 'that' book or go past the library, possibly excessive drinking, drug abuse or self-harming.

NOTE If things have gone on too long or have become worse you may start to show more serious symptoms such as obsessive behaviour, suicidal feelings or depression. If you feel your symptoms are getting worse and you are worried, you must get professional help from either your doctor or the counselling service at your institution. If you do this, make sure you tell your personal tutor so that he or she can make allowances for late work or postpone certain assignments.

5 Do I have a personality that stresses me out?

We are all aware that some of our friends get more stressed than others and we may envy them if we are the one that gets stressed out while they remain calm. We should be aware by now that there are: (a) individual differences in how stressful or challenging we see particular events, and (b) individual differences in how we think we can deal with these events, once we see them as stressful. One of the factors for these individual differences is our different personality styles.

How does your personality affect your stress levels?

In the 1950s, two cardiologists, Meyer Friedman and Ray Rosenman, observed that there was more heart disease in their male patients with high-pressured jobs. This may seem obvious to us now but it wasn't at the time. They also noted that particular personality types were also more prone to heart disease. The personality type they felt was more 'at risk' was their so-called 'Personality A' person. Incidentally, Friedman regarded himself as a 'recovering type A'. The type A personality has now become synonymous with 'driven' people, obsessed with time and perfection. The counter to that is the type B personality that is laid-back and easy going.

Are you a type A or a type B?

Type A and type B are essentially a continuum of personality traits from being uptight to laid-back. They are not an intricate measure of your personality but serve to give you a guideline of where your tendencies are.

Type A personalities tend to:

- be very goal driven (in the extreme, often at all costs)
- be competitive
- need recognition and advancement
- multi-task when under time pressure

- be keen to get things finished
- be mentally and physically alert (above average).

NOTE There is continuing debate as to whether type A personality people are more at risk from heart disease. But the potential anger and hostility aspect of this personality type does seem to be a factor.

Type B personalities tend to:

- be more relaxed
- be more easy-going
- socialise a lot
- be less competitive
- set realistic goals that don't overstretch them.

If you are not sure which personality type you are, the Science Museum has a short online fun quiz that allows you to find out. This can be found at: **www.sciencemuseum.org.uk**. Search on 'stress' from the museum's search engine.

Help! I'm a type A personality and I'm already stressed out about it

Not all characteristics of type A people are bad. You will know yourself if you feel too driven or uptight. If you feel you are a type A person you may feel stressed out: for example, if you can't achieve what you set out to do, or if you see coursework deadlines looming and you think you are going to be late. You may need to re-adjust your personal standards and become a little more relaxed, if you feel you are overdoing things. Some of your friends may hint at your behaviour and you may want to consider if you are being too 'driven'.

Think about yourself and develop your emotional intelligence. Are there ways you can tone down your type A characteristics? Identify some of your characteristics you think you can work on. Also, check out the stress-busting techniques to help you when you need them.

Why bother – I'm a type B personality?

Not all the characteristics of extreme type B personalities are good. You may find yourself too laid-back where nothing stresses you until things get out of hand. You need to submit work tomorrow and suddenly you have got to get into action and you may not have the time to give your best. But, if you are an extreme type B, this may not worry you either! However, try to balance your relaxed style and ensure you are keeping to the goals you have set.

We need to get a balance

As with everything, we need a balance of drive and relaxation. Ideally you should be halfway between a type A and type B person. This way, you can deal with unexpected deadlines and other stressors by calm planning. You feel in control and not stressed out.

So once you have become self-aware, emotionally literate and believe in yourself, how do you approach stressful events?

6 Proactive strategies for dealing with stress

Stress-busting techniques are one way of coping with stress (see Section 8), but they are just that, 'techniques', and they are good to have. However, a more fundamental way of dealing with stress is to be proactive in your management of it. Psychologists have identified two broad types of coping strategy:

- problem-focused strategy
- emotion-focused strategy.

Problem-focused strategy	• Know your stressors. • Analyse what stresses you about an event. • Break down the various components of the situation into manageable chunks. • Identify which part is the problem. • Look at the options. • Develop an action plan. • Check your resources – do you need help?
Emotion-focused strategy	• Know your stressors. • Reflect on how you *feel* when confronted with this stressor. • Resist your feeling to avoid thinking about this. • Reflect on how you can start to change this emotion. • Trust in others and discuss with a friend or counsellor.

Source: Based on coping strategies from Lazarus and Folkman (1984)

If you are already a proactive stress-buster, you may find you have a preference for one or other of the strategies above. Ideally, you should be using both strategies as they tap into your self-belief and your emotional intelligence. Activity 4 asks you to think about how you solve problems.

ACTIVITY 4 Problem solving as a way of dealing with stress

Now think of an example that is pertinent to you. How would you use this problem-solving strategy?

1. Identify a stressful problem.
2. What makes it stressful?
3. How do I feel about it?
4. What can I do now to manage it?

Checklist for proactive coping strategies	Need to work on this ✓
Personal development: • Self-belief (I am a 'can do' person) • Emotional intelligence (I know myself and trust others)	
Personality type: • Type A (perfectionist, driven, high standards) • Type B (relaxed)	
Strategies: • Problem-focused (analyse, action plan) • Emotion-focused (realign emotions)	

7 What makes studying stressful?

Learning can cause stress and your ability to handle some degree of stress will help you. You may well find you are in your comfort zone at the beginning of a course where you feel in control of your learning and you can predict what is going on. However, you may find that as the difficulty increases, you feel less in control of what you know and don't know and very soon fall outside your comfort zone. At this stage you are learning! It is important to recognise that you must go through this stage in order for your new knowledge to find its place and become your new comfort zone. It is important to fit into your new comfort zone, although for some students this takes until the exams before everything starts to fall into place. Look at the graph in Figure 1.1.[1] Where do you feel you are now? Are you happy to be outside your comfort zone while you learn?

Becoming a student can be seen as a 'rite of passage'. It is something you probably feel you want to do; it does mature you. You leave home, make a new home for yourself, make new friends and learn about something you are interested in. These are all exciting challenges and can give you such a buzz **or** completely stress you out. Which is it for you? Activity 5 asks you to identify stressors in academic life.

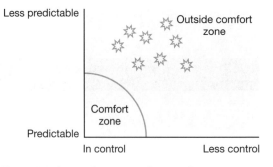

Figure 1.1 Are you in your comfort zone?

ACTIVITY 5 Stressors in academic life

Identify some of the stressors in academic life from this typical scenario. What do you think Joanne should do? Then identify academic stressors that particularly affect you.

Joanne was the first of her family to go on to further study and she was very excited at studying engineering. She made friends quickly through her studies and the clubs she joined. However, now in her third year, money, or lack of it, is an increasing worry. She has taken out several loans but has now decided to take a part-time job to make ends meet and has found herself a job in a local restaurant. She works two evenings a week on four-hour shifts finishing at midnight. She has also taken on another small job in the local supermarket working a busy afternoon shift. While her bank balance is now looking healthier, she feels that the late nights and the extra supermarket job are beginning to affect her work. Her studies are increasingly complex and she has several projects to complete. As this is her third year she needs good grades to get the degree she wants. She is beginning to feel there are too many demands on her life and doesn't know how to cope, especially since her boss at the restaurant is pressurising her to work more shifts.

---

[1] Thanks to Professor Mark Lutman from the University of Southampton who discussed these ideas. He feels that a good learner is one who can cope with being outside their comfort zone – as long as it is not for too long.

	Academic stressors	Coping strategies
Joanne		
You		

Will I/do I fit in?

When you leave home to study you leave behind something you have grown familiar with: your friends, your town, your boyfriend/girlfriend and your family. This familiar environment has helped make you and support you. Although you are excited by leaving all this behind, you may find that once you are away things do not feel as comfortable or safe as they did at home. You are basically homesick. Many of your fellow students will also be feeling the same and you know you have to make an effort to fit in, find new friends and belong. The best time to do this is right at the beginning of your studies when everyone is looking out for new friends. You may find that you don't mix with the right group in the first instance, but by the second semester you will be feeling confident enough to know who you'd like to be with and how to go about it. Being shy may make this process slower, but try and join clubs you are interested in and that should automatically link you with like-minded people.

I never seem to have enough money

The Student Experience Report 2006, carried out by MORI (Unite, 2006), with over 1000 face-to-face interviews with undergraduate and post-graduate students, found that of those sampled, over half reported difficulties managing their finances and one-third had already asked their families to help them out in a crisis. Postgraduate and mature students, however, were least likely to turn to their families for financial support.

Finances are an increasing source of stress for students and finding part-time work is an obvious solution. The trend towards part-time work when in full-time education is growing. The Student Experience Report 2006 reported that four in ten of those interviewed had done part-time work during their studies, and this is set to increase. In a *Guardian Unlimited* article in 2002 it was reported that the National Union of Students in the UK estimated that approximately 42% of students worked part time, whereas the Trades Union Congress's survey in 2000 claimed that 60% of students needed to work to meet basic living costs (Henessey, 2002). Although working gives you that added work experience and responsibility, too much can damage your studies. The UK Government recommends that you spend no more than 10 hours/week in part-time employment.

Lack of money is the route cause of other stressors, e.g. poor accommodation, cheap food and lack of course materials. So getting your finances right is crucial (see Activity 6).

ACTIVITY 6 Budgeting

Budgeting is something we have to do all our lives. However, if finance is a particular stressor for you then you must get to grips with budgeting. This is rarely anyone's favourite activity, but to prevent debts building up you need to know what comes in and what goes out and work within that budget as much as you can.

How do your finances look? Work on a weekly or monthly basis, whichever suits you best.

	Amount incoming weekly/monthly	Amount outgoing weekly/monthly
INCOME:		
Loan		
Part-time work		
Family		
Savings		
Other		
ACCOMMODATION:		
Rent		
Electricity		
Gas		
Water		
Telephone		
Council Tax		
Other		

	Amount incoming weekly/monthly	Amount outgoing weekly/monthly
STUDIES:		
Tuition fees		
Field trips		
Stationery		
Project costs		
Other		
LIVING COSTS:		
Food		
Eating out (evening and day)		
Toiletries		
Mobile phone		
Travel: car		
Travel: bus fares – daily		
Travel: long-distance trips (home?)		
Clothes		
Other (dentist, doctor, prescription, etc.)		
SOCIAL LIFE:		
The pub		
Cinema, clubs		
Sporting activities		
Other		
TOTAL		

Do the incoming and outgoing columns balance?

What should you do if you find yourself in need of financial support? Your institution will have a student support centre where you can find out information on the student hardship fund that it operates. The centre may have other schemes to help you budget more effectively. There are people in your institution whose job it is to help you; you should be proactive and seek them out.

I don't know what my tutors expect of me

A problem for first-year students is the move into Higher Education. You may have come from an 'A'-level course in the UK, be an international student or a mature student returning to full-time education.

Always check your programme and course documentation (see 'Learning in Higher Education') as this describes the aims of your courses and the learning outcomes. Always make sure you know exactly what is needed in an assignment, never assume. Remember: you will be expected to develop an independent style of learning (see 'Learning in Higher Education'). If you are in doubt regarding what is expected, ask either your tutor or a student in the second or third year.

If you have a study buddy or peer mentoring scheme in your institution, take full advantage of it. If not, you may want to ask if one can be set up. See the Peer Assisted Learning website at Bournemouth University in the UK.

I just can't learn everything I am expected to

The academic load and demands of coursework are another area that has been identified as a cause of stress. You may find that your assignments are bunched towards the end of the semester and you struggle to hand in by the deadlines.

Assignment deadline bunching is a problem. But, if you are given the task way ahead of time, you will be expected to time-manage all your assignments (see Chapter 2, 'Managing your time'). Plan when you can fit each assignment in, given the amount of knowledge you know at the time. Sometimes you may have to get started before you have had the lecture, seminar or laboratory class. You can make an outline plan and fit in as much as you can as you go along.

Academic load in terms of sheer quantity of what you are expected to learn will mean that you need to develop some effective academic skills. The chapters in this book are designed to do just that. Actively take what you need from each chapter and **act on it** and this will start to reduce your stress as you begin to feel in control. Activity 7 asks you to identify your stressful events.

The complexity of the material you have to learn will also increase with the years and this has been shown to be another stressor. Don't suffer in silence over something you are struggling with. Ask your tutor and possibly a postgraduate teaching assistant who may be helping on the course. Don't forget that you can ask your friends or student mentors, if you have this set up in your programme.

In 'Learning in Higher Education' we discussed the characteristics of a novice and an expert; you may want to check this out again later.

ACTIVITY 7 Identifying your stressful events

Which of the following, if any, do you find stressful:

■ bunched assignment deadlines
■ the sheer quantity of work to get through
■ complexity of the work
■ lack of understanding of what is expected of you
■ anything else?

How can you be proactive in managing these potential stressors for you?

Complete the concept map below with the different types of study stressors and list ways of dealing with them. Place each study stressor on the first branch and the ways of dealing with it on the lower branches.

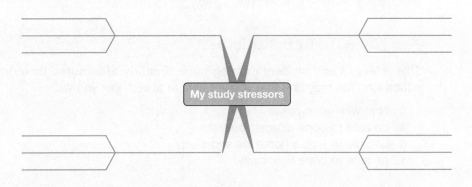

See feedback section for a map of the result of stress on study.

Dropping out: a response to stress?

Dropping out from your studies can be a response to stress, but not necessarily. If you feel that you really have chosen the wrong subject, the wrong place to study and you now know exactly what you want to do and it is not studying, then leave. You will become even more stressed if you stay and will only be staying because you want to 'save face' or not offend someone. According to a BBC article (BBC News, 2004) one in seven students in the UK drop out. However, this varies greatly across institutions. Learning how to keep stress under control and not letting it ruin your life is vital.

If you want to leave because you feel you can't cope or you are generally unhappy, **think again**. With the help of your personal tutor, a student adviser, a friend or a religious leader, discuss why you are unhappy and what your options really are. You will find there are various options and one could be just right for you, enabling you to go on and graduate. **Don't let wanting to leave be a flight reaction to stress**.

Who gets more stressed out?

As we should know by now, being stressed out varies between individuals. However, some groups of students are more likely to feel the pressures than others. Stressors can be external or internal. External stressors refer to things outside of us that we have to deal with, e.g. exams, coursework, finances, etc. Internal stress refers to our own personality characteristics, or if we are dealing with some incapacity or illness. So, all stress is an interplay between what we bring to the event and the event itself. The imbalance between internal and external stressors can affect our psychological and physiological well-being and cause stress (Lazarus and Cohen, 1977).

Since external factors play a role in stress, certain students may find themselves under additional pressures.

Are you a mature student?

This refers to any student coming back to study after some time out of education. You may find that you are unsure about how you will:

- fit in with youngsters
- be able to cope academically
- be able to juggle home life and study
- be able to cope financially.

Are you an international student?

As an international student you also have additional things that add pressure. You will have to deal with:

- setting up home in another country
- being homesick
- understanding the cultural differences (socially and academically)
- working in a language that is not your native language
- facing, possibly, racist comments. Do report this if within the university.

External pressures are discussed in Activity 8.

NOTE You are probably a happy and well-adjusted student even though you may have these added pressures. Please don't feel you have to be stressed out. If you are coping well, you may want to be alert to students in a similar situation to you who are not coping well and you may be able to give them some support (develop your emotional intelligence).

ACTIVITY 8 My external pressures

	Applies to me	Do I need to do anything?
Just returning to full-time education after many years and wonder how I will cope.		
I'm homesick (or may become).		
My English is not good enough.		
I'm not giving enough time to my family.		
I miss my friends back home.		
Can I cope?		

List more pressures that apply to you and check if you think you need to do something about it to keep them in check. What personality type are you – could this influence your reaction to stress? Are you proactive and use problem- and emotion-focused coping strategies (see Sections 4, 5 and 6 above)?

8 Stress-busting techniques: a maintenance strategy

In addition to the personal development and proactive strategies above, we can develop a maintenance programme that enables us to cope with on-going stress that hits us once in a while. Some basic techniques are:

- **Exercise**. This will help the physiological aspect of stress and the release of endorphins will give you a feeling of euphoria as well as help your heart. It is also ideal for getting rid of anger and frustrations. If you want to choose only one stress-busting technique, then choose this one.
- **Relax**. When you are feeling stressed out it is difficult to unwind. You may find you have to make a big effort to do this. It may be better to go to classes such as yoga or t'ai chi. Exercising also helps you to relax. If you want to develop your own relaxation techniques then try deep breathing or meditation. Go out with friends and have a good laugh.

- **Eat well**. Avoid junk food and too much alcohol – both of these can sap your energy and make you feel low.
- **Talk**. Open up to friends and family. They will feel honoured that you trust them enough to discuss your problems. Talking allows you to see things in perspective and get another view.
- **Stress diary**. By keeping a diary you start to articulate what your feelings are and what stresses you out. Once you do this you become conscious and self-aware, which is where you must start in order to cope. You can couple this with talking to your friends.
- **Focus**. When we are stressed we start to feel overwhelmed. Go back and look at the strategies for developing self-belief above and focus on each part of your plan.
- **Get support from others**. There are some problems you can't and shouldn't face on your own. Don't try and be superman or super-woman. Most Higher Education institutions are caring and will have support in place for you. You should make yourself familiar with what is available: for example, student services, Students Union, religious chaplains, counselling services, medical services, your personal tutor and, of course, your friends and family.

Exams – the special case

During revision:

- plan a realistic revision timetable – this will help you stay on top of things
- summarise your notes, make key points, highlight important information and use concept maps for quick overviews
- take breaks so you can stay alert.

During the exam:

- 'feel' calm – breathe slowly and deeply
- feel in control
- read the instructions carefully (very often students don't do this)
- read the questions calmly, underlining key aspects
- mark the questions you want to do first
- allocate time for each question
- allow time to check your work.

9 On reflection

Stress management, as you have seen, is much more than learning a few techniques; it is life changing. It cannot guarantee you a stress-free life, and would you want one? But it will enable you to manage it and keep the health-threatening aspects of stress under control.

Summary of this chapter

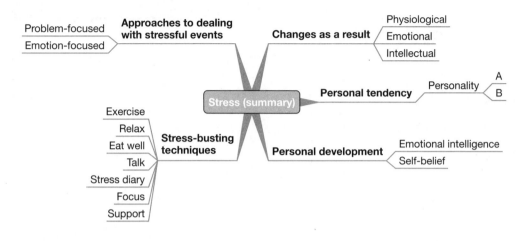

Now reflect on your current abilities to work through a stress management plan and consider what you need to do to improve. You may want to transfer this information to your own institution's PDP scheme.

ACTIVITY 9 Update your personal development planner

Having read this chapter, gauge your confidence again. How does this compare with your confidence levels at the start of the chapter? What can you do to improve? You can incorporate this into your own PDP and of course add anything else that you feel is appropriate.

Grade your confidence on a scale of 1–5 where 1 = poor and 5 = good.

My stress management plan	Confidence level 1–5	Plans to improve
Recognise how I react to stress. *Section 3*		
Check my self-belief. *Section 4*		
Improve my emotional intelligence. *Section 4*		
Recognise my personal tendency to being stressed (personality type A, B). *Section 5*		

My stress management plan	Confidence level 1–5	Plans to improve
Identify proactive strategies in dealing with stress that suit me best. *Section 6*		
Identify what stresses me. *Section 7*		
Identify and use the best stress-busting techniques for me. *Section 8*		

Date: _____

Getting extra help

- Talk to your university counsellor. He or she will be able to give advice on how best to deal with the common problems associated with the stresses of studying.
- Ask friends how they cope with stress – not only will you discover that it's more common than you think, but also they may have some useful stress-busting tips for you.

Consult a few interesting websites:

- **Student Mental Stress: Dstress**. This site is produced by Loughborough University and is full of useful information. It is a good interactive site. See: **www.d-stress.org.uk** [last accessed November 2008].
- **Mind: How to Cope with the Stress of Student Life**. Mind has a guide and a series of tips for getting help if you need it. Search on 'student stress' using the search engine: **www.mind.org.uk** [last accessed November 2008].
- **Channel 4, 4Health**, Student Stress, Wendy Moore. Search on 'stress' using the search engine. 'Most students will feel the effects of stress at some point in their studies and a small number of students may feel stressed or depressed for a lot of the time.' See: **www.channel4.com/health** [last accessed November 2008].

Feedback on activities

ACTIVITY 1 Identifying signs of stress

	Signs of stress	What he/she might be feeling	What he/she should do
Carlos	Becoming withdrawn. Not eating properly. On edge/irritable.	Emotional. This can be weepy, or aggressive. Emotional exhaustion.	Notice that things aren't right and something needs to be done before falling behind with his studies. Talk to someone he trusts – friend, tutor or counsellor. Make sure this doesn't go on for too long.
Lucy	Heavy drinking. Not sleeping well. Disinterested, forgetful.	Feeling unwell and possibly depressed from too much alcohol and not enough sleep. Mental exhaustion.	Be alert to a change in behaviour that is unhelpful. Identify the first thing that needs to be done, i.e. stop drinking. Seek help from a friend or counsellor to prevent serious alcohol damage.

NOTE In these case studies the key to moving on is being alert to your own stress patterns and recognising when they are becoming overwhelming. Seek help and allow your friends to help you. As a friend, you may have to help someone who is trying to push you away. Be patient and try not to abandon him or her during this difficult phase of your friendship.

ACTIVITY 2 Recognising your own symptoms of stress

Here are some symptoms of stress. Check the ones that you have identified. You may recognise more symptoms that you didn't realise indicated stress.

▶

How do you feel? (Include physical and emotional characteristics)	How do you act and behave?
Feeling overwhelmed.	You are disorganised and forgetful. You are over cautious and have difficulty making decisions. You panic. You have lost your confidence. You can't concentrate on your work. Mental exhaustion.
Feeling tired and exhausted.	You have no or little interest in things. You don't sleep well. You cry about things easily.
Feeling anxious and nervous.	You are moody, irritable, aggressive and get angry easily. You may resort to recreational drugs to alleviate symptoms.
Feeling very emotional and tearful.	You react emotionally and are often near to tears … emotional exhaustion.
Feeling sick/tight feeling in stomach/not hungry.	You have diarrhoea and/or lose interest in food.
Heart is pounding.	You perspire more than usual.
Feeling homesick.	You withdraw from your friends.
Being anti-social.	You want to be on your own. People irritate you and you get short tempered.
Feeling depressed.	Everything becomes too much and you have little interest in doing anything.

NOTE If your list was rather short, you might now recognise some of the symptoms you have. Add them to your list in this activity. Being aware of our stress symptoms is very important, as we saw in Activity 1.

ACTIVITY 3 Is it all down to fate?

	Comments
When things go wrong for me, it is just bad luck.	This means that you feel your behaviour doesn't contribute, or contribute much, to things that go wrong for you. You are placing the blame on something external – 'bad luck'.
It doesn't matter how well I plan, what's going to be, will be.	You feel you have no control as your whole life is already mapped out for you.
Friendships are a result of chemistry – they work or they don't.	Chemistry is definitely part of friendship, but not everything. If you don't work at finding and keeping friends, you will be on your own. Social well-being is very important in controlling stress.
Some people have all the luck.	See the first statement above. In this case you assume other people's successes are a result of 'good luck' rather than their efforts.
When things go wrong, I can usually find out who is to blame.	See the first statement above.

Statements of self-belief

I can influence what happens to me.
If I make specific short-term plans I know I will be able to keep to them.
I know friends are attracted to each other, but I can still influence how well I integrate with my friends. I have the interpersonal and emotional intelligence to do that.
When things go wrong, I work out why and sort it out so that it doesn't happen again.

ACTIVITY 7 Identifying your stressful events

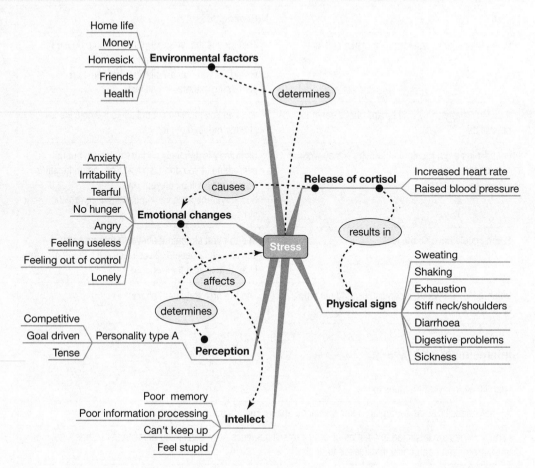

Map of study stressors – summary chart

References

- 6Seconds: Emotional Intelligence Network, available at: http://6seconds.org/index.php [last accessed November 2008].

- Bandura, A. (1997) *Self Efficacy in Changing Societies*. Cambridge, Cambridge University Press.

- BBC News (2004) 'One in seven students to drop out', 30 September, available at: http://news.bbc.co.uk/1/hi/education/3703468.stm [last accessed November 2008].

- Goleman, D. P. (1995) *Emotional Intelligence: Why It Can Matter More Than IQ for Character, Health and Lifelong Achievement*, New York, Bantam Books.

- Hennessy, K. (2002) 'All work and no play makes ... a student', *Guardian Unlimited*, 30 September, available at: http://education.guardian.co.uk/students/story/0,,802009,00.html [last accessed March 2009].

- Lazarus, R. S. and Cohen, J. B. (1977) 'Environmental Stress', in I. Altman and J. F. Wohlwill (eds), *Human Behavior and Environment*, Vol. 2. New York, Plenum.

- Lazarus, R. S. and Folkman, S. (1984) *Stress, Appraisal, and Coping*. New York, Springer.

- Unite, Student Experience Report 2006, MORI, available at: www.ipsos-mori.com [last accessed November 2008].

2 Managing your time

Managing our time is something like dieting. We know what we should eat, we know why we should eat that way and we know the benefits it will bring. However, how often do we start with good intentions and then let things slip? Time management can be similar. We know why we should manage our time, we often know what to do, but we just can't keep to it.

In this chapter you will learn how to:

1. identify your relationship with time and understand how this affects your time management
2. consider your life goals as part of your time management
3. manage your time efficiently and effectively.

USING THIS CHAPTER

Estimate your current levels of confidence. At the end of the chapter you will have the chance to reassess these levels where you can incorporate this into your personal development planner (PDP). Mark between 1 (poor) and 5 (good) for the following:

I can identify my relationship with time and understand how this affects my time management.	I can identify my life goals as part of my time management.	I can get the best out of my time.	I can manage my time effectively.

Date: _____

1 Introduction

How many of us have started each day by stumbling from lecture to seminar to the café, to the pub, and then to bed, only to do the same the next day with little thought of what we are doing? How many of us start the day by looking at the electronic messages and using that as a driver for the morning's activities? At the end of the day you get to bed exhausted because you have been so busy 'reacting'. But what have you actually done that is important in moving you forward? Are you a proactive time manager or a reactive one?

Our relationship to food, stress and time is very personal and in order to move on in all these areas we need to identify our relationship with them. This chapter enables you to identify your own relationship with time and recognise how you manage time now. You will look at the importance of the whole picture in order to fulfil all aspects of your life, not just your studies. Finally, we shall look at the mechanics of time management in order to make things happen.

Seeing time as a resource

We have only to look at the number of idioms in English that relate to time to see that we regard time as a resource. Most of these idioms refer to spending, wasting or saving time, as shown in the figure on the next page.

We are living with technological communications that give us instant access to information and we find ourselves in an environment that demands even quicker responses from us than ever before. We are living in

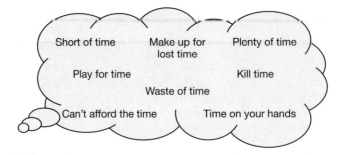

social cultures, be they industry, college or social spheres, where the volume of activity each week has rocketed. This can result in us feeling controlled by time. In a study of how North Americans use their time, the researchers found that 61% of the population reported never having excess time with 40% feeling that time is a bigger problem for them than money (work by Robinson and Godbey, 1997, cited in Boniwell, 2005).

The life of a student is tightly constrained by deadlines, time slots and timetables. How many times have fellow students you know complained about the amount of coursework they have to do and the bunching of deadlines? We increasingly work and play in environments that demand multi-tasking and that suits some and not others. Time affects us all, but how we **perceive time** and handle it varies between individuals.

2 Recognising your relationship with time

We can get an insight into how we deal with time by recognising if we generally 'look forward', 'look to the past', 'work to the wire' or finish one thing before starting the next. When we look at time like this, we realise there can be no 'one size fits all' as we have individual preferences.

First let us look at our preferences for particular time perspectives, as this is one aspect that affects our motivation to study.

Time perspectives

Philip Zimbardo, an award-winning social psychologist from the University of Stanford, looked at how our dominant orientation to the past, present and the future influences our behaviour and especially our ability to manage our time (Zimbardo and Boyd, 1999). Activity 1 helps you to identify some of these different time perspectives in other people.

ACTIVITY 1 Recognising different time perspectives in others

In this activity there are no absolute answers, and it is used to prepare you for recognising your own relationship with time later. Use the scenarios to give you a flavour of the characters and then estimate the following:

1. What time perspective dominates these students' lives at present: past, present or future? There could also be a mixture of these time perspectives.
2. Who do you think are multi-taskers and single-taskers?
3. Estimate their motivation to study.

Adrian is a second-year student living in a house with other students. He is very sociable and really enjoys his time with friends. The highlight of his week is Thursday night when he goes out with friends until the early hours of the morning. These Thursday nights have been so enjoyable he has started extending them to a few more nights as well, as Adrian's philosophy in life is 'to live for today'. Now, in the second semester, coursework and work difficulty is increasing and he is finding it hard to cope with everything, apart from his social life. He has had several warnings from tutors for late hand-ins, but just can't get around to doing more work, but he knows he has to. He finds it quite difficult to juggle social life and coursework.

Ismet is someone you can rely on to have a good time. He often arranges great evenings that are cheap but great fun. He is now in his third year and knows exactly what he wants to do when he finishes studying. His great planning abilities have helped him manage a busy social life and a challenging course. However, he knows he could probably have got a better degree grade if he had put more work in, but he gets such a buzz from juggling all these parts of his life that he is prepared to accept that. Although, having said that, he is heading for an upper-second degree classification.

Rachael always wanted to be an engineer and as a child was fascinated by those Victorian civil engineers who laid the foundations of our cities today. She knows it is tough, and is determined to get a good degree. She works very hard and is setting up volunteering and vacation work to get as much hands-on experience as possible. She also manages to have several pieces of coursework on the go at the same time and seems to be able to cope with it, although she gets a little irritated if she is interrupted while working. Her friends think she needs to relax a bit and at least take some time to enjoy herself now.

Student	Time perspective (past, present, future)	Preference to multi-tasking or single-tasking	Motivation to study (high, medium, low)	Estimated time management skills (poor, OK, good)
Adrian				
Ismet				
Rachael				

Check the feedback section at the end of the chapter.

Now, think about some of your friends. What time perspective dominates their lives? Do you think they are multi-taskers?

What's your time perspective?

Sometimes it is easier to recognise characteristics in others than ourselves, so now you've looked at others, it is time to take a look at yourself and see if you can identify which time perspective dominates you during semester time. In Activity 2 you can select several time perspectives. It would be interesting to see which one feels like you now.

ACTIVITY 2 Identifying your own time perspective

Look at the different time perspectives – which one(s) do you feel dominate(s) you during the semester?

Time persective 1	Time perspective 2
I tend to be impulsive and love excitement. I am happy to take risks as this makes life exciting. My motto is 'Live for today because I don't know what tomorrow will bring.'	My past life was not very pleasant and I too frequently recall events or things I regret doing and it can sometimes affect me now.
Time persective 3	**Time perspective 4**
I know where I want to go and I put plans in place to help me get there. I am prepared to work through boring pieces of coursework as I know it is laying a foundation for later work.	My motto is 'Whatever will be, will be.' I generally feel that I shouldn't worry too much about the future as it will take care of itself and luck plays a large part in how successful one is anyway.
Time persective 5	
I get a warm feeling when I think about the past, my family or cultural traditions. It makes me know who I am. It is very important for me to keep track of my old friends.	

Check the feedback section at the end of the chapter.

Consider how these time perspectives could effect your time management behaviour. Do you think you need to make adjustments to enable your studies?

Ideally we should be balanced between the different positive time perspectives, but not perspectives 2 and 4 as they have a negative effect on our life. Most successful people have a tendency to be 'future oriented' (perspective 3). When you are engaged in your academic studies this should motivate you sufficiently to encourage you to be future oriented. If you are not motivated, then it is going to be hard to engage with your learning or manage your time effectively. However, too much of this orientation can make you a workaholic, so you do need a balance.

We have seen that our time perspective affects our behaviour and our motivation to study and subsequently how we manage time. Our preference to being a multi- or linear tasker reflects our perception of time and how we manage time to complete tasks.

Are you comfortable multi-tasking or not?

An important anthropologist, Edward T. Hall, observed that different cultures had particular preferences when structuring their time. Cultures that see time as linear tend to emphasise the usage of time in discrete slots and complete tasks in a linear manner. Those cultures that see time as more fluid and less exact tend to carry out their tasks in a more non-linear manner and do lots of things at the same time. Work has continued in this field and these characteristics are also observed in individuals and particular jobs.

Different jobs have different time cultures where different time personalities can thrive. Those working with disaster teams, transport crews and surgical teams need people who can estimate time accurately and know what has to be done, when it has to be done, and do it. Those working in more creative fields may find such colleagues stifling. The academic time culture is deadline driven and many institutions will penalise you if your work is not handed in on time. If working to deadlines is not your preferred style then it is important to acknowledge that first and devise ways of coping.

With regard to individuals, those who prefer to do one task at a time are seen as 'linear taskers' while those happy to juggle lots of tasks at the same time are seen as 'multi-taskers'. If you see time as being discrete then you are able to identify slots in which to work and control your time. If, on the other hand, you see time as fluid and continuous you may not see much of a separation between work and your social life and you carry out tasks when the mood takes you rather than working to rigid time plans. How you think of time therefore can influence your tendency to multi-task or not. Activity 3 helps you to identify if you are a multi-tasker.

NOTE   If you want to learn some jargon, a multi-tasker is a polychron (a term first coined by Hall, 1959) and someone who focuses on one task at a time is a monochron! Can you recognise monochrons and polychrons in your friendship group?

ACTIVITY 3 Are you a multi-tasker?

Some of the key time management behaviours that can distinguish multi-taskers from others are: planning, focus and attention, reaction to change, and performing under pressure. You may already know if you are a multi-tasker, but have a look at a few of these statements and check the feedback. Remember: we can all be multi- or linear taskers but we prefer to operate in one or the other. Your preference will determine how you manage your time and how you meet your deadlines.

▶

	Ideally me	But in practice ... I do/don't do this ...
Planning		
1. I like to plan what I am going to do. Although I find it hard, I need to plan my time quite carefully. Without a plan, I feel a little bit lost. [linear tasker]		
2. I don't like working to a detailed time plan. It makes me feel constrained and irritable. [multi-tasker]		
Focus and attention		
3. Once I start on a task I give it my full attention and I dislike it when I am interrupted. [linear tasker]		
4. My focus and attention tends to be spread across lots of different tasks I am doing. It doesn't bother me if I am interrupted, I just deal with that and then carry on. [multi-tasker]		
Reaction to change		
5. Once I have worked out my plan of action, I get annoyed if I have to change it. [linear tasker]		
6. I can make rough plans, but happily change them too. [multi-tasker]		
Performance under pressure		
7. I like to keep track of the tasks I have to do and can prioritise very well. This gives me breathing space and so I can do the work before the pressure gets too strong. [linear tasker]		
8. I work best when I feel under time pressure. I am usually juggling several pieces of work to meet my deadlines. Prioritising is a last-minute approach for me, but I tend to get everything done. [multi-tasker]		
Is your preference multi-tasking or linear tasking?		

Check the feedback section at the end of this chapter for more information.

NOTE   These characteristics are just some indicators of multi- and linear tasking.

Advantages for the multi-tasker

You will probably feel less intimidated by the time pressure as you are able to juggle your coursework. You will probably find this stimulating. You may be a procrastinator as you are happy to leave things to the last minute and get started on many things simultaneously, but make sure you finish them! You have a very flexible working style and can deal with interruptions and changes to your schedule.

Dangers for the multi-tasker

Your preference for working under pressure and leaving things to the last minute does not allow for any mishaps. What if you suddenly realise you don't understand something the night before you hand in your coursework or that you should have completed a set of data before now? Since you can juggle lots of tasks, you may react to all your tasks in the same way. You must remember to plan and schedule and prioritise your activities, at least to some degree. If you try to do too much at one time you can be inefficient as you may just get overloaded and find you don't do anything very well. It may be better to allocate quality time for particularly difficult or important tasks. You may find you are a multi-tasker because you are an urgency addict (see Section 3 below). Now is your time to reveal your true colours!

Advantages for the linear tasker

You consciously want to have control over your time and if you are able to plan and identify time periods when things should be done, you can probably deal with the pressure. As a result of your prioritising and planning, you will be able to focus on key pieces of work.

Dangers for the linear tasker

Studying and the bunching of coursework deadlines can lead to a sense of time stress and the feeling that you can't do anything properly. You need to break down your tasks into smaller chunks and schedule at that level so you feel you are working in a linear mode. You may also need to be flexible enough to find those quality slots at short notice.

Checklist for dealing with your relationship with time

1. Identify your time preference.
2. Recognise if you are a multi- or a linear tasker.
3. Note if you can improve your relationship with time.
4. Recognise how this impacts on your time management.

3 Addressing your life goals: getting a balance

Time management is more than just organising ourselves and writing 'to-do lists'. We also need to make room for our wider goals in life, relationships, friends and family – we need a balance. Just planning and prioritising the tasks we have been given can be rather reactive and in order to account for all aspects of our life that are important to us, we also need to be proactive and ensure we work at them too. In our busy world there is a tendency to be 'urgency driven', reacting to all those demands that cross our path, rather than by those things that are important. We need to make sure we can plan, create and fit in all the things that are important to us in our life.

Traditionally time management training has been concerned with giving us tips to enable us to organise our time and deal with those ever-increasing urgent activities, generally in a very linear manner. Stephen Covey, father of nine children, professor of Business Management and an author of one of the most influential business books, *First Things First*, believes that we need to change our paradigm of time management from being addicted to dealing with what we perceive as urgent to proactively determining what is important. 'Importance' then becomes the new framework for managing our time.

The framework below was devised by Covey *et al.* (1994) to enable us to clarify what is urgent, not urgent, important and not important. Activity 4 asks what is important in your life.

	Urgent	**Not urgent**
	I	**II**
Important	Lectures, seminars, etc. Coursework preparation Assignment deadlines Crises	Preparation – long-term goals Planning – long-term goals Relationship building Creating new ideas/plans Personal development
	III	**IV**
Not important	Interruptions (some) Meetings (some) Some emails	Trivia Junk mail Time-wasting activities

Adapted from Covey, *et al.* (1994)

Quadrant I

Activities here are important and urgent; they have to be dealt with. To deal with activities here, we have to organise and prioritise what needs to be done. If we procrastinate with activities here, there will be serious consequences. In this quadrant we can feel driven and constrained by time, resulting in feeling stressed.

Quadrant II

This quadrant is where we deal with important issues such as planning (to keep quadrant I in check), creating new ideas and working towards our goals for both university and life in general. Keeping fit, doing exercise, broadening our mind, making intellectual leaps in our studies, volunteering, reading, helping friends and family, and developing meaningful relationships are all part of quadrant II. In this quadrant, we feel empowered and we need to deal proactively with the items in it. Don't neglect to do so.

Quadrant III

Many of us who are urgency addicted will deal with items that seem urgent but are not important. You may find you are reacting to other people's priorities at the expense of your own – try and keep a balance, and say 'no' to a few more non-urgent things.

Quadrant IV

This is where we generally waste our time. We might slump in front of the television, read trashy novels, etc. We are all in this quadrant from time to time, but try to limit how much time you spend here. You will find yourself in this quadrant often if you are driven by urgency as you will be stressed and exhausted and this is where you 'drop'. Also, when you procrastinate, you will find yourself in this quadrant.

ACTIVITY 4 What's important in your life?

You may feel very tempted to skip this activity. Please take time to think about it. The questions are quite challenging, but answers will come.

1. What things are important to me across my life?
2. What gives me a buzz?
3. What kind of work would I like to do after my studies? Do I need to be getting experience in place for that?

Now think of some of the steps you need to take in order to operationalise these goals. What could your plan look like if you include some of these things? Remember: these are your quadrant II activities and you need to be proactive in order to make them happen. Quadrant II activities are easier for those with a future time perspective.

This activity is something you need to do on an annual basis as your views do change, and it may need to be revitalised.

NOTE You should be motivated to study and successfully completing your degree should be one of your life goals. If this does not appear in your list, you need to ask yourself why you are studying or if you are studying the wrong subject.

4 Organising yourself

Organising yourself involves planning your time and organising your study space. Your plan tells you what you should do and when you should do it and for how long. Your study space enables that to happen. If you are a multi-tasker you may want to skip this section, but stop and read it as you may be able to maintain your spontaneity and couple this with some degree of planning that can help you. In addition, you should be able to determine the kind of environment that gets the best out of you. Linear taskers will probably be competent planners by now but check where you best learn and ensure you can make that happen.

Of course your degree of motivation for this will depend, to some extent, on your time perspective. Planning encourages the development of a future orientation. If you are dominantly oriented towards the present, you will find it hard to fufil your plans even if you make them. Be careful of this.

How do you organise your time through planning?

Even the worst students of time management don't lurch unconsciously from one thing to another during the day, every day. There is always some degree of planning. However, what is your general pattern on time planning during a week? A plan will give you some idea of where all that time is going and how effective you are at getting those important things done (see Activities 5 and 6). Interestingly, a study in 1997 found that students at a particular university had more study work activity on Monday, Tuesday and Thursday, and fewer studied at weekends. The study found that typically students spend 38.8 hours on study-related tasks (the range was 34–48 hours depending on age, gender and year). Of that study time, 35.5% was spent on assessed work, 12.8% in lectures, 8% on non-assessed work, 7.6% of time in tutorials and 3.2% searching books in the library (Innis and Shaw, 1997).

ACTIVITY 5 Developing a weekly schedule

Look back on a typical week during semester time and try to remember how you spent your time. Include sleep, going out, paid work, private study, group/coursework, etc., as well as attendance at lectures/seminars. Note this down on the schedule below and estimate the time for your activities, using time slots. Are you happy with this or would you have liked it to be different? Is it similar or wildly different to the research above?

A typical week

Approximate times	Mon	Tues	Wed	Thurs	Fri	Sat	Sun
8.00–10.00am				9.00–10.00 Lecture			Catching up with sleep
10.00–12.00		11.00–12.00 Lecture	Seminar				Catching up with sleep
12.00–2.00pm						Paid work	Seeing friends
2.00–4.00pm			**Sport**				
4.00–6.00pm			**Sport**				
6.00–8.00pm			Paid work				
8.00–10.00pm			Paid work				
10.00–12.00pm							

Now think of next week and plan how you should spend your time, given the deadlines you have.

Approximate times	Mon	Tues	Wed	Thurs	Fri	Sat	Sun
6.00–8.00am	Sleep	Sleep	Sleep	Sleep	Sleep	Sleep	Sleep
8.00–10.00am				9.00–10.00 Lecture			Catching up with sleep
10.00–12.00		11.00–12.00 Lecture	Seminar				Catching up with sleep
12.00–2.00pm						Paid work	Seeing friends
2.00–4.00pm			**Sport**				
4.00–6.00pm			**Sport**				
6.00–8.00pm			Paid work				
8.00–10.00pm			Paid work				
10.00–12.00pm							

Next week my main goals are: _____

ACTIVITY 6 Balancing your time

Look at the activities on your weekly plan:

1. Can you identify the quadrants? Label them QI, QII, QIII and QIV.
   - Are any of your activities labelled QI really QIII? You can gain time by weeding out QIII-type activities.
2. Make a new empty weekly planner and start by putting in events/activities that are time sensitive, e.g. a lecture, as these are immovable.
3. Add QII-type activities in the free slots (these may not be on a weekly basis, but possibly a monthly basis). These will be taken from Activity 4, above, 'What's important in your life?' Remember to use the time slots to free up time to do things you want to do.

Organising your study space

You may have read in time management books that you need to have a clear desk (represents a clear head!), be somewhere quiet and not be disturbed. However, when you actually talk to students and ask them about their organisational preferences, it varies. What do you prefer? See Activity 7.

ACTIVITY 7 Your current and ideal study space

Imagine you have to complete a piece of coursework, which could, for example, be an essay or a laboratory report. You know you have to begin this piece of work today and so you sit down to start. Answer the questions in the table below. The examples are just prompts; you can also add your own. You may be happy with what you do: if so, then say so; if not, say what would be ideal for you.

	What you do currently	Is this ideal? If not, what is ideal?
1. Where do you prefer to work?	*At home, in the library.*	
2. Generally how is your work space organised?	*Cleared desk, work on top of other things, work on floor, have papers in a folder, have loose papers.*	
3. When you sit down to work do you find yourself getting up soon afterwards?	*You are hungry, thirsty, just need to sort something out quickly. Check the ritual you have before you finally get started.*	

	What you do currently	Is this ideal? If not, what is ideal?
4. How long do you think it takes you to feel settled and start work?		
5. Do you like to have music on at the same time as studying or have other people around you?	*Some people need to be alone and quiet and others need a certain background noise. What is your ambient preference?*	

There are no correct answers for this except to say that it is advisable to have all the papers you need to start an assignment at hand, as well as knowing **exactly** (not roughly) what you have to do and how long you have to do it. Having a messy desk and working with music and people around you may be what works for you. If so, then keep to it but do check you get the best out of this and it is not just a habit. The essence of this activity is for you to identify how you currently organise yourself, recognise your rituals (this is like doing stretches in the gym prior to your workout; you prime yourself for activity) and recognise that you are getting ready for work. However, if your 'rituals' go on for too long, you may be procrastinating. So be aware. If you are currently working in a space that is not conducive to your learning, now is the time to identify what the problems are and make changes.

Making a piece of work manageable

Some pieces of coursework can be rather daunting, so you need to create smaller chunks that are easier to manage:

- clarify what is needed in your coursework
  - identify any data you need from experimental or practical work
  - identify the pieces of information you need
- make a list of all the parts/chunks you need to complete
  - order the list
- check the hand-in date for your coursework
  - add a time frame to each chunk.

If you are a multi-tasker you may be happy with the main points. If you are a linear tasker, you may want to develop further the sub-points in your list.

5 Time management strategies

In the earlier sections we have looked at individual preferences with respect to our perceptions of time and how this influences the way we organise our time. In some cases time may be handled well and for others, the majority of us, there will be room for improvement.

Time is a resource that cannot be reused or recycled as with some other resources. We have a fixed number of hours in a semester and the only way of doing all those things we want to do and need to do is to manage this resource more efficiently. If you consider how much effort you put in each day you need to ask yourself what the net effect or outcome of all this effort is.

Mechanics of time management – planning, scheduling and using 'to-do' lists

To do this effectively you need to take different time frames and the most appropriate is the semester, the week and the day. Your semester plan enables you to see the overall picture for your studies and plan those important things that can get lost once the semester starts, e.g. develop a new sport, start up a new hobby, do some volunteering work or attending the careers advisory talks/workshops.

The weekly schedule fills in those time-constrained activities like lectures etc., leaving you slots for other important activities.

The 'to-do' list relates to each day and is where all your planning stops and the 'doing' takes place. This time frame is critical. If you consistently don't deliver within this time frame and you are predominantly a linear tasker, you start to feel overwhelmed and out of control. Multi-taskers may condense their 'to-do' lists in a flurry of activity, possibly at the last minute.

The table below gives some idea of how these time management aids work for your studies, but remember: this should also include important things you want to do outside of your studies.

NOTE 'To-do' lists are where the action happens and they should have a time frame and be able to support your goals. Make them SMART: Specific, Manageable, Relevant and Timely.

Recommending a time management strategy

Good time management is about working smart and not about working long hours. Your time is precious and you don't want to squander it on things that are not important, so be:

1. **S**pecific – identify precisely what you have to do. Goals that are too general rarely get finished.

2. **M**anageable – you will need to break large pieces of work down into smaller, manageable chunks so that you can tangibly feel small successes of a larger piece of work or project. By doing this you can more easily stay on track.

3. **A**ttainable – don't set yourself goals that are going to be difficult to achieve as this will only sap your self-confidence. Set sizeable goals that may be challenging, but attainable within the resources you have.

4. *R*elevant – the goal is working towards something you want or have to do within this time frame and for a particular project. Remain focused.

5. *T*imely – know when your task is done. What is your time frame? What needs to be done to make it complete?

Long-term planning	Mid-term planning	Short-term planning
Planning ⟶		Doing (outcome from your time planning)
Semester plan	Weekly schedule	Daily 'to-do' list
Identify your academic goals for this semester. Read unit descriptions to see what is expected of you.	This is similar to the weekly planner in Activity 5, above. Ensure items identified in your semester plan get transferred to the appropriate weekly planner.	This is your present time perspective. Apart from your time-sensitive slots, you should prioritise your other activities according to their importance.
Note assignments and hand-in dates for your courses. Find out who you need to see regarding possible work placements, Erasmus exchange, etc.	Enter your time-sensitive items like lectures, tasks/event that satisfy your key goals and those urgent things that just must get done.	Start your day by setting your 'to-do' list and then **prioritising** tasks according to their **importance** and 'due date'.
Note any software you need to learn or be expected to know and find out how you can train yourself.	Make sure your weekly planner includes your whole life and not just your studies. Many people are increasingly turning to electronic means for this through mobile phones or PDAs.*	PDAs usually have a 'to-do list' function, you may want to use that. Highlight the high priority tasks.
Promise yourself to complete your personal development planner as this will enable you to articulate what you are learning and identify where your strengths and weaknesses are.	Carefully estimate the time it will take you to complete tasks. This takes experience, but it is a characteristic of good time management.	

*PDA is a personal digital assistant. It can be integrated in your mobile phone or a standalone tool. There are also several desktop tools that can be used like a PDA, e.g. Google has a selection of tools and Microsoft Outlook has a PDA-like function built into it.

Checklist for developing good time management strategies

1. Balance short-term with long-term (life) goals.
2. Be importance rather than urgency driven.
3. Plan – in detail for linear tasker and roughly for multi-tasker.
4. Know how and where you learn best.
5. Understand your relationship with time.

ACTIVITY 8 Recommending time management strategies

How should the students below improve their time management skills? Can you identify their issues with regard to time management? A summary of time management is included below to help you work through this activity.

Jane is the first of her family to study at university and she is very excited by it. She lives with a long-term boyfriend who is just finishing a modern apprenticeship scheme. She is in her first year and, although she has worked before, she was not prepared for the amount of independent work she would have to do in addition to keeping her 'old life' together. Jane knows what her goals are, but finds the juggling of tasks difficult as there seems to be so many demands on her time.

Winston has been in the UK for about a year and is enjoying his studies. He knows what he wants to do when he finishes but has difficulty around exam times. He is fine during the year and manages to get his coursework in on time. Revision for exams is somehow different. He doesn't have a set place to revise and some days goes to the library, other times he sits on the floor of his bedroom or in the kitchen. He knows that when he starts to revise he will suddenly feel hungry and then goes to make something to eat. He will come back, ready to start, and then realises he hasn't made a promised phone call, so he does that. He is now ready to start, and a friend calls and they have a chat. By late afternoon he gets some work done but then his friends ring up and invite him out. Since he feels that his day is already wasted, he decides to go. He feels bad about this, but promises himself he will start revising properly tomorrow.

Can you write your own scenario?

NOTE   If you are dyslexic you may have difficulty putting things (mentally and physically) in order. It is important for you to try and identify what you need to do and create a slot for it. If you have persistent problems with this, then it would be advisable to consult a learning differences unit at your institution as it is essential you find a strategy that suits you.

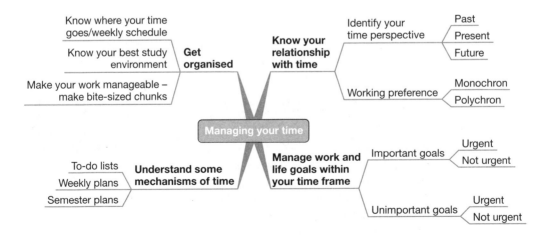

6 On reflection

Time management is about understanding your relationship with time and how that affects your ability to manage time. Looking forward motivates you and enables you to identify your life's goals. Keeping up with old friends, and enjoying yourself now, also balances your life.

Planning, scheduling and 'to-do' lists are mechanisms you can use to keep yourself on track, but ensure that your track is for important issues and not trivia. This will give you a sense of achievement and a feeling of control over your time.

Now, reflect on your own relationship with time and how you intend to adapt your behaviour so that you can spend your time more effectively. You may want to transfer this information to your own institution's personal development planner scheme.

ACTIVITY 9 Update your personal development planner

Having read this chapter, gauge your confidence again. How does this compare with your confidence levels at the start of the chapter? What can you do to improve? You can incorporate this into your own personal development planner. Add anything else you feel appropriate.

Grade your confidence on a scale of 1–5 where 1 = poor and 5 = good.

My time management plan	Confidence level 1–5	Plans to improve
I recognise that my relationship with time affects how I manage my time. *Section 2*		
I recognise that my life goals are as much a part of my time management as course deadlines. *Section 3*		
I know how to get the best out of my time as I know how I study best. *Section 4*		
I now know how I can manage my time effectively and can develop strategies that suit me. *Section 5*		

Date: _____

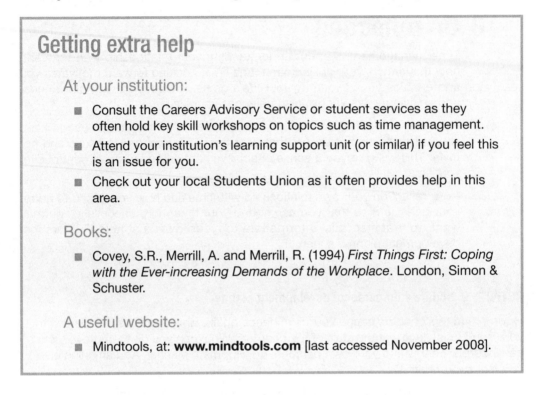

Getting extra help

At your institution:

- Consult the Careers Advisory Service or student services as they often hold key skill workshops on topics such as time management.
- Attend your institution's learning support unit (or similar) if you feel this is an issue for you.
- Check out your local Students Union as it often provides help in this area.

Books:

- Covey, S.R., Merrill, A. and Merrill, R. (1994) *First Things First: Coping with the Ever-increasing Demands of the Workplace*. London, Simon & Schuster.

A useful website:

- Mindtools, at: **www.mindtools.com** [last accessed November 2008].

Feedback on activities

ACTIVITY 1 Recognising different time perspectives in others

There are no absolute answers to this feedback. Here are some interpretations. If yours are different, it may be worth articulating your reasons.

Adrian

His time perspective is very much in the present, especially with respect to his social life and having a good time. From his short description, we might conclude that he is happier doing one type of activity at a time (his social life doesn't seem to vary much) rather than juggling a lot of different activities. His motivation to study appears to be low. His time management skills may be doubtful (poor).

Ismet

His time perspective is dominated by present and future. He is prepared to live now, but keeps his eye on coursework so that he doesn't fall behind. He seems to be a good organiser, and that takes some juggling. He has to do this as well as keep up with coursework, although it seems he pulls back on his social life to get some of his coursework completed. He seems to be a multi-tasker and quite motivated in his studies as well as good at time management.

Rachael

Her time perspective is very much in the future and very much at the expense of living now. She should be careful that she doesn't experience burn-out and needs to re-balance her life. She appears to be a multi-tasker when it comes to her studies, but the fact that she gets irritated when interrupted could mean that she prefers to focus on single aspects of her coursework – doing one piece at a time and liking to stay focused. She is highly motivated and probably a good time manager (motivated people usually manage their time better than non-motivated people).

ACTIVITY 2 Identifying your own time perspective

If you are dominated by time perspective 1, you are 'present oriented'. You really focus on having a good time. For you, it is the now that counts. This is really a hedonistic perspective and we should all spend time in this perspective at some time during a week. If, however, it dominates you, you may find that you will be prone to giving up your work in favour of the addiction to seek excitement and having a good time. Being permanently in this time perspective is very unhealthy for your studies or career in the future as you succumb to temptations that appear more exciting at the time.

If you are dominated by time perspective 4, you are also 'present oriented' but in a negative, fatalistic way. You feel that life is outside your control and nothing you do will change that. You have a general feeling of helplessness. Being predominantly in this time perspective zaps your motivation. You see no point in putting in the effort so your studies and future work will really suffer.

If you are dominated by perspective 5, you are 'past oriented' in a positive way. Your happy memories have helped you develop a positive view of life and given you the stability to move on; we all need this. Research has shown that those in this perspective have a high sense of self-esteem (Boniwell, 2005).

If you are dominated by perspective 2, you are 'past oriented' in a negative way and you may not be able to get over something that was unpleasant in your past. If that is the case, and you feel it is an issue, you may be advised to seek professional help. It is important to deal with negative experiences so they don't run your life. In terms of your studies, you may find you are not meeting your full potential. Negative past events don't have to be traumatic; getting consistently bad marks for essay writing or maths tests, for example, could be enough to determine how you deal with these now.

If you are dominated by time perspective 3 you are 'future oriented'. You have set out your goals and you make plans so that you can fulfil them. You seek out new challenges and opportunities where you can. Research has shown that this time perspective is associated with well-being, persistence and self-confidence (Boniwell, 2005). You can, however, be so concerned with achieving that you forget to enjoy yourself, become a workaholic, experience burn-out and forget to live in the present. You need a balance.

ACTIVITY 3 Are you a multi-tasker?

You will probably find academic life is very much a polychronic culture. More than likely your coursework assignments will be bunched towards the end of your course just when you are thinking of revising for your exams. In some cases you are finishing coursework and sitting exams in the same week. It is important to identify what your working preference is so that you can make adaptations to fit in with the actuality of study life.

If you have identified yourself as a multi-tasker then you will probably fit in well with academic structure. Be careful, however, that you give important pieces of coursework enough attention and don't leave things to the last minute.

If you have identified yourself as a linear tasker, then you need to prioritise your tasks, break them down into small tasks, create a time plan and carry out these smaller tasks in a linear way. You need to work in small chunks so you can get that piece of work finished within your schedule. This will keep you on track in a polychronic environment while you work in a linear fashion!

Multi-taskers (polychrons) prefer ...	Linear taskers (monochrons) prefer ...
time to be unstructured	structured time
not to make detailed plans	to work to detailed time plans
to work on tasks when they are in the mood	to work to their prioritised list of activities
to spread their focus and attention across lots of things	a very focused approach
to go with the flow and if they are interrupted it doesn't matter.	to work without interruption.

ACTIVITY 8 Recommending time management strategies

Jane may have sorted out her major goals and planned well, but she does not seem to be handling her 'to-do' list well. She needs to prioritise, and that includes her home life, and stick to her daily tasks. If she carries on like this, she may feel that she can't cope with her studies and leave. She must work smart and really do what is important.

Winston has problems revising for exams whereas structured assignments seem to be OK for him. He seems to be a classic procrastinator. He needs first to accept that this is what he is doing and then set himself small tasks. He should concentrate on the task at hand and not take or make phone calls during this period. He can then reward himself with a couple of hours out with his friends. He will feel good about himself and enjoy his time out a lot more.

References

■ Boniwell, L. (2005) 'Beyond time management: how the latest research on time perspectives and perceived time use can assist clients with time related concerns', *International Journal of Evidence Based Coaching and Mentoring*, 3(2), 61.

■ Covey, S. R., Merrill, A. and Merrill, R. (1994) *First Things First: Coping with the Ever-increasing Demands of the Workplace*. London, Simon & Schuster.

■ Hall, Edward, T. (1959) *The Silent Language*. New York, Garden City.

■ Innis, K. and Shaw, M. (1997) 'How do students spend their time?', *Quality Assurance in Education* 5(2), 85–89.

■ Robinson, J. P. and Godbey, G. (1997) *Time for Life: The Surprising Ways Americans Use their Time*. State College, The Pennsylvania State University Press.

■ Zimbardo, P. and Boyd, J. (1999) 'Putting time in perspective: a valid, reliable individual differences metric', *Journal of Personality and Social Psychology*, 77, 1271–1288.

3 Learning part time

Although this is a separate chapter on learning part time, the distinction between full-time on-campus students and those of you studying part time is becoming blurred. From a 2008 survey of student lifestyles, conducted by Sodexho – Times Higher Education, it was found that 'almost half of the students with a job in term-time undertake paid work for between 11 and 20 hours a week, and 10% devote between 21 and 30 hours a week to their job' (Attwood, 2008). As a part-timer, you may also feel that you are missing out on all those facilities on campus but, again from the same survey, 67% of full-time students socialise off campus, 63% study in their own accommodation and 91% spend 10 hours or less in the library. So, don't feel you are necessarily missing out on a great social life on campus.

In this chapter you will:

1. become familiar with the key administrative documents on your course
2. understand how to prepare yourself for part-time learning
3. know the range of learning technology that could help you
4. know the online skills you need to develop in order to exploit those technologies.

USING THIS CHAPTER

If you want to dip into the sections	Page	If you want to try the activities	Page
1 Being a successful part-time learner	77	1 Update your personal development planner	92
2 Using technology to learn	83		
3 On reflection	90		

Estimate your current levels of confidence. At the end of the chapter you will have the chance to re-assess these levels and incorporate this into your personal development planner (PDP). Mark between 1 (poor) and 5 (good) for the following:

I am well prepared for my studies.	I am familiar with the learning technologies I can use.	I am a competent online learner with a set of skills to help me.

Date: _____

1 Being a successful part-time learner

As a part-time learner, whether enrolled as a full-time student or not, your main issue will be the competing demands on your time. You can succeed if you prepare yourself and recognise how you learn, remain well motivated, network well with fellow students, know how to deal with the potential stress of it all and manage your time effectively.

Different ways to learn part time

Being a part-time learner can mean several things: you study at home with a book, work to a learning agreement and evidence your learning through work; have day release to attend classes; study part time most of the year, but once or twice a year you have a residential week where you meet everyone. In all of these variations you will probably have some element of online learning, so understanding how to use learning technologies will be vital.

Distance learning

This is a generic term for learning 'off campus' or part time, and it can be paper based, entirely online or a mixture of both. You will need access to a PC so you can log in to your institution. Apart from your course materials you should also have remote access via the Internet to library facilities, the Students Union, the library and most other facilities available to students on campus. You may need to check this out. Your course will have a set of documents that you need to familiarise yourself with (see 'Learning in Higher Education', Section 3 and information below). Since you may not meet your fellow students, you need to network online in order to feel part of a study community (see 'Prepare yourself' below).

Work-based learning

Through this approach you will have registered to study and probably been given a list of things you are expected to show competency in at the end of your studies (learning outcomes). You will be expected either to complete coursework and learning outcomes through your every day work activities or to present a comprehensive portfolio of evidence showing the competencies you have developed. It is very important therefore to ensure that the experience you are gathering does map to the learning outcomes of the course. If it does not, your tutors will not be able to give you a 'pass' as they have to match your developing competencies against the learning outcomes for that course. Understanding what is required on the course therefore becomes vital. Even though the course will be based on your job, you will still be expected to read the academic literature and place what you are learning within conceptual frameworks that align with that literature.

Compact courses

These can also be distance-learning courses, with a week of face-to-face study at your institution. You will probably be given work to do during the semester so you are prepared for this intensive week. Arranging time off from work and family duties is essential and you will probably need to find a week's accommodation. If this is while your institution is closed to traditional students, you may be offered student accommodation.

Day release scheme

Sometimes your institution organises courses that allow you to study one or two days a week. If this is the case, you will be local to your institution and in this mode of learning you will probably have arranged day release from work. You may also be joining a class of students who are studying full time and you may feel under time pressure as your reading and coursework will have to be fitted in. However, good planning and time management will see you through (see Chapter 1, 'Managing your time', and 'Prepare yourself' below).

Prepare yourself

At the start of your course take time to prepare yourself by: identifying why you are doing it, recognising how much you want it and arranging your life to get you through those inevitable dips. Preparing yourself for study is not just for part-timers, it is something all students should be doing.

Understand your course

Although you should look thoroughly at the course you have enrolled on beforehand, you will probably find that you have only given the study detail a fleeting glance. Once you have registered, you must take a closer look at your course. This is particularly important when learning at a distance as you don't have that easy backup that you normally have when with fellow students on campus. Look at the checklist below and ensure you understand this information at the beginning of your course. If you don't know the answers now, make a point of finding out as soon as possible.

Checklist for proactive coping strategies	
	Need to work on this ✓
Regulations: • I know the pass mark and marks needed to gain certain grades. • I know what my options are if I fail a unit or module.	
Learning outcomes: • I understand this is what I should know at the end of the course, and I will have to evidence this through my coursework, portfolio and/or exams.	
Learning materials: • I know where they are stored and how I can access them.	
Reference materials: • I know how to get key texts and access the library remotely.	
Coursework: • I know what is expected, when and how to hand it in.	
Assessment: • I've made a note of the dates and what is expected. I have access to old exam papers so I can practise.	

Also check the information in 'Learning in Higher Education', Section 3, at the beginning of this book.

Your approach to learning

To get the most out of your studies, you need to understand yourself as a learner and through this you can exploit your strengths and work to improve your weaknesses. As explained in 'Learning in Higher Education', Section 1,

Figure A1.1, David Kolb, in 1975, proposed a four-part learning cycle that we still use today: (a) gain experience, (b) observe and reflect, (c) work with abstract ideas and concepts and (d) apply learning to new situations. As we learn new things, we go through this cycle with the end result that we are able to apply our learning to new situations. As learners, however, we tend to feel happier in particular areas of this cycle, but not all of them. So, if you are happy in the 'gaining experience' part of the cycle, then you are more likely to be an activist and happy to get going quickly on a project and not 'hang about'. Similarly, you may not be too happy to 'take time out' to reflect on what you are doing. 'Know yourself as a learner' and 'Learning in Higher Education' expands on this.

As a learner you also have a preference for processing information and one popular way of looking at this is VARK (Visual, Auditory, Reading/writing, Kinaesthetic). This proprietary tool was developed by Neil Fleming, an educational researcher from New Zealand, and Charles C. Bonwell from the USA and considers the four sensory ways we can get information: looking, hearing, reading/writing and hands-on. The authors say that as learners we have preferred senses for taking in information.

Look at the following – which do you think applies to you best and least?

Visual learners learn best through:
- Taking notes and making lists to read later.
- Reading information to be learned.
- Learning from books, videotapes, filmstrips and printouts.
- Seeing a demonstration.
- Working with concept maps.
- Seeing the overview of what is to be learned.

Strategies for visual learners:
- Use highlighters in texts.
- Create concept maps/flow charts
- Use videos.
- Format your texts that visually lay out your information.
- Underline and circle text as you read.

Auditory learners learn best through:
- Listening to lectures and audio sources.
- Arguing and discussing ideas.
- Giving oral presentations as they can generally talk well.
- Using speech recognition software like DragonPlus or Via Voice.

You may be distracted by a lot of noise so your learning environment should be quiet.

Strategies for auditory learners:
- Record your notes through speech recognition software.
- Read aloud.
- Revise by recording your thoughts and playing it back.

Reading/writing learners learn best through …
- Handouts from lectures.
- Good textbooks.
- Writing essays.

Strategies for reading/writing learners:
- Taking a good set of notes in lectures.
- Learn for exams through practice essay writing.
- Learn through your own writing (you often don't know what you know until you write it down).
- Learn through writing things out that you have to learn (often again and again).
- Create lists.
- Create and answer your own frequently asked questions.

Kinaesthetic learners learn best through:
- Doing and practising.
- Taking in information through labs, field trips, excursions, etc.
- Learning from demonstrations.
- Using examples to learn concepts and principles.

Strategies for kinaesthetic learners:
- Walk about while you are learning.
- Take frequent study breaks.
- Learn by handling materials, using models, doing things.
- Create models, posters, images.
- Skim-read books to get an overview first.

NOTE For more information on learning styles see: **http://www.studyskills.soton.ac.uk/ studytips/learn_styles.htm** or an Internet search on VARK.

Take care when using learning-style questionnaires. There are very many of them and they all measure something different. Always listen and reflect on how you learn best and use that if in doubt. The VARK approach above will give you some ideas and you can always add your own.

Motivation

Learning part time and/or at a distance will mean that you need a lot of motivation to keep going. Learning can be difficult and you will hit low spots where you have to pick yourself up and keep going. Without a lot of motivation to study, you may 'lose your way'. Motivation comes from various sources.

Motivation to learn	
Extrinsic	**Intrinsic**
External motivation from parents, employer, partner, friends, etc., and possible rewards such as bonus, promotion, new job. The subject you are studying may or may not interest you that much.	Internal motivation results from something you really want to do and can also be linked to new job prospects. You are particularly interested in the topic.
Success and reward	

Your motivation will probably be a mixture of intrinsic and extrinsic. However, when the going gets tough, you need a good dose of intrinsic motivation and self-belief to 'stay the course'. To keep your motivation up it is important for you to feel reasonably well in control (see the chapters 'Managing your stress' and 'Managing your time'), chunk up your work into manageable bits, set short goals that allow you to succeed and recognise your achievements as you go along.

Confidence

When you are studying part time you are having to juggle lots of things in your life and as your studies become more difficult and make more demands on you, you may feel your confidence drop. This is a natural response, but it is important that it doesn't become too critical. All true deep learning will, at some time, put you outside your comfort zone (see Figure 1.1, in Chapter 1, 'Managing your stress'). Also, check out Sections 4, 5 and 6 in that chapter and remember that self-belief is critical. If you find your confidence ebbing away and you are not recovering, do email your tutor or fellow students and get it sorted out. It is important to talk about it as then you can start to find solutions.

Family and work commitments

This will be the greatest competition for your time. You need to establish a regular time and place to study and, as with all your other activities, this should become a fixture in your diary. As soon as possible establish critical dates for family, work and study and get them in your diary. If there are any clashes, be proactive and negotiate with your family, employer or tutor.

Network and keep in touch

Learning is based on an inner dialogue with yourself in relation to the learning materials and coursework and through interpersonal dialogue with your fellow students and tutors. You need both! It is important therefore to make sure you know who may be studying on your module at the same time as you so you can support each other. Don't forget: your tutor is also part of this network.

Identify a learning space

Find a place where you can study. If you are studying at home and have to move your papers after each study session, make sure you have a handy box that you can put everything into so that nothing gets lost. Also, identify where you can learn best: a quiet place, a busy place, a tidy place or a messy place. We all have our own preferences. Whatever you do, try to establish a learning routine, pace yourself and set reasonable goals.

> **Hot Tip**
>
> Since you will need to have Internet access at home, invest in a wireless-enabled laptop so you can sit anywhere in your house and be online. This will give you maximum flexibility regarding your learning space.

Skills for part-time learning

All learners need to understand themselves as learners and develop skills that best suit them. This is the whole purpose of this book. It is more critical, however, for part-time learners to understand how they learn best as they have to make the most of the small amount of time they will have available. The crucial skills for you as a part-time learner will be your ability to:

- manage stress and time
- motivate yourself during difficult times
- take responsibility for your own learning and
  - be self-disciplined and set your own deadlines
  - reflect on your progress and do something about it if necessary
  - ask if in doubt
- exploit learning technologies.

2 Using technology to learn

Whether you are learning part time or full time, you will probably need to have some technology to keep you going. Ideally you need:

- An Internet connection at home, preferably broadband if that is possible in your area.
- A wireless-enabled laptop so that you can work in the most comfortable place in your house and be able to move around if that space is demanded by others.
- A memory stick so you can back up your material and take your work with you as needed.
- A printer as you may be expected to submit work in paper format.
- An MP3 player if you have access to audio or video podcasts.

Also, as we saw earlier, being a full-time student doesn't mean you are necessarily on campus and socially there. The Sodexho – Times Higher Education survey (2008) also found that 88% of students use social networking sites every week, so take a look in this section to see how you can benefit from them educationally.

Access to information

You will be given a set of materials, such as these: lecture notes, problem sheets, case studies, textbooks or journal articles. Whether you are a campus or a distance student, you will probably have access to a 'virtual learning environment' (VLE). This is an online repository for all the learning materials as well as other online tools. Generally, these systems are now available via the Web and through Internet access on your own PC and a password from your institution, you will be ready to access all your material. Apart from written texts you may also find that increasingly your tutors provide you with audio and/or video podcasts which enable you to download to an MP3 player, for what is now called 'mobile learning'. You should also be able to get remote access through your library to online journals as well as the university catalogue. The file-sharing video application on the Web, YouTube, has also become a host to some educational videos. The Open University in the UK, for example, has launched a set of YouTube videos – you may want to check this out, http://www.youtube.com/ou. (Times Higher Education, 2008).

Collaborate with others

Online tools for collaboration, information sharing and networking are loosely known as Web 2.0 technologies. Some examples of these technologies are: email, chatrooms, blogs, sites like Facebook, office-type documents on Google, and wikis.

Wiki

The most famous wiki of course is Wikipedia, the online encyclopaedia that gets its information from the general public (which is why you should use it with care and never use it as your primary source of information). A wiki allows you to create linked pages of text and multimedia 'assets'. Your tutor may ask a group of you to create a wiki on a topic and this will enable those with permissions to upload and edit information. You may also want to create your own wiki as a study guide or a portfolio. If your institution does not have a Wiki feature on the VLE it uses, you can always try some of the free services that are available, such as 'PB Wiki' . However, since it is a free service, it does have limited capacity. You can see how to use this through a YouTube video.

Blogs

A 'blog' is a shorthand version of 'Web log' and is set up by an individual to publicise his or her views on a particular topic. Blogs tend to be text based but they can also take multimedia items. Blogs can also be used for online seminars where your tutor will set a topic for discussion.

'Google Docs'

Web 2.0 technologies have increased our ability to learn from anywhere and with anyone. We don't necessarily need to be sitting at our own PC. However, when we have our documents on our own PC then we need to be at that PC in order to access them (unless you have emailed them to yourself, or put them on your memory stick). If you use Google Docs, for example, you can access your documents (text, spreadsheet or presentations) from anywhere and you can also allow your colleagues to see and work with them if you want. If you don't have a PC with all the relevant office software, or you want to able to access your documents from anywhere, you may want to consider exploring this. Check out 'google docs' on a Web search engine and follow the video tour. A good place to start if you are interested is: http://www.google.com/google-d-s/tour1.html.

Social bookmarking

This is a way of marking web pages you (and others) are interested in. The standard 'add to favourites' feature on your Web browser allows you to save an interesting site in a hierarchical structure that you have created. You also have to go back to the same PC in order to access your 'favourites'. Social bookmarking software, such as 'Del.icio.us', allows you to post interesting sites to your Del.icio.us account (it is a free service), add key words that help you organise the information (a bit like putting in folders except you can have many key words) and share this with others if you wish. To access your sites, you search on the key words you have used and all sites with those 'tags' appear. You are also able to see if anyone else has used that key word for other sites – giving you a wider view. There are some things you need to know about social bookmarking:

1. You need to 'tag' the sites you post to, let's say your Del.icio.us account. These tags, or key words, relate to how you will use the information and you may be able to use it in several ways, so you will have several tags. The tags will enable you to search for the group of sites you have marked with these tags. Knowing how you want to tag is important. All resources in a library are tagged, but they use a standard sets of tags, e.g. Library of Congress, and this formal tagging system is called a taxonomy. Because it is formal it enables everyone to find the same information using the same search words. However, when we tag our websites in social bookmarking applications, we tag in an informal way and the same website can be tagged in numerous ways by different people. This way of tagging is called a 'folksonomy', a term coined by the information management architect, Thomas Vander Wal (**www.vanderwal.net/about.php**).

2. In these applications you have the option of viewing your tags as a list, you can bundle them (like grouping in folders) or you can view them visually as a 'tag cloud' Figure 3.1). Words appear in cloud format with some words in

larger font if they have more websites tagged using this word. Tags are on single words, but the author in the example below has grouped words that go together to ensure an easier retrieval. However, this does limit your return when using this term to identify similar sites tagged by others.

local authorities	Aerobic
LandRemediation	Landfill
WasteManagement	Anaerobic

Figure 3.1 An example of a tag cloud

For more information on social bookmarking and a list of online tools, see Netsquared organisation at:
http://www.netsquared.org/choosingsocialbookmarking

Skills for online learning

Using learning technologies in your learning is not just for part-time learners. Increasingly full-time students are finding that a lot of their work is online. However, as a part-timer you will find that you have to rely more on e-learning as your main source of literature, learning materials and online activities. All students then need to develop a set of skills that enable them to exploit these technologies to the full.

Netiquette

Netiquette is simply 'etiquette for online communication'. Email-type communications do have certain social rules that you should adhere to:

- Write clear subject headings
  - Be precise – the heading should reflect the content of the message.
  - Keep the header when forwarding or answering so a chain of messages can be identified.
- Organise your message effectively
  - Don't be too verbose, keep your message to the point.
  - Itemise key things where you want a response. Don't hide key information in verbose text, particularly at the end of the email; it will almost definitely be missed.
  - Avoid sending attachments if you can. Remember: you can use applications like Google Docs which allow you to direct people to a document or Flickr if you are using photographs.
- Be aware of your tone
  - Don't use capitals letters as it feels like YOU ARE SHOUTING.
  - It is easy to misread the tone in an email and respond in an aggressive way. If you feel offended, wait and respond when you feel calmer.
  - Don't send 'flaming' angry emails yourself as they can appear more aggressive in this medium.

Working with online groups

Online networking can be formal seminars, groups working on a project, informal forums or study help groups. It can be tricky working in a group online, especially if you have to make a decision about something. When you are sitting face to face in a group, you know where everyone is and that sets up an expectation of how the interaction will be; for example, a person at the apparent head of table has a greater tendency to dominate or lead the discussion. Similarly, how people sit in the meeting, the tone of their voice and facial characteristics give you clues as to how engaged they are with the discussion. When you are working online, these physical cues are not available to you and you need to apply a bit more structure to the proceedings online in order to move forward. Figure 3.2 gives you an idea of some of the structures that you and your group may want to consider.

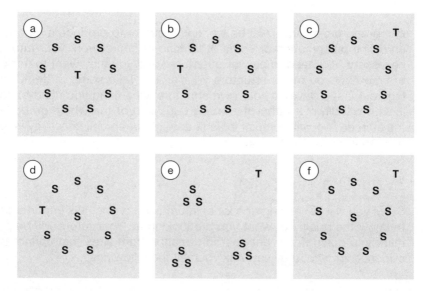

Figure 3.2 Online group structures (S = student, T= tutor)
Source: Maier and Warren (2000)

Online seminars/discussion groups

In formation (a) of Figure 3.2, your tutor holds centre stage and most of the interaction will be from tutor to student. Here the tutor is 'in charge'. You 'listen' to what others say and contribute as you see fit. In this pattern there is rarely interaction between students.

In formation (b) your tutor is one of you, part of the group, but this can be difficult to achieve as you will always feel that the tutor is 'in charge'. More mature students can cope with this better.

In formation (c) the tutor is the quiet observer. He or she may be 'listening in' on the discussion and you may have an uneasy feeling about this. It is easy to feel a little paranoid in an online environment. If this mode is used it is important for the tutor to say so and be explicit about his or her role.

In formation (d) your tutor may select someone to lead the discussion and then be part of the group. If you are selected to lead, you also need to bring your tutor in along with everyone else. This is quite difficult, as you may feel nervous about handling it. Again, this is easier for more mature students.

In formation (e) student sub-groups would have been set up to discuss some aspect of an issue or problem with the view to reassembling to see what others have said or decided. Your tutor may only 'listen in' at the end phase.

In formation (f) your tutor will select someone to lead the discussion as in (d) above. This is a very good skill to learn, as you need to know who is in your group, who has said what, if there are people who have said nothing yet and how can you bring them in. You need to know from your tutor what the goal of the discussion is, how long it should last and what the output should be.

Group projects online

In a group project, you will be working together to produce a report, a wiki, an online presentation or some other kind of coursework your tutor deems necessary. You need to be well structured and you may want to think ahead of time how you might structure your group. Take some of the ideas from Figure 3.2 and develop your own structure. One thing you need to consider is who will direct – either the sub-groups and/or the whole group. Having the attitude 'we will all muck in' isn't enough for an online activity where you need to finish with a product.

Evaluating a website

Since you will be looking at a lot of information online, it is important for you to know the quality of what you are looking at. Your tutors will be quick to mark you down if you get your information from sites that cannot provide evidence for what they say. Ask yourself the following:

What's the purpose of the website?

1. Is the site selling a product or services?
2. Is this an institution or a company promotion site?
3. Is this a self-promotion site?
4. Is this a collection of information/links of interest to the author and others?
5. Is it instructional material?
6. Is it a collection of papers, like e-prints or an online journal website?

What information is there about the origin of the site?

1. Who is the author? Identify the authority of the site.
2. What organisation is the author affiliated to?
3. What is the domain of the site? For example, .edu, ac.uk (education, academic), .gov, .com, etc.
4. When was the site produced or last updated? Determine the currency of information on the site.

What can you deduce from the content?

1. What is the focus of the site?
2. What is the potential readership?

---

3. What impression do you get from the language? Does it use 'persuasive' language or is it objective and backed up by evidence/references?
4. Can you detect any biases?

Websites which naturally have academic integrity are those for online journals. Check out 'Web of Knowledge', but make sure your institution has given you access. If you are a UK student in Higher Education, this will be your 'Athens' login.

Any information you get from general websites needs to be backed up by work that is based on evidence (i.e. research). Remember to cite your websites correctly, see Chapter 13, 'Understanding academic integrity: plagiarism'.

Hot Tip

To search the Web for more academic sites try using Google Scholar (**http://scholar.google.co.uk**) or Intute (**http://intute.ac.uk**). Google Scholar ranks a site according to, for example, its original publication source and citations. The websites listed on 'Intute' have similarly been scrutinised for their academic integrity. However, in both cases, you still need to check for yourself.

Assessment

Assessment comes in two basic forms: formative and summative. Summative assessment is probably what you think assessment to be, and it contributes to your final grade. Formative assessment, on the other hand, is there for you to take advantage of in order to test how you are getting along and identify any areas where you need to do more work. Very often students won't do assessments that don't 'count'. This is very short-sighted and you should take every opportunity given to you for formative assessment. As a part-time learner this can give you a real boost as well as identify where you need to concentrate your efforts.

Quizzes and tests

A quiz sounds very much like something you see in a magazine; however, it has now become associated with formative assessment in online learning. Tests are more formal and often seen as summative assessment.

Tests and quizzes online tend to be (although not exclusively) multiple-choice questions. You will be given a statement and then expected to select the correct answer from a list. You can also have tests where you are expected to match two parts, label diagrams, etc. If you know you are going to have online tests you need to know what kind they are and practise using the software. Very often these tests are timed and you need to know exactly what to do.

Coursework

You will have larger pieces of coursework to do on your course and in fact you may only have coursework as your summative assessment. Make sure you check this at the beginning of your course together with how it should be presented and the submission date.

You may be asked to submit coursework electronically through your institution's VLE and if you do this you usually get an electronic 'stamp' to verify that you have handed it in. If you send by email, ensure you set up your email to ask for a receipt once your email is opened.

Once you hand your work in electronically, it can be checked for plagiarism. In the UK, generally the Turnitin software is used for this. Make sure you understand what plagiarism is (see Chapter 13, 'Understanding academic integrity: plagiarism').

Hot Tip

The excuse 'my PC crashed' for not handing in your coursework on time is no longer a valid excuse. You are responsible for backing up your work. Save your work at short and regular intervals while working, save it to your memory stick or send it to yourself by email.

Exams

Check at the beginning of the course if there are any exams or if it is all coursework. If there are exams you need to know if they are in the form of computer-aided assessment, i.e. online, or if you have to go to your institution to 'sit' the exams under strict exam conditions.

If you are on day release, or have any other form of contact with your institution, you will probably be expected to attend a formal exam hall, if you have to do exams.

Make sure you know how to study well for your exams so you can recall the information when you need it (see Chapter 8, 'Excelling in exams').

3 On reflection

In this chapter you have looked at what it means to be a successful part-time learner and the kind of technology and subsequent skills you will need.

Summary of this chapter

Take a quick look at Figure 3.3 opposite and assess how well you are now familiar with these areas.

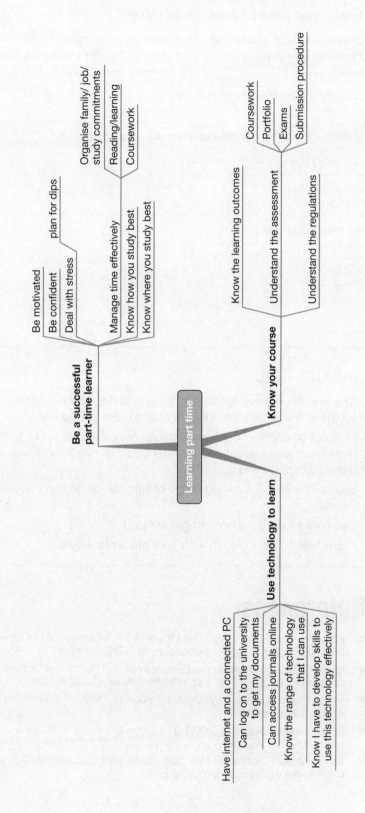

Figure 3.3 Summary of the chapter

ACTIVITY 1 Update your personal development planner

Now reflect on your current abilities and consider what you need to do to improve. You may want to transfer this information to your own institution's personal development planner scheme.

Grade your confidence on a scale of 1–5 where 1 = poor and 5 = good.

My developing skills	Confidence level 1–5	Plans to improve
I am well prepared for my studies.		
I am familiar with the learning technologies I can use.		
I am a competent online learner with a set of skills to help me.		

Date: _____

Getting extra help

- Check with your institution if it has online tutorials or training material for the software or technology it may expect you to use.
- Find out who you should ask if things go wrong with your technology; there is usually a telephone number you can ring. Check you have this before things go wrong.
- Search the Web for a wide range of tutorials on topics you are finding difficult.
- Use your student network to get support.
- Know how to get in touch with your students union.

References

- Attwood, R. (2008) 'Survey finds it's all work, less play for the top-up generation', *Times Higher Education*, 11–17 September.
- Intute Collection Development Framework and Policy, [last accessed 12 September 2008] available at: **http://intute.ac.uk/policy.html**
- Maier, P. and Warren, A. (2000) *Integrating Technology in Learning and Teaching*. Kogan Page, London.
- Times Higher Education (2008) 'The Open University – YouTube opens a video eye on OU', 21 August
- Vander Wal, T. Wanderval.Net. [last accessed 1 October 2008] available at: **http://www.vanderwal.net/about.php**

2 Improve your work

This part emphasises what you can do to get the most out of some of the basic components of your education: note-making, lectures, reading, presenting your work and exams. You may want to find out what your note-making style is and try out different approaches. Remember, you will need your notes to structure your revision later. Lectures are often seen as a passive activity but you can get more out of them if you know how to be an active listener.

You may think that reading is something you learnt in primary scool and you don't need to look at it again; this is not the case. At this level you need to be more aware of how texts work, be critical of what you read and develop efficient strategies. This increased awareness will also improve your writing.

At some time during your studies, team work, oral presentations and poster presentations will be part of your assessment. Your tutors may refer to these as key or transferable skills. This means that once you are aware of how to improve these skills, you can transfer it to other contexts.

Exams are inevitable, so within your busy schedule it is important to know how to organise the revision process, identify the best way to present the information you need to learn and recognise how you best remember things.

Take time to reflect on the skills you are developing in this part through the questions in each chapter.

4 Getting the most out of lectures

If you have to take notes in a lecture, the pace, rate of delivery and framework for presenting the information are all out of your hands. The pressure is on to think on your feet, to try to make sense of the thinking which has gone on behind the scenes in the preparation of the lecture and to be able to record information at speed – in other words, the ability to multi-task. Thus, it is vital that your listening skills and your note-making abilities are in tip-top condition to enable you to get the most out of lectures.

In this chapter you will:

1. assess your own interaction during lectures
2. explore the skills needed to get the most out of lectures
3. examine how to prepare for lectures to develop efficiency
4. develop keener listening skills.

USING THIS CHAPTER

Estimate your current levels of confidence. At the end of the chapter you will have the chance to reassess these levels where you can incorporate this into your personal development planner (PDP). Mark between 1 (poor) and 5 (good) for the following:

I know the skills needed to get the most out of lectures.	I know the different types and purposes of lectures.	I can listen effectively and differentiate the information I am listening to in lectures.

Date: _____

1 Are you a lecture sponge?

Lectures are a waste of time.

Angela, first-year student

A **sponge** learner is ready (or not so ready) to **soak up** information from tutors and lecturers. This sounds comfortable and relatively relaxing, but it is an ineffective way of learning. Did you know, for example, that if you listen to someone (e.g. a lecturer), without actively making notes or participating in some other activity, you will be doing well to remember 20% of what's been said?

There are many reasons why some students do not get as much out of lectures as they should. Often this is because they have not prepared sufficiently and have inappropriate expectations of lectures.

What do you expect to get out of a lecture?

Pitching your expectations high is one of the ways you can yield good results. If you intend to interact with the information you will receive during lectures, you need to have the right mindset (see Activity 1).

ACTIVITY 1 Am I a lecture sponge?

Answer true or false to each of the statements.

	True	False
1. The lecture (or series of lectures) should teach me all I need to know on that subject/topic.		
2. I want to go into the lecture and get all the information I need for my assignment.		
3. I should not need to take notes because the information is provided as handouts or online.		
4. I do not need to think in lectures; I just need to listen carefully.		
5. Lectures should contain pictures, video clips, etc., as well as written and oral communication.		

If you have answered 'true' to most of these statements, you will find that there is a gap between your expectations and what lectures offer. This is neither the fault of your lecturer nor of you. It is simply that the rules of the lecture game do not match what you expect. Most students want value for money from the lectures but it is important to understand the purpose of lectures as a teaching tool. This will help you to get the most out of them.

How to increase your capacity during lectures

Activity 2 explores some of the problems that students have expressed about lectures. Identify your problems and look at the solution hint so that you can go immediately to the appropriate section of this chapter.

ACTIVITY 2 What do I do in lectures?

Problem	Solution
Your expectations for the purpose of the lecture are inappropriate.	Look at the purpose of lectures so that you adjust your expectations.
You are unable to cope with the volume of information because it is **all** new to you.	You need to do some pre-lecture preparations.

Problem	Solution
You quickly go into information overload and give up taking notes.	You need to do some pre-lecture preparations to ensure that you are ready for listening and understanding the information more effectively and at greater speed. You need to sharpen up your listening and selection skills.
You do not recognise or understand some of the new terminology.	You need to do some pre-lecture preparations.
You cannot follow the gist of the lecture and seem to become muddled.	You need to have a tentative information framework upon which to hang the information. You need to do some pre-lecture preparations.
The information seems very detailed and in great depth.	You need to do some pre-lecture preparations so that you have your own framework or skeleton of information before going to the lecture.
Your questions are not answered during the lecture.	This may be the result of a misunderstanding of the lecture format. Have a look at the purpose of lectures.
You are distracted easily by other students who are talking or by rustling of paper.	Either choose where you sit very carefully (if possible) or learn how to cut out extraneous and unwanted noise. Develop more effective listening skills.
The lecturer's style may not match the way you take in information.	You need to be more aware of the way academic tutors present information so that you can choose an appropriate method to take in more information and also to get the information down more effectively. Try to increase your listening skills. Try to vary the format of the presentation of your notes.
Your lecture notes are not used later on.	Match up the purpose of the lecture, the type of lecture and your presentation format so that the notes will be helpful. Develop more effective listening skills.

2 The purpose of lectures

Lectures are not the same as seminars and group tutorials. They serve a different purpose, and consequently the anticipated outcomes for students are different. Lectures last between 40 and 50 minutes. As a teaching tool, they are intended to give information to groups of students. In some ways they are cost effective in that they can deliver information to large student cohorts. The size of the student group will depend upon the subject and the individual university. Some undergraduates are taken aback when they walk into a lecture theatre, and there are up to 500 students present. The size of the group can vary between 25 and 500.

Most departments organise a series of lectures to coincide with specific units of study. At the start of the unit, some students seem unaware of the purpose of lectures. However, this may be a case of crossed messages, and that the lecturers' intentions are not made explicit to students. For example, many lecturers do not usually expect to be interrupted by students' questions during a lecture. Some academics will tell you that they have set aside a little time at the end for questions but many will give their 'speech' and disappear. This is down to individual teaching style and delivery. However, be alert to the lecturer who sets aside time for questions. This may change your note-taking tactics during the lecture in terms of making your questions stand out in your notes as a memory jogger for later. Usually, you are expected to listen to the talk. Many lecturers use PowerPoint slides on a large screen to get across their points. Some lecturers may use an overhead projector (OHP) with transparencies (OHTs) containing information. These may be typed or handwritten. In some subjects, notably Mathematics, lecturers provide examples by writing mathematical workings at speed on a board.

There are various types of lectures, and the efficient student is aware of these types so that most use can be made of the information, format and style. This means that you may need to think on your feet quite quickly to spot the type and be flexible in your response in terms of expectations and note-taking.

Type of lecture	Purpose	Outcomes
Keynote	Keynote lecture is intended to raise issues/questions. Setting the scene and giving a broad overview.	To get you to question information and research. To inform you of the main issues.
Introductory	Introducing a series of lectures. Setting the scene and giving a broad overview.	To provide you with a framework of knowledge/concepts upon which everything else will hinge.
Sequential	Each lecture builds upon the previous one.	An assumption of prior knowledge from previous lectures.
Focus	Takes a specific aspect of a topic and goes into detail. Provides information and detail about specific research.	To fill in or put flesh upon the framework which was provided in the introduction.
Conclusion	Sums up the key points of previous lectures. Draws all the threads together.	To give an overview which can be used in conjunction with introductory lecture notes.

The biggest problem for students is that often the lecturers do not specify which type of lecture they are delivering so you will have to think on your foot at the beginning of a lecture. Of course, you can make some judgements prior to the lecture. If you look at the unit/course handbook this will help you to work out the type of lecture you are listening to. By reading between the lines of the departmental guidance information you can decide upon the type.

Most experienced lecturers follow a logical framework for delivery. There will be a brief introduction, the main part of the lecture and summaries or conclusions. However, these components are discrete and many lecturers do not signal explicitly what is happening. However, you need to be alert to this hidden structure so that you can be prepared. For example, the introduction will help you to anticipate what is to come. Some lecturers will provide a quick overview of the structure, which will help you to be aware of when they are moving on to another section or sub-topic. It is worth making sure that you take down the summaries and conclusions so that you can use these as a check to find out if you have teased out the main points of the lecture. This alerting system will be examined in more detail in the section about listening skills.

3 What skills are involved?

Getting the most out of lectures hinges upon your ability to make connections. The efficient and effective student is able to take in and select the information, while at the same time fitting this into some internal scheme or mental jigsaw. The lecture sponge soaks up the information but does not realise that the facts and knowledge are part of a big picture and so has not developed the flexibility to fit new information into previous knowledge – so the connections are not made and the jigsaw is often incomplete. This will result in notes gathering dust in files or having to spend time trying to make sense of why you made the comments.

There are seven main skills which you need if you are to get the most out of your lectures:

- good listening skills
- concentration skills
- summary skills
- note-taking skills
- organisational skills – both on paper and in your thinking
- critical thinking skills
- multi-tasking skills – the ability to do many of the above at the same time and at speed.

Of course, lectures do not suit all types of learner. Some students' knowledge and understanding is increased by listening to someone tell them about a topic or explaining a concept. However, others do not get as much out of this oral method of getting information because it has no hooks to help them remember and process the information. Thus, you must ask yourself how you are going to bypass your preferred learning style if you rely upon visual and written note cues. Perhaps it is worth considering how you can develop greater efficiency so that lectures are a true source of information. See the sections on pre-lecture preparation and templates for taking down information – in particular the Cornell Method.

As was stated earlier, students who simply turn up for the lecture and listen for 40–50 minutes are missing opportunities. Some work in preparation for lectures is not time wasted. Similarly, reflection and consolidation after the lecture will reap benefits for revision and in helping you to obtain better grades in your coursework and examinations.

Efficient pre-lecture preparations

Spending time preparing for lectures is time well spent and will ensure that you learn more when you go to the lecture and that your note-taking is more effective and meaningful.

Your preparation will pay off because you will be able to recognise and begin to understand new terminology and ideas. This means that you know which key words to listen out for. This will help you to **focus your listening skills** so that you can take better notes. You will, therefore, be able to listen for the clues which are in the lecture to help you make sense of new information and concepts.

There are many sources of information which you can use to help you prepare effectively to get the most out of your lectures:

Source	How to make use of it
Course handbook	
Unit/session overviews	To give you an overview. To give you an idea of what to expect. To inform you of the purpose of specified lectures.
Lecture series titles	To help you to start building that framework or jigsaw of information.
Lecture titles	To enable you to make the connections and links.
Unit glossaries	To help prepare you for new terminology. To improve your listening skills – you know what to listen for. To help you to understand new concepts.
Indicative reading lists	Get hold of some of these and look at the sub-headings in chapters to get a sense of a new topic and to help you to develop your own internal map or jigsaw picture. See if there are any definitions of new terminology so that you are prepared for your lecture.

Source	How to make use of it
Online information	
Department site	Check electronic information which is available. This may be in the form of PowerPoint notes or information sheets. Read this information in advance of the lecture to put you in the right frame of mind and to prepare you for key concepts and ideas.
Internet searches	Download background information to help you understand what the lecturer is getting at.
Library site	Check the subject section to find out what your subject librarian has loaded up for different courses/units.
Yourself	
	Make a list of questions which spring to mind about the topic. See if you can get the answers in the lecture. (If not, at least this is a checklist of things you need to find out.) Get your file/notes organised in advance to save time on the day. Anticipate some sub-headings for your notes.

Making effective use of pre-lecture notes and downloads

In the long term, pre-lecture preparations will help you to understand new concepts and ensure that you are ready to take in new terminology because you have had to engage with the information and have had to think about it. Think about athletes. They always perform warm-up activities to ensure that their muscles are flexed beforehand and to ensure that performance is high. Pre-lecture preparations have the same main purposes and act as a warm-up for the brain or to get you into the right frame of mind to absorb the lecturer's information more efficiently and effectively. The hidden side effects are explained in the following table.

Pre-lecture activity with collected or downloaded information	Purpose/use
You can go through the lecture notes carefully and highlight with a coloured marker pen important information.	This will increase your understanding. This will improve your memory skills. This will help you to retrieve the information later because crucial information stands out and provides a quick-access short cut for the brain.
You can also annotate those notes – make your own comments or questions in the margin.	This will increase your understanding. This will improve your memory skills.
You can highlight key terminology (and put a definition of meaning alongside if necessary).	By putting the definition in your own words, this will increase your understanding and memory – much more so than if you simply copy out someone else's definition.
You can scan the lecture notes into your your computer.	You can customise the layout so that you can make your own additional notes during the lecture alongside the lecturer's notes. (Some students prefer to customise printed lecture notes by double spacing for ease of access; or make space for your own notes parallel to the lecturer's notes.) Once again, reading and making decisions about what to do with the layout will provide valuable reinforcement.
You can scan the notes into your computer and make up your own concept map.	This is useful for those who prefer to have information in this alternative format rather than the traditional linear format. Making yourself do this activity can help you to develop your own map of the information.

Cautionary tale

I haven't got the time to do all this before each lecture. It's bad enough having to keep up with everything as it is.

Sharon, first-year History student

It is short-sighted to think that there is not enough time to do this type of pre-lecture preparation. It will save you time in the long run because you will get more out of the lecture in terms of your understanding; your notes will be of a better quality; and this in turn will boost your chances of doing a better assignment or remembering information for examinations. It boils down to ensuring that you organise your time as effectively as you can and add this element into your weekly schedules. Try out some of these activities over a semester and reflect upon your grasp of the topic and your ability to cope with the process of writing an assignment.

Supposing I did all of this beforehand. What would be the point in actually going to the lecture?

Jim, second-year English Studies student

Jim is not the only student who has made this comment. However, the point he is missing is that during lectures, tone of voice, emphasis and other body language will strengthen your understanding. Remember: some lecturers try to provoke thought by their tone of voice, and this does not come across in the impersonal notes. You can't get all of this from the two-dimensional downloads and information on screen. It is true that some lecturers are more memorable in their delivery than others but this human interface may spark off discussions with your friends, and you will not be able to participate in this further dimension to the purpose of lectures – to generate discussion and questions.

Post-lecture activities: what to do with the information after lectures

What do **you** do with your lecture notes after the lecture? Many students toss the notes into a file, often in a haphazard way. Some have a number of file pads which are used randomly for various lectures, and the notes are left there for filing at a later date. But what happens when you drop your bag, and the notes are scattered everywhere?

If your notes are of real value, you will need to do some work on them as soon after the lecture as you possibly can – while the information is still fresh in your mind. Your notes will be vital for assignment and examination success, so why not spend some valuable time in reviewing, consolidating, tidying up the loose ends and reflecting?

- The organisation of your filing system is personal but the system has to be maintained and each set of lecture notes needs to be carefully filed away into your system.
- Take time to read through your own notes to make sure they make sense to you. You may have to write in full some of the abbreviations you were forced to use in the lecture because of the speed of the lecturer's delivery. Tackling this soon after you have taken the notes means that you can draw upon recent memory of what the lecturer said to improve your notes and make them more understandable.
- Highlight key words and phrases so that they will stand out when you come back to the notes at a later date.
- If you have not had time to do sub-headings, read through a section and put a succinct title to it. Check your sub-heading titles and consider whether you need to change these so that the notes have greater cohesion and you will be able to recognise immediately the framework of the information at a later date when your memory of the lecture has faded.
- Write the key concepts in a different colour in the margin next to important information. This is termed annotating your notes.
- A4 Summary Sheet – if you can discipline yourself to do this, you will reap greater benefits. This is a bullet-point summary of the information and key points. By doing this, you will have to review, reflect and consolidate the knowledge and information and most importantly you will have to put it into your own words. This can be placed at the

beginning or the end of each notes section so that you can get a quick reference to what is contained in the notes to help you decide whether you need the information for an assignment at a later date. These Summary Sheets are also useful for revision purposes.

4 Lecture alerts: behind the scenes

Obviously, lecturers have their own style of delivery and quirky ways. However, there are some features that you might like to look out for in order to alert you to possible outcomes which could affect your concentration and selection of information.

Body language cues	Alert
Speaks very quickly	Need to have good listening skills. Look out for key words/information. It may simply be a sign of nervousness.
Speaks very softly at the beginning of the lecture	This may be used as a ploy to get students' attention and to calm down the 'audience'. If used for this purpose what is said at this point may not be vital.
Reads from notes	This type of lecture places greater pressure on your concentration skills because it can often be delivered in a monotone. The lecturer may be nervous or unsure of the information and needs to rely heavily on notes.
Says some things very slowly	This is a verbal method of underlining and putting information in bold. It is likely that the information is important so you need to record it in your notes.
Repeats phrases and sentences	It could be that the lecturer has lost his or her place in his or her notes! More often it is a way of emphasising important information so you need to record it in your notes.
Pauses occasionally	You have to decide if this is an individual/stylistic feature or not. It could be that the lecturer has lost his or her place in his or her notes! It may be a ploy to make a point that some students are talking during the lecture. It may be the lecturer's way of emphasising important information so you need to record it in your notes.
Turns to screen to go through slide information (be it OHT or PowerPoint)	This is the sign of an inexperienced lecturer. Sound levels will naturally drop so you need to be listening carefully.

Body language cues	Alert
Paces up and down in front of 'audience'	This type of style of lecturing is often accompanied by lack of use of notes. The lecturer knows his or her stuff! It can be distracting for some students, so you must ensure that your concentration levels are high.
Use of rhetorical questions	You are not expected to answer these either by shouting out the answer or by raising your hand. They are used to get students to be critical or to demonstrate the current debates and issues. The lecturer then proceeds to answer his or her own questions. At times they are a device to vary the delivery so that students do not fall asleep in lectures!

Environmental features	Alert
PowerPoint slides	Where are the notes? Are hard copies available in the room? Was I expected to download them myself prior to the lecture?
PowerPoint slide usage	(i) As information handouts only (usually six slides per A4 page) to start off your notes. (ii) As an aide-memoire for note-taking (usually three or four slides per A4 page with lines for you to personalise the information). (iii) Some slides are for information only and are not talked about by the lecturer; others are brought up on screen and additional information is given. If a lecturer uses this style, you must be alert and concentrate so that you do not lose your place!
Overhead transparencies (OHTs)	This is an alternative to PowerPoint. It probably means that there is no electronic version available for download. Each slide contains succinct information which you are expected to record in some way.
Writes information on board	You need to take down this information because it may not be contained in any other source of notes.

An awareness of these features will ensure that you get even more out of your lectures.

5 Template for note-taking

Taking notes in lectures does rely upon the expertise of the lecturer. Style of delivery and expertise varies, and this can have an impact upon your ability to keep up with the notes but more importantly the need to be flexible. This applies to all formats of note-taking.

Your note-taking should ensure that you leave spaces for the lecture's afterthoughts and revisitings. Lecturers are only human and at times suddenly remember information that should have gone with an earlier section. At other times, lecturers can be imparting information from their notes and at the end of a section they want to bring you up-to-date information which they have just read about. This information has to be tacked on and you would need to try to place it in the appropriate section of your notes. If you have left no room, you should ensure that you link the information by arrows or colour coding when you are involved in the post-lecture activities.

On the other hand, one of the problems with making a note of what the lecturer has said in a linear manner is that there is less room for flexibility. A template for lecture notes could solve your problems.

The Cornell Method

This is a method which was developed over 40 years ago by Walter Pauk to help his students at Cornell University (Pauk, 2000). It was intended to increase efficiency and originally consisted of six stages. It was his intention that students:

- record information from lectures
- reduce their notes
- recite the information to aid recall and memory
- reflect
- review the information to make sure they understand it
- recapitulate and make a summary.

The following table shows how you could organise your note-taking, the Cornell way. As you can see, it is a template which could be prepared beforehand, using your word processor. Section A provides vital information to help you to identify your notes at a later stage. Section B is the space where you write your information during the lecture while Section C will allow you to reflect upon what you have learnt during the lecture and give you space to write up distilled and useful information. This could be essential for use in gathering information for your essay or as a start to producing effective revision notes. Of course, the active student will come away from the lecture with some questions unanswered and Section D will provide space for you to summarise the lecture to get a global or overview picture.

A. Lecture title:	Date:	Lecturer's name:	Page number:

B. Space for information taken down **during** lecture

C. Additional notes in post-lecture phase:
key words;
key concepts;
key theorists/names.
Additional information which you have remembered from the lecturer's talk which you didn't have time to record in the lecture.

D. Follow-up:
Questions you might have
Commentary

Uses

Its main advantage is that it is possible to cut down on redoing notes. Again, you have to be well prepared in advance for this way of taking notes. However, once you have got into the routine of preparing your pages in this way, you will quickly adapt and the lecture work space (B) will not seem restricted or limited. It will also provide you with more usable notes for revision. Similarly, if you are searching through your files for information to put into your essays, you need only glance at the summary section to find out if there is anything worth using.

6 Using a laptop during lectures

Electronic notes are now part of a student's life. Writing electronic notes during lectures is down to personal preference but also to the facilities which are available in your college or university. If you have a laptop computer with wireless connections you will have access to many facilities. However, not all lecture rooms are set up in this way at the moment. To help you to decide whether electronic notes are viable for you, consider Activity 3.

ACTIVITY 3 Should I use a laptop in lectures?

Which of the following statements apply to you? Answer true or false.

	True	False
1. I prefer not to work straight onto screen.		
2. I do not feel confident working on a computer under pressure.		

	True	False
3. My keyboard skills are slow.		
4. I am not sure about basic functions of my word processor.		
5. I do not like to read information straight from the screen.		
6. I feel embarrassed using a computer in front of other people.		
7. I am worried that I might press the wrong keys and wipe all my lecture notes.		

If your answers are mainly true, you really ought to consider whether you are ready or really want to make electronic notes during lectures and seminars. You need sophisticated skills of listening, summarising and multi-tasking when coping with lectures. Making electronic notes adds another dimension to this complexity. You need to ask yourself whether using an electronic format during the lecture is the right approach for you. The crucial questions you have to ask yourself are:

- Do I have the necessary skills?
- Is this way of note-taking going to support me or be a barrier to my learning?
- Do I want to take notes in this way?

Of course, if the answer to the final question is 'no', then you will eliminate this mode of 'writing'. However, you need to make sure that in the long term you are not closing doors for more efficient ways of working both at university and beyond.

You need to have a good speed of typing if you are going to stand a chance of keeping up in lectures. This may seem a trite remark but spending some time in a vacation or before you embark upon your course learning how to touch-type or improving your typing speed will be time well spent. The old adage 'practice makes perfect' has never been more true than in these circumstances. The more time you set aside to practise your skills, the quicker you will become. The best case scenario is that you are able to touch-type. This means that you can look at the slides and still type in your information. Being at this level of expertise also implies that you will not be slowed down looking for a specific key. If this happens, the lecturer will be three sentences ahead of you, and you will be constantly chasing your tail. Touch-typing does not imply that you use both hands – though this is better. Many students can type at speed only using two fingers on each hand. You need to ensure that your typing speeds and your knowledge of the word processing program are automatic so that you are not slowed down grappling with the technology!

Reviewing and consolidating your notes is easier on computer, and the final product will be clearer to read at a later date. However, a small amount of forethought can reap excellent rewards when you are under pressure to find information for an essay, for example. Thus, setting up a template on your laptop can be done in advance so that you can move around the document, placing the lecturer's information in its appropriate box or section.

7 Critical listening: ways to increase your listening skills

Listening to a lecture requires skills which you may need to practise in order to increase your efficiency. The student who develops active listening skills is the one who will understand and deal with new and challenging information more effectively and will also be able to remember the information for longer periods of time before having to rehearse the information in some way (see the section on exams in Chapter 8).

Baseline skills

These are:

- concentration
- anticipation
- questioning
- selection/elimination
- analysing
- summarising.

If you are questioning, selecting and summarising spoken information, you will be actively involved in the lecture. The result will be higher levels of concentration because you are being critical – not in the sense of negatively criticising your lecturer's voice or clothes but, more importantly, critical of what is being said. You can improve your concentration skills. It is all very well to be told not to daydream during lectures. It is natural for the mind to wander but you must make sure that you keep yourself in check. Prompting yourself with questions is a way of keeping your mind on the job in hand. Thus, if you think you are getting bored, instead of doodling, start analysing the information you are listening to.

Mental joggers – asking the right questions

These are:

- Why has the information been included?
- How does it link with the rest of the information?
- Is it essential or exemplar information?
- Is this a new section?
- Does what the lecturer is saying fit in with what you have already read or is it controversial?
- What point is the lecturer trying to make?

In addition to concentration, a vital skill to use is that of anticipation because it will set off your own questions, make you listen for the answers you need, and in this process you will be selecting information and tagging some parts of the lecture as being of higher priority than other parts (selection and elimination).

What to anticipate/what to listen out for	What is its use?
Introductory statements	May indicate an overview of the lecture structure so that you can be ready to organise your sub-headings and branches of information.
Signal language	This could get you ready for lists, for example. For more specific examples see below.
Summaries/conclusions	These will help you to develop a framework of information. They can be used as a checklist when you review your notes to make sure you didn't miss anything out. They can deepen your understanding.

8 How to hone your listening skills: we hear what we want to hear

The warm-up

You can double your listening capacity by doing the pre-lecture activities. These activities will make you aware of key terminology and give you a broad framework of information so that you go into a lecture with some hooks upon which to put the new and sometimes challenging information. Although these activities will increase your ability to make sense of new concepts and ideas, you need to do something slightly different to ensure that you prepare yourself for hearing the information.

- Pick out and list key terms, terms with which you are unfamiliar and terminology which seems to be used in a very specific way in the subject. (You will be aware of this because your understanding of the meaning of the word does not make sense in the specialist texts.)
- Check your understanding by defining the terms in your own words. Then, cross-check in a subject glossary to find out if you got them right.
- Say the words aloud or, better still, record them onto a disk and listen to them. This way you will be prepared for hearing the terms, and your brain will not have to slow down to process the information when you are in the lecture.
- If you are working electronically, you can enlist the help of your computer if you have appropriate software. You can type in your list (or cut and paste if you are working from departmental, electronic information), and get the computer to speak the words to you so that you hear them. Voice recognition software such as Text Help has this facility and will even let you decide whether you want to hear a male or female voice!

Now you are in a better position to listen out for the key words in the lecture because your mind has heard them and is looking out for them (Activity 4).

ACTIVITY 4 Listening for key words

Here is the script of part of a lecture. Get a friend to read the text to you or scan the text into your computer and get your computer to read the information to you and see if you can pick out the key words.

The topic of the talk is 'The Dangers of the Sun'.

This is a general talk by the Health Services and is open to all and any students.

Jot down what you would anticipate you will hear about this topic:
1.
2.
3.
4.

You will find answers at the end of the chapter.

Now jot down the key words/terminology which you would anticipate:
1.
2.
3.
4.
5.
6.

You will find answers at the end of the chapter.

Text extract: 'The Dangers of the Sun'

Pick out the key words and points while you listen to this extract:

> For many years dermatologists have warned the public about the dangers of staying in the sun without protection. Exposure to the sun can have dramatic results, apart from the treasured tanned skin. There are three points which I wish to bring to your attention in this talk. Firstly, the sun can damage the layers of the skin. The outer layer can change its appearance. The texture can become leathery with a loss of elasticity. This can result in premature ageing of the skin, causing wrinkles and brown blotches. Secondly, over-exposure can result in skin cancer. The brown blotches may be the outer indicator of cancer. They appear as moles on the skin. Next, extreme exposure to the sun increases the possibility of breaking down our natural protection from the sun's radiation. The effects of UVA and UVB are becoming more well known. Tanning shops promise their customers that they can provide 'safe' tanning. They try to convince us that UVA is a lower level of radiation and therefore less harmful. This is not true! In fact, UVA has been proved responsible for damaging the deeper layers of the skin which destroy structural proteins and thus harming the immune systems ...

Check your notes with the answers at the end of the chapter to see if you picked out the main key words and points.

Listening for main points/ideas

This exercise will help you to improve your skills of selection and elimination. The task is best tackled as a listening exercise so get a friend to read the text to you or scan the text into your computer and get your computer to read the information to you and see if you can pick out the main points.

Text extract: 'Is a bulky diet of eucalyptus leaves the best option for the tiny Koala?'

> Should Koalas change their diet? Are eucalyptus leaves a sensible choice in the changing environment? Is the Koalas' diet appropriate for the modern world? All these questions and more have been asked by biologists in their study of this diminutive and appealing little animal.

The diet of the Koala is limited almost entirely to eating eucalyptus leaves. Environmental issues and the decrease in natural habitats apart, there are drawbacks and advantages to such a restricted diet. The size of the Koalas' digestive system, their metabolic structures and chemical make-up of eucalyptus leaves combine to provide a fascinating forum for discussion.

The dichotomy lies in the leaves and the digestive system. On the one hand the leaves are rich in fibre but contain high levels of lignin. Fibre is not conducive to digestion, and lignin, a woody material found in the cell walls of many plants, is indigestible. So why does the Koala have such a voracious appetite for this source of fuel? Another drawback is that the ratio of an animal's gut volume to its energy needs is dependent upon animal mass. Thus, this tiny creature does not have the capacity and its metabolic system has difficulty coping. The quality of the food is poor so this means that large quantities are needed in order to extract sufficient nutrients. So how does it manage to digest and process poor-quality food for its metabolic needs?

It would appear that the Koala has adapted its digestive system to cope with its roughage-laden diet. Scientists in New South Wales conducted a study in the early 1980s and uncovered three major factors.

Firstly, the Koala can regulate the passage of food through its system, like a rabbit. In this way it has developed a system which discriminates between different sized particles so that the smaller, more easily digested ones can be digested first while the coarser, indigestible matter is expelled almost immediately. This space-saving exercise allows the Koala to increase the rate at which the 'good' material can be put into the system.

Secondly, the Koala is a relatively slow-moving animal compared with others of a similar size so it is able to reduce the fuel it needs. It can be compared with the slow-moving, three-toed sloth.

Finally, eucalyptus leaves have hidden fuels. Although the woody, indigestible lignin is present, there is also a wealth of lipids and phenols which are rich sources of energy. However, the Koala's system cannot cope with phenols so these are excreted, leaving the lipids which provide useful carbohydrate energy in the form of starch and sugar.

So what seems an improbable system has been adapted to take account of animal size, metabolic rates and energy-saving adaptations.

See if you have picked out the main points in the answers at the end of the chapter.

Verbal cues and signals

Your listening skills can be greatly improved if you know what triggers to listen for and the significance of these signals.

Signal	What to expect
Start with	This may be signalling the introduction which will give overviews.
Lecture is divided into ...	Tells you the structure.
However, on the other hand, but, conversely, on the contrary, despite	These signal contrasting or opposing information and evidence.
In addition, in other words, put another way, also, as I said previously	These signal repetition of information or provides you with another definition or explanation.
For example, that is to say, furthermore, another example, such as	These alert you to the fact that what follows will be examples of a main point.
Especially, specifically, most importantly, I cannot stress enough	Lecturers will use these to signal emphasis so listen very carefully because they obviously think the information is vital/important.
Firstly, secondly (etc.), next, then, penultimate (last but one), ultimate, finally, in conclusion	Be ready for a number of points or lists.
Therefore, thus, because, consequently, accordingly, if ... then, as a result of this	Cause and effect.
I'll expand on this later ... I'll give you more detail about this later in the lecture ... I'll take this point up later ...	These mean that you must be on the alert to link up later information with this earlier point. You might even leave space in your notes to accommodate this.
In conclusion, let me summarise, let's recap, in short/in brief, to wrap up, the main points covered were ...	These are useful because they will help you to get the global/big picture because the lecturer has summarised the information for you.

The significance of knowing about these signals when you are listening to someone speak is that you are expecting and anticipating certain types of information to follow. This will aid your understanding and speed up your processing of the information so that ultimately your notes will be of a better quality.

Thus, by a more focused and active approach to your listening, you will be able to make more effective notes and overcome the problem of forgetting what you have heard.

9 Recording lectures

This section explores the use of electrical and electronic devices to record and store information from lectures and seminars. Before you rush off and buy some gizmo, you need to consider its uses, the advantages and disadvantages of different devices and likely academic tutors' attitudes and responses to usage (see Activity 5).

Activity 5 Recording lectures: myth or reality?

Look at the following comments made by students and decide whether you think they are true or false.

Statements made by students If I use some sort of recording device …	True	False
It will take all the hard work out of lectures.		
It will save me time.		
It will mean I do not have to do anything.		
It will help me remember information.		
It will ensure that I understand my lectures.		
I can sell the information to other students who didn't make the lecture.		

To find out if you are correct, look at the answers at the end of the chapter. The implications for these statements are discussed in this section. Some students have been encouraged at school and sixth-form college to use dictaphone-type devices. They may have been useful and appropriate at that stage of study but you need to consider your academic demands now, and whether this type of method of recording is most suitable and appropriate to your individual needs.

Devices

There is a baffling array of gadgets available on the market. Which one you choose largely depends upon what you want to use it for:

- tape recorders
- mini-disk recorders
- mobile telephones
- PDAs (Personal Digital Assistants).

The pros and cons of these gadgets are discussed in the table below.

Device	Pros	Cons	Additional features worth considering
Tape recorders	Cheap to buy. Small and portable. Tape cassettes are inexpensive.	Not very versatile. Information on tape is not easily transferred to other systems. A one-hour lecture takes an expert two hours to transcribe. Sound quality is variable and can be dependent upon where you are sitting in relation to the lecturer.	Variable speed playback enables you to slow down playback so that you can take in information more effectively. There are different sizes of tape cassettes. If you intend to share with others you need to consider compatibility. Is there an advanced facility to 'mark' information while someone is speaking? It aids retrieval later.
Mini-disk recorders	Sound quality on play-back is excellent and not reliant upon sitting at the front for best results. Fairly cheap to buy. Small and portable. Mini-disks are fairly inexpensive. Mini-disk capacity is larger than tape cassette. Navigation is easier – therefore searching for specific information is quicker and less time consuming. Can be used for other purposes, e.g. recording music.	Attractive gadget and therefore stealable. A one-hour lecture takes an expert two hours to transcribe.	Variable speed playback option enables you to slow down playback so that you can take in information more effectively.
Solid-state recorders	Record information onto RAM chips or cards. Easier transfer of information from one system to another. Recording time is longer than both the above. Small and portable.	A one-hour lecture takes an expert two hours to transcribe.	
Mobile telephones	You probably already have one so no additional cost.	Recording space is limited. Only use in emergencies.	Check the memory capacity. Is there an option to plug in memory cards to boost facilities?
PDAs	Small and portable. Voice memo is available on more expensive models.	Expensive if you get one with the options you need for this type of activity. Limited capacity for recording speech. Need to be well organised and to back up information regularly onto another, more permanent system. Attractive gadget and therefore stealable.	Look for MP3 facility to enable you to listen to text.

A final consideration: some machines can record information in a way that is compatible with speech recognition software on your computer. However, your machine has to be set up to recognise the voice before it will download and transcribe recorded speech. This may seem like an excellent solution but the practicalities are such that **all** of your lecturers would have to take time out of their busy schedules to go through the voice recognition programme. However, if you have one lecturer for a lot of your time, it might be worth considering. But be ready for your lecturer to refuse, stating time pressures etc.

Recording protocols

If you wish to record the lectures in some way, apart from cost, utility and meeting your needs, you must also bear in mind other factors. It is important that you get **permission** to use your machine. This means that you might need to email lecturers before the start of their unit to ask for permission. It is also worth briefly reassuring your lecturer about the purpose to which you intend to put the recordings. Some students explain that they are auditory learners and take in information more readily if they hear it while reading handouts and notes. It might be that you need to request a temporary use of a recorder because you have broken the hand/arm with which you write. Many lecturers are uneasy about students recording their lectures. Some are openly hostile. You need to be aware of this so that you are not frustrated or upset by responses to your request. The reasons some lecturers do not want you to record their lectures often relate to copyright of intellectual property or the fact that they can no longer control how their information is used.

'What are they going to do with this information?' is a question frequently asked by lecturers. Some academic tutors are wary of giving permission because a lecture may contain off-the-cuff comments and responses which the lecturer would not want to be used for future purposes. It may be a reflection of the litigious society in which we live that lecturers are on their guard concerning recording of lectures because of the notion of 'evidence which could be used etc.'. That is not to say that this is commendable, but it is certainly understandable.

If you seek permission at the beginning of a unit, this usually means that you do not have to make the request at each lecture. Of course, if there is a stand-in lecturer, it is only polite to inform him or her that you have been given permission to record the lecture.

At university you will be expected to cope with the recording and the machine so that it does not interfere with the smooth running of the lecture. Academic tutors do not expect to be given the machine so that they can turn the recording on and off. This may have been the system at school but it is different in Higher Education settings. You will need to think about the ethics of selling your recordings to other students.

Summary of this chapter

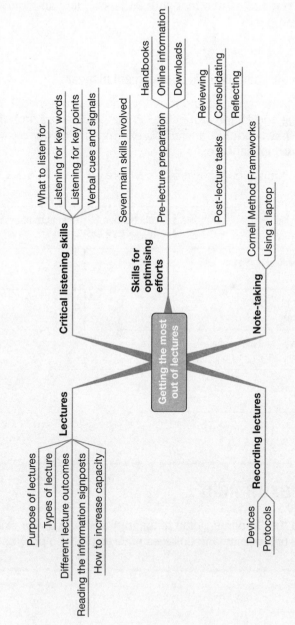

Getting the most out of lectures

Lectures
- Purpose of lectures
- Types of lecture
- Different lecture outcomes
- Reading the information signposts
- How to increase capacity

Critical listening skills
- What to listen for
- Listening for key words
- Listening for key points
- Verbal cues and signals

Skills for optimising efforts
- Seven main skills involved
- Pre-lecture preparation
  - Handbooks
  - Online information
  - Downloads
- Post-lecture tasks
  - Reviewing
  - Consolidating
  - Reflecting

Note-taking
- Cornell Method Frameworks
- Using a laptop

Recording lectures
- Devices
- Protocols

10 On reflection

Organisation and management are key factors to success. Getting the most out of lectures is up to you. Preparing properly, organising your note-taking and developing effective listening skills will help you to gain the added value you need to ensure that your understanding and knowledge of your subject is deepened.

ACTIVITY 6 Update your personal development planner

Now reflect upon how you go about getting the most out of lectures and how you intend to change and adapt your habits so that you can spend your time more effectively. You may want to transfer this information to your own institution's personal development planner scheme.

Grade your confidence on a scale of 1–5 where 1 = poor and 5 = good.

My developing skills	Confidence level: 1– 5	Plans to improve
I know the skills needed to get the most out of lectures.		
I know the different types and purposes of lectures.		
I can listen effectively and differentiate the information I am listening to in lectures.		

Date: _____

Getting extra help

Go to the Students Union to find out where to go for skill development. Many universities and colleges have tutors who provide this service.

Feedback on activities

ACTIVITY 4 Listening for key words

The talk: 'The Dangers of the Sun'

Jot down what you would anticipate you will hear about this topic:
1. Problems of over-exposure
2. Skin protection and radiation
3. Skin cancer
4. Ageing process

Now jot down the key words/terminology which you would anticipate:
1. Skin cancer
2. UVA/UVB
3. Dermatologist
4. Skin layers
5. Over-exposure
6. Cancerous moles

Sample notes

Dermatologists warned about the dangers of over-exposure without protection.

1. Sun damages layers of the skin, changing appearance:
   (a) texture – leathery with a loss of elasticity
   (b) result – premature ageing of the skin, causing wrinkles and brown blotches.

2. Secondly, over-exposure – skin cancer:
   (a) brown blotches indicator of cancer
   (b) appear as moles.

3. Extreme exposure – skin's natural protection from the sun's radiation destroyed:
   (a) effects of UVA and UVB more well known
   (b) tanning shops – UVA is a lower level of radiation and therefore less harmful (not true!)
      (i)   UVA responsible for damaging the deeper layers of the skin
      (ii) structural proteins destroyed
      (iii) immune systems damaged.

Text extract: 'Is a bulky diet of eucalyptus leaves the best option for the tiny Koala?'

Should Koalas change their diet? Are eucalyptus leaves a sensible choice in the changing environment? Is the Koalas' diet appropriate for the modern world? All these questions and more have been asked by biologists in their study of this diminutive and appealing little animal.

Koala diet: limited – eucalyptus leaves
+ & – to restricted diet.

The size of the Koalas' digestive system, their metabolic structures and chemical make-up of eucalyptus leaves combine to provide a fascinating forum for discussion.

Leaves and the digestive system

Leaves
- rich in fibre
- fibre not easily digested by Koalas
- but high levels of indigestible, woody lignin.

Digestive system
- gut volume to energy needed = animal mass
- Koala capacity = small
- eucalyptus nutrients poor so large quantity needed.

System adaptations

1. Koala can regulate food in system:
   (a) differentiates types of food
   (b) expels coarser indigestible matter
   (c) left with smaller, more easily digested particles.

2. Cut down on energy requirements:
   (a) slow moving
   (b) needs less energy
   (c) unlike other small animals
   (d) like three-toed sloth.

3. Koala extracts energy fuel carbohydrate from eucalyptus:
   (a) lipids – rich source of energy
   (b) expels phenols
   (c) gets starch and sugar for energy.

Reference

- Pauk, W. (2000) *How to Study in College*, 7th edn. New York, Houghton Mifflin.

5 Working in a real team

Working with others is always a balance between maintaining our own individuality and becoming a member of a group to which we are proud to belong. The more we join with people 'like us', the more confident we feel in being able to maintain that balance. This balance is often a result of being able to predict how each of us will behave, which in turn builds up trust within a team. However, once we work with people we don't know or with those from different cultures, we are less able to predict how we will react with one another or what our expectations are. Many companies work in multicultural environments, with flatter hierarchical structures on increasingly complex issues, where you will be expected to work in very diverse teams. Being a member of such a team therefore needs more skill and you need to know the components of team building in order to make this work. Hoping to muddle along because you have had experience of working with your friends on many projects is no longer sufficient.

In this chapter you will learn how to:

1. understand what a real team is
2. identify the learning styles of your team in order to allocate key roles
3. engage with the mechanics of setting up a real team.

USING THIS CHAPTER

Estimate your current levels of confidence. At the end of the chapter you will have the chance to reassess these levels and incorporate this into your personal development planner (PDP). Mark between 1 (poor) and 5 (good) for the following.

I understand what a real team is.	I can identify the learning styles of our team in order to allocate key roles.	I can engage with the mechanics of settng up a real team.

Date: _____

1 Introduction

We work and play together in many groupings which are brought together for a variety of purposes, such as: sports teams, informal learning groups, mentoring groups, buzz groups for creative solutions, virtual groups and project teams. We generally lump this all together as 'group work'. However, each of these groupings operates differently. This chapter will develop our understanding of working in a team project as opposed to a loose gathering of individuals, a key employability skill for your future.

The Association of Graduate Recruiters' chief executive, Carl Gilleard, talking to BBC News (2006), said that 'Employers are likely to be looking to graduates who can demonstrate softer skills such as team-working, cultural awareness, leadership and communication skills, as well as academic achievement.'

There is generally no doubt that being an effective team player and/or leader of a team is an important skill and its development starts during your studies. However, you undoubtedly have a view of group work that may not be all that positive, so let's start by revealing that position now (see Activity 1).

ACTIVITY 1 Annoying things about working with others

Below are a series of statements that students often make about group work. How would you deal with these annoying things? Answer these questions now but you may want to change your answers after reading the remainder of this chapter.

Annoying things	I would deal with this by ...
There are always free-riders in a team and their marks are boosted by those who do the work.	
Teams slow me down and that irritates me.	
I have difficulty with the topic the team has to work on and I'm afraid I'll keep the others back.	
Sometimes team members won't complete their tasks [at all, or on time].	
Sometimes teams don't divide the work up fairly.	
Sometimes you get students who just don't care about their grades, but I do.	

Check the feedback section at the end of the chapter for more information (or wait until you have read the remainder of the chapter).

2 What is a team?

A team is a group of individuals with defined goals who work together for a particular purpose. An essential characteristic is that the individuals in a team are interdependent in order to get the job completed. However, just coming together with a group of friends does not mean that you are automatically a team. Most employers know that we have to 'work at' becoming a team and this is reflected in the significant amount of staff development that goes into team building.

Teams are able to deal with complex problems and come up with more creative solutions than individuals alone. In the workplace, teams are increasingly cross-disciplinary, drawing on the expertise of many. More than likely, your student project will be confined to those on your course, but remember: working together with different kinds of people is a preparation for future work. Good teams also enhance commitment and a feeling of community among their members.

Friendship groups and teams

We all automatically want to form a team with our friends and if you are told to form a team, you would probably do just that. The advantages of this are that you are comfortable with each other, you want to support each other and it makes you feel good. The main disadvantage of friends as teams is that your relationship is built on socialising and having fun. The project team could put a strain on that relationship as you may have to behave in a different way with a particular friend in the team than you would do socially.

If someone outside your friendship group joined your team, it may also be difficult for them to feel accepted.

Moving from group to team

The main issue for student project groups is to move from being a group of individuals to being a team. Two management consultants, Jon Katzenbach and Douglas Smith, wrote a best-seller entitled *The Wisdom of Teams* where they looked at the difference between a group of individuals working together and high-performance teams. Their findings are summarised in Figure 5.1.

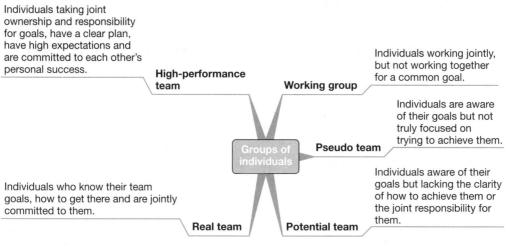

Figure 5.1 How individuals work together
Adapted from Katzenbach and Smith (1993)

Checklist for creating a real team

Members of a team ...

- are absolutely clear of the team's goals
- allocate roles
- take joint responsibility for the goals
- plan how to achieve goals
- allocate tasks to all members
- are good time managers
- value everyone in the team
- identify and deal with hidden agendas
- trust one another to be dependable, honest, fair and objective in their dealings with each other.

Identifying team characteristics

Characteristics	Grouping*	Issues
You are working together as a group to share information, understand assignments and learn together. Each of you will take away information from the group, which will help your own understanding of a topic. The group has no accountability for its output.	Working group	As an informal grouping this can be very productive and supportive during the learning process. Recognise that you are an informal group and that you have no output as a team.
You are in a group that has been assigned a task. As a group you are responsible for the output. However, as a group you are not working collectively in order to try and achieve this. The group appears to have no interest in setting goals, working collectively and coming up with a plan even though you may call yourself a team.	Pseudo team	This is a real problem grouping because you think you're a team when you're not. At this level you have not developed team skills or fully understand how teams work. You need to understand the task, work collectively, identify skills within the team and be mutually accountable for the outcome.
You are in a group that has been assigned a task. You understand that as a group you are responsible for the output. You understand that you need to work together, develop a plan and be collectively accountable. You are trying to do this but it can be very frustrating because the 'team' becomes unfocused and members are not always moving together in the same direction.	Potential team	As the label for this grouping suggests, there is potential here but it is not yet fully realised. By the end of year 2 you should at least be carrying out teamwork at the 'potential team' level. You will further develop your skills in the following year(s). Most problems with student project teams are identified with this kind of grouping (including pseudo teams). Take stock of the team skills you need to develop and make notes in your personal development planner (PDP).
You are in a group that has been assigned a task. As a group you are responsible for the output. All members of the group are committed to the project and understand that they hold themselves mutually responsible for the outcome. As a group you have identified the resources you have in your team, i.e. the skills and knowledge you can bring to the team in order to make your plan more effective. You are also aware that all team members need supporting.	Real team	If you are working at this level you understand how teams work, including the collaborative work and accountability that are needed for the output. By the end of year 3 you should be working on team projects at this level. Student projects working at this level should do very well. Critically reflect on the team skills you are developing. Don't forget to evaluate and evidence your developing skills in your PDP and incorporate in your CV.

Characteristics	Grouping*	Issues
You are In a group that has been assigned a task. As a group you are responsible for the output. All members of the group are committed to the project and understand that they hold themselves mutually responsible for the outcomes. As a team you know the strengths of your members and work with those strengths. In addition, you are truly interdependent and aware that each member of the team needs space and encouragement for personal development, and the team values everyone's contribution. You see the value in reflection and how it can improve your team performance.	High-performance team	This is what you are aiming for. You work with mutual interdependence that reflects the group's skill mix and personal preferences. Your language is aligned to the goals of the task and you have a strong sense of mutual responsibility for the output of the team. Team members feel fulfilled and proud to be part of this team. If you have got to this level before your final year of studies then you are doing very well, but it is a rare occurrence. Aim to be in at least one high-performance team before you finish your studies. Update your PDP with an evaluation of how your skills have developed in this area.

* Terms in this column used by Katzenbach and Smith (1993)

As you work towards being an effective team, you need to consider the various functions that teams perform in order to work well together (see Activity 2). John Adair, who is a leading authority on leadership and the first to be appointed as a professor in Leadership Studies, says that teams need to consider how they achieve the task, build/maintain the team and take care of individual needs. See Figure 5.2.

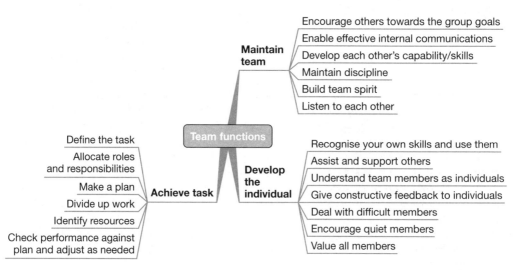

Figure 5.2 Team functions

Adapted from John Adair's model of how teams function (Adair, 1986)

ACTIVITY 2 Understanding team patterns – what's your view?

Each of the three areas identified by Adair (achieving the task, building the team and responding to individual needs) should to be addressed if your team is to work effectively and harmoniously. Just imagine these scenarios and identify the functions missing from John Adair's model and estimate the kind of group you think they are (working group, pseudo team, potential team, real team, high-performance team).

Check the feedback section to compare your answers.

Scenario 1

You are working with a great group – they are all your friends. You often meet in the pub as it gives a good informal atmosphere and you can enjoy the work. It is good because no one in the group nags or bosses anyone else around. You have done some reading around for this project and written a few things down and you hope that it will be useful. You assume everyone else is doing that too; after all, they all turn up and seem engaged.

Assume it is now two weeks before your final deadline.

	Jot down some ideas
What are the dangers for individuals working in a group like this?	
How might such a 'team' appear during the project presentation if they don't change?	
Take stock – what does the group need to do **now**?	
What would you have learned about teamwork from such a group?	
Which function(s) of the Adair model is missing in this example? What type of group do you think this is? working group | pseudo team | potential team | real team | high-performance team	

Scenario 2

You are working with a group of people – they are all your friends. You all sat down and worked out what you had to do and you think someone made a list, but you haven't seen it. A couple of your friends have become really bossy and they tell everyone else what to do, constantly adjusting and fiddling with things and even controlling what you are doing. They have told you to do something that you have no expertise or interest in and do not like how tasks are allocated. You never expected these friends of yours to be like this. You'll be glad when it is all over.

Assume it is now two weeks before your deadline.

	Jot down some ideas
What are the dangers for individuals working in a group like this?	
How will you all be feeling right now? Who will do those last-minute tasks if you all feel fed up?	
How might such a 'team' appear during the project presentation if they don't change?	
Take stock – what does the group need to do **now**?	
What would you have learned about teamwork from such a group?	

Which function(s) of the Adair model is missing in this example?

What type of group do you think this is?

working group | pseudo team | potential team | real team | high-performance team

Scenario 3

You are working with some people you know and some you don't know. Things are going well and you have even developed ground rules, appointed a group coordinator and have regular meetings. However, as time goes on problems arise as two group members aren't 'pulling their weight'; one has even stopped coming to meetings and hasn't produced anything yet. The group is getting annoyed as the members see all their hard work being compromised by those who aren't contributing effectively.

Two weeks to go – what would you do from the following? Select 'yes' if you would carry out this action or 'no' if you wouldn't.

Action	Yes/no	Possible reasons
Find out if person X has a genuine reason for not doing the work		He or she may be ill, have family problems or just be finding life pressures difficult at present. Depending on the answer, as a group you could give that person support or you may need to encourage him or her to seek help. Other reasons?
Ignore person X and do his or her work yourselves		It is the only way to complete the project. The tutor is only giving one mark for the completed project, so you have to. This is not ideal and it will only cause resentment. Other reasons?

Action	Yes/no	Possible reasons
Assuming there are no mitigating circumstances, then contact person X and say you need him or her to do his or her share – refer to ground rules and what the person has to do to complete the project. Discuss with the person and then put it in writing – email or letter – from the whole group; ensure a date for reply/action and retain a copy.		Person X realises the group is serious. Keep a record of your communication – you may need to say what you will do if you get no/little response. Other reasons?
Report person X to your tutor explaining which part of the project person X is responsible for.		This should be a last resort, but may be necessary in extreme cases. If you do this, you should tell person X and give him or her a chance to put things right. It should all be transparent and 'business-like'. Your reason?
Some of your ideas …		

Which function(s) of the Adair model is missing in this example?

What type of group do you think this is?

working group | pseudo team | potential team | real team | high-performance team

3 Getting started as a team

Before looking at your task or problem, everyone should:

- introduce themselves (often seen as breaking the ice)
- agree a set of ground rules
- estimate the learning styles they have in the team as this will impact on the tasks and roles the team members are happy to do
- allocate role of coordinator.

Set your ground rules

Ground rules are vital if you want to establish an effective team. Ground rules will be the foundation for a strong working relationship based on: trust, honesty and an awareness of the expectations of each other. Social groups also have ground rules, but these tend to have developed over time and are very often unspoken. However, if someone in a social group violates these 'rules', they are often made to feel acutely aware of it. In a team, where individuals come together to start working as a team, making ground rules explicit is very important. Make sure this is the first thing you do so that when any member of the group feels things are going wrong, he or she can refer to them and remind everyone of their agreement. Be honest with the group and say what is important for you when working with it. Activity 3 helps you to consider how to establish ground rules.

ACTIVITY 3 Establishing ground rules

Develop ground rules that can be used by a team – some examples are below. List three more that would be important to you when working with a team. If you are already working in a team do this together and make sure you make a note of your rules.

Ground rules
1. Take responsibility for your own learning, actions and reactions (i.e. accept accountability).
2. Be honest and open (especially if you don't understand or agree with something).
3. Carry out your work on time.
4.
5.
6.

Determine your team profile

Teams start with a group of individuals who need to become a team. You need to recognise each other's individual differences as a resource and in order to do that it is useful to look at your individual learning styles.

Peter Honey and Alan Mumford, two British psychologists and leading experts in learning and behaviour, have developed a set of learning styles that determine whether you are: an activist, a reflector, a theorist or a pragmatist (Honey and Mumford, 1992). See the diagram below. Activity 4 asks you to identify your team's profile.

Concrete
thinker

Activist: doing

Reflector: reviewing

You are a person who enjoys the present and are flexible and open to new experiences. You tend to act first and think about the consequences later. Activity is often centred around you. You are less happy when you have to listen to long explanations, working on your own, or following precise instructions.	You are cautious and tend to hold back and observe first. You are happy collecting and analysing data but slow to commit yourself to a conclusion. You are able to maintain the 'big picture' perspective. You can have problems with deadlines because of your reluctance to reach a conclusion or be rushed.

Active
person

Reflective
person

You enjoy putting theories and techniques into practice. You work confidently with ideas and put them to work for you (or the team). You need to see the immediate benefit of some idea/concept and are less happy with the purely theoretical. You are uncomfortable with endless discussions that become unfocused.	You like thinking through problems in a logical and rational way. You are very objective and weigh up the evidence. You like a structured situation with a clear purpose and hate activities that are poorly briefed. You are less happy working with others who have different learning styles or if you have to discuss your feelings.

Pragmatist: planning

Theorist: concluding

Abstract
thinker

ACTIVITY 4 Identifying your team's profile

What's your team's profile? Using the diagram above identify which quadrant most describes you when working on a project. Try and do this as a team so you can identify your team's profile. If you are not currently working in a team, identify the profile that usually suits you when working in a team.

Look at the descriptions in the quadrants above. You may find you can identify yourself in several quadrants. However, rank the description where it is:

1 = like me most of the time
2 = like me some of the time } Dominant profile
3 = rarely like me
4 = never like me

Now put your rankings in the next table:

▶

Team member	Activist	Reflector	Theorist	Pragmatist
Example: person A	4	1	2	3
Me				
Number of members ranking 1 or 2 on a given type				

In the example above, person A is predominantly a reflector/theorist. If most of the other members of your group also have this profile, you may have difficulty producing your goals on time. Knowing this in advance can alert you to the potential weakness of your team. This allows you to take corrective action early on.

According to personal rankings your team predominantly comprises:

Type	Number of members with this tendency/profile
Activists	
Reflectors	
Theorists	
Pragmatists	

Ideally, a team has a member from each of these categories, but more than likely you cannot change your team members, so use this exercise as a guide to consider how best to achieve your task with the individuals you have. Use this information to allocate roles for your team (see Section 4).

Remember: as a team you still all need to consider how you will fulfil other functions like maintaining team spirit and ensuring that everyone is valued (see Figure 5.2).

4 Becoming an effective team

Now you have the basics in place, you can start planning, allocating roles and making good decisions.

Develop a plan of action

Without a plan you will not be able to work as a team. Once you have identified a coordinator/leader, you can start working on your plan. The plan includes not only a list of activities, but also protocols for the team (based on ground rules), e.g. dealing with meetings and what to do if individuals don't fulfil their tasks etc. The designated coordinator needs to ensure there is a workable plan and **everyone** understands it and is committed to it. You can then further develop the roles of the team.

When planning:

1. Read carefully the brief given to you by your lecturer.

2. Agree what you have to do, by when and in what format(s).

3. Divide the brief into various sub-tasks.

4. Allocate team members to the various tasks.

5. Set a timetable with milestones.

6. Set out how you will handle meetings: regularity, minute taking/storing, decisions taken and actions set.

7. Establish reporting procedures and mechanisms for revising the plan, and keeping records and minutes of meetings.

8. Have a mechanism to ensure open communications with the ability to resolve conflict.

9. Plan how you will present your work.

Develop team roles

Use the information from this section and the one above to establish the kind of roles you would like in your team. You may find you have to split up along thematic lines as you may be expected to hand in work as a team, but with identifiable parts for each participant's grade. However, you do need to establish who does what and, whatever you decide, you will need to have a coordinator – someone who keeps the team 'on track' and 'on time'. There will be other roles and some people may have two roles, one on the task and another related to some element of team maintenance.

First allocate your coordinator then develop your plan (see Activity 5) and return to complete your team roles later.

ACTIVITY 5 Allocating team roles

Name	Role(s)
	Coordinator (checks milestones, group performance generally) + sub-topic task
	Record-keeper + sub-topic task

Make good decisions

Decision making can be difficult in teams. You may be more of a risk-taker than others, look at evidence selectively, have certain prejudices (often unknown to yourself) and be swayed, or not, by group pressure. All these lead to a flawed decision outcome.

There are various ways for teams to come to an agreement and make a decision:

1. **Consensus** – this agreement means alignment of the team as a whole with the goals set. Those who may have disagreed are prepared to cooperate for the success of the team and not take up defensive positions.

2. **Unanimous** – here everyone has to agree before a decision is taken.

3. **Majority** – this can be, for example, if 51% agree then the decision is taken, but this can split your team.

Ideally you want to have a consensus decision, which means you are all prepared to accept the decision made. A fairly simple technique you can use as a team to air the issues during the decision-making process is the *Six Thinking Hats* proposed by a leading authority on creative thinking, Edward de Bono (1999).

Each 'hat' looks at an issue from a particular point of view. This can also reduce confrontation as people are working within the confines of their 'hat'. You don't physically have to wear different hats, but they are used to symbolise a different viewpoint. It is more objective if you adopt a hat that does not directly correspond to your own position:

- **White Hat** – with this hat you focus on information, reports and any data that are available. It is an objective position.

- **Red Hat** – with this hat you make a decision based on your opinion, intuition and feelings. It is a subjective position.

- **Black Hat** – this is a pessimistic and critical review of the decisions being taken. You focus on what may not work with this decision and what could go wrong. You are essentially looking for the weak points and the team should be able to address and counter these. This position will help you make more reliable decisions. It is an objective position.

- **Yellow Hat** – this is an optimistic viewpoint, and helps you see all the benefits and value of a decision.

- **Green Hat** – this is the hat for creativity and intuition. This position is very important when the team feels it can't move forward. Sometimes you need to harness this creativity and take risks.

- **Blue Hat** – this is the overview position or the 'meta-hat'. The team coordinator or the person chairing your meetings may want to have this hat. The person wearing this hat should know when to call on the other hats in order to come to a decision.

Once the team has heard all the views from the different hat perspectives a decision is made.

NOTE Only take time to use a technique like this for important decisions.

ACTIVITY 6 Being your own troubleshooter when teams go wrong

It is usual to go to your tutor when things go wrong in your team. This is invariably about someone not fulfilling their part, you feeling that you are doing too much or being left out. It is easy to turn to someone else, but before you do that, try troubleshooting your own problems. In the table below there is a list of things that can go wrong. You may want to add your own as well and consider how you could put things right.

If you are expected to reflect on your teamwork as part of your project then do reflect on how you sorted out your own problems. This can only gain you marks for initiative and being an independent learner.

Tick what might be going wrong in your team and think how to remedy it. ▶

What's happening in the team?	Tick	Possible remedies (and make cross-references to places in this chapter that could help)
Not clarifying what your task or objective is		
Not checking on progress		
Not checking on time		
Not clarifying or recording what has been decided		
Not clarifying who is going to do what		
Not clarifying what has to be done by when		
Not establishing procedures for handling meetings		
Not keeping to agreed procedures		
Not listening to each other		
Allowing individuals to dominate and others to withdraw		
[some are] Not turning up for meetings		
[some are] Not doing the work allocated		
[some are] Not doing the work allocated very well		
[some are] Not recognising the feelings of members of the team		
[some are] Not contributing equally to the progress of the team		

Keeping your team going

Teams can work well and then go wrong. Make sure you keep communication channels open as your team develops, so you can keep it working well. Bruce Tuckman (Tuckman and Jensen, 1977) showed us that teams go through a repetitive cycle of:

- **forming** – characterised by dependence on the coordinator, but little consensus on the aims
- **storming** – where members take up positions, establish themselves within the group, form sub-groups and challenge other team members
- **norming** – where agreements are met and adhered to, members feel they have their role and can make decisions, and the coordinator can work without major challenges
- **performing** – where the team knows what it has to do, and all members are committed and feel accountable for the outcome.

You may find you cycle several times through storming, norming and performing as your project develops. Be aware of these cycles, see them as part of the process and find a way to deal with it. If you feel inclined to seek help from your tutor, check to see if you are just in a storming phase which you need to work your way out of as a team.

Working in a diverse team

There are various aspects of working in a diverse team and this section is just a brief discussion of some of the issues. We live with diversity across our lives: different types of people, different abilities, different subject disciplines and different cultures. Diverse teams make the working with

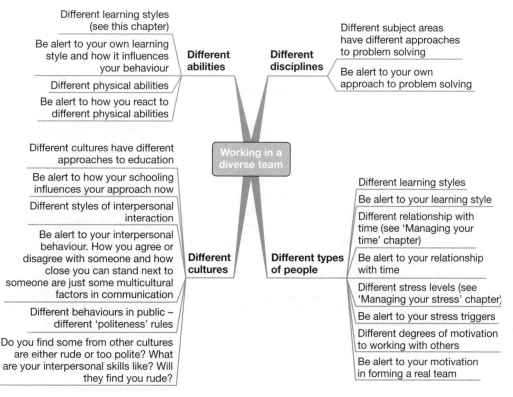

Figure 5.3 Working in a diverse team

diversity more formal and it is this aspect of teamworking that requires more attention as we have to work harder at creating the trust necessary for effective team work.

Figure 5.3 outlines some of the issues to consider.

5 Tools of the trade

While students on campus and living close can easily work face to face, not all students are full time or living close enough to do this. Forming a virtual team for those off-campus students is the only way to progress this. Although it is easier to make decisions face to face, virtual teams will gain experience of working together in an approach to teamwork that is becoming more common in the workplace.

Both virtual and face-to-face teams should be using technology. The virtual teams will be using it to communicate and store information, while the face-to-face group will probably limit it to file storage with the odd email and mobile call. Virtual groups should ensure that the technology they use offers a mix of synchronous and asynchronous communication possibilities.

There are various pieces of technology that can help groups keep on track:

- **Mobile phone (synchronous communication)**. Only use your phone for the cancellation of meetings. This is too awkward for arranging meetings because you are just talking to one person at a time.

- **Email (asynchronous communication)**. Make sure you have each other's email address. You can keep in contact easily, share documents and arrange meetings.

- **Using electronic group facilities: 'a must' for virtual groups**. Many institutions now have portals or similar software where you can set up your own groups. You can use this to keep in touch, upload key documents and generally use for team administration. Also, if your team members either study part time or live far away from each other, you can use an online group facility to store all your documents. If you are a virtual group, you will also want to check if your institution has software for online chatroom facilities or online conferencing software so you can have real-time conversations (synchronous). If your institution does not have these facilities, you could investigate social networking sites.

- **Developing a good filing system**. You will have your documents on your own PC, but you also need a joint filing system for all the team's documents and this can be done using some online group facilities at your institution. Also, remember to organise your files to reflect your team's plan and keep well-labelled versions of your documents so that you know which document you are working with.

NOTE Make sure you back up all your documents regularly. 'I couldn't hand my work in because I had a computer crash' is becoming an increasingly lame excuse and your tutor will view it like that. Be responsible and back up your work as you go.

Checklist for a copper-bottomed approach to teamwork

1. **C**ommitment: you all take joint responsibility for the success of the team and be inclusive to all.

2. **O**bjectives: you take time to make the objectives and goals for the team clear to all.

3. **P**urpose: in order to keep the team motivated you all need to be clear why you are involved with this team and have clarity of purpose.

4. **P**lan: you need to plan how to solve the problem set you by breaking the task down into sub-tasks **and** establishing how you work together as a team.

5. **E**xpectations: as a team state what your expectations are and work towards a set of high expectations.

6. **R**oles: make sure you allocate roles to your team members so that you can act on your plan. Recognise individual differences when allocating roles.

---

6 On reflection

Through this chapter you should be able to articulate the essentials of working in a real team, reflect on your experience of working in student project teams and know what you need to do to improve the next team. At an interview for a work placement or once you leave your studies, you may be asked how well you work in groups. Now you have started to reflect on and articulate your skills, it will make this kind of question a lot easier for you to answer.

Go back to Activity 1, 'Annoying things about working with others', and see if you would now answer it differently. You should have developed some more awareness of how you would deal with these potentially annoying aspects of working with others.

Take time to reflect on your experience in project teams and the skills you feel you need to develop to make yourself a more effective team member. You may want to transfer this information to your own institution's personal development planner scheme.

ACTIVITY 7 Update your personal development planner

Having read this chapter, gauge your confidence again. How does this compare with your confidence levels at the start of the chapter? What can you do to improve? You can incorporate this into your own personal development planner. Add anything else you feel appropriate.

Grade your confidence on a scale of 1–5 where 1 = poor and 5 = good.

My teamwork skills plan	Confidence level 1–5	Plans to improve
I understand what a real team is and I am developing my skills to achieve this. *Section 2*		
I have identified my learning style and know how it can affect team performance. *Section 3*		
I know the mechanics of setting up a real team and put those steps in place when I work in a team. *Sections 3, 4, 5*		
I understand that a major challenge is working in a diverse group. My team is aware of the issues involved and alert to possible problems. *Sections 2, 3, 4, 5*		

Date: _____

Getting extra help

- Your institution or course probably offers team-building training. Take advantage of this and take time to reflect on what you are learning.
- See the references at the end of the chapter.
- A general web search on 'team building' or 'working in teams' will bring up a host of information for you to choose from.

Feedback on the activities

ACTIVITY 1 Annoying things about working with others

Annoying things	I would deal with this by ...
There are always free-riders in a team and their marks are boosted by those who do the work.	Start with ground rules for your team. Agree what you will do in advance if someone doesn't do their share. If the situation persists let your tutor know (rationally, not in a whingeing manner) of what you have done and that it has not improved.
Teams slow me down and that irritates me.	Listen to what other team members are saying rather than assuming they can't contribute. Recognise the different types of contribution they bring. If I am better at the technical side, I am happy to share this with the team as we are all interdependent.
I have difficulty with the topic the team has to work on and I'm afraid I'll keep the others back.	I will let the team know of my worries and offer to do some things that I know I am good at.
Sometimes team members won't complete their tasks [at all, or on time].	Check if our ground rules are being flouted. Enforce our rules and if this does not improve inform our tutor. State the measures taken in order to improve this ourselves.
Sometimes teams don't divide the work up fairly.	The team may be working as sub-groups within the team. This has to be stopped. This issue has to be talked about so that everyone feels they are being heard and valued.
Sometimes you get students who just don't care about their grades, but I do.	The team needs to be convinced that the members are interdependent and let others down if they don't work. This is part of the ground rules and if it cannot be solved by the group, it needs to be discussed with the tutor.

ACTIVITY 2 Understanding team patterns – what's your view?

Scenario 1

Type of group

This is more of a 'working group', i.e. a group of people who are not really pulling together as well as they could. These individuals are probably working informally as a 'working group' without realising it and possibly see themselves as a team. They have assumed that since they all worked well together before, it would be successful. However, as a team they have to work differently and very often working with friends is not a good idea as old and established ways of getting along may not be appropriate for this task.

Adair group functions

The group lacks a focus on the task and the members aren't building their team, although it is working at a very social level (maintenance). The group needs to redefine itself as a team.

Scenario 2

Type of group

The group is more of a 'pseudo' to 'pseudo team'. You started out identifying your goals but you don't seem to have shared that. Why didn't you ask to work on the identified goals, rather than just moaning that you haven't seen them? Some of your friends realise they need to behave differently if they want to get the job done, but seem to be doing this in a unilateral way. It appears they have taken the lead instinctively, without discussion, which makes them appear bossy. If this group wants to stay together as a group of friends **and** a team, it needs to discuss openly how it can achieve the task set and the different roles it will have to adopt in order to do that.

Adair group functions

This group is basically lacking the team-building function. Some of you are trying to achieve the task while others are still operating as a social group. This group needs to think of itself as a team and of ways to bring everyone together on task and be mutually dependent.

Scenario 3

Type of group

This group is more of a 'pseudo' to 'potential team' and with a little effort and the development of interdependence and joint responsibility for the goals it could be a 'real team'. It may be that this team didn't fully discuss the task and identify the resources within the group at the very beginning. Management theory refers to the importance of frank discussions within a group so that all are in agreement (aligned) with what has to be done, how it has to be done and who has to do it. Remember: a 'real team' has shared responsibility and is moving in one direction towards the goal.

Adair group functions

This group appears to be achieving most of the Adair functions but not as effectively as it could. As the group develops, it may need to reassess some of its earlier decisions as to the needs of individuals in the team and how the team spirit should be maintained. Keep lines of communication open so that problems can be ironed out before they become obstacles to achieving the task.

ACTIVITY 6 Being your own troubleshooter when teams go wrong

What's happening in the team?	Tick	Possible remedies (and make cross-references to places in this chapter that could help)
Not clarifying what your task or objective is		You haven't gone through the planning process. See Section 4.
Not checking on progress		You haven't developed a mechanism for checking how things are going. You can't leave everything to your coordinator. Go back to your planning document and put something in there that you can all sign up to. This is very important.
Not checking on time		As above. It is part of your progress-checking mechanism.
Not clarifying or recording what has been decided		Include as part of your planning mechanisms for recording your decisions. See Sections 4 and 5.
Not clarifying who is going to do what		You don't seem to have allocated roles, see Section 4, and in order to do that you need to understand the learning styles of your group, see Section 3.
Not clarifying what has to be done by when		This means as part of your planning you have not established a timetable with milestones.
Not establishing procedures for handling meetings		Again this is part of your planning process, see Section 4. Devise an electronic method for storing your decisions/actions from meetings, see Section 5.
Not keeping to agreed procedures		Check you have your ground rules in place, Section 3, and how you deal with individuals who flout them, Section 4.
Not listening to each other		If you remember, being a real team means collaborating and appreciating all in your team. Look again at the team functions from John Adair, Section 2.
Allowing individuals to dominate and others to withdraw		See above and this relates again to the functions in a team.
[some are] Not turning up for meetings		Your ground rules and procedures for making them work should be applied here. This is why it is important to set these up **before** things go wrong. See Sections 3 and 4.

▶

What's happening in the team?	Tick	Possible remedies (and make cross-references to places in this chapter that could help)
[some are] Not doing the work allocated		As above. However, you may want to check that this person really did agree to do this work. If it really is a problem, you may need to reallocate tasks. Be flexible enough to do this.
[some are] Not doing the work allocated very well		It is quite likely that you will get some high-flyers in your team and others that are struggling. If you feel the work some do is not up to standard, bring the team together and work out a way of resolving this. Should someone else do that aspect; do they need some quick coaching? Find out the problem.
[some are] Not recognising the feelings of members of the team		This relates back to the 'develop the individual' aspect of John Adair's model. Every member of your team is important and every team member needs to recognise this.
[some are] Not contributing equally to the progress of the team		First check why this is happening. Maybe those concerned feel they are contributing well. Be honest and clarify the situation. Again, with a good plan and clear milestones you should be able to go back and identify where things are going wrong. You may need to make adjustments.

References

■ Adair, J. (1986) *Effective Team Building*. Aldershot, Gower.

■ BBC News (2006) 'Graduate demand outstrips skills', 7 February, available at: **http://news.bbc.co.uk/** and search on the title of the article.

■ De Bono, E. (1999) *Six Thinking Hats*. London, Penguin.

■ Honey, P. and Mumford, A. (1992) *The Manual of Learning Styles*. Maidenhead, Peter Honey.

■ Katzenbach, J. R. and Smith, D. K. (1993) *The Wisdom of Teams*. New York, HarperBusiness.

■ Tuckman, B. W. and Jensen, M. A. C. (1977) 'Stages of small group development revisited', *Group and Organizational Studies*, 2, 419–427.

6 Presenting your work

Being able to present your work well as a student, and later on in your job, is an invaluable skill. You have probably sat through countless talks already and looked at many posters, so you instinctively know the kind of presentation that bores you. Now is your opportunity to articulate your instincts and hone your presentation skills for both posters and talks.

In this chapter you will learn how to:

1. prepare information for posters
2. design posters for visual clarity and coherence
3. design slides for clarity
4. recognise what makes a good and bad oral presentation
5. know how classic mistakes in oral presentations affect your audience and how to avoid them.

USING THIS CHAPTER

Estimate your current levels of confidence. At the end of the chapter you will have the chance to reassess these levels and incorporate this into your personal development planner (PDP). Mark between 1 (poor) and 5 (good) for the following:

I can understand the key elements of poster design.	I can understand key elements of slide design.	I can understand the characteristics of effective oral presentations.

Date: _____

1 Introduction

Being able to give a good and clear presentation to a public audience is a skill that you and your future employer will value greatly. Prospective employers invariably ask for your experience in using these key skills during interviews. You need to be able to articulate what makes a good and poor presentation and offer evidence for your knowledge. So, when you are asked to give a talk or produce a poster as part of your studies, recognise the importance of developing the skills of delivery as well as conveying the content.

Posters and oral presentations are forms of presentation that enable you to develop your confidence in different ways. Posters check your ability to present information succinctly, and present it in an attractive and message-focused way, while oral presentations allow for more information and a more in-depth delivery. In both modes you will probably find yourself taking questions and explaining your ideas.

2 Poster presentations

Assessed coursework can take the form of a poster presentation. This can be, for example, an individual piece of research, a group project or a visual essay where you present the ideas of a particular topic. Whatever the content of your poster, a poster is a visual presentation format and as with any other form of communication, it should 'tell a story'.

Before you do anything, start with a checklist:

> **Checklist: clarify what is expected from your poster assignment**
>
> 1. The purpose of the poster and the intended audience.
> 2. The size of the poster required.
> 3. Any specifications for the production, e.g. does it have to be through particular software, can you produce it by hand, or use a cut and paste method (not advisable)?
> 4. Expectations regarding display, e.g. do you need to print it out or display via a PC/laptop?
> 5. Printing quality, i.e. can you print out in draft form as this is much cheaper?
> 6. The presentation, e.g. in a conference setting with your poster set up in a room or as part of an oral presentation.
> 7. The assessment criteria.

Information regarding the checklist is discussed in this section.

Planning what you want to say

Identify your audience

Establish who your audience is. Your tutor should give you guidance here. Don't just assume that you are writing for your tutor because there is a tendency to think he or she knows this material already and you don't need to explain it in such detail. So, it is be better to assume your audience is an intelligent 14-year-old.

NOTE Researchers are now asked by some research councils to write an abstract of their research that could be understood by an intelligent 14-year-old.

Identify your message

The key to any poster is deciding *what* your message is. In order to do this you need to distil the key points of your work onto some rough paper and arrange the order of your 'story'.

If you are reporting on work from your individual research project or a group project it is good to write a short section at the beginning (approximately 200 words) which outlines:

- why you did this research (gives a context)
- how you did it (method)
- issues it raised (there may be some interesting things to solve on the way)
- key findings/conclusion/recommendation.

This is similar to an 'abstract', which is found at the beginning of a journal paper in order to prepare the reader for the content of the paper. Once you have the abstract, you have the key ideas for your poster and your introduction.

If you have not carried out any data-gathering research, you may be asked to present a poster on a topic. This is something like a visual essay and you will also need to start by jotting down a summary of your reading by:

■ stating the importance of this topic (gives context)
■ listing the key points/issues/positions (as theoretical positions, key researchers, key solutions, etc.)
■ offering critical reflection on what you have read and a concluding remark.

Once you have summarised what you have found, you have the key ideas for your poster and they can be part of your poster introduction.

Secondly, your poster must have a very clear message. The information in your abstract or introduction can be further developed in the boxes on your poster (see 'Designing your poster' below).

How we read a poster

A poster is not a jumble of things that can be read in any order (unless you are using the poster as a form of art). Generally, we read a poster from the top left and work our way down to the bottom right, as with any page we read. However, you can break this rule if your route through the poster is clear and logical.

Coherence (progression of ideas) is important in any written document and a poster is no different. Make sure your start and end-points are obvious. More creative subjects may want to flout this rule and offer a more visually demanding display. If this is the case, you need to decide if your reader needs to come away with key pieces of information and how you will visually identify them.

Remember, readers will probably spend no more than about five minutes reading your poster. In that time you have to convey your message through words and images. Identify key pieces of information (see 'Identify your message' above).

Designing your poster

Layout

A fairly transparent way to design your poster is to allocate text and picture boxes to the size of paper you have. Your first decision is the size (A1?) and the orientation (portrait or landscape?) of your poster. Figures 6.1–3 show different layouts.

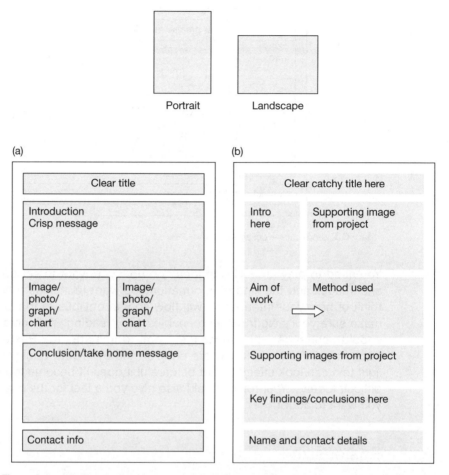

Portrait　　　Landscape

(a)

Clear title

Introduction
Crisp message

Image/
photo/
graph/
chart

Image/
photo/
graph/
chart

Conclusion/take home message

Contact info

(b)

Clear catchy title here

Intro
here

Supporting image
from project

Aim of
work

Method used

Supporting images from project

Key findings/conclusions here

Name and contact details

Figure 6.1 Portrait: mixed column solutions. (a) Predominantly single column with lined boxes. (b) Predominantly double column with or without lined boxes

Clear precise meaningful title

Intro

More detail

Conclusions/
findings

Image/
graph

Image/
graph

Image
or
graph

Image
or
graph

Future work

Contact details

Figure 6.2 Landscape: a more visual poster

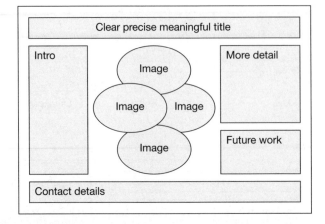

Figure 6.3 Landscape – collage effect[1]

You need to play around with ideas on how you want to set out your text and images and the kind of information you want to include. Remember to think of how your information will flow so it is obvious to the reader. Also, make sure your colour scheme enables easy reading. Your colour scheme should enhance the message, not dominate it. Pastel-coloured backgrounds with dark text are easy on the eye. Dark backgrounds with light text can look effective, but be careful it doesn't become too garish and difficult to read. Your topic should also give you a feel for the colour scheme you want to adopt.

Poster size

Paper sizes are standardised and the ISO (International Organization for Standardization) paper sizes we use are labelled as 'A' size papers ranging from A7 to A0; the smaller the number, the larger the paper size. The paper size we use most often is A4. Most student writing blocks are A4 size and it is also the standard size for most photocopiers and printers. The usual size for a poster is A1.

Some paper sizes are as follows:

> *A5 + A5 = A4 (height 29 cm × width 21cm)*
>
> *A4 + A4 = A3*
>
> *A3 + A3 = A2*
>
> *A2 + A2 = A1 (height 84 cm × width 59 cm)*

---

[1] Acknowledgement: thanks to Adam Warren from the University of Southampton for the inspiration of poster making through these diagrams.

Text: size of font and choice of font

Remember that people will be standing some distance away from your poster, so make your text easy to read from about 1.5 metres. You may want to use fancy fonts, but be careful – simple, clear and well-proportioned fonts are better. Try to use a point range between 20 and 35, though the size you choose will depend on the font as some can appear clumsy when too big.

Some of the options you have are:

Typeface: serif or sans serif?

The basic choice is between serif and sans serif fonts.

Many studies have shown that sans serif and a wide-letter look are easier to read.

Times New Roman is a serif font but with a rather narrow-letter look. This generally rates poorly on readability tests. It is also now considered rather 'old fashioned'.

Garamond is also a serif font but the letters look a lot wider and this makes it easier to read. If you prefer to use a serif font, this is probably better than Times.

Arial is a sans serif font and the letters combine a narrow look with an uncluttered letter shape.

Verdana, on the other hand, is also a sans serif font, but the letters have a wider look which makes it easier to read.

Font size

This will depend on the typeface you use, but as a guide: the main title at approximately 100 points, sub-headings 50 points and the main text 25 points.

Emphasis

You may want to emphasise key points. Below are some possibilities. However, only use two, at the most, in one poster. You can:

- use bold, italics, underline or capitals
- change the text colour
- put text in a graphic or box.

Alignment

The human eye can detect very quickly if text is not aligned and this can make it look unprofessional. It is like wearing clothes that are not ironed. Make sure your text does align and if you have a list ensure that all the first words in your list start the same, i.e. don't use a mixture of capitals and lower case.

Line length

Line lengths that are too long or too short interfere with the speed of reading. A good average line length to work with is approximately 39 characters long.

Graphics

Select graphics that enhance your text. Some stray images will look very odd.

Checklist: dos and don'ts

- **Don't** have lots of different typefaces.
- **Don't** use lots of different point sizes.
- **Don't** use your emphasis features for a large block of text.
- **Do** have a consistent layout.
- **Do** include white space around your text as this gives contrast to text and rests the eyes.
- **Do** print a draft copy to check before the final print.

Hot Tip

Don't use an unusual font as the printer may not recognise it.

Tools to use

The preferred way to produce a poster is by using a software package. Check with your tutor how he or she wants you to prepare your poster. Part of your assignment may in fact be the use of a particular piece of software.

Microsoft PowerPoint is a natural choice for most as it is already part of Microsoft Office. As a UK student (of recent years) you will probably have used this software for school coursework. Before you start you need to set up the page size and orientation you want to use. To do this in PowerPoint for an A1 poster, open a new file and click **File > Page Setup > Custom**, select a **Width** of 60 cm and a **Height** of 84 cm, and choose either portrait or landscape orientation.

You can then save your PowerPoint file onto a memory stick and take it to someone who can print it at the size and weight of paper you require. Try to get an A3 (twice as big as A4) draft copy of your poster to check the layout and colour scheme before printing at A1 size.

NOTE If you have had no experience of PowerPoint, check to see if your institution is running any ICT sessions or tutorials.

Displaying your poster

There are several ways of displaying your poster:

- on a display board
- hanging from nylon thread (need heavier weight paper for this or mounted on card)
- sticky tape on a lecture room wall.

NOTE If you are going to present your paper outside your institution, you may need to have it laminated (your institution should have facilities for this). You will also require a cardboard roll to transport it safely to your venue.

Checklist for your poster

There is nothing worse than hanging up your poster only to find an obvious spelling mistake. Poster language must be correct. You (or better still, someone else) need to:

1. Check your message for clarity.
2. Reduce the number of words and still keep it clear.
3. Check for spelling mistakes.
4. Check your images support your text.
5. Check the order of information for cohesion.
6. Get a draft A3 copy to check layout and colour (see Figure 6.4 for a summary of posters.

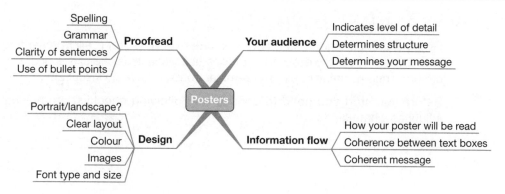

Figure 6.4 Poster summary

Talking about your poster

Although your poster sits there for all to read, you will probably be close by and may be asked some questions. You should practise explaining in a simple way what your work was about, why you did it, any problems you had to overcome on the way, and the outcomes and conclusions. If your poster is an 'ideas poster' on a topic, you need to be able to explain the central message and issues of the topic presented in your poster. Your poster may be the visual aid for an oral presentation in preference to slides.

See Section 3 for some information on oral presentations.

Having your poster assessed

Your tutors will tell you how they are going to assess your work. Some of the things that they may look for are listed below:

Criteria	Description
Knowledge	The knowledge presented is accurate and relevant to the title; key points are clearly evident.
Structure	The poster has a clear beginning and end. The text boxes have clearly defined pieces of information.
Language and images	Language is clear, concise and easy to understand. It is appropriate for the intended audience. No spelling or grammatical errors. The images enhance the text.
Amount of information	There is enough information to inform the audience of the topic and not too much to require lengthy reading.
General impression	The poster is visually attractive. The content presents new information or information from a different angle. It has some novel/interesting things to say.

3 Oral presentations

Giving a talk can mean standing up alone or with a group and presenting your ideas or your project work. You can use visual aids like slides or, if you are presenting a small paper in a seminar context, have no visual aids.

Before you start you need to consult the following checklist as this will influence what you do.

1. The topic – identify and present the key issues.
2. The talk – group or individual.
3. The purpose of the talk and the intended audience.
4. The length of time you have to talk.
5. The length of time for questions.
6. The method of presentation, e.g. overhead projector, via a computer, with no visual aids at all.
7. The handouts – are you expected to provide them; if so, how many?
8. The room layout: where will you stand, where can you put your papers? If you are a group, how will you arrange yourselves in the space?
9. The running order for presentations – are you one of many that afternoon?
10. The rehearsal – use to decide who says what in a group talk.
11. The assessment criteria – address them in the preparation.

The oral presentation assignment

Once you have provided answers from the checklist above, you can start preparing your talk.

Organising what to include

The amount of detail you put into your talk will be determined by the purpose and the audience, but your talk must always have a beginning, a middle and an end.

If you are presenting an individual or group project you need to:

- contextualise the project – lead-in
- state how you carried out the project
- mention problems you may have experienced
- state your findings and conclusions.

If you are presenting an idea you need to:

- contextualise the issues
- state where you researched the issues (a broad-brush approach to show where you have your evidence)
- discuss controversial issues
- state any conclusions.

NOTE A common mistake with many student presentations is that the talk fails to have a proper introduction that contextualises and introduces the audience to the topic. Many students jump straight into the fine detail of their work. Don't do this, as the audience has to work hard to 'catch up' in order to understand you. You have to assume that your audience may not know as much about the topic as you and providing an introduction is a key element in a talk.

Timing

Check how long you have for your 'slot' and confirm if this includes question and feedback time afterwards. As a rule of thumb, work on the following for a 15-minute slot:

- 10 minutes talking
- 5 minutes questions and/or feedback.

Again, as a rule of thumb, if you assume one slide per minute then you should have a maximum of 10 slides for a 10-minute talk.

The method of presentation

The most common ways of giving a presentation are as follows:

- via a computer using presentation software
- using an overhead projector (OHP)
- with no visual aids at all.

When using an overhead projector you will need transparent slides either to write on, with a marker pen, or to print to from your computer. You can use a presentation package, like Microsoft PowerPoint, and print directly onto OHP slides. It is not recommended that slides are handwritten as this can appear messy, unless you have particularly clear handwriting. Graphics would also have to be hand drawn and that is not a good idea.

When using a piece of software you can present via your computer. This gives a clearer presentation and enables you to add graphics easily, include colour and use hyperlinks if necessary. If part of your work was to produce a website, then this would be vital, as you would be able to show it.

Giving a talk with no visual aids is quite difficult. The traditional example of this is reading a paper in a tutorial. This can be very tedious. If you were expected to use this mode of delivery, it would be wise to put your key ideas on cards and talk around the ideas, rather than reading directly from your paper.

Slide design

As with posters, the design of your slides is important. Your audience will not want to read a lot of text from your slides. You are not there to read from your slides; that is pointless and tedious. Your slides are there as visual aids to set the scene for the topic you are talking about and give a visual anchor around which you can talk. Therefore, the more visual you can make your slides, the better – as long as they don't look like a comic! We all remember:

- images
- diagrams that show connections/processes
- key words and phrases (especially if they are repeated often enough).

We don't remember dense text or bullet points very well.

Software packages like PowerPoint have built-in slide designs, but there are only a few that are really usable and not too fussy. We have all seen those designs too often and this can create boredom in the audience before you start. So, avoid the template designs in the software and create your own, if you can (Figure 6.5).

Try using more images than text, but make sure your images are related to your work.

Your slides should be clear and uncluttered in order to be understood. Select a font that is easy to read, and be guided by the suggested font sizes in PowerPoint (point size 32 for main bullets and 28 for sub-bullets).

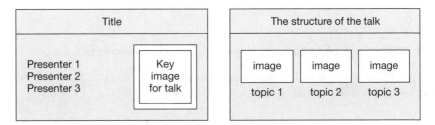

Body of talk: topic 1 [mixture of images and text]

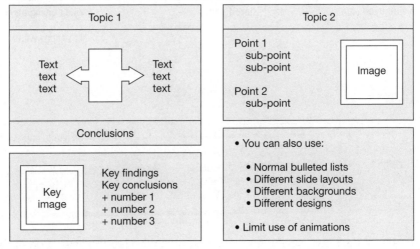

Figure 6.5 Slide designs

> **Hot Tip**
>
> Take as many digital photographs as you can of your work while you are doing it so you can include them in your presentation. This can be, for example, your team, the equipment you used, the results (if visual) and simplified graphs. This will really bring your presentation to life.

What audiences remember

Your audiences will only hear what you have to say once; they have no opportunity to go back and check. What you say at each point should be clear. We all remember how things 'fit together' better than a list of things. If you can show how things are connected (via diagrams), how processes work (flow diagrams) and how things look (images, pictures) then this will make your presentation memorable. Identify your 'take home message' and make sure you say this at the end in a clear voice with visual support.

Characteristics of oral presentations

Activity 1 will look at our experience of listening to and/or giving a talk.

ACTIVITY 1 Good and bad characteristics in oral presentations

For a moment, consider the numerous talks and lectures you have listened to and complete the table below.

Characteristics of talks you have enjoyed ...	Characteristics of talks that bored you ...	Your strong and weak points when giving an oral presentation
		I'm happy with ...
		I'd like to improve ...

Were any of your own strong and weak points in the feedback section at the back? Check to see the effect they can have on an audience.

Dealing with nerves

Many people get nervous when they have to speak in front of others, even if they have been presenting for years. You may think your lecturers are fine at giving talks, but invariably the first few lectures of a semester cause a few 'butterflies', even to long-standing performers. Having some nerves is good as this gets the adrenaline flowing and keeps you alert and on top of the subject. You may find that you are nervous at the beginning of the talk, until you get into the swing of it, and then you are fine. This is very common. Problems only occur when your performance nerves overtake you.

Some of the things you may be nervous about are:

■ an overwhelming feeling of being watched
■ feeling that others will think you're stupid
■ forgetting what you want to say
■ losing your thread and getting muddled.

Some of the signs that tell you that you're nervous are:

■ shaking
■ forgetting certain words
■ stuttering
■ sweating
■ your voice becomes higher than normal
■ you speak too quickly
■ being tongue-tied.

You may be able to recognise some of these characteristics when you give a talk, and the effect can be distressing.

Dealing with performance nerves

The first thing you need to do is take back control, and you do this by increasing your confidence in your own ability by being well prepared and in control of the topic you are presenting. Rehearse your talk so that you practise the words and phrases you are going to use and assess how long your talk will last so that it is within your time limit. Most student project presentations are approximately 15–20 minutes, but if you are presenting as part of a group you may only have 5 minutes for your part. Never go over your time limit. When you rehearse, you should identify areas that don't flow, where you are unsure of the point, or where you've included something that you are now unhappy with. A rehearsal will also identify the key sentences you need to link between slides.

The next thing you need to do is deal with your emotions. As stated before, some nerves are good, but not too many. Your aim is to calm yourself down so that you can think and speak clearly. Try visualising a speaker you admire. Identify why you admire that speaker and try to visualise yourself presenting like him or her. You need to do this regularly so that it becomes a habit and when you stand up, there you are 'in character'. If that doesn't work for you, deep breathing is often recommended in order to lower your heart rate and reduce your nerves. Finally, reflect honestly with a friend on your performance. You may feel, for example, that you were hesitating a lot, but more than likely the audience didn't notice it. Your perceptions of your performance are therefore often different from the audience's. Essentially, you have to find out what works for you, and it is important to be proactive in achieving that.

Activity 2 helps you to recognise if you have performance nerves.

ACTIVITY 2 Recognising if you have performance nerves

Indicate for yourself: 1 = rarely me , 2 = sometimes me , 3 = always me.

Characteristics of performance nerves	This is me: 1–3	What I plan to do
An overwhelming feeling of being watched		
Feeling that others will think you're stupid		
Fear of forgetting what you want to say		
Fear of losing your thread and getting muddled		

Check the feedback section at the end of the chapter.

Delivering your talk confidently

First, remind yourself that giving a talk is not the same as writing an essay that you then read out. Reading aloud from a script will result in poor marks for the 'communication skills' aspect of your assessment (see feedback for Activity 1). So, writing an essay or long-hand notes, and then reading them, is not an option! What you will need is some form of notes – perhaps 'prompt cards', unless you are confident enough to rely on PowerPoint slides or transparencies to act as prompts for you.

When written text is read aloud it always sounds monotonous, and it is easier to read it than to listen to it! Free speech is much more interesting, and it does not matter about the odd 'um' or 'er' – that's natural and allows some 'processing time' for your audience.

The key features that you need to consider during the delivery of a talk are your:

- voice and pace – vocal formatting
- engagement with the audience
- manner of handling of questions.

Voice and pace

In Activity 1 you may have identified some voice characteristics that illustrate a poor talk. Being alert to your voice and pace are key attributes to public speaking. Check out Figure 6.6 and, when you rehearse your talk, check your voice and pace characteristics.

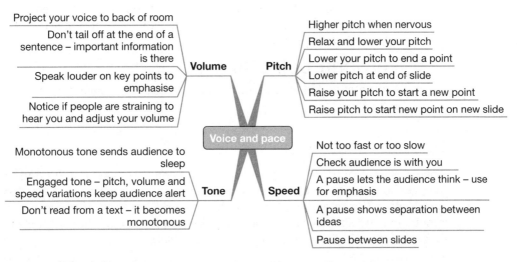

Figure 6.6 Voice and pace summary

NOTE Use language markers, e.g. and now ... the next point ... in contrast ... in conclusion ... and finally ... plus voice tone to indicate a change or a new point. This can be done by raising your voice, speaking more slowly and pausing slightly before moving on; this helps the audience to follow the flow of your talk.

Engagement with the audience

For those of you in the process of developing your oral presentation skills, you can tend to focus on yourself as the speaker and forget about the audience. This is a cardinal mistake. Once you accept that the audience is there and you want to engage with them, then your talk will become an interactive event and you will enjoy it. To engage your audience therefore you should:

- stand for eight seconds at the beginning of your talk looking at the audience – just scan across the room and don't look at anyone in particular, which cues the audience that you are ready to speak
- introduce yourself while scanning the audience
- start positively and not with an apology because something didn't work – your audience is only interested in what you have to say now
- look and sound interested in your talk and the audience
- tell your audience the structure of your talk
- maintain the right pace and use voice features mentioned above
- thank the audience for listening and invite questions.

NOTE If you read from a paper you will not be able to engage with the audience as you will lose eye contact, start to mumble into your paper, be monotonous and read too fast. If you find that slides are not enough and you feel quite nervous, use notes on a card, or a paper with large print – around

Verdana point size 16.

Add notes to tell yourself to look at the audience, pause or stress a point.

Handling questions

This is always harder for the individual presenter. However, you need to prepare as well as you can for questions. Make a list of your key messages and look at the questions that could be asked for each. If you are in a group, you should answer questions relating to your contribution to the talk. Question areas to prepare for include the following:

- Why you chose to research the topic using a particular method.
- Did the work of a key author influence you in any way?
- How did you arrive at your conclusions (possibly the choice of statistics used)?
- What difficulties did you find during your research and how did you overcome them?
- If you did this work again, what changes would you make?

NOTE If you get questions you can't answer, be honest. It is always obvious when a speaker tries to invent an answer. You can always thank the questioner for that question, as it will move your thinking on.

Planning a talk

Whether you are planning your talk for yourself or with a group, the key features remain the same. However, group presenters have the added task of deciding how each presenter contributes to a coherent talk (see Chapter 5, 'Working in a real team').

ACTIVITY 3 Oral presentation: time check

If you are involved in preparing for a presentation use Activity 3 to check your progress.

Fourteen preparation time check tasks	To do	Doing now	Done
In the weeks or days before the talk			
1. **Understand your research topic** and ensure you know enough background to feel confident with your particular angle on it. This will also give you confidence in question time.			
2. **Structure your talk** by identifying key messages and points for development within those sections. If you are presenting as a group you will divide the sections between you. Make sure you have a beginning (stating what you will do), a middle (develop your arguments) and an end (present a conclusion). Remember: group presentations need to allocate responsibilities.			
3. Decide on the **visual style** you will use and prepare your slides well. Make sure they are uncluttered and easy to read.			
4. **Decide on a title** for your talk. Try and make it short but informative. Use the 'Baked Beans' approach – 'it says what it is' – you can always have a fun strap line (like a sub-heading), but it must be catchy.			
5. **Write brief notes** onto 'prompt cards' to help make sure that you cover the ground you intend to, and in the right order.			
6. **Practise** giving your talk and timing it – either to friends, or between yourselves.			
7. **Check the room layout for the talk** and make sure that you know where you will stand or sit, where your audience will be, and the equipment you will use.			
8. Identify your '**take home message**' and how you are going to deliver it.			
9. **Assessment criteria**: do you think your talk will meet the assessment criteria. If not, what changes do you need to make?			
On the day of the talk			
1. **Re-read your prompt notes** and any supporting material, such as handouts you may have prepared for the audience, to make sure you 'get on-message'.			
2. **Get to the venue early and check the equipment**, if you can.			
3. Remind yourself of the simple but vital **rules for delivering your talk confidently** (voice, pace, audience, questions).			
4. **Support each other** in a group presentation. Identify where you will all stand, and how you will link between speakers.			
5. **Relax, breathe deeply** to keep those nerves in check (see above) and remember that your audience is on your side!			
You're on! Go for it!			

4 On reflection

This chapter has looked at only two aspects of presenting your work: posters and oral presentations. Essays, reports, making and producing things and portfolios are just examples of other ways you can present your work. In all of these, be clear what is expected of you, how it should be presented and what your message is. You should also pay attention to the coherence of your message, and to the general look and feel of the product. When you present your work you should feel proud of the content and how it looks.

ACTIVITY 4 Update your personal development planner

Having read this chapter, gauge your confidence again – how does this compare with your confidence levels at the start of the chapter? What can you do to improve? You can incorporate this into your own personal development planner and of course add anything else you feel appropriate.

Grade your confidence on a scale of 1–5 where 1 = poor and 5 = good.

My presentation skills development plan	Confidence level 1–5	Plans to improve
I can condense information relevant for poster presentation.		
I can design a good poster using the key elements of design.		
I can identify key messages when giving a talk.		
I am gaining confidence in recognising and reflecting on my strengths and weaknesses when giving a talk.		
I understand the principles of slide design.		
I can engage the audience when I give a talk.		
I know how to deal with questions.		

Date: _____

Getting extra help

- Check your institution as most universities have web pages giving you support for a range of study skills. These are usually there to provide brief tips.
- The website *Mind Tools*. There is a wide range of self-help tips on this site. The material is directed towards business people, but advice is suitable for anyone wishing to develop their skills in these areas. See **www.mindtools.com/CommSkll/PresentationPlanningChecklist.htm**.
- If you are expected to use ICT and presentation software you are unsure of, check your institution. Your options should be a paper, virtual or hands-on tutorial.
- Look for books on 'public speaking'.

Feedback on activities

ACTIVITY 1 Good and bad characteristics in oral presentations

Some of the key factors that determine the quality of a presentation are shown in the following table:

Characteristic	Effect on the audience	Solution
Little or no eye contact	'Hello, we are here as well!'	Make every effort to look at your audience. Look around and try not to look at just one person. If you look at one person all the time it becomes embarrassing and the new focus of attention for the audience.
Mumbling	'What is he or she talking about?' After trying to understand for a while, the audience will give up.	Practise your talk beforehand and either record it, or get a friend to listen. You need to project your voice. Always talk to the back of the room rather than those at the front.
Monotonous voice	A monotonous voice becomes a drone and the audience can't work out what is important in your talk. If this goes on for too long the members of the audience start to daydream, go to sleep or just wish they were somewhere else. Avoid the EGO (Eyes Glaze Over) effect.	The message in a piece of written text is delivered via headings, sub-headings and paragraphs. Your voice has to format your text for you. You can use **pitch**, **loudness** and **pauses** to create effect. Use these to show movement between ideas and emphasise important points.

Characteristic	Effect on the audience	Solution
Reading from the paper	Your audience feels bored. If you read from the paper, first you tend not to look at the audience very much and, second, your reading speed will be faster than free speech.	Read from cards if you feel you have to read something. Make the font large as it is difficult to read large font quickly. Also put notes on your card telling you what to do, e.g. 'look at audience', 'make reference to diagram on visual', etc.
Little or no structure	Your audience feels 'what is this all about?' Audiences are very forgiving at the beginning of a talk and usually assume it will get better. But if after five minutes it is not clear how you are going to structure your talk, the audience will get annoyed and only have you to focus on instead of the content.	Remember: if you get lost in a book, you can flick back through the pages. You can't do that when listening to a talk, so it must provide visual and oral help to reinforce the structure. Pause between sections and speak louder at the start of a new section. See these as vocal formatting techniques.
Too much information	'Oh no, not another graph I can't read or another slide full of tightly packed bullet points.' The audience can only take very tightly packed information for a few minutes, then there is overload and it switches off.	Identify your key messages for your talk and expound them. Better to present too little rather than too much. What is the 'take home message' from your talk? Make sure the audience at least remembers that.
Bad visuals	Your audience feels annoyed. Poor graphs, small images, tightly packed text all add up to 'noise'. The audience can't read it so why use it?	If you are using graphs, create a visual of the trend for your presentation. If you want the audience to see detail, give it as a handout and talk around it.

ACTIVITY 2 Recognising if you have performance nerves

Characteristics of performance nerves	What you can do
An overwhelming feeling of being watched	Once you engage with your audience and start looking at it, you should start to reduce this feeling. Try and think how you feel when you are having a conversation. If you don't look at people, this feeling could intensify.
Feeling that others will think you're stupid	This is a confidence issue. Make sure you practise your talk, know how to explain difficult things and be comfortable with the order and content of your slides.
Forgetting what you want to say	This is also part of a lack of confidence and something that you fear when you get stressed. If you practise, you should have the key phrases and concepts ready for use.
Losing your thread and getting muddled	This happens when you feel stressed. You need to start by feeling positive about your talk. You have practised, you may not say everything in an ideal way, but no one will notice. If your structure is clear, you can't get muddled.

7 Taking control of your reading

You probably, and quite rightly, see yourself as a proficient reader; you have after all passed sufficient exams to take on higher studies. However, as you progress through your studies, you will find that reading can be more of a challenge than you thought. You need to develop the tenacity to read through complex technical texts for background information, specific facts, to see how things work and to apply theories.

You are now at a stage where you need to become a smart reader and be able to identify quickly documents that suit your purpose and then read them efficiently with a critical eye.

In this chapter you will:

1. recognise key textual features that help you read quicker
2. know how to identify appropriate texts through your reading list (and beyond)
3. develop strategies for the effective reader.

USING THIS CHAPTER

Estimate your current levels of confidence. At the end of the chapter you will have the chance to reassess these levels and incorporate this into your Personal Development Profile (PDP). Mark between 1 (poor) and 5 (good) for the following:

I understand how features of a text can help me read more efficiently.	I know how to identify what I have to read, and don't just read anything that looks vaguely appropriate.	I have a set of reading strategies that I can and do use.

Date: _____

1 Finding your way around texts

As a reader you do not always consciously take note of how tests are constructed because you are concentrating more on the message contained in the text. However, if you are to negotiate texts more efficiently, it is well worthwhile exploring how they are put together.

Finding your way around texts is often reliant upon:

- Your knowledge of how texts are assembled and put together. In other words, the style of the text.
- Your understanding of text types that you read most.

You can increase your reading speed and improve your comprehension by being familiar with the way text is written for your subject. This is called 'genre' or the style of the text. You might also examine how the text is organised and how the author has analysed (broken down) the material in order to set up an argument. Be aware that different disciplines (e.g. engineering, sociology, philosophy, psychology, neurology, etc.) will have different ways of arguing, so the text may be set out in a different format and adhere to different 'rules'.

Different types of texts

Expert readers are able to navigate texts more quickly than novice readers and one of the reasons for this is that they know what to expect from different types of texts. In other words, they can recognise the hidden features of a text so that they are aware of the purpose of the text, and what they can get out of it.

During your studies you will be reading mainly textbooks, 'readers', your lecturers' notes, manuals, and texts on the Web. Textbooks help you understand a topic and are often accompanied with a list of key concepts, diagrams, pictures, examples and questions that enable you to test yourself. Textbooks therefore simplify and 'teach'. Some of course are better than others.

Readers are books that tend to have multiple authors and are written to provide more in-depth information on a topic. Each author often has a topic to develop and it is generally written in a discursive style (e.g. presenting an argument, explaining a concept in relation to another concept, arguing against a theory).

Manuals are like recipe books with a set of instructions. Unfortunately they are often lacking in clarity and you may find you have to 'find your own way' through the instructions.

Texts on the Web can range from full peer-reviewed articles that you can access through your institution's library to blogging. Be careful how you use web sites (see Chapter 3, Section 2, 'Skills for online learning').

Journal articles are the published result of a researcher's work. You find these articles in academic journals that are either physically in your institution's library, or available remotely. These journal articles are the key resource for all research, and have been peer reviewed before going to print. You can also use journal articles to trace a community of scholars active in an area.

NOTE You must reference all the resources you use, otherwise you could be accused of plagiarism (see Chapter 13).

Hot Tip

Try to familiarise yourself with bibliographic software such as EndNote or Reference Manager to manage your references (and notes from readings) during larger projects.

Key features of a text

Different types of texts have different features and it is important for you to understand what they are and how they can help you get a quick overview of a text. Most of the characteristics you will know, but do you really know how to use them effectively?

Heading	Sub-headings
Summary/abstract	Paragraph
Bold/italic print	References

ACTIVITY 1 How do you use textual features?

Text features	What do you do?
1. How do you use headings and sub-headings?	1. I don't really think about it; I just start reading to the end. 2. Skim through the text to see what it is about. 3. Use them to structure my notes.
2. Do you read the abstract?	1. I don't know what this is. 2. I don't bother with this as it is outside the main text where all the information is anyway. 3. I always read it before deciding if I should read any further.
3. How do you use summaries in texts you read?	1. I just read; I don't think about it being a summary or not. 2. I read an abstract or summary first to get an idea, 3. I understand a summary can be at the beginning or the end of the text, so I look for it.
4. Do sub-headings help you understand how the writer thinks?	1. I have not really thought about it. 2. I know they are there and take notes under sub-headings. 3. I use sub-headings to get an overview of the text before I start reading properly.
5. What's a paragraph for?	1. It breaks the text up on the page so it doesn't look to dense. 2. It is the writer's way of explaining something.
6. Do you use the revision section of a textbook (if it has one)?	1. I don't usually have time for this. 2. I do look at the revision section at the end. 3. I look at the revision section at the beginning and the end.
7. Do you take any notice of key terms or concepts that are sometimes used in texts?	1. Generally, no; I just read and take notes. 2. Yes, I take a look to give me an overview of what will be in the text.
8. What do you do with the references?	1. I've never really thought about looking at them. 2. I use the references to see who the key researchers are in this area, and how I can extend my reading.

See the feedback section for further explanation.

Some more about paragraphs

The writer will use the paragraph to build up his or her argument. How writers do this depends on what they are talking about: for example, a process, a definition, a description, etc. Being able to identify quickly how the paragraph is structured will help you read more efficiently. See also Chapter 14, Section 2.

Some simple ways that ideas are developed by the authors are through:

- **Definitions** and/or **descriptions** using link words such as: *is defined as, comprises, refers to*, etc. The author may be looking at descriptions or definitions that are under dispute, adding his or her own definition, or referring to some standard definition.
- **Comparing and contrasting** using link words such as: *similarly, on the other hand, is different from, compared with, however,* etc. The author will be, for example, comparing results from various experiments or contrasting different views.
- **Cause and effect** typically use link words such as: *as a result, therefore, if … then …, because*, etc. This is usually found when an author is discussing how things work.
- **Processes** or **sequences** typically use words that indicate a sequence of events such as: *first, second, then, next, finally*, etc. Processes can refer to the flow of an event and/or the time sequence.

It is important to look out for these link words and underline some of them as you skim through the text. You should prime yourself if the writer says 'There will be four key changes to … .' Skim the text and underline the key link words that introduce these 'four changes'. Understanding link words tells you how the text is organised.

In addition, a good writer will use the first or second sentence in a paragraph to indicate what that paragraph is about. This is called the 'topic sentence' (see also 'Skimming' in Section 3). Once you know this, you can use it effectively.

Text ingredients

Look at Figure 7.1 to see how the paragraph develops.

As you can see, sentences have a function in the text and this is the way the author can guarantee that the text fits together, or in other words, that it has coherence.

ACTIVITY 2 Identify key link words and their function in a paragraph

Look at the text in Figure 7.1 and underline some of the key link words and their function in the paragraph.

See the feedback section for further explanation.

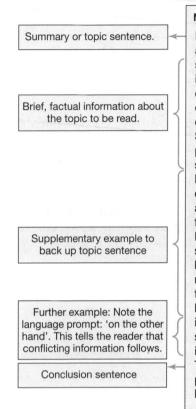

Maximising the earth's resources

Biodiversity is the interactivity of diverse plant and animal life in a particular habitat in order to sustain equilibrium in the ecosystem. A look at invertebrates can demonstrate some of this complexity. Invertebrates are known as ectotherms and are dependent upon their environment for many metabolic functions. Scientists are beginning to investigate ways of preventing disease in invertebrates and in doing so can demonstrate that they may be part of a large food pyramid. Giant millipedes are an example of this. Most live in moist rainforests and eat decaying plant material. As they forage for food they become covered in parasitic mites. Human natural instinct would be to kill these small parasites because they are thought to be harmful and irritating to the host. However, in millipedes they perform a vital role: they eat the fungi which grow in the joints. If the mites were killed, then fatal fungal infections would develop in the millipedes. On the other hand, in another species mites can be harmful. Varroa mites can infest bees and have been found to be irritants. Thus, scientists need to examine the role of parasites in the eco-systems to provide stable bio-diversity for the future.

- Summary or topic sentence.
- Brief, factual information about the topic to be read.
- Supplementary example to back up topic sentence
- Further example: Note the language prompt: 'on the other hand'. This tells the reader that conflicting information follows.
- Conclusion sentence

Figure 7.1 Paragraph development

Technical texts

Science, maths and engineering texts can be difficult to read as they generally do not have narrative style. When reading a narrative text, your understanding will flow with the 'dialogue'. More technical texts, on the other hand, concentrate on explaining, for example, concepts and their relationships, characteristics and properties of substances/materials and cycles of events.

Since these texts are less narrative style, new facts and information are packed very tightly into each page and you will find yourself faced with a bunch of new vocabulary and acronyms, mathematical equations, symbols and formulae, diagrams and flow charts.

Be very clear of the purpose for reading such texts, so you can concentrate on getting what you want from them. You will need to read these texts in small chunks and take your own notes. If you can reformulate what you have read, or create your own mind map to show how concepts relate to one another, then you will develop your own understanding. Be prepared to do this in small chunks.

If you are finding some concepts difficult, search around on the Web until you find a file that can give you a simpler explanation. Sometimes you just need someone to say the same thing in a slightly different way in order to unblock it for you. Acronyms can be a stumbling block to the flow of a text, but there are many websites that provide full acronym lists for your subject; find a good one and keep it to hand (or post it to your Del.icio.us bookmarking site – see Chapter 3).

2 Knowing what to read

What you read will depend on the purpose of your reading. When you look for a text, you need to be clear why you are reading. It can be quite general if you just want to get an overview of an area, or it can be quite specific if it relates to a piece of coursework.

Identify suitable texts

Suitability of text is not just about choosing the right book for the assignment. It is also about choosing the right book *for you* at your stage in the learning process or your level of understanding. It is important for you to manage this.

The books are too hard

While choosing books to suit *your* needs depends upon what you already know and bring to the task, you must remember that sometimes your tutors put books on their lists which are too difficult for many students. They have introduced these books to challenge you. Their expectations are high!

If the books are too hard for you, then you must draw upon strategies to cope with this. You need to start examining the suitability of the text for your purpose.

Is this text suitable for *you*?

Just because a tutor has placed a book in the Reserve Collection or on Short-Term Loan does not always mean that you are ready to access that particular book. Some students forget that one of the elements of successful reading is the knack of matching their level of understanding with the relevant reading for their coursework.

You may become disheartened when you can't understand a text on the 'book list'. This may be because you are still grappling at an early stage of understanding with both the new concepts and the new terminology. Some books may be just too complex for you at this stage. If this applies to you, you should choose a text that gives you more of an overview. If the subject is new to you, the Idiot's Guides on the market are a 'must'! However, there may be some excellent 'A'-level textbooks which serve this purpose before you start reading more complex journal articles. It is important that you seek advice from your department, tutors and postgraduate students about what is available. You can of course always try your institution's second-hand bookshop and see what other students bought.

NOTE   This advice may seem to contradict what your academic tutors tell you. There are few who would recommend 'The Idiot's Guide to …' or Wikipedia. This is because tutors expect their students to have a higher starting point. You need to assess the knowledge *you* bring to this activity and choose accordingly. However, only use these resources to get you started.

Is this text suitable for my studies?

The question you need to ask yourself is 'Does this book or chapter or article contain the information or evidence I need for my assignment or task?' If it does then it is worth using. However, you will probably find that there is no one book which conveniently and neatly contains all the information you need for your specific assignment. So you are expected to dip in and out of books, chapters and journal articles. Identifying key words, and working with your writing plan (see Chapter 15), will enable you to make effective decisions about what to use and what to discard.

Remember: the books or chapters or articles have not been written especially so that you can answer the question posed by your tutor! They may go into a lot of complicated depth which is not relevant to your current needs, so only read what you need to read to gain an understanding and the information you want.

ACTIVITY 3 Selecting appropriate books

Try this out with a selection of books for one of your assignments. You will need to have a list of key words available. Mark it as 'a possible read' or 'discard it'.

Write book title:
Has this book been mentioned/recommended by my tutors?
Is it on the reading list?
Are there some of my key words (or equivalent) in the title?
Is the book fairly recent? Remember: if the publication date is too old, the information may be out of date.
Look at the back cover of a book. Do the summaries indicate that there may be some useful sections?

▶

Look at the list of contents at the beginning. Are there any of my key words in the titles? If so, note the specific chapters in the 'possible' column.

Look at the index at the back of the book. Search for specific key words (or equivalent). Note the page numbers in your 'possible' column.

Sample some of the chapter sub-headings. Do you think some sections may be of use? Make a note of page numbers in the 'possible' column.

Sample a small section of a chapter. Is the information accessible to me? Remember: if the style of writing is too academic or filled with many technical words which you don't know, you may not be ready for it yet.

ACTIVITY 4 Is this the right journal article?

Try this out with a journal article you have come across. Mark it as 'a possible read' or 'discard it'.

Write article name:
Has the article been mentioned/recommended by my tutors?
Is it on the reading list?
Are there some of my key words (or equivalent) in the title?
Read the 'Abstract'. This gives an overview of the article. Does it contain any useful information for my assignment?
Examine the key words (usually located after the Abstract). Is there a high match factor?
Is the article fairly recent? Remember: if the publication date is too old, the information may be out of date.
Sample some of the sub-headings. Do you think some sections may be of use?
Sample a small section of the article. Is the information accessible? Remember: if the style of writing is too academic or filled with many technical words which you don't know, you may not be ready for it yet.

Reading lists

I'm so confused by the reading lists. I've been told to choose the best books but how do I know which are the best. I wish they would just give us a few books to read for an assignment.

First-year Geography student

The tutors think they are being so helpful giving us detailed reading lists. Frankly, I find them daunting. When am I going to find the time to read them all?

Part-time Psychology post graduate student

You may not realise that your tutors expect you to take control of your learning and that this also applies to the reading lists! They assume that you will make choices in your reading. Thus, they will provide course handbooks with lengthy reading lists, unit reading lists, lecture handouts with lists of references and electronic course notes with further reading lists. This can be confusing and overwhelming. Do they expect you to read every single text to which they refer? The answer to this question is usually 'no'. So why do they give so many lists? Most academic tutors are aware that their students come from different academic and cultural backgrounds, with a variety of prior learning experiences. Reading lists therefore have to cater for these different needs, but you may be able press your lecturer to give you a 'must read' list.

The tutor's perspective

Some tutors want to provide a rich source of background reading for their subject and will provide students with detailed reading lists. They do this because they want their students to 'read around' the subject and not be blinkered into reading only a few texts, which would get them through the assignment. Often, these lists are for guidance. If a student has little or no knowledge of the content of the unit, then the list must include some texts which enable this student to build up concepts and knowledge. The reading lists have to take this into account and provide some basic texts and some more advanced texts to challenge and develop thinking.

As academic tutors, we provide substantial lists because we are concerned about the availability of texts in the library, particularly for our part-time students. Therefore, we may include books about the same topic by different authors. These will contain very similar information. We do not expect students to read every book but we are reassured that by including this variety the important texts will be accessible and available in the library.

Managing reading lists: personal control

Looking down a long list of guided and suggested reading can be daunting. Making skilful choices about what to read and what to leave aside for the present are important features of managing your reading.

Reading lists must be used selectively to suit *your* needs. This means that there are some simple rules you can apply when searching the library or the Web for your reading material for your assignment:

ACTIVITY 5 Pragmatic decisions for reading lists

Ask yourself ...
Is this book available when *I* need it?
Is the book only available in the reference section of the library? (This means that I have to make sure I plan my study reading so that I can do this in the library and not in my flat or room.)
Is the book pitched at a level which I can understand? (Sample a chapter to see if you understand the ideas.)
Does the book contain chapters/sections which would be useful to help me complete my assignment? (Remember to go back to your assignment title to check what you are being asked to do.)
Is the book too difficult for me to understand? (Then you need to choose a book which you can understand before moving on to more complex books.)
All of the books on the reading lists have already been taken out by others on my course. (Use your key words to search for other resources.)

The shelves are bare!

It is important to understand how the library works with respect to reading lists. Many essential reading resources are placed in a 'Reserve' or 'Reference Only' section in the library. This means that there will be many of your fellow students chasing these precious texts. You need to ensure that you find out in advance the 'loan availability' of books. In most college and university libraries this is divided into:

- Reserve/Reference Only/Short-Term Loan.
- One-week loan.
- Three-week loan.

Of course, if you have left it very late to look at your reading lists, the chances are that your fellow students have got there before you and taken out the books. Thus, it is vital that you organise and manage your work routines to ensure that you do not leave your reading to the last minute.

3 Developing efficiency through reading strategies

You are expected to do a considerable amount of reading at college or university. However, you do not have all the time in the world to read. Therefore, it is essential that you become an efficient reader.

ACTIVITY 6 What reading strategies do you use?

Look at these questions to find out more about the way you tackle background reading, reading for assignments, reading for literature reviews and reading to increase knowledge and understanding.

Answer yes or no to the following statements:

Your reading strategies	Yes	No
1. Do you read a chapter or journal article from start to finish and have a vague idea of what was said?		
2. Does it take you longer to complete the reading for your course, compared with your friends?		
3. Do you find that what you read seems to go above your head?		
4. Do you read word by word?		
5. Do you 'say' the words silently to yourself in your head as you read?		
6. Do you find you have to read and reread sections?		
7. Do you try to avoid reading complicated/advanced texts and articles?		
8. Do you vary the pace of your reading?		

Check the feedback section at the end of the chapter to find out solutions.

Reading speed

If I read more slowly it will help me to understand difficult concepts and texts which seem inaccessible because of the way they are written.

Mary, first-year Engineering student

Sometimes reading slowly can impair your understanding. Slow readers are more likely to miss the point or get bogged down with minute detail.

If I read a chapter/article/section of text over and over again I will be able to understand the concepts.

Kate, second-year Chemistry student

Perhaps you are tackling a text which is too difficult initially for you or that you have no clear idea of what it is that you want to get out of the text and are simply reading as a large sponge with the hope that something will soak in!

- Did you know that the average university student can read at 250 words per minute?
- Did you know that efficient readers can skim a block of words in less than a quarter of a second?

ACTIVITY 7 A speed test in reading

■ Choose a passage to read which is unfamiliar to you. You may wish to use one of your recommended course books.

■ Time yourself for 10 minutes.
■ Count how many words your have read in this time.
■ Divide your total by 10.
■ Your answer will tell you how many words per minute you can read comfortably.

If it is less than 150 words per minute you need to work on this skill.

Of course, you must remember that personal reading speeds vary according to the complexity of the text and its novelty for you. If you pick up a chapter in a children's textbook about your subject, your reading speed will be high because of your own level of knowledge in relation to the complexity (or otherwise) of the text. However, if you take up a cutting-edge journal article which goes into great detail about intricacies of a new theory, your reading speed will naturally slow down to cope with the complicated concepts and sentence structures and very specific use of key technical terminology.

Increasing reading speed

Train yourself to ...	Try this ...
Read faster.	The more you practise reading quickly, the better you can become. Try to increase your rate by choosing texts which are easy to start with.
Increase the amount of information your reading brain can take in. You can 'see' words out of the corner of your eyes.	Try reading a phrase at a time rather than individual words. With practice, you can increase the length of phrases you read at speed.
Read more quickly to improve comprehension.	Read a difficult section quickly twice. This is better than reading it slowly once!
Improve the flow of reading.	Avoid backtracking when reading. Backtracking is when your read and reread a few words or a section.
Recognise the 'look' of new terminology.	Practise reading lists of key subject words. Time this activity – allow five minutes per day when encountering new terminology.
Avoid 'sounding out' words in your head as you read.	Give your eyes and brain practice at just looking at the words. Try to get your eyes to move forward and time yourself to see how quickly you can get to the end of the line or the next full stop.

Speed readers can read both vertically and horizontally because they are absorbing information visually and letting their brain take in many pieces of evidence at the same time. Many now appreciate the value of power walking; 'power browsing' is the equivalent in reading and can help you to 'digest' the main themes of a book in 10 minutes! There are many websites which you can visit and which help to improve and increase your reading speed. Tony Buzan's books give many tips and practical hints, e.g. *Speed Reading* (2006).

Skimming

Skimming is a particular style of reading. It is a way of gathering as much information as possible from text in the shortest time possible. Skimming is primarily a visual activity and is used for getting the gist or impression of a chapter/section of text. You are not reading the whole page in the usual way, and your eyes do not move from left to right along the line as they do when reading a whole text.

Skimming is one of those reading strategies which takes confidence. Many people read in their head – in other words, they say the words silently to themselves. This process often helps readers to remember and understand what they are reading. However, with skimming the brain takes in the information in a different way. It uses only the visual clues to gather up the text on the page.

Expert skimmers tend to look for key words, nouns (these inform the reader what the content and information is), verbs (these give the reader clues about the relationship between the nouns) and link words in that order to help them get a quick overview. A reminder of some link words is: *however, thus, on the other hand*, etc. They are the glue of the text and help to stick the text together in a specific manner, depending upon the viewpoint or arguments, which the writer wishes to put across.

Skimming is useful to help you make decisions about whether a text is useful for your assignment. It is also vital for those learners who like to have the big picture before reading in detail.

The expert skimmer

Let's look at the way an expert skimmer operates.

Skin regrowth

There are specific <u>age cycles</u> with human skin. <u>Between</u> the ages of <u>15 and 25</u>, apart from the odd blemish, the skin has a <u>youthful</u> look to it. It can take a beating with <u>too much sun, alcohol and convenience food</u> and <u>still</u> look <u>good</u>. This is <u>because</u> the <u>cell growth is rapid</u> during these ages and can occur on a <u>19 day cycle</u>.

This reader has picked out the underlined words and sent this information to the brain via a visual fast-track route. Notice that some of the 'glue' words help to make the highlighted information make sense: 'Between', 'too much', 'still' and 'because'.

Try this for yourself with a passage from a newspaper. Choose a topic in which you have some interest and try to stop yourself from reading the words silently to yourself.

Use the topic sentence in each paragraph to skim a document

You can also quickly skim a document by using the structure of the paragraph. Remember that the first sentence (or two) in a paragraph should highlight what the paragraph is about (topic sentence), so by just reading the first sentence or two of each paragraph in a document you quickly get an idea of how the text develops (see Chapter 14, Section 2).

On-screen scanning

Computers can speed up and support your skimming through searching a text for a particular word. Adobe Acrobat files have a function where they provide a list of all instances in the text of your search word. You can see instantly how often it occurs and where. This way you can find out if the text is going to be useful for a specific assignment.

The interactive reader

Being an 'interactive reader' is the opposite to being a 'passive reader'. If you do not engage with your reading effectively, you will simply waste your time. You may say to yourself that you spent two hours reading in the library and feel very pleased, but stop and think what you got out of those two hours. If you weren't engaging with the text (being an interactive reader), the chances are that you got very little out of it.

There are many ways of becoming more interactive with your texts. A popular method is the SQ3R method. It will enable you to make the most of the time you spend reading as it helps you focus and structure your thoughts. It stands for

| Survey | Question | 3R |
| | | Read, Recall, Review |

First of all you need to get a taste of the chapter/article you have chosen to read so you will need to skim the text to see if it is suitable for your purpose (Survey).

Next, ask yourself why you are reading the text and what you want to get out of it so that you read with a specific focus. Your comprehension improves if your mind is actively searching for answers to questions (**Q**uestion).

Then, read carefully, breaking up your reading into small sections, looking for the main ideas. Annotate the text and make notes (**R**ead).

After this, mentally go through the ideas you have just read and pick out the main points and see how things 'hang together'. Check that you can answer your initial questions and that you have assimilated and gathered the information you need (**R**ecall).

Finally, look back and reread selected sections, expand your notes if necessary, to see if the passage has answered everything you wanted (**R**eview).

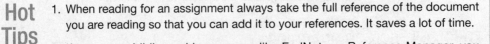

Hot Tips

1. When reading for an assignment always take the full reference of the document you are reading so that you can add it to your references. It saves a lot of time.

2. If you use a bibliographic manager, like EndNote or Reference Manager, you can save your notes into this database with the possibility later of searching your notes

The critical reader

The 'interactive reader' is the process by which you engage with the text, whereas the 'critical reader' is taking this a step further and looks at how you challenge a text. You want to know the authenticity of what is being said, the authority of the author, how he or she has used evidence to state a claim. You will work towards being a critical reader through your studies and this will be one of your key graduate skills.

They keep mentioning critical reading. But what are they getting at? I just read.

First-year Biological Sciences student

In a survey of academic skills at Southampton University in 2000, the gulf between what the academic tutors expected of their students and the skills the students thought were needed for study was great. Academic tutors expect their students to be able to 'interact' with documents in an intelligent way. This means evaluating and being critical of what you read.

ACTIVITY 8 Are you using your critical skills [reflection]?

Are you using critical reading skills?	Yes or No
1. Do you think about what you are reading and question what the author has written?	
2. Do you take what the author has said as the truth?	
3. What credibility does the writer have in the subject area?	
3. Do you challenge the ideas as you are reading?	
4. Are you able to distinguish different kinds of reasoning used? (See Chapter 14, Section 1.)	
5. Are you able to synthesise the key information and make connections between what one author and others are saying?	
6. Can you make judgements about how the text is argued?	
7. Can you evaluate how the information could be better or differently supported?	
8. Can you spot assumptions which have not been well argued?	

The questions above demonstrate what it means to become a critical reader.

ACTIVITY 9 Weighing up the evidence

Now you are in the right frame of mind for approaching your reading in a critical manner, you need to practise and generalise your skills. Here are some questions to get you to interact with and think about your texts. Gathering the evidence is the first stage; weighing up what you have found is the critical thinking you will have to apply.

Take a document or a website and look at the following questions and consider where the evidence is in the text.

1.	Who is the author?
2.	Who is the author's audience?
3.	What are the central claims/arguments of the text?
4.	What is the main evidence?
5.	Give examples of how this is substantiated.
6.	What assumptions lie behind the evidence or arguments?
7.	Is adequate proof provided and backed up with examples of evidence?
8.	What are the general weaknesses of the threads of the argument/evidence?
9.	What are the general strengths of the threads of the argument/evidence?
10.	Give examples of what other leading authors have to say on the same subject.

For more information on criticality, see Chapter 14, Section 1.

4 On Reflection

In this chapter you have looked at what it means to be an efficient reader.

Summary of the chapter

Take a quick look at Figure 7.2 and assess how well you are now familiar with these areas.

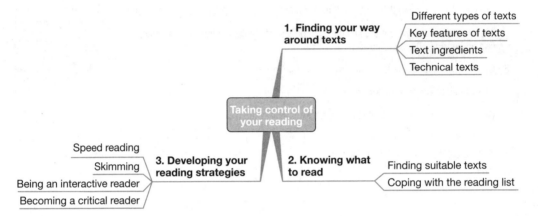

Figure 7.2 A summary of this chapter

Now reflect upon how you go about managing your reading and how you intend to change and adapt your reading habits so that you can spend your time more effectively. You may want to transfer this information to your own institution's personal development planner scheme.

ACTIVITY 10 Update your personal development planner

My developing skills	Confidence level 1–5	Plans to improve
I understand how features of a text can help me read more efficiently. *Section 1*		
I know how to identify what I have to read, and don't just read anything that looks vaguely appropriate. *Section 2*		
I have a set of reading strategies that I can use. *Section 3*		

Getting extra help

- Your institution should have student support services available if you find you have problems with your reading. Don't be afraid to go, this is not a literacy problem. You probably need to get your technique honed.

- There are plenty of self-help websites on various aspects of reading; check them out. Remember: always read what is appropriate for you at the time and as your knowledge increases you can progress to more difficult texts.

- Go and see your personal tutor if you are really concerned about your reading.

Feedback on activities

ACTIVITY 1 How do you use textual features?

Text features	What do you do?
1. How do you use headings and subheadings?	a. I don't really think about it; I just start reading to the end. b. Skim through the text to see what it is about. c. Use them to structure my notes.
You should actively use the headings and sub-headings to skim a text and see what it is about. If you only use it to structure your notes then you will just get a summary of that text. Make sure this is what you want. If not, think how else you can take notes. A smart reader shouldn't being doing 'a'.	
2. Do you read the abstract?	a. I don't know what this is. b. I don't bother with this as it is outside the main text where all the information is anyway. c. I always read it before deciding if I should read any further
You should always read the abstract if there is one. This gives you a quick overview and can prevent you reading something that is not appropriate.	
3. How do you use summaries in texts you read?	a. I just read; I don't think about it being a summary or not. b. I read an abstract or summary first to get an idea. c. I understand a summary can be at the beginning or the end of text, so I look for it.
Always look at the summary or abstract first to get a feel for what it is about. You should be doing 'b' and 'c'.	

Text features	What do you do?
4. Do sub-headings help you understand how the writer thinks?	a. I have not really thought about it. b. I know they are there and take notes under sub-headings. c. I use sub-headings to get an overview of the text before I start reading properly.

You should answer 'c'. Only take notes under sub-headings if you want a summary of the text to work from.

5. What's a paragraph for?	a. It breaks the text up on the page so it doesn't look too dense. b. It is the writer's way of explaining something.

The answer is 'b'. Since each paragraph is an idea, you can see how the writer builds up his or her ideas/concepts/arguments.

6. Do you use the revision section of a textbook (if it has one)?	a. I don't usually have time for this. b. I do look at the revision section at the end. c. I look at the revision section at the beginning and at the end.

You should really be doing 'c' if you want to understand fully what this text is about. Reading the revision section at the beginning can prime your reading.

7. Do you take any notice of key terms or concepts that are sometimes used in texts?	a. Generally no; I just read and take notes. b. Yes, I take a look to give me an overview of what will be in the text.

The key terms are important as they give you the scope of the text and you see which terms are familiar and unknown to you in advance.

8. What do you do with the references?	a. I've never really thought about looking at them. b. I use the references to see who the key researchers are in this area, and how I can extend my reading.

If you are carrying out a larger piece of work, like an extended essay, a large project or a dissertation, it is important you use the references to piece together who is doing research in this area. For smaller pieces of work, you probably won't need it.

ACTIVITY 2 Identify key link words and their function in a paragraph

Biodiversity is the interactivity of diverse plant and animal life in a particular habitat in order to sustain equilibrium in the ecosystem. A look at invertebrates can demonstrate some of this complexity. Invertebrates <u>are known as</u> ectotherms and are dependent upon their environment for many metabolic functions. Scientists are beginning to investigate ways of preventing disease in invertebrates and in doing so can demonstrate that they may be part of a large food pyramid. Giant millipedes are an example of this. Most live in moist rainforests and eat decaying plant material. As they forage for food they become covered in parasitic mites. Human natural instinct would be to kill these small parasites because they are thought to be harmful and irritating to the host. However, in millipedes they perform a vital role: they eat the fungi which grow in the joints. If the mites were killed, then fatal fungal infections would develop in the millipedes. On the other hand, in another species mites can be harmful. Varroa mites can infest bees and have been found to be irritants. Thus, scientists need to examine the role of parasites in the ecosystems to provide stable biodiversity for the future.

Are known as –	Indicates a description of a term
However –	making a contrast – why we shouldn't kill millipedes
If … then … –	tells what would happen if the mites were killed
On the other hand –	contrasting here the effects in another species
Thus –	summing up how to treat this dilemma/complexity.

Most of this paragraph refers to explaining the complexity of the topic through comparison of the metabolic function of invertebrates (ectotherms).

ACTIVITY 6 What reading strategies do you use?

Reading strategies	Solutions
1. Do you read a chapter or journal article from start to finish and have a vague idea of what was said?	• Set reading targets. • Ask yourself what information you are looking for. • Read a section which you think gives you the information you need. • Read a short section, cover up the text, write brief notes about what you think you have understood and read. Then check your notes with the text.
2. Does it take you longer to complete the reading for your course, compared with your friends?	• You might be choosing texts which are too advanced for you at this time. • Focus your reading more by posing questions to which you require answers. • Set manageable targets. • Give yourself some questions so that you can find out the answers.
3. Do you find that what you read seems to go above your head?	• You might be choosing texts which are too advanced for you at this time.

Reading strategies	Solutions
4. Do you read word by word?	• You might be choosing texts which are too advanced for you at this time. • Build up your self-confidence as an academic reader. Do this by letting your eye flow over a phrase at a time. Practise this with magazines and newspapers.
5. Do you 'say' the words silently to yourself in your head as you read?	• This slows you down; let your eye flow over a phrase at a time, and visually take in chunks of text.
6. Do you find you have to read and reread sections?	• This might be because you are tired or have lost concentration. If you are tired, take a short rest. • If you have lost concentration, you need to reset your focus and set yourself new and possibly shorter targets. • Ask yourself what you think the section is going to be about before you read it and then check to see if you are correct. • You might be choosing texts which are too advanced for you at this time. • Take notes.
7. Do you try to avoid reading complicated/advanced texts and articles?	• It is the flexible and effective reader who makes appropriate decisions about the level of the text to read.
8. Do you vary the pace of your reading?	• To start with, make a conscious effort to monitor your pace of reading. Evaluate its effectiveness. Then adjust according to the task.

Reference

■ Buzan, T. (2006) *Speed Reading: Accelerate your speed and understanding for success*, 3rd edn. Harlow, BBC Active.

8 Excelling in exams

Examination success is the final hurdle. Examination marks often form part of your overall mark and thus count towards your final degree. Success depends upon knowing what is expected, good organisation, appropriate notes and effective memory techniques. This chapter will help you to explore what works and why. It will increase your skills and productiveness.

In this chapter you will:

1. examine the purpose of revision
2. explore new and effective techniques for efficient revision
3. learn about memory strategies
4. learn how to organise yourself during the examination.

Estimate your current levels of confidence. At the end of the chapter you will have the chance to reassess these levels where you can incorporate this into your personal development planner (PDP). Mark between 1 (poor) and 5 (good) for the following:

I can manage and organise the whole revision process effectively.	I can recognise which revision notes system to use for different purposes.	I understand how to control pressure and stress.	I understand the characteristics of productive memory strategies.	I can use effective strategies during the examination.

Date: _____

1 Introduction

What are the most common reasons why students do not get the marks they anticipate?

Some students dread examinations while others will admit that they enjoy the adrenaline rush. However, many students are at some time disappointed with their grades. Unexpected failure or low marks do not always mean that the student has not revised or does not understand the subject. A survey of tutors and examiners highlighted a number of common problems (see Activity 1).

ACTIVITY 1 Where do I stand?

Reflect upon your previous examination performance. What do you think could be improved? Look at the following table and be honest with yourself. In the right-hand column there are suggestions for methods to improve your performance, and cross-references to some relevant sections in the book.

This chapter will take you through the solutions so that you can increase your performance and get better grades.

Problem	Has this happened to you? Answer yes or no	Solution
Failure to answer the question set.		BUG technique (see Chapter 12).
Misinterpreted the question.		BUG technique (see Chapter 12).
Answered the wrong number of questions.		Get to know what is expected of you (see Sections 3 and 4).
Insufficient examples to support ideas/arguments.		Get to know what is expected of you. Improve your revision mapping techniques.
Insufficient knowledge.		Get to know what is expected of you. Distil information into manageable revision notes.
Illegible handwriting.		Practise writing at speed to maintain legibility.
Incoherent writing – long, rambling sentences which do not make sense to the reader.		Concept maps to connect information more effectively will have an impact upon your written communication and organisation.
Not all the questions answered. This may have occurred because you have run out of time or spent too long on the early questions.		Be strict and stick to time allocations worked out prior to the examination during revision. Memory recall strategies and techniques need to be strengthened. Practise recalling information under timed conditions.
Forgot the information on the day.		Relaxation techniques. Have a good night's sleep. Do not drink large amounts of alcohol and caffeine before the examination.
Course materials not referred to sufficiently.		Get to know what is expected of you. Listen out for tips and guidance during lectures. More effective revision notes. Increase your memory techniques.
Irritating errors – spelling mistakes, weak and incomplete sentences, silly errors in calculations, etc.		Leave some time at the end of the examination to check through your work for irritating errors.

2 What is revision?

Perhaps this question is jumping the gun, and the first question should really be 'Why have examinations?' Examinations and revision are closely interlinked. Examinations are a way of finding out what you have understood from your course. Many lecturers refer to 'learning outcomes', and examinations are a method of testing your grasp of those outcomes. Contrary to popular belief, examinations are not a fiendish method, devised by your tutors, to trick you!

The answer to the question 'What is revision?' may seem obvious, but it is important to make sure that you understand the purpose of revision so that you optimise your efforts. In its literal sense revision means 'seeing again', and this is what you will be doing when you go over your notes and look back on the information you have gathered over your units and modules. However, if you want to be an effective reviser, revision is much more than reading your notes. You need to develop an active approach. This will ensure that you get better grades. So what makes a successful reviser?

- preparation
- organisation
- memory and recall.

Activity 2 asks you to identify your problems with revision.

ACTIVITY 2 Common difficulties with revision

Which of these apply to you?	Tick ✓
1. I am often frustrated at examination times.	
2. I am often *very* nervous at examination times.	
3. I often find that I can't sleep properly at examination times.	
4. I seem to spend a lot of time revising and not getting the good results.	
5. I am not sure if my techniques are the most efficient.	
6. I mainly leave revision until it is almost too late.	
7. I put off my revision and find myself looking for other things to keep myself occupied.	
8. I have vast amounts of notes to help me revise.	

Check the feedback section at the end of the chapter to find out how to start changing your working patterns.

3 Productive revision

Be prepared

Most students come to university with some ideas about how to go about revising for examinations. However, the strategies you have used in the past may have been effective for the type of examinations you did then, but are not necessarily the most efficient now. Preparation is not only about drawing up a timetable and arranging your files and books on your work space! Activity 3 asks you to reflect upon how you have tackled revision in the past; you should analyse what worked well (you got good results) and what didn't work well (you got poor results).

ACTIVITY 3 Productive working habits

Which of these revision techniques worked well for you and which didn't?

	Yes/No
1. Writing out my notes again and again helped me to remember facts and information.	
2. Reducing information into shorter notes helped me to remember facts and information.	
3. Memorising essay answers.	
4. Writing out sample essay answers under timed conditions.	
5. Using concept maps, mind mapping or diagrams helped me to remember facts and information.	
6. Putting important information onto audio tapes and playing them over and over again.	
7. Revising with friends.	
8. Using colour (coloured highlighters, for example) to help me to summarise and understand key points and to remember facts and information.	
9. Reading my lecture notes (without any other activity).	
10. Writing out essay plans from past questions.	
11. Spending long periods revising a week before.	
12. Using memory triggers to help me remember.	
13. Using key words as the basis for understanding.	
14. Any other method you have used.	

In certain circumstances, these are all useful techniques either on their own or, more appropriately, in combination. However, you now need to consider their role and value in the context of study at university level. Think about why and when certain techniques worked well for you and why others did not, and develop your own approach.

4 Countdown not meltdown

Be organised

Preparation, organisation and memory recall are the essential elements of good revision. It is important that you have a clear revision strategy leading up to examinations so that you do not experience 'meltdown' or excessive anxiety during your examinations. This section explores:

- how to develop the right 'mindset'
- the tricks of the trade, i.e. the best strategies for maximising time and results
- dealing with examination nerves
- last-minute countdown.

The right 'mindset'

Preparing for examinations is not just about learning and memorising facts and information so that you can regurgitate them in a timed examination. It is also about:

- knowledge of what is expected of you by your tutors
- consideration of the assessment criteria
- selection of important theories, ideas and evidence
- realistic self-expectations
- development of efficient note-making systems
- development of organisational strategies
- increasing your memory capacity
- ability to 'crack the code' of the examination questions
- getting a buzz from understanding your subject.

Knowing what to expect and, equally importantly, what is expected of you are vital parts of the revision process. These two factors should drive your preparations and inform your strategies. See Activity 4.

ACTIVITY 4 Knowing what to expect

The table following will get you actively involved with your revision right from the start of your unit/module. Use it as a memory aid and keep it prominently displayed at your workstation (wherever you do most of your studying) as a constant reminder. If you are studying for Joint Honours or have examinations set by more than one department, it is vital that you check each department's rules and regulations. Do not assume that they are the same.

What to expect	Source of information	Fill in your answers in this column
List the number and title of papers/ examinations I have to take this semester.	Course handbooks. Departmental online information. Examination office – some of the larger institutions have a central office to deal with the organisation of examinations and have a section on the college/university website.	
What am I allowed to take into the examination room (e.g. calculators, statutes for law tests, course notes)?	Course handbooks. Departmental online information. Check with the unit tutor.	
What will be provided for me in the examination room (e.g. periodic tables, molecular models, scientific calculators, law statutes)?	Course handbooks. Departmental online information.	
What do I need to take into the examination room (e.g. pens, pencils, coloured highlighter pens, etc.)?	Examination officers (either departmental or institutional) will let you know the regulations.	
What type of questions can I expect in the various papers?	Past papers: take care that there are no changes for your year. Course handbooks. Departmental online information.	
How many sections are there in each paper?	Past papers: take care that there are no changes for your year. Course handbooks. Departmental online information.	
How many questions do I have to answer?	Past papers: take care that there are no changes for your year. Course handbooks. Departmental online information.	
Where are the instructions on each paper?	Past papers. Course handbooks. Departmental online information.	
What is the length of the examination paper?	Past papers: take care that there are no changes for your year. Course handbooks. Departmental online information.	
What is the marking allocation for the questions in the paper?	Course handbooks. Departmental online information. Check with the unit tutor.	
What are the assessment criteria for the unit/module?	Course handbooks. Departmental online information. Cross-check with learning outcomes.	
What are the expected 'learning outcomes' for this unit/module?	Course handbooks. Departmental online information. Lecture notes from your tutor – some tutors display these at the beginning of units or lectures.	

As you can see, a lot of information can be gathered from your course handbooks. The library is another source of information. Many departments deposit past papers in the library (often in a reference section) and more and more are available electronically. Collecting photocopies of past papers of the relevant examinations that you will be taking is essential.

Hot Tip

Much of this information can be gathered before you start your new academic year because you will have discussed with your tutor which units/modules you will be taking. So before you dash off on holiday, why not get this information and store it in a safe place, clearly marked? October is always a hectic time, and you will be bombarded with a lot of information at the start of your courses. Consequently, many students do not feel they have time to collect information for events that will not take place for months! This is short-sighted. The other advantage of getting the information before you are plunged into a new academic year is that libraries, in particular, are less busy at the end of June and early July and you will be able to gather your information more quickly.

What type of examinations will I have to take?

Your tutors use many different ways to test your knowledge and understanding. Some subjects traditionally use essay questions, while others use multiple-choice questions, calculations or problem solving. Knowing a little about the different types of questions can inform your revision strategies because the different test types tap into different skills and memory techniques. These are summarised in the table following.

Some people have the knack of remembering vast amounts of facts and being able to regurgitate them quickly. These people can score highly on multiple-choice questions. There are others who need time to mull over information and gather their thoughts together. Without lots of timed practice, they will not score well on multiple-choice questions. In an ideal world it would be good if you could choose the type of examination format which suits you best. The reality is that the type of assessment and the ways in which examinations are traditionally set, as yet, do not reflect different learning styles. Besides, the variety of methods for assessing students test different skills, as you can see from the table following. Sometimes your tutors want to find out if you have remembered important facts. This could be the case with the viva that medical students have to take: a sort of oral, fast-paced test of factual information. Multiple-choice questions also enable your tutors to test this type of knowledge. However, most examinations will demonstrate your understanding of the subject and your ability to draw out relevant information to answer the question which is posed. In other words, the ability to handle information which you have stored in your memory.

Type of examination question	Definition	Skills needed
Multiple choice	A statement followed by a choice of answers which are often short and succinct. They test your knowledge of facts.	Good memory for facts. Quick memory recall. Reading accuracy and fluency.
Short answers	These questions require you to write brief paragraph answers and test your knowledge of facts.	Good sentence writing. Succinctness and summary skills. Selection of information.
Essays	These are the same as your course assignments and require you to write coherently and convincingly. They test not only facts but your interpretation of them.	Cracking the code (question analysis). Summary skills. Selection of information. Paragraph/sentence writing. Good grammar and punctuation.
Open book	This type of examination allows you to take in course texts and notes. Some students are duped into thinking they do not test memory.	Selection of information. Location of information. Linking and mapping information.
Take home tests	Students are given three or four essay titles and have to prepare for these in advance. They do not know which question they will have allocated to them until they enter the examination.	Good memory. Selection of information. Summary skills. Organising thoughts in coherent written format.
Problem-solving/case studies	Some departments prefer to set these types of examination questions. Students are expected to marshal facts and put them into real-life, imaginary settings.	Cracking the code (question analysis). Selection skills. Linking and mapping information.
Practice tests	Medical and Health Professional students, for example, are often tested on their practical ability to apply knowledge.	Application of knowledge and understanding. Good memory. Speed of recall and assembly of information.

How organised are you?

The key to success in many circumstances is organisation – not just in your studies but also in the way you run your life. However, organisation pervades every aspect of revision. It relates to your physical environment – for example, where you keep your revision notes, how you categorise your information – as well as the information you have to remember. A well-organised student also has better control of his or her inner self and is thus able to deal with concentration, motivation, stamina and examination nerves.

When should I start my revision?

It is never too soon to start the revision process. Many students leave it too late to do a proper job. Have you ever said: 'If only I'd started earlier with my revision?' Revision is an activity which should be ticking over quietly throughout your unit or module, reaching a crescendo of activity in the weeks and days before the examination. Many students put themselves under unnecessary pressure in the last few weeks before the examination by trying to make their revision notes at the same time as learning and committing information to memory. It is no wonder that the brain and memory are overloaded and less effective! Try to pace yourself and start the revision process at the beginning of your units instead of at the end.

Overview of the revision process

The table following provides you with guidelines for pacing yourself and maximising your efforts. Once you get into the 'Before, During and After' routine you will find that you can improve your grades in examinations.

Before (the start of your unit)	During (while your lectures and the unit are taking place)	After (at the end of your unit in the time before the start of examinations)
1. Collect all the necessary past papers and store them in the appropriate revision file. It is useful to analyse the examination questions so that you can get an overview of the topics which are set and those which come up frequently.	5. After a series of lectures and seminars on a particular topic/ theme, gather together all your information from different sources. These could be handouts, electronic information provided by tutors, your own lecture notes and notes you have made for background reading (possibly in preparation for an assignment).	8. Read through your revision notes and information to ensure that they still make sense and that you understand what you have gathered together in '6'.
2. Purchase some special files in which to keep your revision notes – these are different from your course and lecture notes as you will see later in this chapter.	6. Distil all this information into dedicated revision notes.	9. If you have gaps or your notes do not seem to make sense, you will need to go back to the original notes and information to improve your revision notes.
3. Section off your revision files with clearly labelled dividers. You will need to cross-reference these sections with the examination themes and topics.	7. It is a good idea to sub-divide your topic information into the following sections: • key words • concept map • list of important facts/theories • key theorists • selection of quotations.	10. Begin the memory stage of your revision – memory techniques are explained later in the chapter.

Before	During	After
(the start of your unit)	(while your lectures and the unit is taking place)	(at the end of your unit in the time before the start of examinations)
4. This is for those who like to use technology to help them with revision. Set up a separate folder on your computer for revision. Divide the folder into files which match the topics/themes that are to be assessed. Perhaps you could code the files with an 'R' for revision to make sure that they do not get muddled with ongoing coursework and lecture notes.		11. Practise recall of information under timed conditions. Various techniques are explained later in the chapter.

The multi-dimensional revision map

For some students, revision is like a journey. To reach your destination in good time, it is worth investing in accurate maps. You need to keep in mind your journey's end, even at the start of your revision. On a journey there are times when you have to plot and plan out the whole journey and for this you need to see all the road networks and how they link together. At other times you need to focus on the minute details of street plans. Thus, in the examination there will be occasions when you will need to have the big picture of a topic to help you to make decisions about which elements or networks are applicable to the question. At other times, when working on your essay answer, you will be dealing with individual facts. You need to be able to manipulate both the whole and the parts to answer questions effectively. These are the mental acrobatics you will have to employ when you are in the examination room. Good revision will help you to be in control of your map and to know when to switch from the big picture to the fine details. However, what makes examinations so special is that they put you under timed pressures.

Time-controlled conditions put an added dimension to the revision process. Not only are you expected to be able to recall factual information accurately, to manipulate this information to meet the demands of specific questions and to assemble information from different mental storage areas, but you also have to do this under the pressure of time. Think of each topic as a big map. The way you organise the storage of facts and figures, theories and quotations will determine how quickly you can assemble the relevant information for a given task or question. However, it does hinge upon good networks which are adaptable and can provide you with quick routes to get you to where you want to be. The better organised your information is, the smoother, and therefore quicker, it will be to map out your information effectively.

What is your filing/storage system like?

Use different-coloured files to gather and store your revision notes for each of your examinations. Believe it or not, this simple start to your organisation will reduce stress in the final countdown to your examinations. You will have all the relevant information at your fingertips and will not have to waste time searching through lecture notes and various topics to carry out your memory routines. Keep your backups on a memory stick and in a safe place.

It is a good idea to stick to one system for organising each section of your files. As suggested in the text above, you will need:

- key words with your definitions
- list of important facts/theories
- key theorists
- selection of quotations
- concept maps.

Suggestions for building up these sections in your files is given in Section 5, 'Tricks of the trade', below.

Once your storage framework is in place, using either separate files or computer folders and files, you can start gathering and distilling information in readiness for storing it in your memory systems.

5 Tricks of the trade: good revision notes

This section provides you with ideas for techniques for formatting your notes. It also explores ways in which you can produce more effective revision notes which in turn will increase your memory capacity and strengthen your knowledge and understanding of the subject.

Examinations can help you to consolidate your knowledge and bring together lots of different strands from your unit. During revision time you may find that the 'penny will drop' for you on some topic that you found puzzling during the semester. Making effective revision notes will help in this process and will ultimately give you an indication of what you understand and where the gaps are in your knowledge. In Activity 5 you are asked to identify and analyse your personal preferences for revision notes.

ACTIVITY 5 My revision notes techniques

Have a look at the different types of note systems presented in the table opposite. Decide upon your personal preferences for using the different types. Then analyse and evaluate whether they have been of real help in remembering information for examinations.

Note types	Preferences 1 = frequently used 2 = not often used	Memory lubricators: ask yourself if the note type has helped you remember information for examinations
Lists		
Linear notes in bullet points		
Diagrams (some subjects lend themselves more to this than others)		
Notes in prose format (sentences/paragraphs)		
Concept maps		
Flash cards		
Posters		
Ceiling maps		
Audio notes		
Grids/tables		
Time lines (useful not only for History students but when you have to know about the progress or development of an innovation etc.)		
Other		

What sort of notes you produce and how you distil a whole series of lecture notes into revision notes is to some extent personal preference. There are a variety of ways of producing effective notes which you may want to consider. It is vital, however, that whatever system you choose it provides you with useful notes and is an efficient use of your time and effort.

Hot Tip

Remember: revision should not be a passive activity. Making your revision notes, by whatever technique or combination of techniques you choose, is only a means to an end: effective tools for memory stimulation and ultimately obtaining better examination grades. However, these notes are merely one part of the whole process. Sitting back and admiring your notes will not get your desired outcomes. It is the interaction between your mind, the information (subject context), memory stimulators and your examination systems which gets results.

If you always do the same things to revise, how do you know if they are really working? Could you be more efficient? Could you have remembered the information if it had been presented to you in a different format? It is just as important to evaluate what you did linked to your results. The type of information you are dealing with will also have a bearing upon your success or otherwise. For example, trying to remember the intricacies of the respiratory system, with its high level of difficult subject terminology, might be best approached using labelled diagrams rather than linear, bullet-point notes.

How good are you at customising your notes for revision purposes?

ACTIVITY 6 Customising your notes

Grade your effectiveness judged against past examination performance, where 1 = very useful; 2 = useful; 3 = just adequate; 4 = not effective.

Revision notes	Allocate grade
1. I only use the notes I made for an assignment/essay on this topic.	
2. I only use my lecture notes.	
3. I put all my notes from different sources together in a file.	
4. I only use my lecturer's handouts and downloaded electronic information from the departmental intranet.	
5. I make a new set of notes from all my sources.	
6. I do not have revision notes.	

If you only use one source of notes, you have to be confident that they are comprehensive. Remember that notes made for another purpose, e.g. for an assignment/essay, may not be right for the job of revision. If you gather all your notes from different sources into one file or section, you must be careful that there is not repetition of information. This can cause a drag on your time and sap your energy and memory.

If you make a new set of notes having gone through all your sources, do you end up with more or less notes? In these circumstances, more is not necessarily good as you will see. Besides, if your revision notes are greater than your other notes, you need to ask yourself whether the increased volume helps or hinders memory.

Some students find that they have amassed a lot of lecture notes and notes made from books and articles for a specific assignment. It may seem rather daunting to try to consolidate these a couple of weeks before the examinations! It may be an impossible task and as a result you are immediately put off doing what is a very important aspect of revision that involves not only memory techniques but understanding.

If you have organised your lecture notes carefully, at the end of each topic/unit you might find it useful to make revision notes while things are fresh in your mind. It is often a good idea to place your revision notes at the beginning of the section and identify them in a different colour so that they stand out when you come to the final stages of revision in the build-up to the examinations. Many students use different-coloured paper for this or a range of coloured pens or coloured fonts.

You can customise your revision notes in many ways. Broadly speaking, you can start by drawing up a big route map (concept mapping notes) or you can draw small, detailed maps (information notes). You must decide which is the best way for you to work. There is no right or wrong way, simply personal preference.

How to customise your revision notes

If you want to provide the best support for your memory and retrieval systems so that they can work at speed under pressurised, timed conditions, you need to categorise and compartmentalise information into different maps.

Revision maps

At different times in your examination you will need to draw upon different parts of information to show off your knowledge and understanding to the examiners. There will be occasions when you need to use the subject terminology correctly and with confidence. For this you will need to have key words with your definitions at your fingertips. Sometimes you will gain marks for factual detail which is accurate. You will be drawing upon your store of important facts/theories/processes. If you want to demonstrate the depth of your knowledge and understanding you will need to be familiar with key theorists, leading figures or important innovations. Being able to draw from a selection of snappy and relevant quotations is impressive. At other times your examiners want to find out how well you really understand the topics/subjects and will set questions whereby you will be expected to select and assemble information to bring out the connections. Revision or concept maps enable you to perform in this way.

During the course of your lectures and seminars it is always good to have an eye on creating your revision maps.

Key words/subject terminology

Whether you set up a dedicated file in your revision folder on your computer or whether you prefer to work using paper and pen, it is vital that you have an ongoing list of key terminology. Science and engineering subjects have a vast amount of terminology and acronyms that you must be familiar with. In some subjects, such as Nursing and Medicine, there are many words which look very similar but have totally different meanings. Thus, it is vital that not only do you list the key words but that you know what they mean. Copying a definition out of a dictionary will not aid memory recall. The definitions need to be in your own words so that you can understand them. This will give you confidence and speed when using the terminology under pressure in examinations.

A simple two-column table is the most effective way of gathering the information as you go along and is clear and easy to read when you get to the memory stage of revision (see Activity 7).

ACTIVITY 7 Key word map notes

Choose one of the topics/units which will be examined. Start to fill in the table. Keep this in your revision file.

Key word/phrase/acronym	Your brief definition (if unsure of this, check the accuracy with a knowledgeable friend)

As part of the ongoing nature of revision, this is a two-stage process:

- Stage 1: Collect the most important key words and terminology as you go along throughout the lectures and seminars. This will be a random activity.
- Stage 2: Can the lists be regrouped in any way? This might help you look again at the terminology to make decisions about how to map the information mentally. Some students use colour at the regrouping stage so that they are preparing for memory storage and map connections later on.

Factual information

If your revision notes are to be of any use, you must distil the information you have. As soon as you have come to a natural pause or finishing point with one of your units, you need to distil your information into manageable revision notes. Summarising notes or handouts into 'distilled' notes (key words, phrases) should take up no more than two sides of A4 for each topic.

If you look at some of your notes from different sources, you will find that some of the information is repeated, though in different words.

1. Read through all your notes/sources of information on a topic.

2. Identify the parts where repetition has occurred.

3. Shorten this information into your own words.

4. Pick out the key points first, followed by examples or subsidiary information.

You will have to choose a revision notes system which is suitable for your information, so try out different systems. The type of format you use will depend upon personal preferences to some extent but is often triggered by the type of information with which you are dealing.

Which note format do you prefer?

Here is some information in two frequently used formats: mind mapping and linear. Look at both and see which one makes sense to you.

An example of linear/branch notes

Family: family perspectives[1]

Feminist perspective

- Black feminists
- Radical feminists
- Feminist Marxists
- Liberal feminists
- Marxist feminists
- Common themes:
  - patriarchal institution
  - familial ideology

▶

---

[1] With grateful thanks to David Bown, Sociology lecturer, for supplying these helpful mind maps and branch notes.

- ◆ power structures
- ◆ women's experiences
- ◆ division of labour

New Right perspective

- Promotes traditional family
- Opposition to lone-parent families
- Boys suffer from absent fathers
- Dysfunctional families in underclass

Functionalist perspective

- Loss of functions theory:
  - ◆ Talcott Parsons: two 'basic and irreducible' functions
  - ◆ George Murdock: four universal residual functions
- Multiple functions family:
  - ◆ Ronald Fletcher: 'multifunctional family'
  - ◆ Eugene Litwak: 'non-bureaucratic functions'
- William Goode: movement to nuclear family
- Dysfunctions:
  - ◆ Vogel and Bell: emotional scapegoats

Marxist perspective

- Michelle Barrett: docile workforce
- Christopher Lasch: haven in a heartless world
- Reproduction of labour

Interpretive studies

- Studies of ordinary family life
- Meanings of family life

An example of mind-map notes

As you can see in Figure 8.1, information in mind-map notes is categorised by colour (or shade) rather than as a separate linear branch. The five main headings are in bold so that they stand out as the main branches or stems from the central theme.

An example of a table/grid format for recording: theories/famous people/innovations/inventions

Depending upon your subject and your topic, you can gain marks in examinations by showing off your knowledge about how development and progress has been made. For Education students, it is important to be

Figure 8.1 An example of mind-map notes

aware of the educational system and how it has evolved to become an inclusive educational system. You would need to know key names and dates; you would have to be able to state ideas and theories as well as solutions. Law students have to be aware of the Criminal Justice System, its development to today's system, and who the key players were and are.

Engineering students may need to know about processes: who invented such systems and what is involved, or the theory upon which the system is based. Psychology students may to have know about of the measurement of intelligence and would need to know the different theories of what makes up intelligence.

This type of information is often given along the way during lectures and in the course of your background reading. It is as well to keep a separate section in your revision file to keep this type of information all together. Using grids and tables is often one of the most efficient methods of gathering this type of information. It enables you to memorise the facts but also to obtain an overview of information from which to compare and contrast (see Acitivites 8 and 9).

ACTIVITY 8 Key theories and people map notes (1)

The table below is part of a worked example to demonstrate how you can record this type of information.

Theory	Definition	Named person(s)	My comments
One general intelligence	'g' factor: general ability to reason. Many common abilities classified under this. To do with neural processing speeds. Linguistic, logic and spatial skills.	Cattell Spearman	Cattell – introduced 'fluid' and 'crystallised' intelligence. 'Fluid' – is memory dependent and deteriorates with age. Abstract reasoning and problem-solving abilities. 'Crystallised' – increases with age; attributes can be taught. Performance on culturally loaded tasks. Spearman – developed factor analysis.
Three stratum	Built upon Cattell and Spearman's foundations. Incorporates reaction time.	Carroll	Three layers. Hierarchical layers. Notion of quicker the reaction time, the higher the IQ.
Multiple	Humans have combinations of different types of intelligence. Not limited to single/one general theory.	Gardner	Reaction to 'g' factor and its components. Multiple – started with seven and then identified nine types of intelligence, e.g. musical, interpersonal, intrapersonal, mathematical, logical, linguistic, spatial, kinaesthetic, naturalistic.
Triarchic	Componential theory of analysis of intelligence.	Sternberg	Opposed Gardner. His categories are analytic (academic) and practical.

The development of thinking relating to the notion of intelligence and comparisons and differences can be drawn out of this table. Thus, the basic framework of information is given together with personal commentary. These notes are the foundations for a compare and contrast type of essay, yet the information could be used more generally as background information to a debate about nature versus nurture.

ACTIVITY 9 Key theories and people map notes (2)

Now try this out for yourself with one of your units by using the two grids provided.

Theory	Definition	Named person(s)	My comments

Name a theory or concept related to the chosen topic	Who supports this theory or concept?	Who opposes this theory or concept and why?

Relevant quotations

During the examination, if you can give a punchy and relevant quotation to back up and strengthen what you are writing about and the point you are trying to make, you can gain some valuable extra marks. However, you have to balance up whether (a) you have the time to search such quotations out and learn them, and (b) you have the memory capacity to remember them. Writing an inaccurate or irrelevant quotation is just as bad, if not worse, than not quoting at all. Your choice of quotation is also crucial because it must be linked to an important point or a unique saying/idea. Thus, it is vital that you remember the accurate quotation but also that you know what point it is making.

Hot Tip

Taking into account the above advice, it is better to learn short quotations or phrases which will do the job you want. You should be on the lookout for these while you are conducting your research reading and while you are going through various handouts. It is worth alerting your consciousness to pick up on these when they are given in lectures. Often they are throw-away remarks but can be used most effectively in examinations.

Revision/concept maps

No revision notes section should be without an A4 or A3 revision/concept map of the whole unit. These maps are invaluable for ensuring that you make the connections with all your information. These will help you to obtain a greater depth of understanding of your subject. They are most useful to help you forge links between ideas in a theme or topic.

These maps tend to be fairly complicated, depending upon your topic. Figure 8.2 gives an example of a simplified map to show you how the general ideas are linked together.

Having a concept map at the beginning of each section of your revision notes can fuel your final countdown. You can also use it to test yourself in the final stages of the revision process.

Poster displays

These are similar to concept maps but on a larger scale. The best type of poster display for revision purposes is on A3 size paper. This size allows you to incorporate visual information which could stimulate memory later on. Posters should be kept in a prominent position.

I always put one on my ceiling above my bed so that when I'm lying in bed forcing myself to get up, I gaze up and see the poster. It's sort of like a subliminal thing to help me remember.

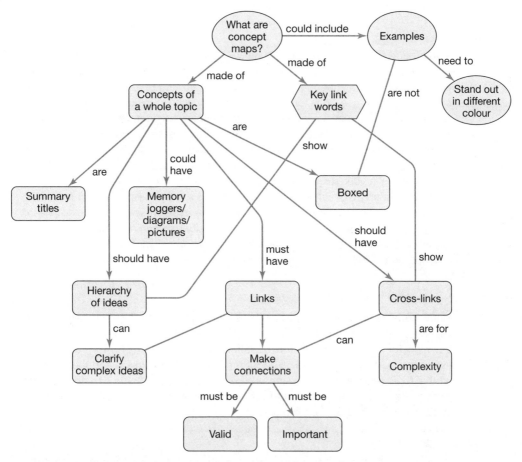

Figure 8.2 A simplified revision/concept map

Adapted from: **www.mc.maricopa.edu/dept/d43/glg/Study_Aids/concept_maps/conceptmaps.html**

Hot Tip Strategic revision

Look back at Activity 4, 'Knowing what to expect', where you were asked to find out what your examination papers will be like. You can make good use of past papers in many ways. Obviously, your tutors would like you to learn everything connected with the unit. However, you need to be ready for the format of the examination. You have to apportion time properly and be ready for the way in which the tutors word the questions. You will not have much time to figure out what a question is getting at and what information is required under the pressure of the actual examination. Therefore, your preparations should cover all eventualities of which you have control.

Time allocations

If your paper consists of essay-type answers, then it is important to work out how much time you should spend on each question so that you can pace yourself in the examination. You will need to take into account allowing yourself reading time and choosing the best questions for you as well as allocating some time for checking your answers. Some papers do not allow you to do any working for the first 10 minutes. This ensures that students read the paper through and start to make decisions about which questions to answer. Some departments assume that students will do this and do not ring-fence or protect any time within the examination. Make sure you know what happens in your subject so that you can calculate the amount of time you have for actually writing your responses. If your paper is a mixed response type (one short section, with short answers, or multiple-choice type, followed by a couple of essay-type responses), you also need to consider matching time allocation to maximum marks per question. It would be foolish to spend a lot of your precious time on a question which only gives you a few marks.

Question spotting

Many students look at papers which have been set over the previous two or three years so that they can get a feel not only for the topics which come up (patterns) but also for the wording of the questions (manipulation of information). For example, you may have learnt all about the Industrial Revolution and the question on this topic requires you to weigh up the impact of this upon a certain sector of people. This could have an effect upon the way you make up your revision notes in readiness for memory learning and recall.

If you have managed to work through all the 'Tricks of the trade' section, you will now have a well-organised revision file which is properly compartmentalised. It will provide you with all the information you need to move on to the next stage in your revision, which is making sure that you can memorise all that is contained in your file sections.

6 Memory stimulators

However effective we are at preparing and organising revision and gaining an understanding of the material, we have to commit it to memory for an examination. The more thoroughly we understand a topic, the more easily we can deal with unexpected and/or complex examination questions. So, it is important not to rely totally on pure memory recall or rote learning (learning chunks of information by heart). We need to develop strategies to help us remember.

Why do some people seem to have good memories and others struggle to remember what day it is? Perhaps those with good memories have developed strategies for remembering, and they have worked out ways of remembering which suit them best. **Rote learning** may have worked in the past for some examinations but at university this is not a sensible strategy because of the volume of information you will have to deal with and because you are overloading your memory without understanding the subject. This type of learning uses up a lot of brain capacity, and, in particular, memory capacity. The problem with this is that it leaves little spare capacity for other activities which go on during an examination. It is difficult to remember isolated strings of information, but when you have found a way to connect them, then you have a deeper understanding of the material (concept maps will support this), and this makes it easier for you to recall the information you need.

Wouldn't it be wonderful to cast your eyes over a page of information and automatically be able to remember everything on the page? There are very few people who have got photographic memories to enable them to do this. Most students have to work at developing memory capacity and, as one gets older, it is neccesary to keep the memory lubricated by constant practice. Many students have a negative view of their memory ability. You will be surprised how much you can do if you use the right stimulators. There are different types of memory, and knowing how the memory operates can help you make strategic choices to get the most out of the time and effort you put into memorisation at revision times.

How the memory works

The brain is like a living computer. It relies upon hard disk storage (long-term memory), portable storage facilities (short-term or working memory) and a robust operating system. The operating system has to be able to make decisions about where to go for information and to ensure that linkages and connections are made smoothly between the different parts of the system.

The memory system needs you to stimulate it effectively. Using the computer analogy, Figure 8.3 illustrates the various stages of memory interaction.

INPUT
- Short-term memory
- Working memory

PROCESSING
- Working memory
- Long-term memory

OUTPUT
- Working memory
- Long-term memory

System needs to be primed to take in information

System needs to be well organised so that it stores the information ready for quick access

System needs to be prompted to retrieve and recall information

Figure 8.3 The stages of memory interaction

This system has to be finely balanced to get the most out of it. If you overload one part of the system, then you reduce the effective working and processing of other parts of the system. Just like a computer, this reduction will lead to sluggish operation and retrieval. Many of you will, at one time or another, have complained bitterly that your computer takes forever to load up stored information. Some have said that it is possible to go away and make a cup of coffee while the computer chugs on and displays the irritating hour glass to let you know that it is loading and retrieving your information from within its filing and operating systems. Rote learning, mentioned previously, clogs up your systems. It saps a lot of the energy from your processor and output systems. Consequently, if you are taking in further information, such as reading a part of an examination question, the balance of your system is skewed and everything starts to slow down – just what you do not want in timed, pressurised conditions.

For optimum working the memory system needs:

- motivation
- minimal stress distracters
- concentration surges.

Therefore give your memory system a chance to work well by ensuring that you are in control of your stress levels, cut out unwanted distractions, and utilise memory joggers to provide the concentration surges and lubrication for your memory system.

What sort of memory strategies (joggers) do you use?

Think about how you remember. Answer the following questions:

- What was your first day at school like? (episode)
- What is your home postal code? (fact)
- Where did you have your last lecture? (episode)
- How do you open a document on the computer? (procedure)
- What is a key concept in your favourite topic? (knowledge)

Our long-term memory is organised so we can remember facts, episodes, knowledge and procedures. These use different aspects of our memory. In addition, how facts and knowledge are remembered (written text, diagram, mind map, etc.) could reflect your ability to recall that information. Certain subjects can be remembered effectively by drawing and labelling diagrams, e.g. the intricacies of the blood system, but this would not be suitable for learning the causes of poverty in the last century, where a grid chart may be better. However, if you have set up revision files you are well on the way to strengthening better storage in your memory system.

You may find yourself better at remembering some types of things than others. Can you identify your memory strengths and weaknesses? See Activity 10.

Check the feedback section at the end of the chapter to see a sample of two topics and the strategies appropriate for each topic.

These strategies help you to prime your memory input system so that you give it the best chance to work. They will also provide effective organisation systems for storage during the processing stage.

ACTIVITY 10 Memory strategies/joggers

List two topics you will be studying (select quite different types of topics):

TOPIC A _____

TOPIC B _____

Memory strategies	Topic A	Topic B
Mind mapping, diagrams and flow charts		
Associations – making links with the information (concept map)		
Writing out information		
Remembering information in lists – rearranging the order of the list so that the first letters of each word on the list make up something silly or amusing, a memorable mnemonic		
Using shapes and colour		
Saying the information – to yourself or out loud		
Poster display – similar to a concept map but incorporating visual clues as well		
Customised fridge magnet displays		
Chunking or grouping information		
Devising a story about the facts		
Flash cards		
Anything else you have found useful		

Of course, controlling your environment will also ensure that you give the whole system the best chance to operate. Distractions will weaken the effectiveness of the memory system so it is imperative that you evaluate what distracts you and how you are going to eliminate these (see Activity 11).

ACTIVITY 11 Controlling distractions

	Your answer	Ideal? Better to …?
Where do you revise?		
Is it noisy?		
What about comfort factors?		
Do you take regular breaks?		
Do you set realistic targets for what you can memorise in a specified time?		
Do you prefer to revise alone or with friends/both?		
Do you need to spread out your notes?		
Do you walk around when you are memorising information?		
What is likely to distract you?		
What time of day do you prefer to revise/study?		

Bursts of concentration are better than setting aside long periods to revise. Research suggests that we can only sustain **productive** concentration levels for 40 minutes at a time. The memory retains more when you concentrate for short periods of time. If you have set aside a three-hour chunk of time for specific revision and memory learning, make sure that you split it up into small 15-minute chunks and then take a brief break – stretch your legs, make a drink (preferably not containing caffeine or alcohol) and do some relaxation exercise.

How do you prepare for timed conditions? The output stage

If I had plenty of time, I could recall loads of information.

Emma, second-year Environmental Science student

I can produce a really good essay which flows if I had more time.

Andrew, first-year History student

Most of us would agree with these students at some time during examinations. However, the trick is to ensure that you are prepared for the real circumstances and that you can trigger your brain to recall information from the different storage areas at speed. It is no good having all the information to answer a question if you do not show it off in the examination itself. It is well worth reminding yourself of the time you have apportioned for each examination response (see 'Hot Tip: Strategic revision', above).

Once again you need to give your memory the best chance for success and this will mean a two-staged attack.

Stage 1: Getting the information to stick in your long term memory

The memory is better lubricated when it has small chunks of information to deal with initially. So break down your facts etc. into bite-sized portions. Go over them regularly to imprint them and then see what you can remember. Gradually put the chunks together so that your memory makes the connections and so that you can recall larger and larger sections.

Stage 2: Retrieving or recalling the information at speed

The knack in examinations is bringing the information out of the depths of your memory. This means that you must set aside time to rehearse this. Practising recall of facts and timing yourself is important. On the day not only will you have to do this but in response to a specifically worded question, you might have to pull out parts of one of the storage drawers or files in your long-term memory and combine these with others. This slows the process down so you need to make sure that your speed and accuracy of recall is good. Many students practise recalling information at speed by getting hold of previous examination papers and timing themselves with specific questions. Try out a number of strategies in Activity 12.

ACTIVITY 12 Recall speed strategies

Try out some of these strategies. Remember that your subject matter may determine which ones are the best.

Recall speed strategy	Recall time	How to improve ...
Labelling a diagram		
Drawing a cycle of information		
Listing main facts/events		
Drawing and labelling how things work (e.g. for procedures)		
Constructing an essay plan for specified questions (e.g. for take home examinations; questions from past papers)		
Writing out prepared essay questions		

7 Controlling the pressure

The mind and body function well on a certain amount of stress. Levels of adrenalin can keep you ready for action which is needed during the examination. Certain levels of stress can keep you on your toes, more alert and ready for action. Stress also means that your motivation is stimulated so that you have a positive attitude to your revision. However, too much anxiety and adrenalin can be counter-productive. To keep a check on your levels, go back to Chapter 1, 'Managing your stress'. This provides excellent advice and guidance. Learn to recognise your stress levels and carry out some of the solutions which are contained in Chapter 1. Here are some reminders for you.

Stress-busting techniques

1. **Exercise**. This will help the physiological aspect of stress and the release of endorphins will give you a feeling of euphoria as well as help your heart. It is also ideal for getting rid of anger and frustrations. If you want to choose only one stress-busting technique, then choose this one. It is important not to remain static while you are revising. Many students walk around while using their memory strategies.

2. **Relax**. When you are feeling stressed out it is difficult to unwind. You may find you have to make a big effort to do this. It may be better to go to classes such as yoga or t'ai chi. Exercising also helps you to relax. If you want to develop your own relaxation techniques then try deep breathing or meditation. While you are revising, make sure that your shoulders, neck and hands, in particular, do not tense up. Regularly do some relaxation exercises for these areas while you are sitting. See if relaxation tapes can help you to unwind.

3. **Eat well**. Avoid junk food and too much alcohol – both of these can sap your energy and make you feel low. During revision time, some students drink excessive amounts of caffeine which can be found in coffee, tea and cola-type drinks. There is the popular idea that drinking coffee will keep you awake so that you can revise all through the night before your examination. While this liquid intake may keep you awake, it has an adverse effect upon your memory capacity and functioning.

   I kept myself awake all night with mugs of coffee so that I could learn and memorise my notes the night before my exam. The coffee certainly kept me awake but I had a memory blank in the exam and felt exhausted. I did worse in that exam so I'm not going to do that again.

   Peter, second-year Chemistry student

   Of course, if you have paced yourself in the weeks before examinations, you should not need to take these drastic measures.

E-day pressure countdown

Examination day or e-day has finally arrived. This is another source of stress and anxiety. Remember that anxiety can cut down on your memory's performance so carry out the following countdown checklist to give yourself the best possible chance in the examination.

Checklist: e-day countdown

- Make sure you get a good night's sleep the night before the examination.
- Think positively: your hard work in the build-up to the day will pay off.
- Avoid groups of 'friends' who want to talk about what they have learned. This can be a source of worry. Panic rises when you listen to what they have done because it is different from yours. If you have carried out the stages of revision set out in this chapter, you will be well prepared. Anyway, who is to say that your friends are right?
- After the examination it is better if you avoid groups of 'friends' who want to talk about what they did in the examination and what they wrote. This is another source of anxiety. There is nothing you can do to change what you wrote in the examination. Besides, who is to say that your friends are right?

---

8 Last-minute countdown

Rushing around at the last minute or on the day of the examination places you under unnecessary pressure. Go through this routine. It will keep you calm and positive as e-day approaches.

- Double-check the day, place and time of your examination.
- Check that you have a good pen and at least one spare ready for use.
- Check that the other equipment you can take into the examination is in good working order.
- If you are allowed to take in notes or a textbook, make sure that you have followed the regulations. Some departments require you to erase all your supplementary notes on textbooks so that they are 'clean' for the examination.
- Minimise your personal belongings – money and mobile telephone.
- Switch off your mobile telephone before entering the examination room.

9 The examination: 10-point plan

Stress can be minimised by getting into routines which take your mind off your anxiety levels. This section looks at what to do at the beginning of the examination, during the examination and at the end.

The beginning

1. Remind yourself of your worked time allocations. If necessary, jot these down on your answer booklet in pencil.

2. Read through all the questions carefully.

3. Categorise the questions:
   (a) the ones you can do
   (b) questions for which you have some of the information
   (c) questions which you cannot answer.

4. Decide on the order in which you will answer the questions. Start off with the ones you are most confident about and which will give you a chance of gaining the most marks.

During

5. Now take each question in turn.

6. Read the question carefully and do the BUG technique (see Chapter 12) to work out exactly what information you need to include and how to handle the information.

7. For essay questions, do a framework plan or a mind map. This means that you download all the relevant information before you start writing. This will take pressure off your memory and enable you to produce a more coherent and cohesive response.

8. Remember your reader – get to the point and then expand upon it.

After

9. Try not to do a post-mortem of your performance.

10. Do not check with others about what they did. Remember: if it is different from what you did, who is to say that they were correct?

10 Special examination arrangements

Some students can be granted special arrangements for examinations. These students will need some sort of proof of entitlement. Usually, this is provided when eligible students have applied for the Disabled Students' Allowance (DSA). In these circumstances, the student's needs are known well in advance and are unlikely to change over time. There may be occasions when something unexpected happens which could affect examination performance: for example, breaking a hand or arm, family bereavement, etc. Your institution can respond to both of these circumstances but it needs to know as far in advance as possible to organise the best arrangements for you.

What are special arrangements?

There are a variety of types of arrangements:

- additional time
- separate room
- a reader
- a scribe

■ an amanuensis (reader and scribe)

■ a computer.

If you think you are eligible, you need to discuss how special arrangements can be organised. Your personal tutor, the Disability Officer or the Dyslexia Coordinator are usually the best sources of information.

NOTE Do *not* leave this to the last moment or you may be told that nothing can be organised at short notice.

11 On reflection

This chapter has focused upon revision and examinations. You have been taken through suggestions, advice and guidance for ways to tackle the whole process. Some sections may have challenged the way you currently work and you may find that your skill levels and working habits have changed. It is vital that you constantly reappraise the way that you go about your revision and preparation for examinations to make sure that you maximise your efforts to gain the best marks and grades.

Summary of this chapter

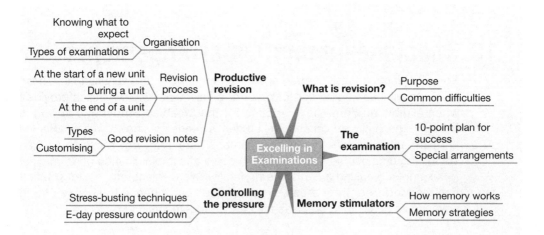

ACTIVITY 13 Update your personal development planner

Now reflect on your current abilities and consider what you need to do to improve. You may want to transfer this information to your own institution's personal development planner scheme.

Grade your confidence on a scale of 1–5 where 1 = poor and 5 = good.

My developing skills	Confidence level 1–5	Plans to improve
I can manage and organise the whole revision process effectively.		
I can recognise which revision notes systems to use for different purposes.		
I understand how to control pressure and stress.		
I understand the characteristics of productive memory strategies.		
I can use effective strategies during the examination.		

Date: _____

Getting extra help

- Go to the Students Union to find out where to go for skill development. Many universities and colleges have tutors who provide this service.
- Some departments organise special revision sessions. Check to see if these are available.
- Revision buddies: some students find that getting together with others on the course is a useful and interactive method of revising. To get the most out of this, you need to plan this with your friends so that you all are at the same stage of revision when you meet. It is frustrating if you have worked on a section but the others haven't.
- If you have a particularly bad stress reaction to exams, first talk to your personal tutor. He or she may advise you to go and see the counselling service within your institution.

The following books will help you to improve your examination technique:

Buzan, T. (2006) *The Ultimate Book of Mindmaps*. London, Harper Thorsons.

Buzan, T. (2006) *Brilliant Memory: Unlock the Power of your Mind*. Harlow, BBC Active.

Feedback on activities

ACTIVITY 2 Common difficulties with revision

Which of these apply to you?

	Tick ✓
1. I am often frustrated at examination times.	
2. I am often *very* nervous at examination times.	
3. I often find that I can't sleep properly at examination times.	
4. I seem to spend a lot of time revising and not getting the good results.	
5. I am not sure if my techniques are the most efficient.	
6. I mainly leave revision until it is almost too late.	
7. I put off my revision and find myself looking for other things to keep myself occupied.	
8. I have vast amounts of notes to help me revise.	

If you have ticked one of these then it is time to start thinking about how to improve your revision strategies.

If you ticked '1'

You have not perfected an efficient system of revision. Your memory strategies may not be the most effective. You need to try out different techniques. (Read this chapter carefully to identify where you could make improvements.)

If you ticked '2'

Most people are nervous at examination times. However, if you are excessively nervous, you may need to learn how to control your examination nerves more effectively (see Section 7, 'Controlling the pressure').

If you ticked '3'

This may be a sign of your growing anxiety. It is also an indication that you may not be using the most productive strategies for revision (see Section 3, 'Productive revision', Section 5, 'Tricks of the Trade', Section 6, 'Memory stimulators', and Section 7, 'Controlling the pressure').

If you ticked '4'

Your revision may be without a proper focus and plan of campaign. You may not know how to prepare for revision. You need to try out different techniques (see Section 4, 'Countdown not meltdown'; Section 5, 'Tricks of the Trade', and Section 6, 'Memory stimulators').

If you ticked '5'

You are stuck in a rut and no one has told you how to revise properly. You need to try out different techniques (see Section 3, 'Productive revision', and Section 5, 'Tricks of the trade').

If you ticked '6'

Your time management is in need of an overhaul (see Section 4, 'Countdown not meltdown' and Chapter 2, 'Managing your time').

If you ticked '7'

This is often a sign of procrastination. Of course, it may be that revision has been an unpleasant experience in the past. It may be that you are dithering because you don't have a plan of campaign or you don't know how to revise.

If you ticked '8'

Having large files of notes is not necessarily appropriate for revision. It takes time to search through lots of information to find what you need. This may be time you do not have. For some students, a thick volume of revision notes is like a security blanket. However, you need to ask yourself if your notes are time efficient. Remember that it is quality not quantity which matters! You need to explore ways in which you can distil your information (see Section 5, 'Tricks of the trade').

REMEMBER! If you always do what you have always done,

you will always get what you have always got.

Now is the time to take stock of your revision habits.

ACTIVITY 10 Memory strategies/joggers

List two topics you will be studying (select quite different types of topics):

TOPIC A The cardiovascular system

TOPIC B Handover procedures on the hospital ward

Memory strategies	Topic A	Topic B	Uses and relevance
Mind mapping, diagrams and flow charts	✓	✓	Topic A: Labelling a photocopied diagram. Topic B: Numbered flow chart helps to remember procedure.
Associations – making links with the information (revision/concept map)	✓		Topic A is interconnected while B is more sequential.
Writing out information	✓	✓	Write out either the diagram or flow chart to help make mental links.
Remembering information in lists – rearranging the order of the list so that the first letters of each word on the list make up something silly or amusing, a memorable mnemonic			Not relevant for B – correct order is essential.
Using shapes and colour	✓		Topic A lends itself more readily to colour associations for flow of blood etc.
Saying the information – to yourself or out loud	✓	✓	Useful to reinforce most information.
Poster display			
Customised fridge magnet displays	✓		Pictures of different parts of the system more easily displayed than text.
Chunking or grouping information		✓	Topic B procedures can be grouped.
Devising a story about the facts Flash cards	✓		Photocopied pictures of parts of system and definitions of terminology can reinforce memory.

3 Apply your skills

One of the unique aspects of science, engineering and technology courses is the experimental work undertaken in the laboratory or out in the field. Many courses also ask you to learn some computer programming, and you may also find there is a design aspect where you are required to think creatively to come up with new products or processes. In fact, these aspects of your studies may well be the ones you most looked forward to when you decided to study in this area.

In 'working in the laboratory' and 'handling errors' you will learn about some of the skills needed to undertake practical work and see how careful analysis of the errors and uncertainties in your measurements can help you to make a more critical evaluation of your work, leading to well-expressed conclusions about what you have achieved. This ability to draw realistic and valid conclusions about your experimental outcomes is one of the most important skills you can develop as an experimentalist.

In the first part of 'solving by design' you will learn how to make life easier for yourself by writing a computer program. This is not a section about how to program in a particular language, but it will introduce you to some of the ways that good programmers write programs with maximum efficiency and minimum frustration. In the second part of this chapter you will be introduced to good practice in design exercises. The hardest part of these is often coming up with a good idea, so learning about formal techniques to enhance your creativity will help you avoid mental blocks when you need to get your assignments done.

9 Working in the laboratory

In science, engineering and technology courses, experimental work plays a large part. It is quite likely that this more practical element is one of the main things that attracted you to your subject in the first place. If you can make effective use of your time in the lab you will be able to increase your understanding of the theoretical aspects of your course as well as learning skills and techniques used by professionals in your field as part of their day-to-day work.

In this chapter you will:

1. learn about different styles of work you may be set in the laboratory
2. consider how to prepare for experimental work
3. recognise good approaches to recording experimentation
4. start to develop your critical abilities for drawing realistic conclusions.

USING THIS CHAPTER

If you want to dip into the sections	Page	If you want to try the activities	Page
1 Styles of experiment	232	1 Basic Rules for Laboratory Safety	235
2 Before you start	233	2 Reasonable conclusions?	238
3 Carrying out the work	236	3 Update your personal development planner	240
4 Drawing conclusions	238		
5 On reflection	239		

Estimate your current levels of confidence. At the end of the chapter you will have the chance to reassess these levels where you can incorporate this into your personal development planner (PDP). Mark between 1 (poor) and 5 (good) for the following:

I am aware of the different types of laboratory work I will meet.	I know what to do before or at the start of a laboratory session to prepare.	I understand how to carry out and record my experimental work effectively.	I can draw valid conclusions from my experimental work.

Date: _____

1 Styles of experiment

During your course you will probably be expected to carry out experimental work. This is usually done in a laboratory often working individually, in pairs or in a small group. The aims of this kind of work can be very broad and a given experiment might be designed to help you do one or more of the following:

- understand how a theory or law works in practice
- learn how to use a standard piece of equipment or a standard method of analysis
- observe a physical effect or process
- define a theory or law from observation
- test a hypothesis.

In addition you may develop your skills in:

- recording and analysing data
- assessing the reliability of data
- communicating scientifically
- problem solving
- working in a team
- planning and time management
- thinking critically.

The work you do in the laboratory may be real, hands-on stuff or it may be virtual, a computer simulation in which you can control and vary different parameters to see their effect on a given system. Some people find simulations less exciting than using experimental apparatus, but they can have the useful advantage of giving you more control of a variable than might be possible in reality. They can also allow you to observe how a system behaves at extreme, and even unsafe, values of particular quantities such as very high temperatures or within highly radioactive environments. Simulations can also be just as effective as more traditional lab work in helping you to develop the more generic skills in the list above.

We can divide experimental work into two broad classes each with its own strengths: **experiments to demonstrate** and **experiments to find out**.

Experiments to demonstrate

These are laboratory exercises designed to enhance your understanding of something you have already learned about. Perhaps you have previously covered the theory, process or concept in a lecture or tutorial; the aim of the lab session is to see it working in practice. Normally at the end of such exercises you will find the expected result, so they are not experiments in the sense of having unknown outcomes. However, that does not make them a pointless undertaking. They can give you valuable insight into a process, making something that was rather abstract in the lecture into a concrete concept that you can appreciate more readily. They can also help you to get a feel for experimental errors of various types and the process of measurement and recording of data. Sometimes, although you know the law you want to demonstrate, the method is not given to you and you are asked to design a suitable experiment to achieve your goal.

Example titles of experiments to demonstrate:

- Experiment to show that a mass sliding down a slope obeys Newton's second law.
- Experiment to illustrate the effect of latent heat of fusion on the cooling of a material.
- Experiment to demonstrate the method of titration.

Experiments to find out

In this kind of lab work you are asked to make an investigation without knowing the expected outcome. This is much closer to the way researchers in your field use experimentation and the most significant example of this kind of work in the majority of science, engineering or technology degrees is an extended individual research project towards the end of the programme of study.

Experiments to find out are also known as problem- or enquiry-based learning. Often this kind of experiment feels more 'real' to students. Equally it can be rather frustrating, leading you down blind alleys with the result that your understanding of the scientific concepts involved does not advance much, especially if the time allowed is quite limited. If that happens to you at some point, try to remember that even unsuccessful experiments can teach you about the process of experimentation and help you to develop many aspects of your skills for the future.

Examples of experiments to find out:

- Experiment to find the relationship between the applied force and the resulting extension of an elastic band.
- Experiment to determine how temperature affects the rate of a chemical reaction.
- Experiment to investigate the effect of internal resistance on terminal voltage in an electrical circuit.

2 Before you start

In lab work you get the opportunity to go at your own pace and to take time to explore concepts and theories. It is common to hand out lab sheets that explain what you are expected to achieve as a result of a particular piece of work and perhaps tips for how to go about it.

For experiments to demonstrate it is worthwhile doing some preparation before you start to experiment. If you have the lab sheet or know the title of the lab in advance of the session then you can look over the relevant theory to see how well you understand it. Even if you don't get the sheet until the lab, a quick scan of the relevant lecture notes to refresh your memory is a good idea. Do you know what the expected result of the experiment is? Are there parts of the theory you don't follow so well? Can you see how the experiment might help you to clarify these? Are you going to use a standard piece of equipment or process used in your field? Can you find a description of how to go about this? What other, more generic skills might the experiment help you to develop?

It doesn't matter if you can't get a clear view of every aspect of what you will do and what you will learn in advance; the preparation you do will get you thinking about the topic and help you to make more connections and clarifications to your understanding once you get started on the practical work.

For experiments to find out the preparatory work is even more crucial. You may need to design your own experimental method and decide how to record and analyse your observations to achieve your goal. You may also need to think about how you can evaluate your results to decide if you have achieved the aim. Careful thought and planning in advance can save you from a lot of frustration.

The checklist below gives suggested questions for planning the various stages for each type of experiment.

Checklist for preparing lab work		
	Experiments to demonstrate	**Experiments to find out**
Experimental aim	Is the aim clear from the lab sheet?	Is the aim of the investigation specified or do you have to define it yourself?
Theory	How well do you understand the theory related to this topic?	What theory that you have covered may be relevant to your investigation?
Apparatus and method	Do you know how to use all the equipment you will need? Do you understand how you are expected to use it to achieve the aim?	What apparatus will you need? How will you use it to achieve the aim?
Results	Do you know what you should measure and how to do it? How will you display your data?	What will you need to measure and how will you do this? How will you display your data?
Analysis	How will you analyse your results? Do you need to define a method or is it given?	What kind of analysis will be required to achieve the aim?
Evaluation	Do you see how to evaluate your results to decide if you achieved the aim satisfactorily?	What kind of evaluation will be required? How will you define successful achievement of your aim?

Whichever kind of experiment you are undertaking, a vital part of the planning process is an assessment of the associated health and safety risks.

Considering health and safety

Before you start any practical or experimental process you **must** make an analysis of the associated health and safety risks. This needs to become second nature both in the university or college laboratory and during your professional practice after your studies have finished.

ACTIVITY 1 Basic rules for laboratory safety

There are some basic safety rules that **always** apply in the laboratory. Many of these are common sense.

Can you add any more to this list?

Make sure you know the layout of the lab, including the location of emergency exits.
Put your bag and coat where nobody can trip over them. The lab may have lockers or a special area for this.
Read the lab sheet before you start work, taking special note of any instructions relating to safety. Read also any data sheets for the materials and equipment you will use.
Follow any instructions about safe storing or handling materials and equipment.
Follow the rules about safe use of electrical equipment; in particular avoid spilling liquids on electrical equipment.

See the feedback section.

As well as these basic rules that always apply, you need to think about any specific hazards involved in each piece of work you do in the laboratory.

Once you have identified a list of potential risks you can assess the risk of each one by scoring the likelihood it will occur and multiplying that by the severity of the situation its occurrence would lead to. Finally you need to decide what control measure you will take to minimise the effect of each hazard. The control measure should be proportionate to the risk, so if a risk is low, the control may simply be to keep an eye on things, but if the risk is high, a more formal control measure may need to be implemented.

The lab where you do your practical work may have a standard form for risk assessment which includes a table for risk analysis. The risk analysis table below has a typical format and has been completed for an experiment to measure the extension of an elastic band as weights are applied to stretch it.

Hazard identified	Likelihood of occurrence (grade 1–4) (A)	Severity (grade 1–4) (B)	Risk (likelihood × severity (A × B)	Control measure
Damage to eyes if elastic band snaps.	2	3	6	Keep work on bench at below eye level. Wear eye protection when measuring extension of elastic band.
Minor injury to fingers when elastic band snaps.	1	1	1	Observe elastic band to determine likelihood of imminent failure.
Weights fall off elastic band and cause injury to feet.	1	2	2	Ensure feet are not directly below apparatus when adding weight. Wear enclosed footwear during experiment.

3 Carrying out the work

In Chapter 15 there is information on the way an experimental report in a lab logbook might be structured. In this section we will concentrate briefly on specific pieces of information you should record in each section of your lab logbook. Figure 9.1 shows a page from a student logbook. Notice that while it is presented in a tidy way, it is a working record and contains corrections where necessary.

Some particular points to note are:

- The date. All lab work needs to be dated.
- The apparatus list. Note the model and/or serial number of any items of apparatus. If you repeat your experiment another time and get

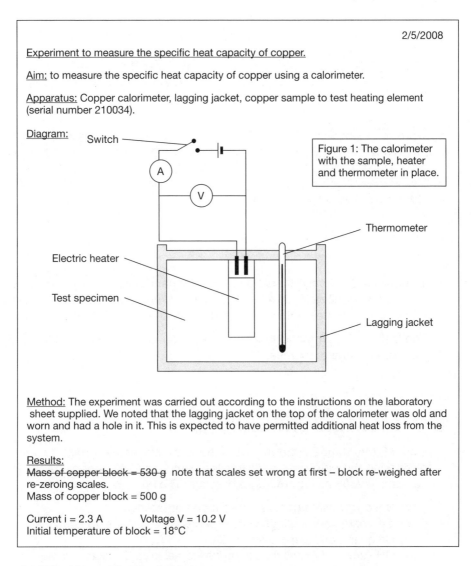

2/5/2008

Experiment to measure the specific heat capacity of copper.

Aim: to measure the specific heat capacity of copper using a calorimeter.

Apparatus: Copper calorimeter, lagging jacket, copper sample to test heating element (serial number 210034).

Diagram:

Switch

A

V

Figure 1: The calorimeter with the sample, heater and thermometer in place.

Thermometer

Electric heater

Test specimen

Lagging jacket

Method: The experiment was carried out according to the instructions on the laboratory sheet supplied. We noted that the lagging jacket on the top of the calorimeter was old and worn and had a hole in it. This is expected to have permitted additional heat loss from the system.

Results:
~~Mass of copper block = 530 g~~ note that scales set wrong at first – block re-weighed after re-zeroing scales.
Mass of copper block = 500 g

Current i = 2.3 A   Voltage V = 10.2 V
Initial temperature of block = 18°C

Figure 9.1 Extract from a laboratory logbook

different results you may want to check if this is due to changes in the apparatus used.

■ The method section. If you get instructions about how to carry out the experiment on a lab sheet you may not need to copy them out again. You should check what is expected with the lab supervisor. In any case, you will still need to record anything that isn't quite as expected or anything you do differently to the suggested process.

■ The diagram. A diagram of the apparatus is always a useful thing to record and much more effective than describing it in words.

■ The correction. If you get something wrong, cross it out neatly and explain what the problem was.

- The numerical accuracy. When recording numerical measurements think about how many decimal places to record. Don't write down lots of digits just because you can see them on the display of an instrument. To what accuracy do you want your answer? Work to the accuracy of the least sensitive piece of equipment as this is the limiting factor on the accuracy of your final answer.

Hot Tip

Think about the graphs you need for your analysis. If you decide in advance, you can make a rough plot as you make your measurements. You will easily spot data values that seem strangely large or small if you have a visual representation and you can check if they are really valid before it's too late to make repeat measurements.

The results and analysis section of your experimental record usually comes next in the logbook. We will look at some simple methods of analysis and consider how to deal with experimental error in the next chapter.

The last section in the logbook is where you draw your conclusions about the experimental outcomes.

4 Drawing conclusions

One of the things students find hardest about experimental work is discussing the outcomes and drawing useful and valid conclusions. This is something you can improve with practice. The basic rules are:

- Base your statements on evidence not feelings.
- Compare your findings with expected outcomes if you can.
- Be quantitative wherever possible.
- Give error estimates for any numerical values if possible (see Section 10).
- State whether you have achieved the aim of the experiment or not.

You may also give suggestions about the sources of experimental errors and ways you might improve the experiment if you were to repeat it.

ACTIVITY 2 Reasonable conclusions?

Consider the statements in the table below. Do you think they represent well-thought-out conclusions or not? Can you say why you came to each decision? Use the bullet points above to help you decide.

	Good ✓ or bad ✗	Reason
Errors may have been introduced when measuring the length of the sample as it was difficult to line the ruler up sufficiently close to the edge.		
In our opinion the experiment turned out quite well.		
In the end we proved Boyle's law to be true.		
Most of the errors were probably due to human error.		
The hypothesis was that objects of different masses would undergo the same acceleration and this was found to be the case.		
The value found for the acceleration due to gravity was quite close to the expected value.		
The value found for the acceleration due to gravity was within 2% of the value given in the data book.		

See the feedback section.

5 On reflection

This chapter has asked you to consider how to prepare for and carry out work in the laboratory. Many of the techniques considered apply equally well to other forms of practical work such as fieldwork. You have seen that preparation is an important part of the process both to familiarise yourself with what you are going to do and to make sure you have thought through the safety implications of your activities. You are now aware of the kind of information that must be included in each section of a lab logbook and in Chapter 15 you can find out more about the structure of a logbook entry. Finally you should now have a reasonable grasp of how to write good discussion and conclusion statements.

Summary of this chapter

Have look at Figure 9.2 and make sure you are familiar with the concepts.

Figure 9.2 Summary of how to prepare for and record your work in the lab

ACTIVITY 3 Update your personal development planner

Reflect on your current abilities and consider what needs to improve. You may want to transfer this information to your institution's personal development planner scheme.

Grade your confidence on a scale of 1–5 where 1 = poor and 5 = good.

My developing skills	Confidence level 1–5	Plans to improve
I understand how different styles of work in the laboratory may develop different sets of skills.		
I understand how to prepare for lab work before I start.		
I know how to record my experimental work.		
I can draw valid conclusions from my work.		

Date: _____

Getting extra help

- Laboratories are often staffed by postgraduate demonstrators and/or technicians who will be pleased to help you with technical issues in the lab
- The lab supervisor can help you to understand what you should record in your logbook and how to do this.

Feedback on activities

ACTIVITY 1 Basic rules for laboratory safety

You may also have thought of....

Make sure you know the layout of the lab, including the location of emergency exits.
Put your bag and coat where nobody can trip over them. The lab may have lockers or a special area for this.
Read the lab sheet before you start work, taking special note of any instructions relating to safety. Read also any data sheets for the materials and equipment you will use.
Follow any instructions about safe storing or handling materials and equipment.
Follow the rules about safe use of electrical equipment, in particular avoid spilling liquids on electrical equipment.
Safety goggles and gloves should be worn when appropriate.
No food or drink is allowed in the laboratory.
Long hair should be tied back.
No experiment should be undertaken unless the process has been authorised.
Special care must be taken when handling and assembling glass apparatus.
All containers must be clearly labelled as to their contents.
Protective clothing such as lab coats should always be worn where provided.
Hazardous chemical and biological spills on floors, benches or equipment should be reported to an appropriate member of staff.
Any faulty equipment should be reported.
Apparatus must not be set up and left unattended unless permission has been obtained and clear instructions are displayed indicating action to take in an emergency.
Laboratory chemicals must not be sniffed, inhaled or tasted.
All accidents and incidents must be reported immediately to an appropriate member of staff and recorded on an accident/incident report form.
Throughout and at the end of a practical, the working area should be cleaned and tidied, hands should be washed and equipment switched off unless marked otherwise.

ACTIVITY 2 Reasonable conclusions?

	Good ✓ or bad ✗	Reason
Errors may have been introduced when measuring the length of the sample as it was difficult to line the ruler up sufficiently close to the edge.	✓	This statement is clear and precise about the potential source of error. It could form the basis for thinking about how to improve the experimental method another time.
In our opinion the experiment turned out quite well.	✗	This is just an opinion. No evidence is offered to support the belief and 'quite well' is a very vague evaluation.
In the end we proved Boyle's law to be true.	✗	To prove that a physical law is true you need to show that it holds for every possible case. This would need an exhaustive experiment to be carried out. Be very careful about using the words 'proof' and 'prove' in experimental studies. They are best avoided. A better statement would be: The experimental study supported the validity of Boyle's law under the conditions tested'.
Most of the errors were probably due to human error.	✗	Human error suggests something you did wrong that you could have got right. This is also a very vague statement. You should try to be more specific in identifying the causes of errors.
The hypothesis was that objects of different masses would undergo the same acceleration and this was found to be the case.	✓	This is a good statement about the achievement of the experimental aim.
The value found for the acceleration due to gravity was quite close to the expected value.	✗	What is meant here by 'quite close'? It is very vague and you want to aim always to be precise. If possible the relation between an expected and an experimental value should be expressed quantitatively.
The value found for the acceleration due to gravity was within 2% of the value given in the data book.	✓	This is a clear and quantitative statement of the closeness of an expected value to one found experimentally.

10 Handling errors

Every experimental measurement you take has an error or uncertainty in it. This is an unavoidable fact as no measurement can ever be perfect. In order to evaluate the quality of the outcome of an experiment you need to be able to make an estimate of the size of the associated error. A good grasp of how errors can be estimated and how they combine when you make calculations will help you to draw proportionate and valid conclusions from your experimental data.

In this chapter you will:

1. understand that there are different kinds of error
2. see how to estimate and record errors
3. find out how errors from separate measurements combine.

USING THIS CHAPTER

Estimate your current levels of confidence. At the end of the chapter you will have the chance to reassess these levels and incorporate this into your personal development planner (PDP). Mark between 1 (poor) and 5 (good) for the following:

I know there are different kinds of experimental error and understand the difference between them.	I can estimate errors well and record them in a standard format.	I know how errors combine when measurements are used to make calculations.

Date: _____

1 Types of errors

Whenever you take a measurement there is a degree of uncertainty or error (the two terms are interchangeable) in that measurement. The size of the error depends on the measurement technique used to obtain the data. Some measurement methods are more accurate than others, but all leave you with a certain amount of error. Much effort is expended by engineers and scientists in finding ways to minimise the error in a measurement or designing new techniques with inherently less uncertainty. To draw valid conclusions from your experimental measurements you need to understand about errors, why they are always there and how to estimate and interpret them.

A measurement presented without an estimate of the error is of very little use if we want to compare it with other measurements. For instance, if you measure the height of two students and get an answer of 170 cm for one and 173 cm for the other you might think the second student is sure to be taller than the first. However, if you are then told that the ruler you used has an uncertainty of ±5 cm then you can't be sure that the measured difference is real. The height of the first student could be anywhere between 165 and 175 cm and the second student could be from 168 to 178 cm tall. In fact, with this much uncertainty the students could be exactly the same height!

The errors or uncertainties in experimental measurements can be of three types.

Systematic errors

Systematic errors are errors where the measurement is always shifted up or down from the true value by the same amount. Often they arise from poor calibration of equipment. For instance, think of measuring the length of an object with a ruler as shown in Figure 10.1.

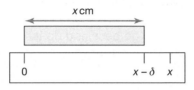

Figure 10.1 Systematic errors

The true length of the object is x cm. Unfortunately the ruler has somehow become stretched. Perhaps it has been kept under tension for a long time during another experiment. Now the ruler always gives a value a bit less than the true value when you use it to measure. The difference, δ cm, between the true value, x cm, and the measured value $(x - \delta)$ cm is a systematic error. Every time you measure a length that should come out as x cm with this ruler it gives you the same slightly smaller value.

We could imagine another ruler that has somehow shrunk and always overestimates the length of the things you measure.

A common source of systematic errors in experiments is not setting the output of a piece of equipment, such as a voltmeter or ammeter or a set of scales, to zero when the input is zero. These are called **zeroing errors** and they add a small positive or negative value to every measurement you make with the equipment.

Careful calibration of equipment before you make a measurement can reduce the size of systematic errors.

Random errors

Random errors are not predictable. In any given measurement taken with a piece of measuring equipment there will be random error with a size that depends on the measurement technique used. It will not be possible to predict whether the random error has increased or decreased the measured value compared with the true value. Repeating the measurement under the same conditions and with the same piece of equipment will give you a slightly different value every time, sometimes bigger than the true value and sometimes smaller.

Random errors can be due to the inherent limitations of the equipment or measuring technique or to the limitations of the scale from which the measurement is read.

Human errors

Human errors are simply mistakes caused by using equipment or implementing experimental techniques incorrectly. If you become aware that you have made a human error during an experiment then the results are invalid. You will have to go back and do the experiment again if you want to draw any valid conclusions from your measurements.

2 Estimating and recording errors

When you make an experimental measurement you must always try to estimate the size of any associated errors or uncertainties. Measurements presented without an error estimate in scientific work should be treated with deep suspicion. If you don't know the associated error how can you use the measurement with confidence?

For example, the National Institute of Standards and Technology (NIST) in the USA quotes, among others, the following physical constants with their associated uncertainties:

Values of some physical constants and their associated uncertainty as given by NIST		
Constant	Value	Uncertainty
Avogadro constant N_A	$6.022\,141\,79 \times 10^{23}\,\text{mol}^{-1}$	$\pm 0.000\,000\,30 \times 10^{23}\,\text{mol}^{-1}$
Newtonian constant of gravitation G	$6.674\,28 \times 10^{-11}\,\text{m}^3\,\text{kg}^{-1}\,\text{s}^{-2}$	$\pm 0.000\,67 \times 10^{-11}\,\text{m}^3\,\text{kg}^{-1}\,\text{s}^{-2}$
Planck constant h	$6.626\,068\,96 \times 10^{-34}\,\text{J}\,\text{s}$	$\pm 0.000\,000\,33 \times 10^{-34}\,\text{J}\,\text{s}$

Note that every entry in the table has units as well as an uncertainty. You need to include units so a reader can understand exactly what your measurement means.

The error is expressed in a standard format with a ± sign between the value and the error estimate to show that you do not know if the error acts to increase or decrease the difference between the measured and true values. This gives you an estimated range for the error. For example, if you say that your height is 160 ± 3 cm you mean that it lies somewhere between 157 and 163 cm.

The errors in the table are given as **absolute errors**. Absolute errors are expressed in the same units as the measured value itself. We may also quote error estimates as **relative** or **fractional errors**. In this case the error is given as the ratio of the absolute error to the measured value:

$$\text{relative error} = \frac{\text{absolute error}}{\text{measured value}}$$

Or if you prefer to express the error as a percentage:

$$\text{percentage relative error} = \frac{\text{absolute error}}{\text{measured value}} \times 100\%$$

ACTIVITY 1 Relative errors

The NIST website gives the value of the Avogadro constant and its absolute error as:

$N_A = 6.022\,141\,79 \times 10^{23} \pm 0.000\,000\,30 \times 10^{23}\ \text{mol}^{-1}$

Express the error in relative terms.

The relative error is given by

$$\frac{\text{absolute error}}{\text{measured value}} = \frac{0.000\,000\,30 \times 10^{23}}{6.022\,141\,79 \times 10^{23}} = 4.981\,616\,35 \times 10^{-8}$$

or $4.98 \times 10^{-6}\%$.

So we can express the constant as $N_A = 6.022\,141\,79 \times 10^{23}\ \text{mol}^{-1} \pm 4.98 \times 10^{-6}\%$.

Note that once the error is expressed as a relative error or a percentage it has no units and we must associate the units with the measured value only.

Now you try to make the conversions for the remaining values in the table.

You can find the answers in the feedback section.

If you want more practice, the value, absolute and relative error for many more constants can be found on the NIST website.

So which error should you quote: the absolute error or the relative error? Well it depends on the circumstances. If you want to know whether to consider an error as significant or not then the relative error may be the best choice. If you see a measured length of an object recorded as $0.234\,53 \pm 0.001\,38$ cm it is hard to decide if the error is large or small relative to the measured value. Converting to relative error and expressing as a percentage gives a length of $0.234\,53$ cm $\pm 0.5\%$, which makes it easier to judge whether, for any given application, the error may be considered as small or not. On the other hand, if you only know that the error is 5% it doesn't give you much feel for how big it really is and that may matter depending on your application. For example, if you know you have to fit your object through a hole with a length of 0.2359 cm then the absolute error tells you more readily whether it is likely to fit. As you get used to estimating errors in different circumstances you will find it easier to judge the most useful way to represent them in each case.

How big is the error?

How do you know how big the error in a given measurement is? You almost always have to make an estimate, and for this reason it is usual to give only one or two significant figures when you write down an absolute error. It is unlikely that you can give a more realistic estimate.

Sometimes you will be able to make separate estimates for the systematic and random errors. If this is the case you can record each as a separate figure if you wish. So if you measure a weight with scales you know are poorly zeroed and which also have a random error due to whether the spring has released all its tension from the previous measurement or not, you could record the weight as, for example, 1.249 ± 0.3 ± 0.1 kg where the first uncertainty is random and the second is systematic. Often we cannot separate the types of errors and must estimate them all together.

So how can you make a good estimate of the size of the uncertainty in a measurement? Well in a single measurement it is rather difficult to know what the error might be. If you have no special information about your measurement technique or your measuring equipment, such as a manufacturer's estimate of the likely error, the best you can do is a rule of thumb:

A reasonable estimate of the random error in a single measurement is about half a unit on the scale used to make the measurement.

For example, on a ruler marked in centimetres you can say that the length of an object is $x \pm 0.5$ cm. If the ruler is marked in millimetres then the length of the same object can be estimated to be $x \pm 0.5$ mm. On digital meters we usually assume that we can measure to half the last decimal place on the display. If the display on a voltmeter says 0.123 453 4 V we would record the measurement as 0.123 453 ± 0.000 000 5 V.

If we can make more than one measurement of a quantity that is expected to have a random error then we can reduce the uncertainty in the measurement by averaging the multiple measurements and working with their mean value as the best available estimate of the true value. The spread of the values is characterised by the standard deviation of the set of repeated measurements.

Example

Look at the measurements of the length of an object in the table below:

2.54 cm	2.52 cm	2.56 cm	2.53 cm	2.52 cm

To get an estimate of the variation first we take the mean of these estimates by adding them up and dividing by the number of estimates we have

mean length = (2.54 + 2.52 + 2.56 + 2.53 + 2.52) ÷ 5 = 2.534 cm (to 3 decimal places)

More formally we can state that the mean, $\bar{x}$, of a set of n measurements $x_1, x_2, x_3, ..., x_n$ is given by:

$$\bar{x} = \frac{1}{n}\sum_{i=1}^{n} x_i$$

To get the standard deviation of the n measurements, first subtract the mean value from each measurement:

0.006	−0.014	0.026	−0.004	−0.014

Next, square each number in the table above and then add up all the squares:

sum of squares = 0.001 12

Finally divide by one less than the number of measurements, 5 − 1 = 4, and take the square root of the answer.

The standard deviation is 0.017 (to 3 dp).

The standard deviation, s, can be defined formally as

$$s = \sqrt{\frac{\sum_{i=1}^{n}(x_i - \bar{x})}{n-1}}$$

If you have a very large number of measurements a spreadsheet may be the quickest way to calculate the mean and standard deviation.

ACTIVITY 2 Mean and standard deviation

For each row in the table calculate the mean and standard deviation.

								Mean	Standard deviation
0.977	0.866	0.136	0.749	0.200	0.493	0.720	0.253		
7.0	3.8	8.6	2.2	0.4	4.0				
0.97	0.93	0.84	0.84	0.86					

See the feedback section.

> **Hot Tip** Sets of measurements with small standard deviations are closely clustered around their mean values. Sets of measurements with large standard deviations have a much wider range about the mean.

If you have multiple measurements and you average them, what is the uncertainty in the averaged measurement? This quantity is called the standard error in the mean, σ_m, and is given by

$$\sigma_m = \frac{s}{\sqrt{n}}$$

where s is the standard deviation of the measurements and n is the number of measurements. If you increase the number of measurements the standard deviation of the data set may not change, but if s stays the same then as n increases in size the standard error in the mean, σ_m, will get smaller. As you take more and more measurements therefore you can have more confidence that the mean value you calculate is close to the 'true' value.

ACTIVITY 3 Standard error in the mean

For each of the data sets of Activity 2, find the standard error in the mean. See the feedback section to check your calculations.

> **NOTE** Averaging reduces the random error because of the statistical properties of uncertainties. It has no effect at all on the size of any systematic errors.

Often there is some confusion in students' minds about the difference between the standard deviation and the standard error in the mean, so let's finish this section with a really clear statement:

- The standard deviation is related to the probability that any given measurement lies within a particular range about the mean value. If you calculate the mean of a set of measurements to have a value of $\bar{x}$ and the standard deviation to be s, then, assuming the deviation is due to random error, the probability that a given measurement lies within the range $\bar{x} \pm s$ is about 68%. That is, in any 100 measurements you expect 68 to lie within that range. The probability that any given measurement lies within the range $\bar{x} \pm 2s$ is close to 95%. So in any 100 measurements you can expect about 95 of them to lie in this range. To understand why this is true you need to learn about the normal probability distribution. You can find out about this in any elementary statistics textbook such as *Statistics for Technology* by Chris Chatfield (1983).

■ The standard error in the mean is a measurement of the confidence you have in your calculated estimate of the mean value. A small standard error indicates a high confidence in the mean value calculation. Note that the standard error in the mean will never become zero however many measurements you average.

3 Propagation of errors

Imagine you have measured two different things, each with an associated uncertainty. You want to combine your two measurements, perhaps by adding them together or by multiplying the two values. What will the error be in the resulting sum or product?

For example, if you have made repeated measurements of the distance, y, between two markers and repeated measurements of the time, t, for an object to travel between them at a constant speed so that you know that the mean value ± the standard error in the mean for each measurement is

$y = 1.2 \pm 0.2\,\text{m}$
$t = 3 \pm 0.5\,\text{s}$

you can easily calculate that the speed of the object is $v = yt = 3.6\,\text{m s}^{-1}$, but how do the errors combine? What is the uncertainty in the speed? The combination of errors in calculations is called the propagation of errors.

In the following sections we will not go into the mathematical derivation of the way that errors combine but merely state the results. When you need to understand error propagation more deeply you can find the details you need in a suitable textbook such as Bevington and Robinson (2002).

All the rules you will see below regarding error propagation rely on an important assumption:

The errors in the quantities that you are combining must be independent.

That is to say, if your timing device is running fast (or slow) you don't expect it to affect the accuracy of your ruler, and similarly longer or shorter measurements of the distance don't automatically lead to longer or shorter measurements of the time in any systematic way.

Adding and subtracting

Let $x = \bar{x} \pm \sigma_x$ where $\bar{x}$ is the mean value of x and σ_x is the uncertainty in $\bar{x}$.

Let $y = \bar{y} \pm \sigma_y$ where $\bar{y}$ is the mean value of y and σ_y is the uncertainty in $\bar{y}$.

Then if $z = x + y$, the error in z, σ_z, is given by

$$\sigma_z = \sqrt{\sigma^2_x + \sigma^2_y}.$$

This is often expressed by the phrase: *Random errors add in quadrature.*

Note that the expression for σ_z is the same whether $z = x + y$ or $z = x - y$.

Example

If you have measured the length of two pieces of copper rod and found the lengths to be

$L_1 = 5 \pm 0.1\,\text{cm}$

$L_2 = 15 \pm 0.2\,\text{cm}$

what will be the length of a new rod made from gluing the two rods together end to end? You can assume the layer of glue has no thickness when you make your calculation.

The sum of the lengths of the two rods will be $5 + 15 = 20\,\text{cm}$. The error will be given by

$$\sqrt{0.1^2 + 0.2^2} = \sqrt{0.01 + 0.04} = \sqrt{0.05} = 0.22$$

You can state the final length calculation as $15 \pm 0.22\,\text{cm}$.

ACTIVITY 4 Adding and subtracting errors

1. If the weight of a horse is $425 \pm 2\,\text{kg}$ and the weight of the rider is $65 \pm 0.5\,\text{kg}$, what is the weight and associated uncertainty for the weight of the horse and rider combined?

2. If the initial temperature of a body is $17 \pm 0.5\,°\text{C}$ and the final temperature after heating is $37 \pm 0.5\,°\text{C}$, what is the change in temperature and the associated uncertainty in your estimate?

See the feedback section for answers.

Hot Tip

If you are adding up more than two measurements then you just add up more errors in the same way, so if $a = b + c + d + e$ then

$$\sigma_a = \sqrt{\sigma^2_b + \sigma^2_c + \sigma^2_d + \sigma^2_e}$$

and so on.

Multiplication and division

When we want to multiply and divide quantities it is easier to work with the relative error rather than the absolute error. We will indicate the relative error expressed as a percentage by, for example, $\sigma_x\%$, $\sigma_z\%$ and so forth. Once you have calculated $\sigma_x\%$, $\sigma_z\%$ you can always convert it back to an absolute error if you prefer that format.

Multiplying by a constant

Let $x = \bar{x} \pm \sigma_x\%$ where $\bar{x}$ is the mean value of x and $\sigma_x\%$ is the relative uncertainty in $\bar{x}$ expressed as a percentage.

Then if $z = ax$ where a is a constant with no uncertainty, $\sigma_z\% = \sigma_x\%$, where $\sigma_z\%$ is the relative uncertainty in z expressed as a percentage. That is to say, multiplying by a constant leaves the size of the relative error unchanged. The same is true when you divide by a constant.

Multiplying variables

Let $x = \bar{x} \pm \sigma_x\%$ where $\bar{x}$ is the mean value of x and $\sigma_x\%$ is the percentage relative uncertainty in $\bar{x}$.

Let $y = \bar{y} \pm \sigma_y\%$ where $\bar{y}$ is the mean value of y and $\sigma_y\%$ is the percentage relative uncertainty in $\bar{y}$.

Then if $z = xy$, the relative error in z, $\sigma_z\%$, is given by

$$\sigma_z\% = \sqrt{\sigma_x\%^2 + \sigma_y\%^2}$$

Note that the expression for $\sigma_z\%$ is the same whether $z = xy$ or $z = x \div y$.

Example

If the distance travelled by an object is measured as $y = 1.2 \pm 0.2$ m in a time $t = 3 \pm 0.5$ s, what will be the absolute uncertainty in the estimate of the velocity of the object?

First convert the absolute errors to percentage relative errors:

$$\sigma_y\% = \frac{0.2}{1.2} \times 100\% = 16.67\%, \ \sigma_t = \frac{0.5}{3} \times 100\% = 16.67\%$$

Estimated velocity $yt = 1.2 \times 3 = 3.6$ m s^{-1}.

Percentage relative error in z is

$$\sigma_z\% = \sqrt{\sigma_y\%^2 + \sigma_t\%^2} = \sqrt{16.67^2 + 16.67^2} = 23.57\%$$

Absolute error in z is

$$\sigma_z = \frac{z \times \sigma_z\%}{100} = 0.85 \, \text{m s}^{-1}.$$

ACTIVITY 5 Multiplication and division of errors

1. If the sides of a rectangle are measured to be $x = 3 \pm 0.1$ m and $y = 5 \pm 0.3$ m, what will be the absolute error when calculating the area of the rectangle?

2. If $p = 3T$ where $T = 15 \pm 0.4$ units, what will the percentage relative error in p be?

3. In an experiment to calculate the acceleration of a block of metal along a plane, the force applied to the block is measured repeatedly and the average value is found to be $F = 2$ N $\pm 3\%$. The mass, m, of the block is measured to be 4 kg $\pm 0.2\%$. What will the percentage relative error in the acceleration, a, be if the formula for its calculation is

$a = F/m$?

See the feedback section

Just as for addition, if you have more than two measurements to multiply together then you add up more than two squared percentage relative errors to get the final estimate of the uncertainty.

More complicated arithmetic combinations

What if you have a mixture of addition, subtraction, multiplication and division in your formula? Well you just apply the methods above to each part in turn until you reach the final answer.

Example

If

$$z = \frac{(a + b) \times c}{d - e} \text{ with}$$

$a = 5.47 \pm 0.45$ $d = 6.87 \pm 0.97$

$b = 4.54 \pm 0.74$ $e = 0.36 \pm 0.50$

$c = 7.99 \pm 0.26$

calculate the percentage relative error in the estimate of z.

First find the error in $a + b$:

$$\sigma_{a+b} = \sqrt{\sigma_a^2 + \sigma_b^2} = 0.866$$

and the value of $a + b = 10.01$.

Next find the relative error in $(a + b)$ and in c:

$$\sigma_{a+b}\% = 8.65\%, \quad \sigma_c\% = 3.25\%$$

Then

$$\sigma_{(a+b) \times c}\% = \sqrt{8.65^2 + 3.25^2} = 9.24\%$$

Now for the bottom of the fraction.
The absolute error in $d - e$ is

$$\sigma_{d-e} = \sqrt{0.97^2 + 0.50^2} = 1.901$$

and the value of $d - e$ is 6.51.

The percentage relative error in $d - e$ is $\sigma_{d-e}\% = 16.76\%$.

Finally the percentage relative error in z is

$$\sigma_z\% = \sqrt{\sigma_{(a+b) \times c}\%^2 + \sigma_{d-e}\%^2} = \sqrt{9.24^2 + 16.76^2} = 19.1\% \text{ (to 1 dp)}$$

Raising to a power

If $y = x^n$ then $\sigma_y\% = n \times \sigma_x\%$.

Example

If a square has a side of length 9.24 m $\pm$ 3%, what is the percentage relative error in the estimated area, A, of the square?

Let the length of the side of the square be x. Then the area of the square A is given by $A = x^2$.

The percentage relative error in A is $\sigma_A\% = 2 \times 3\% = 6\%$.

NOTE The rule for powers holds whether n is a positive whole number, a negative whole number or a fraction.

Non-arithmetic functions

For non-arithmetic functions you can still calculate an error estimate providing the error in the original measurements is small.

Example

If $y = \ln x$ and $x = 14 \pm 0.5$, what is the absolute uncertainty in y?

First calculate the upper and lower limits for x.

The maximum value is $14 + 0.5 = 14.5$ and the minimum value is $14 - 0.5 = 13.5$.

Then find the natural logarithm of the maximum, minimum and mean values of x:

$x = 14.5$, $\ln x = 2.6741$
$x = 13.5$, $\ln x = 2.6027$
$x = 14$, $\ln x = 2.6391$

Now find the difference between $\ln 14.5$ and $\ln 13.5$ and divide the answer by 2 to give 0.0357.

So $y = 2.6391 \pm 0.0357$.

ACTIVITY 6 Non-arithmetic functions and errors

If $y = \sin x$ and $x = 24° \pm 0.5°$, what will be the error in the estimate of y?

4 On reflection

You may be a bit surprised at the amount of space devoted in this book to the discussion of handling errors in experimental measurements. However, good error estimates allow you to make valid comparisons between measurements and to minimise the uncertainty in your experimental outcomes. This in turn allows you to draw valid conclusions from your experimental work, which are soundly based on the evidence you have acquired. This is one of the skills that marks out the excellent student from the merely good or average student and is therefore well worth spending a little development time on.

Summary of this chapter

Have look at Figure 10.2 and make sure you are familiar with the concepts.

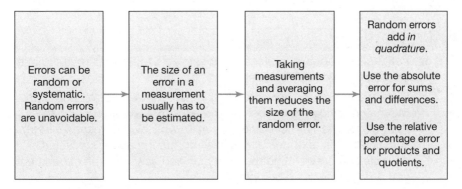

Figure 10.2 Summary of error handling procedures

ACTIVITY 7 Update your personal development planner

Reflect on your current abilities and consider what needs to improve. You may want to transfer this information to your institution's personal development planner scheme.

Grade your confidence on a scale of 1– 5 where 1 = poor and 5 = good.

My developing skills	Confidence level 1–5	Plans to improve
I know the difference between the different types of errors.		
I can make good estimates of the errors in my measurements.		
I can record errors in standard formats.		
I know how errors combine during calculations and can calculate error estimates in sums and products of measured values.		

Date: _____

Getting extra help

■ Ask the lab supervisor or the demonstrators to explain anything in this chapter that you don't understand.

■ If you want to study error handling in more detail and to understand the mathematical theory behind the rules try *Data Reduction and Error Analysis for the Physical Sciences* by Philip Bevington and D. Keith Robinson. This textbook also gives information about statistical analysis and curve fitting that you may find useful as the experiments you do become more complex.

Feedback on activities

ACTIVITY 1 Relative errors

Newtonian constant of gravitation G	$6.67428 \times 10^{-11}\,m^3\,kg^{-1}\,s^{-2}$	$\pm 1 \times 10^{-4}$ or $\pm 1 \times 10^{-2}\%$
Planck constant h	$6.62606896 \times 10^{-34}\,J\,s$	$\pm 5 \times 10^{-8}$ or $\pm 5 \times 10^{-6}\%$

ACTIVITY 2 Mean and standard deviation

For each row in the table calculate the mean and standard deviation:

								Mean	Standard deviation
0.977	0.866	0.136	0.749	0.200	0.493	0.720	0.253	0.550	0.324
7.0	3.8	8.6	2.2	0.4	4.0			4.3	3.0
0.97	0.93	0.84	0.84	0.86				0.89	0.06

Don't forget: if you have n measurements divide by N to get the mean and $n-1$ to get the standard deviation.

ACTIVITY 3 Standard error in the mean

Mean	Standard deviation	Standard error in the mean
0.550	0.324	±0.115
4.3	3.0	±1.2
0.89	0.06	±0.03

ACTIVITY 4 Adding and subtracting errors

1. Weight of the horse and rider combined is 490 ± 2.06 kg.

2. Change in temperature is 20 ± 0.7°C. Note that even though the mean quantities are subtracted, the errors **add** in quadrature. The error in the result is always bigger than the error in the individual measurements.

ACTIVITY 5 Multiplication and division of errors

1. The absolute error in the area will be 1.03 m^2.

2. Percentage relative error in p will be 2.67%.

3. Percentage relative error in a will be 3.01%.

ACTIVITY 6 Non-arithmetic functions and errors

$y = 0.4067 ± 0.0080$

References

- Bevington, P. and Robinson, D. K. (2002) *Data Reduction and Error Analysis for the Physical Sciences*, 3rd edn. Maidenhead, McGraw-Hill Higher Education.
- Chatfied, C. (1983) *Statistics for Technology: A Course in Applied Statistics*, 3rd edn. London, Chapman & Hall.
- NIST website: **http://physics.nist.gov/** [last accessed 14 January 2009].

11 Solving by design

Two common types of practical work that are found in science, engineering or technology degrees are computer programming exercises and design exercises. Both of these kinds of work need slightly different skills to experimental work carried out in a laboratory. Although programming might seem to require a mainly logical approach, it also needs lots of preparation and a little creativity if you are to write successful programs. Design exercises might seem to need mainly creativity, but again careful preparation and a little logic can come in handy.

In this chapter you will:

1. see how to approach a programming exercise systematically
2. understand how to make your code readable
3. learn about the importance of documenting your work
4. get an overview of some structured ways to think creatively.

USING THIS CHAPTER

If you want to dip into the sections	Page	If you want to try the activities	Page
1 Programming systematically	262	1 Breaking down the steps	262
2 Creativity on demand	268	2 Applying creativity	271
3 On reflection	271	3 Update your personal development planner	272

Estimate your current levels of confidence. At the end of the chapter you will have the chance to reassess these levels where you can incorporate this into your personal development planner (PDP). Mark between 1 (poor) and 5 (good) for the following:

I know how to get started on a programming exercise.	I can write code that is easy to read, follow and debug.	I understand the importance of documentation.	I can think creatively when required to do so.

Date: _____

1 Programming systematically

In this section you will think about how to make a start on a programming exercise, how to write code that is easy to read and debug and how to describe what you have done. Most programming exercises start with a statement telling you about the program to be written, what it will do and any rules you must stick to in coming up with your design. This is called the specification for the program. You won't be learning the syntax of any particular programming language here, but you will see how to apply good design and analysis principles to help you to move from the program specification to a documented solution.

The aim of this section is to tell you about some of the things that good programmers do to make their lives easy when they write a program. These hints will help you whether you are writing some simple code on your own, or producing part of a larger project where your code must integrate with that of other programmers.

The first step in getting to a working program is to take a little time to understand the problem before you start to code.

Planning your approach

You need really to think about what your program needs to do. The better you understand the requirements for the program, the more likely you are to be able to get the code working quickly and efficiently once you start to write it.

- What is your program supposed to do?
- Can you summarise it clearly for yourself?
- Do you understand all the terminology in the specification of the exercise you have been given? If not look it up.
- Make a list of all the inputs to the program. What data needs to be supplied to it for it to work? Where will the data come from?
- Make a list of all the outputs of the program. What format might they take? Saved files? Graphics? Text on the screen?

The second step is to break the process that the program will follow down into the smallest steps you can. It is usually easiest to do this in stages. Think of the steps and then ask yourself if they can be broken down into smaller steps or not. If they can, write down the smaller steps and then ask yourself again. Are there smaller steps still?

ACTIVITY 1 Breaking down the steps

Listed in the table below are the steps for making a cup of tea. Each column breaks the tasks down a bit further. Can you think about how to complete the table for the remaining steps?

Put the kettle on	Fill the kettle with water	Turn on the tap
		Take the lid off the kettle
		Put the kettle under the tap
		Wait until the kettle is full
		Take the kettle away from the tap
		Turn the tap off
	Switch it on	Attach the kettle to the electricity supply
		Press the 'on' switch
Get a cup ready	Get a cup	
	Get a teabag	
Make the tea	Put the water in the cup	
	Add milk	

See the feedback section.

The step-by-step process you just followed is similar to the process you use when you design a program. First you break the task down into largish sections and then you go back and break each section down further and further. How do you know when to stop? You stop when the parts are small enough that you can begin to see how you will implement them as program instructions. You may notice that there are a lot of similarities between the way you approach designing a program and the way you approach a mathematical problem as described in Chapter 16.

There are two main kinds of languages you may meet when you are learning to program: sequential languages (such as C or Pascal) and event-driven languages (such as Visual Basic). In sequential languages the program specifies the order in which operations will happen. In event-driven languages the order in which things happen depends on the user. Often event-driven languages have a graphical user interface (GUI) and the user makes things happen by clicking with the mouse.

A systematic design process is particularly important in programs where more than one person will write the code. If the design is haphazard, the different bits of code may not communicate with each other properly. You could come across this problem in group projects, and it is a real difficulty when writing big commercial programs. Getting into good design habits early minimises the risk of this kind of problem and will help you avoid a lot of frustration in the future.

Once you have the basics of your design, you need a way to record it. Different styles of record suit sequential and event-driven programs.

For **sequential programs** the flow chart (see Figure 11.1) is the classic way to record the design. A flow chart shows the major functions of the program and indicates the order in which they will happen. Different-shaped boxes indicate statements and decisions. You might produce several flow charts, for a single program, each with more detail than the last as your design develops.

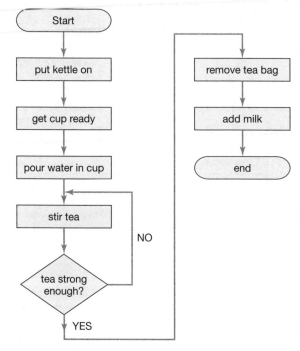

Figure 11.1 Flow chart for making the tea

For **event-driven programs**, there is no clear order in which the different sections of the program will be executed. A flow chart that shows how one operation follows another is not necessarily going to help you get started. A good place to start for event-driven programming is often a series of use cases. A use case is a functional description of the interaction between the user and the system for one action the user might take.

As an example think about the use case for a menu with a **Save File** function:

Example: Save file

Normal operation

The user clicks on **Save** in the menu with the left mouse button to save the current data to the hard disk. The system shows a dialogue box that asks for the filename and directory where the file will be saved. The user inserts the information and the file is stored using the specified directory and name.

Other options

The filename the user gives already exists. The system asks whether the existing file should be overwritten. The user responds with yes or no. If the user says yes, the file is overwritten; otherwise, the dialogue box asking for the filename and directory is displayed again.

> *The filename contains invalid characters*. The message **Invalid File Name Please re-Enter** appears in a warning box, the user clicks OK to acknowledge this and the dialogue box asking for the filename and directory is displayed again.

Notice that the use case is written in easily understandable prose. Once you have specified a use case for each action the program user might take, you can start to think about how they link together and if there is any particular sequence in which they must happen. For instance, an **Open File** function might need to be completed before the option for a **Save File** function is offered to the user.

Whether your programming language is event driven or sequential, taking the time to plan the structure of your program means you will write better and more efficient code that is easier to debug and get running.

Starting to program

Once you have a clear idea of the structure that your program needs, you can begin to code. The precise implementation depends on your choice of language, but there are some useful tactics that can make it easier for you:

- Use a smart editor. Smart editors support programming languages by, for example, colour coding the code so comments are in a different-coloured font from commands. They can also automatically indent your code so that all the commands associated with a particular loop have the same left margin. These things make your code easier to read and easier to debug. Look at the code in the table below and decide for yourself. In which format is the structure of the code easiest to follow?

| ```
begin
clear all;
action 1
for i=1:n
    command 1;
    command 2;
    if x = 3
        action a;
        action b;
    else
        action c;
    endif;
    command 3
endfor;
action 2
action 3
end
``` | ```
begin
clear all;
action 1
for i=1:n
command 1;
command 2;
if x = 3
action a;
action b;
else
action c;
endif;
command 3
endfor;
action 2
action 3
end
``` |

- Start with the top level of your program.
  - For sequential programs:
    - Write a main program that calls each subroutine of the program in turn.
    - Code each subroutine so that its only function is to print a message to the screen giving its name.
    - Run the main program to make sure it calls each routine as expected.
    - If the name of each routine has appeared in the expected order then you will know that the top level of program control is working correctly.
  - For event-driven code:
    - Create a routine for each event that simply writes the name of the event to the screen.
    - Test each event in turn to make sure you get the expected response to each user input.
- Once the top-level control is functioning you can start to write the detail of each routine or event. As you expand the code for each routine or event gradually to give it its full function, keep testing at regular intervals to make sure the whole program still functions as expected. If you get a bug, sort it out before you add more code.
- Give your variables, routines and events useful names that tell you something about what they will do. Code with routines called routine_1, routine_ 2, routine_3, etc. (or event_a, event_b, event_c), is harder to debug than code with routines called save_file, open_file, delete_file (or blue_button_press, green_button_press, red_button_press).
- Don't forget to include code that handles errors. This is particularly important when you are going to test the value of one variable against another. For instance, if you ask the user to input Y or N for 'yes' or 'no' make sure that you have accounted for the case where the user presses, say, M by mistake. You want your code to go back and ask for a new, valid key-press, not to crash completely.
- Put comments in your programs. A header at the top to say what the program does and comments next to the lines of code help you to understand your thinking when you return to a routine later. It takes a little time initially but it saves a lot of head scratching if you need to edit in the future. When you are writing code for an assessment, it also helps the marker to follow your design more easily.

Debugging your code

There are two mains types of errors you will come across:

1. *Compiler or code errors*. The system cannot understand the code you have typed for some reason. Perhaps you have used the wrong syntax, forgotten an 'end' statement or to close some brackets, or used a reserved word as a variable name. The system usually gives you a hint, at least about where in the code it has detected the error and sometimes also about what the problem might be. You will need to work through the

code carefully to see if you can spot what is wrong and correct it before your program will run. Some people find it easier to do this with a print out than by reading directly from the screen.

2. *Run time errors*. The syntax of your code was fine, but it produces a logical error or a variable takes a forbidden value when you try to use it. If the error causes your program to crash then you may get some hint from the system about what is wrong. Alternatively your code may run without error but produce unexpected or invalid outputs. In either case the most likely way to find the problem is to use a debugging tool. Most programming environments have one. This allows you to run the program a step at a time and to examine the value of each variable between steps. You need to be systematic and it is helpful to devise a test data set for your inputs that should lead to known outputs. A testing strategy to make sure your program operates as expected is part of good programming practice.

There is no quick way to find the cause of your bugs, but if you take the time to understand what you are trying to achieve before you start to code and you have made a careful design for your program, you have a far better chance of resolving them quickly.

The following hints may help with debugging:

■ Only change one thing in your code between each test.
■ Look out for which line of code causes the problem. The programming environment may help you to identify this.
■ Work through reported bugs in their order of appearance – do the ones near the beginning of the code first.

Documenting your program

Whether a program is part of an assignment for your course or part of a commercial undertaking, produced by a professional software company for a client, it needs documentation so that somebody else can understand and use what you have produced. The program specification should tell you what documentation you are expected to produce and the list may include:

■ Functional description. What the program does.
■ Architecture description. How you have structured the program.
■ Technical description. The listings of the code and descriptions of the algorithms you have implemented.
■ User manuals. Instructions for users and/or for system programmers about how to use and/or maintain your code.

During your studies you also need to provide clear documentation because:

■ It is good practice.
■ It shows the marker of your work that you understand what you have produced and how it works. Apart from anything else, good documentation gives the marker confidence about the academic integrity of your work.
■ The documentation is likely to have a considerable portion of the marks attached to it and you want to get a good grade.

> **Hot Tip**
>
> Most programming languages come with a library of routines and you can get an idea of good practice in documentation by looking at the information provided with these.

2 Creativity on demand

Design exercises are pieces of work where you start from a specification and end with a product. It might, for example, be an electronic circuit, a mechanical device or a more ergonomic consumer product. As with programming exercises, this kind of practical work usually starts with a design specification or brief that details what you are expected to do and the limitations within which you must work, such as the materials available to you, the maximum cost of the finished product, the permissible dimensions, etc.

In many respects the steps you need to take to be successful with this kind of work mirror those described above for programming and in Chapter 16 for mathematical problem solving:

■ Take time to understand what is required. What is the specification asking for? What are you expected to produce at the end of the exercise? A paper design only? A prototype?

■ What documentation of your design process and outcomes are you required to submit?

Don't expect to produce a perfect design immediately. Designing is normally an iterative process: you think about what is required, produce a draft idea or prototype, test it and revise it on the basis of your test. Figure 11.2 summarises the process.

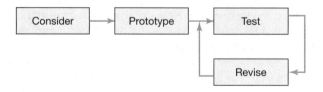

Figure 11.2 An iterative design process

The aspect of design that most people find difficult is having a creative idea on demand. Creativity is often thought of as something you are born with; some people have it and some don't. In fact it is more like being able to play a musical instrument. Most people have a certain amount of musical ability 'built in' but it is mainly through practice that they develop into good players. If you take the opportunity to use your natural creativity whenever you can, you will find that it grows into an ability you can rely on.

Having a good idea

If you find yourself unable to have a creative idea when you need one, there are a number of more formal methods for stimulating your brain. Using one or more of these methods can help you to come up with ideas individually or as a group. Different methods suit different people best, and some methods are more suited to a given type of problem than others. Below are some brief introductions to some formal methods for developing creative ideas.

Brainstorming

You have probably come across the idea of brainstorming already. The process consists of coming up with as many ideas on a given topic as you can. The important point is that brainstorming is a two-phase process: first you come up with the ideas and then you assess them. This means that during the ideas development stage, no idea is to be considered too unworkable or too eccentric. Judgements of that kind are only allowed in the second phase once all the ideas are on the table. The theory is that removing the judgement from the idea-generation process allows people to feel freer and be more creative. Brainstorming is often most useful during the initial, scoping part of a design exercise.

Problem reversal

Problem reversal consists of thinking of ways to achieve the opposite of your final goal. For instance, suppose you want to improve the safety of an electric kettle. Using problem reversal you would try to answer the question 'How would I go about making a really dangerous electric kettle?' Once you have identified all the potential hazards in this way you can more easily go back to your original question and look for ways to minimise the risk.

SCAMPER

This is a technique, created by Eberle (1997), which provides a checklist for thinking through changes you might make to improve an existing product or system. The acronym stands for:

- Substitute – use a different material or component; get someone else to do it.
- Combine – mix parts together or with new parts; integrate processes or services.

- Adapt – alter a part or the whole thing; change the function; use part of something else.
- Modify – make it bigger or smaller; change the colour or shape; increase or reduce in scale.
- Put to another use – use it for something else rather than its original purpose.
- Eliminate – get rid of functions or parts; simplify it.
- Rearrange – turn inside out or upside down.

The outcome of the SCAMPER process is often a set of ideas, like those from brainstorming, which might need further evaluation or refining before they are usable.

Questioning

Ask a question such as 'Why?' and then keep asking until you get to the root of the problem. For example:

Why do we need to improve our kettle? Because it boils too slowly.

Why does it boil too slowly? Because the element gets covered in lime scale.

Why does the element get covered in lime scale? Because the water is hard.

So ... we could improve the kettle by incorporating a water softener.

Instead of 'Why', you might ask 'How?', 'What?', 'Where?', 'When?' or 'Who?'.

There are many other formal systems designed to stimulate creative thinking or to help with problem solving and a web search with creative thinking techniques or problem-solving methods will help you to find out about them. A well-known expert in the field of creative thinking is Edward de Bono, inventor of the phrase 'lateral thinking' and author of numerous books on the subject. If you are interested in learning more formal methods of creativity, his website (see the References section) could be a good place for you to start.

It might also help if you are aware of some of the most common blocks to creative thinking:

- Searching for the 'correct' answer: don't start with the idea that the person who wrote the specification has a single correct solution in mind.
- Worrying about being wrong: have a go, come up with something and then evaluate it to see if it will do the job. If not, try again. You can learn a lot from mistakes.
- Thinking that you are not creative: just relax, let your imagination run riot, don't worry about logic or seriousness and see what happens. Above all, don't give up; the more you try to use your creative skills, the easier it will become to have an idea.

ACTIVITY 2 Applying creativity

Apply one or more of the creativity-enhancing techniques described above to find ways to improve:

- an alarm clock
- safety equipment for motorcyclists
- teabags.

3 On reflection

In this chapter you have learnt about two common types of practical work: programming exercises and design exercises. For both types, careful preparation will pay off in the long run. You need really to understand your specification before you get to the hands-on part of the process. Once you have a prototype, systematic testing and careful revision of your ideas as a result are also crucial.

Keep in mind that for a course assignment many of the marks are likely to come from the documentation you submit with your program or design. Clear documentation shows the marker that you understand what you did.

For design exercises you will frequently find getting started the hardest part. Remember that there are plenty of formal techniques for helping you to structure your thinking when you need to be creative.

Summary of this chapter

Have a look at Figure 11.3 and make sure you are familiar with the concepts.

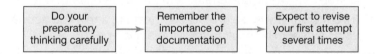

Figure 11.3 Summary of some key ideas in programming and design

ACTIVITY 3 Update your personal development planner

Reflect on your current abilities and consider what needs to improve. You may want to transfer this information to your institution's personal development planner scheme.

Grade your confidence on a scale of 1–5 where 1 = poor and 5 = good.

My developing skills	Confidence level 1–5	Plans to improve
I have a structured way to think about designing programs before I start work.		
I always write comments in my code, indent the sections logically and use helpful names for my variables.		
I understand the purpose of documentation for progams and/or designs.		
I know that there are ways to stimulate creative thought and I can use them in my work.		

Date: _____

Getting extra help

- Many programming and design projects are set as group work. See Chapter 5, 'Working in a real team', for advice about this.
- If your creativity is really blocked, try doing a relaxing activity or some sport and coming back to the problem later.
- Talk through your ideas with a friend; it can help you to sort them out in your own mind.

Feedback on activities

ACTIVITY 1 Breaking down the steps

Put the kettle on	Fill the kettle with water	Turn on the tap Take the lid off the kettle Put the kettle under the tap Wait until the kettle is full Take the kettle away from the tap
	Switch it on	Turn the tap off Attach the kettle to the electricity supply Press the 'on' switch
Get a cup ready	Get a cup	Open the cupboard Take a cup Place near the kettle
	Get a teabag	Open the box of teabags Take a teabag out Place in the cup
Make the tea	Put the water in the cup	Wait until kettle switches off Pour water into the cup Stir with a teaspoon until tea is strong enough Remove teabag
	Add milk	Take milk out of fridge Add milk to tea Stir tea

References

- Eberle, B. (1997) *Scamper: Creative Games and Activities for Imagination Development*. Prufrock Press, Waco, Texas.
- Edward de Bono: **http://www.edwarddebono.com/Default.php** [last accessed 23 January 2009].

4 Develop your technical writing

Having chosen to study one of the SET (Science, Engineering and Technology) subjects, you may feel relieved that you don't have to worry about your writing anymore – after all, you are not doing an English degree. You may also think you write well enough and you don't need to learn to write again! In this section we are simply looking at how you can *improve* your writing and make it more professional; you are simply moving 'up a grade'.

Being able to write well, both technically and academically, is important as it enables you to develop a more rigorous thought process where you need to argue, evaluate and interpret information, a vital skill for work in this area.

Once you have left education, you may become a scientist or an engineer and you will need to communicate your ideas to a variety of colleagues and clients. A major part of that communication will be technical documents where you will be expected to write with clarity and precision.

The following chapters in this part will help you develop these lifelong skills and enable you to: take control of the writing process so you can handle all aspects of an assignment (Chapter 12); understand what plagiarism is and how to avoid it (Chapter 13); and develop your technical writing ability (Chapters 14 and 15).

12 Taking control of the writing process

Writing essays, reports, literature reviews and a variety of other documents is an essential part of your studies. Not only do you learn the subject by writing about it, but also you learn to convey what you know in a logical and coherent manner that is appropriate for those going to read your work.

In this chapter you will:

1. learn to manage the writing process effectively
2. know how to unpack a question or title so you can focus your answer
3. develop a technique for categorising and recording information
4. know how to edit and proofread your work effectively.

USING THIS CHAPTER

Estimate your current levels of confidence. At the end of the chapter you will have the chance to reassess these levels where you can incorporate this into your personal development planner (PDP). Mark between 1 (poor) and 5 (good) for the following:

I know how to manage the writing process effectively.	I can analyse what is required of a question or title correctly.	I have a system for collecting relevant information linked to a title or essay question.	I know how to edit and proofread my work effectively.

Date: _____

1 Becoming a writer

Being able to write is much more than writing the way you speak and much more than just knowing the grammar of a language. Being able to write well is a series of demanding intellectual processes where you need to decipher the question or title you have been given, know how to break that down and collect the relevant information, categorise the information you have, plan a structure, start writing, edit and revise. This is definitely not a simple activity, which is why you read books like this and attend writing classes.

In this section we shall briefly look at the characteristics of expert and novice writers, recognise the writing process and understand how to decipher that question in order to get the marks you deserve. Misreading the question or not writing 'on target' is one of the most common errors for poor marks in student work.

Recognise expert and novice writers

Researchers Bereiter and Scardamalia have spent the last 30 years exploring what makes a writer an expert writer. They have examined how school children and academic writers go about the process. One of the interesting findings is that expert writers manage their writing process differently from novice writers (Bereiter and Scardamalia, 1987). Novice writers adopt a linear approach to their writing and tend to take each of the writing process elements in turn (see Figure 12.1 below). The reason they do this is because they are not at the stage of managing and controlling more than one element at a time, and, for example, may gather information for a document without giving any thought to how they are going to use the information at a later stage in the writing process.

On the other hand, expert writers keep a mental map of the finished product or essay in mind while they are gathering information and writing a draft. They keep moving backwards and forwards through the various activities in the process with ease and skill, and, with practice, so will you.

ACTIVITY 1 Do you have novice or expert writer characteristics?

Novice writer	Mark along the line where you feel you are					Expert writer
	1	2	3	4	5	
I don't read very much.						I read as much as I can to gain an overview.
My reading is mainly from websites.						My reading is from books, articles and websites.
I often read something, take a few notes and then start writing.						I read, take notes, plan a structure (even if it changes later).
When ideas come to me while writing I just fit them in as I write.						I make a note of ideas that come to me while writing so I can fit them in the correct place.
When I write, I usually just paraphrase what I've read.						I paraphrase and critically challenge or evaluate what I've read.
I never need to make a draft copy. I can hand my work straight in.						I usually write several drafts before handing my work in.
I never or rarely proofread or edit my work.						I always proofread and edit my work – often several times.

See the feedback section at the end of the chapter.

How do you rate yourself? Check the expert writer characteristics and use this book to improve yourself as a writer.

Understand the writing process

It is easy when writing something to get wrapped up in the small detail and forget the larger picture. It is important to understand and take control of the whole writing process in order to stay on top of your work. Figure 12.1 will give you an insight into the writing process.

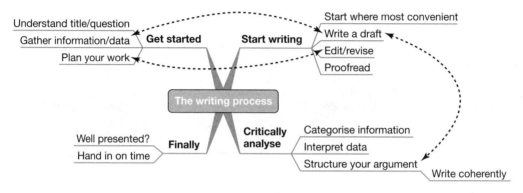

Figure 12.1 Understanding the writing process

To get started, the first things you will have to do are:

1. Understand the title given. The title you are given provides the framework and focus within which to work – see 'Crack the code' below.

2. Gather information and data. You will need to have done some research and read key texts or collected data in the laboratory – see Chapter 4.

3. Plan your structure. You may not get the exact plan at the beginning, but it is a plan for you to start from, even if you make changes later. Starting without a plan or a structure will make it more difficult for you to structure your thoughts and your reader will feel that your work is incoherent and rather random. This is the most common criticism of students' writing – see Chapter 14, Section 1.

Once you get the first three steps sorted out, the other aspects of the process will be up to you and you will find yourself shifting between the writing, drafting and editing activities. Like expert writers, you will also develop a more sophisticated way of working to respond to the more complex needs of writing at university.

Crack the code: unpacking the title or question

When you have been given a title to work with, it is important that you are able to 'decode' it effectively so that what you write is 'on target'. If you are able to write 'on target', i.e. answer the question asked, you will gain good marks. Most lecturers complain that students haven't answered the question properly, so take time to understand the title fully and focus your research and answer.

Understanding the question or title

Fully understanding the title and 'cracking its code' will help you to:

- narrow your research and enable you to focus your reading more carefully
- look for the right evidence and information to include in your work
- answer exam questions effectively – see Chapter 8, 'Excelling in exams'.

If you are not sure what you are supposed to do when you read the title, you need to develop some strategies to help you to decipher just what it is getting at and what is expected of you. The BUG technique can help you do that, and this stands for:

Box *put a box around action words. These are words in a title that tell you what you have to do, e.g. 'Explain', 'Evaluate', 'Analyse', etc. These are important words because they are telling you something about the type of structure expected for your work.*

Underline *Underline the key words in the question. This will help you sort out not only the content expected but also tell you any limitations, e.g. only a specific time scale or one facet to be analysed.*

Glance back to check *Have you missed out any words which are important and change what you have to do?*

The BUG technique is a system which has been developed by Geraldine Price in response to concerns expressed by university students (Price, 2001). It has been used successfully by hundreds of students in different subject areas. Here is what a student had to say:

I used to frequently get comments like 'you have not answered the question' from my tutors. I couldn't understand what they meant because the way I read the essay title, I thought I had done what was asked. When my tutor told me I wasn't tuning myself into the language academics use and showed me the BUG I found that at last I had something which I could use for any essay title or exam question. It's brilliant and saves so much time.

Dave, second-year Mechanical Engineering student

The reason it is important to box and underline specific words is that it helps to differentiate the function of the language used. It is easy to pick out the type of essay or question required because the clue word(s) is boxed. This also serves as a quick reminder when you come back to the title at different times.

If you go through the process of <u>underlining the key words</u>, you will have had to weigh up which words you think are important, and also eliminate words which are not so vital. By doing this activity, you will have started the thinking process and will be analysing the language that will help you get to the heart of what is required. Similarly, the physical act of underlining chosen words helps them to stand out so that they act as memory joggers later on when you are embroiled in your sentence construction and writing – a time when you could forget your way and wander from the point.

The ⇐ 'glance back' is the part which is often overlooked by students anxious to get started with the essay. However, this is the part which helps you to develop critical skills. More importantly, it is a self-check to ensure that you have not got stuck in a 'thinking rut' and taken things for granted. This makes you check that you have done the job properly.

Unpacking your essay title: BUG in practice

Let us explore how this works with some essay titles across science and engineering:

1. *Compare and contrast the benefits of different steel hardening techniques.*

2. *Assess the viability of reintroduction schemes from captive breeding programmes.*

3. *Comment on three ways in which lasers have improved life.*

4. *Describe the UK's potential for the generation of renewable energy.*

5. *A stoppered flask is known to contain hydrogen, nitrogen or oxygen. How would you identify the gas?*[1]

6. *Is land remediation sustainable?*

If we take essay title 1, *Compare and contrast the benefits of different steel hardening techniques,* the first thing we do is to **box** the action words and in this example they are: **compare and contrast**. This tells you immediately how to structure your essay. You know you have to look at the various techniques and weigh up the pros and cons. It will be important, therefore, for you to know how you are going to structure your argument and how you are going to group possible different techniques so you can tell 'your story'.

Next we <u>underline</u> the key words in the title and these are **different steel hardening techniques**. This tells you the subject area in engineering and where you will do your research. Many students would have compared and contrasted these different techniques and not got many marks because they failed to see other key words, namely **the benefits of**. When you **glance back** that is when you would pick up these words if you had not spotted them earlier.

---

1 From The Bunsen Learner at: **http://www.chem.ed.ac.uk/bunsen_learner/august20041bh_sectionb.html** [last accessed June 2008].

In this essay you need to know what the various techniques of hardening steel are, but the key aspect for getting good marks will be how you structure your argument in relation to the 'benefits'. You should get some clues from your lectures. However, if you don't you will need to define how you are going to deal with this. You may want to consider the benefits, for example, in relation to a specific use for the steel, showing how the various techniques alter the steel's properties making it less or more beneficial for a particular use. This essay title could be made more explicit, for example: *Compare and contrast the benefits of different steel hardening techniques in relation to the use of steel for a permanent way (railway track).*

Hot Tip

It is worth spending time solving the language of the title – the key to good marks starts with cracking the code of the essay title. Remember also to use this in exams.

Clarifying the 'instruction words' in an essay or exam question

As a general guideline the following definitions give an indication of what you are expected to do and what sort of essay you are supposed to be structuring. The list below gives some of the most frequently used terminology. It gives general guidelines for working out what kind of essay is required. You are advised to check with your department, as some terminology is used in a very specific way by different departments.

Account for	Give the reason for. Don't confuse this with 'Give an account of' which is only asking for a description.
Analyse	Describe the main ideas in depth, showing why they are important and how they are connected.
Assess	Discuss the strong and weak points of the subject. Put your own judgement clearly in the conclusion.
Comment	State your views on the subject clearly. Back up your points with sufficient evidence and examples.
Compare	Look for similarities and differences.
Contrast	Show how the subjects are different.
Criticise	Give your opinion/judgement about the merit of theories/facts. Back this up by discussing the evidence or reasoning involved.
Define	Give clear, concise meanings. State limitations of the definition.

Describe	Give a detailed or graphic account of how something is or how it works.
Discuss	Give reasons for and against; examine implications.
Evaluate	Weigh things up; look at the strengths and weaknesses and assess.
Examine	Look closely at all aspects of the topic.
Explain	Give reasons for something.
Illustrate	Make clear by the use of examples/diagrams; clarify points.
Interpret	Express in simple terms. You are usually expected to include your own judgements.
Justify	Show adequate ground for decisions/conclusions/ideas/theories.
Outline	Give the main features or general principles of a subject – should not include all the details.
Prove	Establish that something is true by presenting factual evidence or giving clear, logical reasons.
Relate	Show how things are connected to each other, how they affect each other.
Review	Make a survey of something.
State	Present brief, clear information.
Summarise	Give a concise account for the main points – should not include details.
Trace	Follow the development of a topic.
To what extent …	Another way of saying evaluate, but suggests that you bring out how much (or how little).

Sometimes the action word may be missing and you have to make assumptions yourself (or clarify with your tutor) as to what is meant. The essay title above, *is land remediation sustainable?,* is without an instruction word. Here you can imagine adding *discuss* or *evaluate* at the end.

ACTIVITY 2 Debugging the question or title

Look at the essay titles above and complete the following:

■ Apply the BUG technique on the titles.
■ Identify what you should do to get good marks.

See the feedback section.

You can do this exercise even if you don't know about the subject. You are expected just to unpack the title and see what would be expected of you.

Having worked out what your tutor wants in the essay, it is important to develop efficient ways of gathering information so that you group and categorise information/ideas/arguments at an early stage. Doing this systematically will help you 'join up your thinking' and enable you to write coherently.

2 Gathering information

Some students spend too much time and effort on this part of the writing process. It is easy to 'get stuck' at this stage as you may feel you need to keep reading to understand more before you can start writing. Try to make sure that you streamline this activity and then have the confidence to stop.

In this section you will identify how you gather and record your notes and then discuss a structured way of categorising and recording information that maps onto your question or title.

ACTIVITY 3 How do you gather information in preparation for writing?

Ask yourself ...	
1. Do you spend a lot of time gathering information for an essay?	Yes/no
2. Do you find that you have gathered information that is irrelevant or wandering off the point?	Yes/no
3. Do you find it difficult to decide what is needed from the information you have?	Yes/no
4. Do you end up with lots of notes and spend too much time picking out information that you need when you come to write?	Yes/no
5. Do you feel overwhelmed by the amount of notes you have made?	Yes/no
6. Do tutors comment that you have not answered the question and that there are irrelevant sections/information in your work?	Yes/no

See the feedback section for some help.

Categorise and record information using a matrix

To overcome some of the problems listed above, you need to develop a system. One system you can use employs a matrix or a grid which can:

- help you categorise and compare information
- help prevent copying out word for word what is in books and journals because there is limited space available for making notes
- prevent plagiarism if you do not copy out word for word information into your matrix
- develop your summary skills

- be useful for those who like to see an overview of information
- be very good for those of you who have difficulty with sequencing and structuring your work because once you have your information in this format you can then order the information as you wish.

Link the matrix to an essay question or title

Let's use the title which was used earlier to unpick the language:

Compare and contrast the *benefits of steel hardening techniques*.

Your 'evidence' can be collected from different sources and as you find information on the various techniques you can place your summarised bullet points in the most appropriate part of the grid.

Steel hardening techniques

Keep this title in mind so you remember what it is you have to focus on.

Steel hardening techniques	Criterion/focus for your comparison *e.g. for use in a railway track*		Short reference** to remind you where this is from
	Pros*	Cons	
1.			
2.			
Your quick summary/overview/observations***			

* The pros and cons will depend on the criteria that you select (e.g. use of energy, resulting steel properties) – you may not be able to decide that until you have done sufficient reading. Your lectures should also indicate the focus you should be taking.

** Remember that all your notes should have the full reference. See Chapter 13.

*** Adapt your grid to suit your question and how you best work.

It is important to use the language of the question in your matrix. This will act as a constant reminder of what you are supposed to be finding out and keep you 'on track'. Set up the grid **before** you start your information gathering and reading so that you can focus better. This means that as you conduct your background reading, you can decide which box the information goes into.

If you are using printouts of e-articles from your university website, you can colour code the information so that it fits into your matrix or grid. For example, all steel hardening techniques could be highlighted in a specified colour, which then gets transferred to your grid. This way you can quickly identify and categorise information from an article or chapter to suit your purpose.

If you are concerned about how to get your ideas to hang together in paragraphs, you might like to see Chapter 14 where more detailed information about writing is discussed.

3 Making changes and spotting errors

Having drawn up a comprehensive matrix of evidence for your essay you are now ready to manage the drafting and editing stages. Are you aware that these are different activities? Some students start to compose or draft their ideas into prose and at the same time edit what they are writing. For novice writers, it helps to keep these activities separate. Some students have said that they don't have the luxury of time to go through the drafting process and then go through the whole essay again editing what has been written. It is **not** a luxury. Students who try to combine these activities are often unaware of the purpose of the two processes. Trying to cut corners by combining these activities may lead to a drop in the quality not only of your sentence and paragraph structure, but also in terms of the overall structure of your essay. Go back and see how you responded to Activity 1.

In this section you will recognise the importance of editing and proofreading your work. This is a task that many students avoid, but which is such an essential stage for the expert writer.

Draft

Drafting is often referred to as the composing part of the writing process. At this stage you are ordering and structuring your ideas. It should be considered as the first stage of your finished product. During the drafting phase you have the chance to put your initial thoughts into sentences and paragraphs. When you are writing your draft, it can be enough of a struggle just to get the ideas down in the right order. Do not add to it by worrying too much about finding the right word or a particular reference. In fact, when you're stuck, it is often better to leave a gap and fill it in later. If you do this, you must develop a consistent technique that enables you quickly to spot where you have left unfinished parts. You can use the highlighter function in a word processor and then visually go through to see where the gaps are. Alternatively, you can use letters or symbols: for example, XXX is ideal as no word has three consecutive Xs and therefore you will pick up your gaps easily using the 'search' function. After XXX you can always put a note to yourself to remind you what it is about. Remember to devise a method that will best suit your working style.

Edit and proofread

Editing and proofreading are very similar and often carried out as one process when it is your own work. Proofreading is simply going through your work and detecting errors and does not necessarily involve any rewriting or major editing work. Generally, the nature of errors is grammatical, spelling or formatting. Editing, on the other hand, involves not only correction but also a reorganisation of ideas or a rewriting of parts to make them flow better. When you edit you are refining your work and when you proofread you are searching out 'surface' errors.

In order to edit or proofread your work, you need to put some distance between you as the writer and you as the editor; do this by leaving your work for a day or two and coming back to it (build this into your time management). Many people find it helps to print out the first draft and mark it up in a different-coloured pen. That way you can choose the alterations you would like to make without losing sight of the original text. Read the essay as if someone else had written it. Now is the time to check that you have included all the references you need and filled in any blanks that you left in your draft. When you are happy that you have marked up all the changes which you can cope with, go back and edit the document.

Checklist for editing and proofreading

This is a complex activity and you will find you are switching between macro concepts, such as 'is this relevant to the question set?', and micro activities, such as grammatical error spotting. When you carry out this activity decide if you are working at the macro or micro level as switching between the two is less productive and you could miss things. This will mean, of course, reading and rereading several times. Use the following questions to guide you:

Checklist: guide to editing and proofreading		
Macro level (editing)	**R**elevance	• Is my analysis of the topic correct? • What can be deleted as not relevant to the topic?
	Organisation	• Is this the best way to structure the sections? • Can I move paragraphs/sections around for more clarity?
	Coherence	• Does the information flow well between sentences? • Do the first two sentences of a paragraph develop the idea within that paragraph? • Do the paragraphs link well?

Micro level (proofreading)	Grammar +	Have you checked: • Spelling? • Grammar (read aloud to hear grammatical errors)? • Abbreviations (do you say what they stand for)? • Labelling (figures, equations, diagrams)? • Formatting (is it consistent across your document)? • Contents page if necessary • References • Your name, and title of the work?

Using the checklist above, carry out some editing and proofreading of your own work. For small samples of text just work at the 'C' and 'G' levels.

How to spot your errors

You can of course use word processor functions to spot grammatical and spelling errors. However, do check as sometimes the program does get it wrong for your context. Generally Microsoft Word, for example, will tag words as misspelled if they do not conform to US spelling. Similarly, the program does not like the use of the pronoun 'which', which is used in UK English grammar, and Microsoft offers 'that' instead. Overcome these by setting your system to UK English and to do this go to the top menu in an open document and select the button marked **Tools**, then **Language**, then **Set Language** (for a Microsoft Word document) to UK English.

In addition to a word processing program you can always read your work aloud. By reading aloud you slow down the speed of reading and because you can **hear** what you say, you can detect errors better. This is particularly true for grammatical errors or where your line of argument is disrupted. Of course, you could let the technology help you. Using voice recognition software can be useful for those who prefer to work alone. You can listen to your sentences and paragraphs being read aloud to you by the computer so that you can hear if your work makes sense.

Proofreading 'buddies'

These may be difficult to find, especially from your own year group, because of the work pressures of your fellow students. However, it may be a useful service that you and a group of friends can provide for each other. You have to decide on a mutual deadline and place to get together to form a 'proofreading' group to examine each other's work critically and make helpful suggestions.

Get a proofreading 'buddy' to read your work aloud while you listen for errors in construction and structure. You have really to trust your buddy and not feel embarrassed or threatened as he or she reads your work while sitting next to you. This often appeals to auditory learners who can spot their own errors when they hear what they have written.

Learning from errors: frequency patterns

If you want to improve your writing, you need to reflect frequently upon your writing. It is frustrating and time consuming to keep making the same errors. Therefore, you ought to reflect upon the types of errors you make so that you can make a difference in the future. Look for spelling error patterns – do you frequently get certain words incorrect? Do you often miss off the endings of words or the middle bits? By findings patterns of errors you will get a focus on what you need to tackle to improve.

If you know you have persistent problems with spelling, you may want to invest in software that can help you. The student support services at your institution should be able to give you advice. It is also good to identify those words that you consistently misspell and devise a way of trying to remember their spelling. Take care to master everyday words that you tend to misspell as tutors get particularly irritated by this, e.g. advice/advise, practice/practise. It gives a bad impression to your tutors who are marking your work. Finally, really get to grips with the correct spelling for the technical words in your field. If they are not spelled correctly, the quality of your work (whether correct or not) is put into doubt.

Hot Memory Tip

Remember: a 'noun' represents a **thing** and a verb an **action**. Sometimes words look alike but they have a different function:

AdviCe is a noun, e.g. the advice you gave me was excellent.
AdviSe is a verb, e.g. I was advised well.

Trick to remember:

'Cent' is a noun, so is advice, practice.
'Sent' is a verb, so is advise, practise.

Now devise a way to remember the difference between: *effect* and *affect*, *stationery* and *stationary*.

4 On reflection

If you explore how you take control of the writing process, you will be well on your way to becoming an expert writer. Taking the pragmatic approach set out in this chapter will make a difference not only to the quality of your work but also to your time management.

Excellent writing relies on your organisation and management of the whole process and not just on digging out the information. If you take control of the process from the moment you are given the title, you give yourself a better chance of producing coherent and critical work (see Chapter 14 for writing critically and developing coherence).

Summary of this chapter

Take a quick look at Figure 12.2 and assess if you are now familiar with these areas.

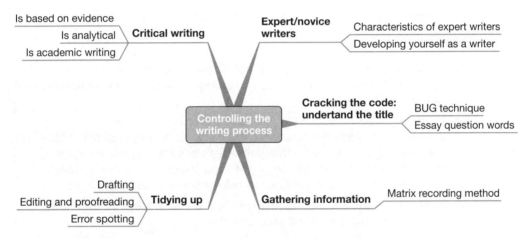

Figure 12.2 Summary of how to control the writing process

ACTIVITY 4 Update your personal development planner

Having read this chapter, you can see that organisation and management play key roles in academic writing. From the moment you receive an essay or report title to the time you hand your work in, you need to be in control of the process. Using the personal development planner below reflect on how you can take control of the writing process and how you intend to change and adapt your habits so that you can spend your time more expertly. You may want to transfer this information to your own institution's personal development planner scheme.

Grade your confidence on a scale of 1–5 where 1 = poor and 5 = good.

My developing skills	Confidence level 1–5	Plans to improve
I know how to manage the writing process effectively.		
I can analyse what is required of a question or title correctly.		
I have a system for collecting relevant information linked to a title or essay question.		
I know how to edit and proofread my work effectively.		

Date: _____

Getting extra help

- Go to the Students Union to find out where to go for skills development. Many universities and colleges have tutors who provide this service.

- If you are unsure about what you have got to do, make an appointment to see the academic tutor who set your essay title. Make sure you have given some thought to the possible ways of interpreting the question so that you have specific questions to ask, and it does not look as if you want the tutor to help you write your essay.

- Find out if there is a proofreading service at your college or university, if you have trouble spotting your own errors.

Feedback on activities

ACTIVITY 1 Do you have novice or expert writer characteristics?

Novice writer	Mark along the line where you feel you are					Expert writer
	1	2	3	4	5	
I don't read very much.	*If you don't read much, it will be difficult to form arguments and write properly.*					I read as much as I can to gain an overview.
My reading is mainly from websites.	*If all your references are from websites, your lecturer will know that you are not getting to grips with the topic. Your reading should be a mixture of websites (properly referenced), books and articles.*					My reading is from books, articles and websites.
I often read something, take a few notes and then start writing.	*Resist reading and writing in one sitting. Read and take notes, collect your notes and from that plan what you want to say. Give yourself a reading limit, read key texts and then work out what you want to say. Make sure all your notes are fully referenced.*					I read, take notes, plan a structure (even if it changes later).
When ideas come to me while writing I just fit them in as I write.	*It is very obvious to your lecturer if you are coming up with ideas while you write. It is so obvious it almost jumps off the page and can disturb your flow. When you have a good idea, make a note of it and when you edit, see if it fits in properly. Or, if it is a really good idea, then stop and reassess your plan.*					I make a note of ideas that come to me while writing so I can fit them in the correct place.
When I write, I usually just paraphrase what I've read.	*Novice writers tend to limit their writing to paraphrasing what they have read, i.e. being simply descriptive, while more experienced writers will take a more critical look at what they are reading and evaluate in the light of evidence. This is a premium graduate-quality skill. Look at the section on critical writing in Chapter 14.*					I paraphrase and critically challenge or evaluate what I've read.
I never need to make a draft copy. I can hand my work straight in.	*No writer, worth his or her salt would dream of handing in the first draft. You have to build in time for editing and refining your work. It always shows.*					I usually write several drafts before handing my work in.
I never or rarely proofread or edit my work.	*Without proofreading you will hand in work with silly and annoying mistakes. You will not have checked the formatting so it will also look messy. As above, build in time to do this.*					I always proofread and edit my work – often several times.

ACTIVITY 2 Debugging the question or title

Let's explore how this works with some essay titles across science and engineering.

1. *Compare and contrast the benefits of different steel hardening techniques.* Already analysed.

2. *Assess the viability of reintroduction schemes from captive breeding programmes.* The action word is 'Assess' where you need to look at the arguments and develop your own judgement, given the evidence. You need to research the different types of captive breeding programmes (you may want to limit this to a particular group of animals and, if so, state this at the beginning of your work) and how the animals are reintroduced into the wild. The key to success in this essay is your analysis of the **viability** of these schemes. How will you 'measure' viability and what does the literature say about that?

3. *Comment on three ways in which lasers have improved life.* The action word is 'Comment' where you will be expected to state your views and the topic is the application of lasers that have improved life. You need to restrict your essay to three areas and to find information about these improvements.

4. *Describe the UK's potential for the generation of renewable energy.* The action word is 'Describe' which means you have to give an account of what is available. You are not expected to make any evaluative comment or compare and contrast (although do check with your tutor as sometimes tutors use 'Describe' but also mean 'Evaluate') information. The key here is the **potential** for generating renewable energy, which may be different from what is actually happening currently.

5. *A stoppered flask is known to contain hydrogen, nitrogen or oxygen. How would you identify the gas?*[2] Although there is no action word here, it is, by default, 'Describe' or 'State'. Here you need to know what the tests are for hydrogen and oxygen and how you would go about identifying them in a stoppered flask.

6. *Is land remediation sustainable?* There is no action word, but, again by default, you can assume it is 'Discuss' or 'Evaluate'. However, do check with your tutor. You need to find out information on the different types of land remediation, group them in some way (e.g. *in situ*, *ex situ*, chemical, mechanical) so they are easier to deal with and then discuss the sustainability of these techniques. You may also want to state how you are interpreting 'sustainability' in this context.

---

2 The Bunsen Learner: at **http://www.chem.ed.ac.uk/bunsen_learner/august20041bh_sectionb.html** [last accessed June 2008].

ACTIVITY 3 How do you gather information in preparation for writing?

Ask yourself ...	Possible solution
1. Do you spend a lot of time gathering information for an essay?	*This sounds as if you are not really sure what you are looking for. Carry out the BUG to clarify what your tutors want.*
2. Do you find that you have gathered information that is irrelevant or wandering off the point?	*Go back to the title and do the BUG to find out exactly what you need to find.*
3. Do you find it difficult to decide what is needed from the information you have?	*Check back at the underlined words in your title. Ask yourself how relevant your notes are and whether you have information to answer the question.*
4. Do you end up with lots of notes and spend too much time picking out information that you need when you come to write?	*You have no system for gathering notes. You need to be more efficient. Look at the section on making notes and look at the different ways of making notes.*
5. Do you feel overwhelmed by the amount of notes you have made?	*You have no system for gathering notes. You need to be more efficient. Look at the next section.*
6. Do tutors comment that you have not answered the question and that there are irrelevant sections/information in your work?	*This is probably because you have not carefully analysed the wording in the essay and conducted the BUG.*

References

- Bereiter, C. and Scardamalia, M. (1987) *The Psychology of Written Composition*. New York, Lawrence Erlbaum.
- Price, G. A. (2001) *Report of the Survey of Academic Study Skills at Southampton University*. Southampton, University of Southampton.

13 Understanding academic integrity: plagiarism

Academic integrity is a code of practice which is strongly adhered to in any type of academic writing. You must ensure that you are able to give recognition to the work of others in your own writing. To do this effectively, you need to understand the rules of referencing your work and how to cite others' work within your text. If students do not reference their work properly they are in danger of being accused of plagiarism. Learning how to reference the work of others also demonstrates your background reading.

In this chapter you will:

1. learn that there are different forms of plagiarism
2. learn steps to prevent plagiarism
3. learn how to cite references in your written work
4. learn how to build up a bibliography or reference list
5. find out how to organise and manage your bibliographic data.

USING THIS CHAPTER

Estimate your current levels of confidence. At the end of the chapter you will have the chance to reassess these levels where you can incorporate this into your personal development planner (PDP). Mark between 1 (poor) and 5 (good) for the following:

I know the variety of ways in which plagiarism can take place.	I know the difference between presentation of in-text citations and references at the the end of my written work.	I know the difference between a bibliography and a reference list.	I know the rules for presenting different types of references.	I am able to manage the collection of references in a systematic manner.

Date: _____

1 What is academic integrity?

Your tutors set great store by academic integrity. Two essential ingredients of this are plagiarism and how you reference your written work. They are closely linked as you will see by exploring this chapter. Referencing your work properly will substantially ensure that you are not accused of plagiarism. However, some students are genuinely unaware that they have plagiarised work because they do not understand what plagiarism is. It is much easier nowadays to fall inadvertently into the trap because of the ease of access of information. Andrew Hammett, the Principal of Strathclyde University, stated that many students are part of the 'Google Generation' (Hammett, 2006), which results in the authorship boundaries being blurred, which could lead to more frequent instances of plagiarism.

Academic integrity is a code of practice which is strongly adhered to in any type of academic writing or exposition. It relates not only to essays but to PowerPoint presentations, examinations, dissertations and theses.

2 What is plagiarism?

I didn't know that I'd plagiarised things. I took words and phrases on the Internet and re-arranged them into my own sentence. I was shocked and humiliated when I was told to go to my tutor about cheating.

Chris, first-year Geography student

Plagiarism can take many forms. *The Oxford English Dictionary* gives a straightforward definition:

> **PLAGIARISM**: *to take and use as one's own, the thoughts, writings or inventions of another.*

It cannot be stressed strongly enough that plagiarism is grounds for failure on your course. All universities and colleges have regulations which can be found on the main institutional website or repeated in your course handbooks and departmental guidelines. The wording is strong to emphasise the severity of the offence.

> *It shall be an offence for a student knowingly ... To represent as one's own any idea or expression of an idea or work of another in any academic examination or term test or in connection with any other form of academic writing, i.e. to commit plagiarism.*

University of Southampton (2006)

Of course, the significant word is 'knowingly'. Like Chris, the first-year Geography student above, some students are not aware that they have plagiarised. However, trying to establish your innocence when you are being questioned by your tutor may be difficult to prove. Therefore, it is vital that you are aware of what plagiarism is and its many forms (see Activity 1).

ACTIVITY 1 What constitutes plagiarism?

Look at these statements and answer 'yes', 'no' or 'possibly'.

Which of the following are considered plagiarism?	Yes/no/possibly
I wrote the words from my textbook in my essay.	
I used inverted commas around the words I took from a text I was reading.	
I used different phrases from different sources and put them into a sentence in my essay.	
I used information from an Internet page which did not have a title or author so it is not plagiarising.	

Check the feedback section at the end of the chapter to find out the answers.

Plagiarism defined

You will be accused of plagiarism if you:

- borrow or copy words from texts
- copy words/phrases word for word from texts
- do not identify and acknowledge all your sources of information
- download text from the Internet and do not acknowledge the source
- play around with the text of others to create your own text
- copy another student's words without acknowledgement
- use someone else's ideas or theories without acknowledgement
- download pictures and diagrams from the Internet without acknowledgement.

Fiona Duggan, Manager of the Plagiarism Advisory Service (PAS), is convinced that many students in the early part of their studies are not aware that they are committing an offence against academic integrity (Curtis, 2004).

3 Steps to prevent plagiarism

Sticking too closely to the words of others without acknowledging or referencing the source can be avoided. These problems stem from weak reading techniques as well as inexperienced writing strategies. Some of these problems are identified in Activity 2.

ACTIVITY 2 Problems and solutions to plagiarism

Students often lack confidence in their own ability to write authoritatively, which is understandable. Look at the following statements and reflect upon which ones apply to you. They could be the precursors to plagiarism.

Check the feedback section at the end of the chapter to find out the solutions to your problems.

Do any of these statements apply to you?	Yes or no
I can't possibly write this better than the author.	
When I look at the notes I've made on the texts I've read, I can't remember which are my words and which are ones from the author's text.	
I can't remember where I got the information to make my notes so I can't check whether the notes are in my own words or not.	
My sentences and paragraphs are like a patchwork quilt. That's how I write up my information.	
I think I can avoid plagiarism just by listing every single source in the bibliography at the end.	

Although plagiarism is detected at the final stage of your writing, i.e. when you are drafting your ideas, prevention measures have to be taken much earlier on in the writing process. It often begins unwittingly at the note-making stage. Thus, it is vital that you distinguish in your notes direct quotations and your own paraphrasing. See if you can idenitfy the text that contains plagiarism in Activity 3.

ACTIVITY 3 Can you spot which texts contain plagiarism?

Read the original text and the following samples and identify which are cases of plagiarism.

Original text

The cognitive resources used in the writing process are considerable, and memory capacity and storage are often overloaded by competing, simultaneous operations. The ability to synthesise information is one of the essential skills required by HE students. Price (2006)

Version A

The cognitive resources used in the writing process are great and memory capacity and storage are often overloaded by many mental, simultaneous operations.

Version B

In Higher Education, the cognitive resources used in the writing process are often overloaded by competing, simultaneous operations. One of the essential skills needed is to synthesise information.

Version C

As Price (2006) indicates in her research, writing is complex and draws upon many of the mind's resources. One of the difficulties is that at times the writer runs out of memory space because of the need to do many tasks at the same time.

Check the feedback section at the end of the chapter to find out which texts would be considered to contain plagiarism.

Hot Tip

You can prevent plagiarism occurring by:

- **organising** the way in which you collect information for your essay or written work

- developing good **summary skills** so that you put information in your own words and are not tempted to use the words of others

- getting into a routine of **accurately recording your sources** – using either your own lists or an electronic reference manager program.

The key to success is management and organisation right from the start. Efficient strategies will support your way of working. To ensure that you develop the appropriate skills, techniques and strategies, explore the chapter on writing, where you will find information to help you to develop methods for recording information systematically which will reduce your chances of plagiarising work.

Although students find referencing confusing, once you understand the logic and principles behind it you will be able to ensure that you do not lose valuable marks in your essays and project work.

4 Referencing your work

Referencing your work accurately is a means of demonstrating the ownership of information. It is also a way of showing off the background reading which you have conducted in order to formulate your ideas on a subject. Citing references provides your tutor with confirmation that you are aware of what is going on in your subject and the research field. Thus, it has a positive effect if it is carried out properly.

Referencing is complicated because there are three different systems which are closely related to one another:

- citations within the text (in-text citations)
- references: a reference list at the end of your work from authors you referred to
- bibliography: a list at the end of your work from authors you referred to and who informed your work.

In-text citations are short but are linked to the reference list or bibliography at the end of your essay. The latter should provide the full information about the item which has been cited within your text.

Is a reference list different from a bibliography?

A reference list and a bibliography serve similar purposes. Some departments use the two terms interchangeably and make no distinction between the two. Other departments have a preference for one or the other, while still other departments like to see both included at the end of your work. You must check your department's guidelines about this.

A **reference list** is a full and accurate description of all of the citations which are found in your text. Some departments prefer these to be listed chronologically. Thus, each item in the list is in the order in which it occurs in your text. This means that it is *not* alphabetically presented but rather the items appear in a numbered list which is cross-referenced with each in-text citation. However, many departments ask students to prepare 'references' at the end of the essay, and these are formatted in alphabetical order.

A **bibliography** has a different purpose. It contains an alphabetical list of **all** the books, articles, Internet information, etc., you have used in the process of formulating your ideas and thoughts about the subject. Not all of the items in this list will be given an in-text citation. For example, you might have read a chapter in a book to help you understand a difficult concept but you have not used this as a specified citation in your essay. In a sense it is a hidden resource which has helped in the accumulation of your knowledge.

5 How to present citations and references

The key purpose of any citation and its corresponding reference is to enable you, or someone else who is reading your work, to identify and locate the original text. So, be accurate and give full details. There are a variety of different conventions for the compilation of in-text citations and references for bibliographies. Two of the most common are the Harvard system and the British Standard Numeric system.

In-text citation rules

The Harvard system

The Harvard system is the most commonly used. In this system each in-text citation must contain the author's name and the year of publication together with page numbers if a direct quotation is used. For example:

Price (2006) states that ...

In a recent study, Price (2006, p. 21) demonstrated that 'memory capacity and storage are often overloaded by competing, simultaneous operations'.

The British Standard or Numeric bibliography

The British Standard or Numeric bibliography allocates a number to each citation and uses footnotes with numbers for references in the text. This is used often by the Humanities. Engineers use a similar numeric system from the Institute of Electrical and Electronics Engineers (IEEE – pronounced 'i triple e').

For example, round or square brackets are chosen (be sure to be consistent in use) and the citation is given a number which is cross-referenced to the reference list at the end of your essay or writing:

Price (1) states that ... (round brackets)

Price [1] states that ... (square brackets)

A recent study[1] ... (as a superscript number)

It is likely that your department or subject area will have a preference for one particular system, and it would be wise of you to use that system.

> **Hot Tip**
>
> Whichever system you choose, you must use it consistently, accurately and following the rules. It is also worth checking individual academic tutors' preferences. This is especially important for those following joint honours courses in two departments. Do not be worried if there is inconsistency of approach within a department.

What information is needed for referencing?

For each reference that appears in your reference list or bibliography you must record specific pieces of information. It is vital, therefore, that you get into a routine of noting down this information in a safe place. This will be dealt with later in this chapter. The presentation of the information has to be carefully punctuated, and the source of your information will have a different method of presentation. However, the main details that you need to collect are:

- author's or editor's surname and initials
- title, with any sub-titles
- year of publication
- edition if other than the first
- location of the publisher
- name of the publisher
- the name, volume number, part number and pages of the journal
- for electronic resources, the web or email address.

The remainder of this section contains information and examples of how to record a wide range of resources and draws upon the Harvard system because it is the most widely used. You may choose to practise creating references for the types of resources that you feel you will need to use in your studying. The most common sources for students are books, chapters from edited books, journal articles and websites.

Books

References to books should include the following details:

author's name and initials

year of publication, in brackets

title of the book, underlined or in *italics*

edition, if other than the first

place of publication

publisher.

For example, Smith, P. and Jones, W. (2006) *The Art of Academic Referencing*, 2nd edn. London, Made-up Publishing.

Chapters from edited books

Some books contain chapters written by a number of different authors. These books will have an overall editor who has compiled the book. You should include the following details:

name and initials of the author of the chapter

year of publication, in brackets

title of the chapter,

title of the book, underlined or in *italics*

edition, if other than the first

place of publication

publisher

page numbers of chapter.

For example, Smith, P. (2006) 'The role of punctuation in referencing', in Smith, P. and Jones, W. (2006) *The Art of Academic Referencing*, 2nd edn. London, Made-up Publishing, pp. 56–72.

Note that the main source, i.e. the book into which you have dipped, is still the part which is in italics *not* the name of the chapter.

Journal articles

References to journal articles should include the following details:

author's name and initials

year of publication, in brackets

title of the article (not underlined or in *italics*)

title of the journal, underlined or in *italics*

volume no. and (issue no.)

page number(s).

For example, Price, G. A. (2006) 'Creative solutions to making technology work: three case studies of dyslexic writers in Higher Education', *ALT-J Research in Learning Technology*, 14(1), 21–28.

Electronic information

There is a wide variety of types of information which you might use from electronic sources. The main ones are:

- Internet pages (Uniform Resource Locators or URLs)
- articles in electronic journals
- electronic books
- articles in Internet journals
- photographs and images
- information from your department's virtual learning environment, e.g. Blackboard
- online newspaper articles
- personal email correspondence (with a leading researcher, for example)
- course discussion board information.

As a rule of thumb it is important that you provide the URL and the date upon which you accessed the information. The rules for books and journal articles remain the same, with the additional URL and accession date:

author's name and initials

year of publication, in brackets (if there is no date, put [n.d.] – and use square brackets)

title of the website, underlined or in *italics,* followed by '[online]'

place of publication

publisher (if ascertainable)

available from: URL [date accessed] – use square brackets: the http:// may be left off if the URL also contains 'www'.

For example, Williams, S. (2002) 'Avoiding plagiarism' [online]: New York, Hamilton College. Available from: **www.hamilton.edu/academic/Resource/ WC/AvoidingPlagiarism.html** [accessed 18 December 2006].

Overview of components of references:

	Author	Year of publication	Title of publication	Title of article/chapter	Issue	Place	Publisher	Edition	Page no.	URL	Date accessed
Book	✓	✓	✓			✓	✓	✓			
Chapter in book	✓	✓	✓	✓		✓	✓	✓	✓		
Journal article	✓	✓	✓	✓	✓				✓		
Internet	✓	✓	✓							✓	✓

Punctuation of citations and references

There is nothing more irritating to your tutor than to have to correct incorrectly punctuated citations and references. It is imperative that you are meticulous in this to maintain your academic integrity. It is also important to ensure that you do not lose vital marks because of silly errors, omissions and lack of proofreading. The examples above provide you with the correct punctuation so it is worth spending a bit of time looking carefully at these and using them as templates for your own work.

In-text citations

Short quotations – single words or short phrases – are included in the body of your text and brought to the reader's attention by single inverted commas. For example,

> Price (2006, p. 21) intimated that a person's capacity, the 'cognitive resources' are significant.

Longer quotations are best delineated from your text by placing them in a separate, indented paragraph. The reader is alerted to the fact that you are going to use someone else's words by a colon. For example:

> The centrality of using language in particular ways in subject disciplines is at the heart of the sociolinguistic theory relating to discourse:
>
> > The student who is asked to write like a sociologist must find a way to insert himself into a discourse defined by this complex and diffuse conjunction of objects, methods, rules definitions, techniques and tools … In addition he must be in control of specific field conventions, a set of rules and methods which marks the discourse as belonging to a certain discipline.
>
> Ball *et al*. (1990, p. 357)

Note that the quotation was taken from a book by Ball *et al*. '*Et al*.' is Latin for 'and all of the rest'. This is a shorthand method of referring to a number of different authors. Note also the punctuation of this.

If you have paraphrased information and ideas which are related to your reading of a specific author, you can strengthen your statement by letting your tutor see that you have read a relevant text. It is important to note where this is located in your text in order to avoid confusion. For example:

> Expert writers need to be able to multi-task when they are drafting their ideas (Price, 2006). They have to draw upon …

Notice that the full stop does not come until after the brackets, thus indicating to which sentence the reference is related.

> **Hot Tip**
>
> Make sure that the minute you put a citation in your own writing, you also take time to put it into your reference list or bibliography.

6 Frequently asked questions

Do I have to name every author or just the first one in my work?

It depends upon the location. In-text citations require the first author only followed by '*et al.*' if there are more than two authors (see example above). If there are only two authors, it is usual to name both in your text. For example, Smith and Jones (2006) state ...

How do I cite and make reference to something which is referred to in a book or chapter which I have read?

These are called **secondary sources**, and the rules for dealing with these are slightly different. The important thing to remember is that you are showing, by your citations and references, which sources you have actually used. If a secondary source is not properly identified it will be taken that you have read the original text or research – which clearly you have not. This would be less than honest.

In-text citation:

According to a study by Smith (2001, cited in Jones, 2005).

When you transfer this into your reference list or bibliography, you can only include the Jones (2005) reference because this is the only one which you have actually read. You have not read Smith's original research but rather Jones's interpretation of it. Thus, Smith is a secondary source.

Do I have to keep repeating a citation from the same book?

If you have used the same reference on a number of consecutive occasions in your text then a way round this would be to use the Latin term **Ibid.**, which means 'from the same place'. However, it is often not used with the Harvard system.

What if I want to refer to a number of books by one author?

One method of getting around this with your in-text citation is to use the Latin term **Op. cit.**, which literally means 'in the work cited'. It is often used to refer to the work of the same author which you have last cited. However, it is often not used with the Harvard system.

7 Bibliographic reference management

Remember that your bibliography should include all the resources you have used to complete your assignment. This means both resources you have referred to in the text of your document and relevant background materials that you have used, but not necessarily discussed. It is essential that you keep meticulous records. A little time spent recording the details of a book, a chapter, an article or an electronic reference will be time well spent.

What advice would I give to future students? It's simple. Keep a record of everything you read in the proper format so that you can use it for your written work. I know my tutors kept impressing on us the need to do this but you know how it is. I was in a rush, didn't think I had time to get out my list and update it. I was convinced that I would remember the reference anyway. So what happened? Yes, when it came to using the reference for my essay I didn't have the correct information. I could not believe how much time it took me to find that one single reference.

Natasha, third-year Fine Arts student

Natasha's advice is so important if you want to become an efficient student and prevent the disproportional amount of time it takes searching for vital references.

There are different ways of recording your information and much depends upon what you prefer. However, if you are doing a lengthy project which will depend upon a lot of references, it is often well worth spending time learning how to manage software which is dedicated to this purpose, such as EndNote or Reference Manager. While, such programs can be used in a simple way, they, nevertheless, take time to master. If your third-year project starts in the summer term of your penultimate year, it is worth setting aside the Easter vacation to get to grips with the software. It will save you much time and stress later on.

Whatever system you use, it is imperative that you record all the details, accurately following the system used by your department. Check with your tutor or the course handbook if there is a preferred style and look carefully at the rules which govern this system.

Low-tech management

You can use either a handwritten list or separate card index system. The handwritten list has the advantage of being accessible at all times if you carry this paper around with you. However, the disadvantages are that the lists are not automatically put into alphabetical order and, secondly, you will have to enter the separate items into a text document eventually.

Writing out separate index cards is another option. The key to success of this system is that each reference is written on a separate index card. There is usually sufficient space to jot down page references and useful quotations. However, you can also add your own notes to bibliographic software. The advantage this system has over the handwritten list is that you can shuffle them around into alphabetical order manually before you enter the separate items into a text document.

Dedicated bibliographic software systems

If you are using or would like to use a bibliographic database like EndNote (see below or refer to the user guide) or Reference Manager, then this is an ideal way for you to keep track of your notes and references. Although it does not always appeal to those who are not comfortable with computers, it is nevertheless a time-saving method, once you have mastered some of the basics. The advantage of this type of system is that the computer will sort out your lists into alphabetical order, you can cite-while-you-write by clicking a reference in your list and the citation is automatically in the text and in a list at the end of your work. In addition, you can also add notes to each entry – quite lengthy notes as well as key words. This enables you to do a search on your notes as well as the author later.

Finally, for these or more extended projects, you can link to remote databases (through your institution) and download key references and abstracts.

Disabled Students' Allowance

Remember: if you are eligible for this allowance, ask for EndNote or Reference Manager software to be purchased for your sole use. This means that it will be installed on your machine and you will be entitled to individual software training.

> **Hot Tip** **Tips for management**
>
> - Put everything you read for a topic into your database, or bibliographic software.
>
> - Key-word the items in your database so you can find a group of references on a related topic you are working on.
>
> - Store the hard copies (if photocopies or paper articles) in alphabetical order, but always make a note in your database if you have a hard copy and where it is.
>
> - Finally, if you make notes on something you've read, also record where your notes are on your database entry too.

What will electronic bibliographic managers do for me?

The specific program that you choose will depend upon:

- the preferred system used by your department – for example, many medical departments use Reference Manager
- personal preferences
- the system to which your university or college has subscribed – many institutions now provide a cut-down version of EndNote for undergraduates which is found on the network system at workstations around your university. It is worth looking into this before you rush out and purchase the costly full program out of your own money.

This sort of software is very powerful and can save much time, providing that you have set it up for your personal use. Many students (and tutors) do not use the full potential of these programs but rather are content to select the features of most use to them.

Common features of electronic bibliographic managers

Electronic bibliographic managers allow you to do the following tasks:

- Create a separate reference 'library' for each of your assignments.
- Add information for each entry – this can be personalised to include key words (for later grouping of references) and a set of notes.
- Choose the referencing style you need to use (most software provides extensive lists from which to choose).
- See an example of what each item in the list will look like at the end of your writing.
- Sort the items in your 'library'. There are many options available for sorting your data so that you can extract the specific items for any written assignment.
- Search for authors or key words (if you have meticulously put these in).

- Automatically create term lists from the author, journal title and key word fields.
- Create term lists – these are particularly useful if you regularly consult specific journals, and to ensure that key words are being used consistently as an additional research tool.
- Use the system with Microsoft Word so that you can select a reference from your database and cite-while-you-write. This means that the referencing and cross-referencing are carried out by the software, and it can save you time.
- Sort your selected bibliography into alphabetical order at the touch of a key.
- Import references from remote databases for more research-oriented projects.

These are just some of the basic tools available in these systems. However, like all technology, you must set aside time to become familiar with its workings and use it frequently so that you do not forget the procedures for carrying out specific operations.

Hot Tip

A comprehensive and accessible booklet on the subject of citing and referencing is *Cite Them Right* by Pears and Shields (2005). It is inexpensive and provides a wealth of examples of different types of references which might be applicable to your subject.

---

8 On reflection

Being aware of the pitfalls and the regulations for referencing your written work will ensure that you are less likely to be guilty of plagiarism. An awareness and understanding of the principles which are behind the regulations is essential. With this knowledge you can begin to appreciate why your tutors are so particular about your referencing.

The essence of this is to organise and manage your time and efforts effectively. Getting into good routines early on in your studies will reap rich rewards and higher grades.

Summary of this chapter

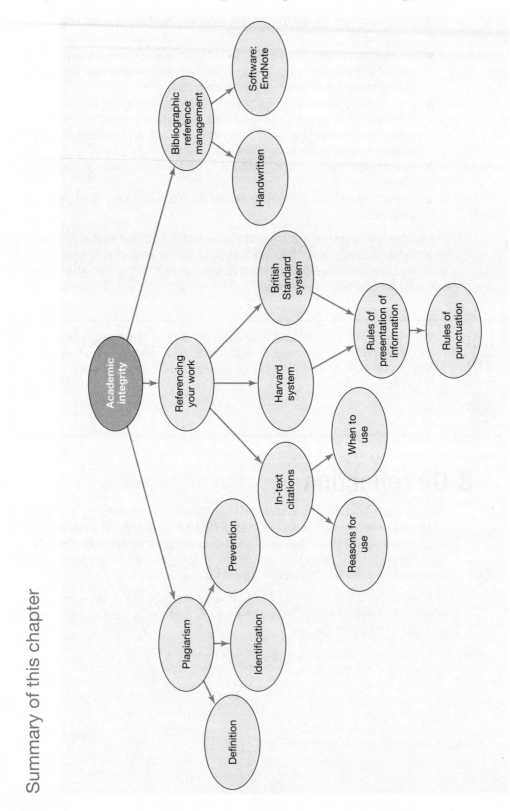

ACTIVITY 4 Update your personal development planner

Having read this chapter, you can see that organisation and management play key roles in the way you reference your written work. Knowing the rules for in-text citations and compiling accurate bibliographic data will ensure that you do not plagiarise work.

Grade your confidence on a scale of 1–5 where 1 = poor and 5 = good.

My developing skills	Confidence level 1–5	Plans to improve
I know the variety of ways in which plagiarism can take place.		
I know the difference between presentation of in-text citations and references at the end of my written work.		
I know the difference between a bibliography and a reference list.		
I know the rules for presenting different types of references.		
I am able to manage the collection of references in a systematic manner.		

Getting extra help

- Go to the Students Union to find out where to go for skill development. Many universities and colleges have tutors who provide this service.
- Closely examine your department's guidelines to make sure that you are aware of their rules and regulations.

Consult the following:

Pears, R. and Shields, G. (2005) *Cite Them Right: Referencing Made Easy*, 2nd edn. Newcastle, Pear Tree Books.

Feedback on activities

ACTIVITY 1 What constitutes plagiarism?

Look at these statements and answer 'yes', 'no' or 'possibly'.

Which of the following are considered plagiarism?	Yes/no/possibly
I wrote the words from my textbook in my essay.	Yes
I used inverted commas around the words I took from a text I was reading.	Possibly
I used different phrases from different sources and put them into a sentence in my essay.	Yes
I used information from an Internet page which did not have a title or author so it is not plagiarising.	Yes

'I wrote the words from my textbook in my essay.'

If you wrote the words of others and do not acknowledge that you have used the words of others, this is considered plagiarism.

'I used inverted commas around the words I took from a text I was reading.'

Just because you have put inverted commas around the quoted words, does not mean that you have not plagiarised work. If you have not stated your source as well, this is considered plagiarism.

'I used different phrases from different sources and put them into a sentence in my essay.'

Patching together lots of phrases from different authors and sources without showing the reader that it is not your own words still constitutes plagiarism. Just because you have put the words into your own sentence does not exempt you.

'I used information from an Internet page which did not have a title or author so it is not plagiarising.'

Many students think that because there is no obvious author or title to the work that they can use such Internet information freely. This is not the case. You are still expected to indicate where you got the information.

ACTIVITY 2 Problems and solutions to plagiarism

Do these statements apply to you?	Yes or no	Solutions
I can't possibly write this better than the author.		A. Read what the author has said. B. Cover up the text. C. List the key words/ideas in your own words. D. Try to explain it simply in your own words.
When I look at the notes I've made on the texts I've read, I can't remember which are my words and which are ones from the author's text.		There are two solutions to this: 1. Colour code your notes so that you can immediately 'see' which are the notes written in your own words. 2. Improve your summary skills by following A–D above.
I can't remember where I got the information to make my notes so I can't check whether the notes are in my own words or not.		The solution to this problem is to adopt a more organised routine to recording your notes. You need to record not just the 'what' but the 'where' – using cards/software/electronic lists will help. (See Section 4, 'Referencing your work' in this chapter.)
My sentences and paragraphs are like a patchwork quilt. That's how I write up my information.		First, develop your reading skills in getting the global picture. Second, become a more critical and active reader of information.
I think I can avoid plagiarism just by listing every single source in the bibliography at the end.		You need to incorporate your acknowledgements into what you are saying to avoid plagiarism. (Go to Section 4, 'Referencing your work', for examples of how this is done effectively.

ACTIVITY 3 Can you spot which texts contain plagiarism?

Read the original text and the following samples and identify which are cases of plagiarism.

Original text

The cognitive resources used in the writing process are considerable, and memory capacity and storage are often overloaded by competing, simultaneous operations. The ability to synthesise information is one of the essential skills required by HE students. Price (2006).

Version A

The cognitive resources used in the writing process are great and memory capacity and storage are often overloaded by many mental, simultaneous operations.

Comment: This is clearly plagiarism. Even though there has been some attempt to substitute some words, the original author's sentence structure is intact and no acknowledgement has been given.

Version B

In Higher Education, the cognitive resources used in the writing process are often overloaded by competing, simultaneous operations. One of the essential skills needed is to synthesise information.

Comment: This is still plagiarism. Although the writer has moved the sentences around a little, it is too close to the original and this version does not acknowledge the source. In addition, this version does not use inverted commas to identify the original text, e.g. 'cognitive resources used in the writing process', 'overloaded by competing, simultaneous operations' and 'to synthesise information'.

Version C

As Price (2006) indicates in her research, writing is complex and draws upon many of the mind's resources. One of the difficulties is that at times the writer runs out of memory space because of the need to do many tasks at the same time.

Comment: There is no plagiarism with this version. This version clearly indicates the source and appropriate paraphrasing of the original has taken place.

References

- Ball, C., Dice, L. and Bartholomae, D. (1990) 'Developing discourse practices in adolescence and adulthood', in Beach, R. and Hyndes, S. (eds), *Advances in Discourse Processes*. Norwood, NJ, Ablex.
- Curtis, P. (2004) *Guardian*, 30 June.
- Hammett, A. (2006) *Guardian*, 17 October.
- Pears, R. and Shields, G. (2005) *Cite Them Right: Referencing Made Easy*, 2nd edn. Newcastle, Pear Tree Books.
- Price, G. A. (2006) 'Creative solutions to making technology work: three case studies of dyslexic writers in High Education', *ALT-J Research in Learning Technology*, 14(1), 21–8.
- University of Southampton (2006) *QA Handbook: Guidance for Schools. Section 1V: Encouraging Academic Integrity – Procedures for Handling Possible Breaches of Academic Integrity*. Southampton, University of Southampton.

14 Improving your technical writing

If you read a book on how to ride a bike, you would have theoretical knowledge of bicycle riding but still not be able to ride. You have to get on and fall off that bike in order to learn. Reading about writing, actually doing it, and getting it in an acceptable form are similar. The bicycle and writing examples are both a set of skills, which cannot develop without practice. You may be someone who has managed to avoid doing too much writing in your earlier education, or you have found that your writing is OK. Whichever way, learning about writing, actually writing and getting feedback on your writing, is very emotive. Very often students get annoyed when they have sessions on writing because they either feel they are already acceptable writers or that it was something for primary school. Both reasons for shying away from improving your writing are wrong. Once you reach higher education, your writing skills need to step up to the mark and become more professional. This marks you out as a graduate.

In this chapter you will:

1. recognise how you use feedback
2. understand how to write critically
3. understand the mechanics of coherent writing

USING THIS CHAPTER

Estimate your current levels of confidence. At the end of the chapter you will have the chance to reassess these levels where you can incorporate this into your personal development planner (PDP). Mark between 1 (poor) and 5 (good) for the following:

I know the kind of feedback I want and what to do with it.	I understand the importance of critical evaluation in writing.	I know how to develop my ideas coherently.

Date: _____

1 Understanding your tutors' feedback

Feedback from your tutors or fellow students will enable you to improve. However, very often students are simply keen to get the mark and move on. Other students on the other hand feel that they are not getting enough feedback and feel 'let down' when they don't get it. Neither group is working optimally. You should be given sufficient (not copious) feedback to give you some headlines on how to move your work forward. It is then up to you to make the most of it and identify how these comments can be taken forward into your next piece of work. However, it may take you a while before you start to see an error pattern in your work that can be improved.

Working with feedback

Giving and receiving feedback is not as easy as it sounds. When giving feedback, let's say to your friend, you need to be careful that it is given at the right time and delivered in a positive manner. Receiving feedback can also be quite difficult. It is important to look at or listen to the feedback objectively (easier said than done) and not be defensive about it. If you want to be proactive in getting the feedback you want, you could ask your tutor for particular feedback when you hand your work in. That way, it will address your needs specifically.

ACTIVITY 1 How do you deal with feedback?

Are you satisfied with the grades you are getting for your assignments? Do you think you could do better? When you get your grade or mark you may want to ask yourself a few questions; circle 'yes' or 'no'.

1. Did you do as well as you expected?
   Yes – can you explain why?
   No – where do you think it went wrong?

2. Do you feel your mark was correct?
   Yes – can you explain why?
   No – where do you think it went wrong?

3. Did you get the kind of feedback you wanted?
   Yes – can you explain why it was good?
   No – what kind of feedback did you want?

4. Can you read your tutor's comments?
   Yes?
   No – go and see him or her.

5. Can you understand the comments from your tutor?
   Yes?
   No – go and see him/her.

6. What have you learnt from this work in terms of: content, structuring your work, writing, time management?

7. I'm only interested in the mark I get.

ACTIVITY 2 Understanding your grade

Do you understand what your tutors mean when they comment on, for example; 'lack of coherence', 'weak structure' or 'didn't answer the question'? Have any of the following statements applied to you? What do you need to do to improve?

Some typical comments from tutors	Applies to me (yes/no)?
1. You haven't answered the question.	
2. You haven't given evidence in the essay/report of having met the objectives.	
3. Your work is too descriptive – you need to evaluate more.	
4. Your work lacks analysis.	
5. You have just listed ideas in paragraphs, but you have failed to integrate what you have read.	
6. The structure of your work is unclear and not well organised.	

Some typical comments from tutors	Applies to me (yes/no)?
7. You don't seem to understand the purpose of a paragraph and you have too many single sentence paragraphs, which read like a disconnected list of things.	
8. Your sentences can be difficult to understand as you tend to link lots of ideas into one sentence.	
9. Your tables and figures have not been numbered or labelled, which makes it difficult to integrate them in your work.	
10. You've got tables and figures in your work that you do not refer to; I'm not sure why they are there.	
11. You've got a lot of spelling errors and typos; it doesn't look like you've checked your work before handing it in.	
12. You have developed a clear and sound argument.	
13. You have provided supporting evidence for arguments made.	
14. You have selected appropriate information, theories and issues.	
15. You have shown evidence of understanding the subject by synthesising (pulling together) other people's ideas and views.	
16. You have used referencing systems with accuracy.	

See the feedback section for further guidance.

Hot Tip

If you are not getting feedback, then make sure you ask for it. If you are only interested in your mark and not the feedback then it will be difficult for you to improve your work.

Writing critically

In your early years at university, you will probably be writing in a very descriptive way. Such essays or pieces of writing tend to be more reporting on things you've read or done without attempting to interpret and critically evaluate them. In your early years you may find your tutors make no or little comment about this. However, as you move through the years, you will find that your tutors' comments change and you will start to see: 'this is just a list of things you've read', 'where is the analysis of the subject?', 'you haven't looked at the topic critically'. All of these comments should tell you that you need to rethink how you deal with the material you are writing.

Critical writing involves critical thinking, which is the synthesis, evaluation, analysis and reflection of what you've read. It becomes your analysis, based on the evidence you've read, and through it you develop your own analytical skills. This is the essence of academic writing.

When you read a text think about how the author:

- Used arguments to state a point. (Do you think the arguments are valid or flawed?)
- Supplied evidence to support those arguments. (Was the evidenced used sound?)
- Interpreted that evidence. (Is the author making links that are not justified by the evidence? Evidence can be from, for example, laboratory data, case studies, fieldwork.)

You need to show in your writing that you can take part in academic debates. You will be judged on:

- how you state your argument/evidence/information
- how you back up your argument/evidence/information
- how you analyse the issues
- how you evaluate all the evidence, both supporting and opposing your claims.

This will mean that you need to read good sources of information and interact with the text while you are reading. You need to question things as you read them, make notes in the margin, highlight key points and how they are evidenced. You also need to keep track of your own thoughts while reading, so make notes in the margin as you go through.

NOTE One of the problems using Wikipedia as your main source of reading is that you cannot guarantee that the statements made have been verified or supported by others. It is not a sound source of evidence for your arguments. Use Wikipedia to get a feel for an area and then go to more academic sources that will be on your reading list.

Being able to think, read and write critically means developing your reasoning powers. Some areas of reasoning that you might use for this are:

Ways of reasoning	Why do this?
Compare and contrast	Identify an issue or topic that you want to compare. This enables you to see the different opinions or positions on a topic. Decide how you will make comparisons between them.
Check for errors	You do this to see if there are any flaws in the logic of the argument, the tests used to substantiate a claim or simple maths. You decide what to check for.
Classify	Identify an issue you want to work on and group ideas and issues together to see what is common between them. You are basically looking for patterns.
Analyse logically	Check that an author's reasoning for a particular opinion/issue does not have logical flaws or compares/contrasts with others. Identify any logical inconsistencies.

You will not want to evaluate critically a document on all of these aspects. Choose what is best for your assignment.

This is the most intellectually challenging part of your studies. Being able to think, read and write critically will take time and this is something you have to work at. So, don't feel despondent in your early years if this is not happening, but it is exactly this skill that will mark you out as a true graduate.

Hot Tip

It is important that your main argument/hypothesis or idea is clearly set out at the beginning (see Chapter 15, Section 2). This is the point from which you develop your supporting arguments, and you will gain marks for substantiating your argument by using various sources.

2 The mechanics of writing – paragraph development

As you probably realise, writing is a complex activity and a simple search on the Web, using the search strings, for example, 'online writing laboratory' (known as OWLs), 'technical writing' or 'scientific writing' will provide you with a mountain of sites to go through. The topic is huge and there is a lot to say about it. This is because it is a complex cognitive activity and writing is an interplay between many systems. These include the systems for grammar (sentence level), document structures (known as text grammar), style (writing in the correct style for a given audience, known as genre) and finally making sure that the whole document hangs together and tells 'a story' (its coherence). Figure 14.1 gives you a visual representation of this. In this section we shall look at how we can improve our writing in these areas.

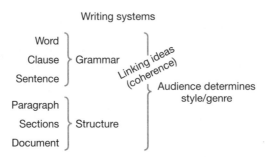

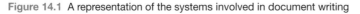

Figure 14.1 A representation of the systems involved in document writing

Characteristics of technical writing

If you were writing a novel or marketing literature, your style would be quite different from a technical report. A novel is designed to keep us, the readers, in suspense and surprise us. Marketing literature is there to convince and influence us to buy. In each style, or genre, you use a different set of vocabulary; you express yourself differently and present material in a different way.

Understanding the genre of academic writing is therefore very important as your tutors will have their 'pet hates' with regard to student mistakes. The tutor rage-O-meter below will give you some idea of the general feeling towards not writing correctly in certain areas.

A mark of a good technical writer lies in being able to be: objective, precise, critical and clear.

Be objective: get this wrong, rage-O-meter = 8

Academic, technical or scientific writing that is not objective is not deemed fit for purpose. It has been given an 8 because your tutor will expect you to develop this. If you are in later years, this will rise to a 10!

It is essential that you present your argument in a balanced way and take care not to write your opinions as though they were facts. You avoid words like: *obviously*, *surely* and *of course*. You critically reflect on the work of others, report the findings and then interpret the evidence (see 'writing critically' in Section 1 above). Similarly, when you present your own data and talk about your own work, you maintain a distance and simply present your own findings and your analysis.

Most technical writing uses the passive construction as this concentrates on what has been done rather than on who did it and grammatically gives an objective feel.

what was done   and not   *who did it*

↓   ↓

PASSIVE   ACTIVE

NOTE There are many websites that offer good guidance on all aspects of grammar. If you are uncertain about using the passive, then find a suitable site that can help you.

The passive is used extensively in the method section of a report where you state what you did (or what was done), and since you carried out your procedure in the past, you will use the **past passive tense**.

Active	Passive
From the moisture content, *I calculated* the void ratio, the specific volume and the unit weight of the sample at the end of the test. *I assumed* that the sample was fully saturated before doing this.	From the moisture content, the void ratio, the specific volume and the unit weight of the sample *were calculated* at the end of the test. It *was assumed* that the sample was fully saturated before doing this.

NOTE   Your lab notebooks and professional diaries will not need the passive. There is also a move to encourage simplicity by writing in the *active* form only. Some websites will say that it is bad practice to write in the passive. However, in the academic world, the passive is still used. It is wise to check with your tutors to find out what they expect of you.

Be precise: get this wrong, rage-O-meter = 7–8

Vague writing, as with not being objective, is a poor marker for scientific or academic writing. Your tutor should be picking up any sloppy habits in this area. Again, in the early years you may find your tutor is less strict, but you should be aware of this as you will eventually lose marks if you don't tighten up your work.

Your sentences are precise and not woolly and you don't make general sweeping statements without evidence. One common error in this area is forgetting to state the units of your data. The units may seem obvious to you, but it is not precise writing if you don't include them. You also avoid making vague statements that could be misinterpreted.

ACTIVITY 3 Focus on precision

The following sentences are examples of vague writing around the use of frequency and quantity. How would you make them more precise?

- The measurements were recorded at frequent intervals.
- The apparatus was stable, so it was rarely checked.
- A substantial amount of reagent was applied.
- An appropriate amount of sulphur was added.

See the feedback section.

Now take another look at some of your work. Do you think there is room for improvement with regard to precision writing?

Be critical: get this wrong, rage-O-meter = 3–10

Your tutor rage-O-meter will depend on your year of study. It can be as low as 3 in your very early years and as high as 10 in your third and fourth years. This is a major error if you are a postgraduate student.

You are able to be dispassionate and evaluate your own work (and that of others). You can weigh up the evidence, and offer an interpretation (see 'writing critically' in Section 1 above).

Be clear: get this wrong, rage-O-meter = 5

There is a fairly wide tolerance range with tutors regarding clarity, as they will always try to make the best out of what they read. We all do this as readers. If you want to gain good marks you need to demonstrate clear and logical thought and that will be through clear writing.

You write clear sentences that are put together logically, showing evidence of clear scientific thinking. Your ability to write clearly is essential in gaining good marks. It displays the clear, dispassionate and logical thinking that your tutors are looking for. Make sure you plan what you want to say early on (see Chapter 15, Section 1) and don't just write as you think about it. If you do that, it is obvious and can appear very muddled. The remaining sections in this chapter will help you develop this clarity.

Structures

Documents you write, whether they are essays, reports or small laboratory write-ups, will all have their own structure (see Chapter 15, Section 2, for the technical report). In this section we shall look at the basic structure of the paragraph and the essay.

If you get your essay structure wrong, you could be looking at a rage-O-meter rating of between 4 and 8 which will depend on your year of study. However, you will be expected to arrive at university being able to write a coherent essay and understand how essays are structured. If your work is very badly structured, you will get a comment from your tutor about the lack of structure, so take note of it. If you are in doubt, look at the section below.

The basic essay structure

The basic framework of any essay is its paragraphs. Grouped sentences (paragraphs) provide a mechanism for communicating your thoughts and ideas in a logical and structured manner. These paragraphs should be linked coherently so that the document you write hangs together and develops a thread of ideas or line of argument. A group of paragraphs forms a section of an essay.

Novice writers often ask how many paragraphs/sections an essay should contain, but this depends on what you have to write and any word limits imposed by your tutors. However, as a general guideline the five-section model is often used (Figure 14.2).

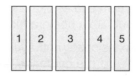

Figure 14.2 Standard five-section essay model

This is a schematic representation of the essay and you will find that the five sections can stretch across many paragraphs. Sections 1 and 5, where there is an introduction and conclusion, tend to be smaller than the main body sections 2, 3 and 4 where most of your argument lies.

Section 1 will constitute the **introduction** and will contain the following:

- A motivating statement – this is *optional*. You may find you add this statement after you have found an interesting fact or position that sums up what you want to talk about. It could be a provocative question. Whatever it is, its role is used to catch the readers' attention.
- A thesis statement – this is *essential*. The topic statement is a clearly focused statement as a result of your research and analysis for the essay. It makes a clear statement about what the essay will cover and the structure it will take (see Chapter 15, Section 2).

The role of the introduction is to lead the reader to the ideas which will be discussed and elaborated on in subsequent paragraphs. It is the place where you can set out your stall and identify areas or topics which will be written about and explained in detail later.

Sections 2, 3 and 4 will constitute the body of your essay:

- Section 2 will be your first topic for discussion. You may have indicated in your introductory paragraphs the topics you will be discussing, so the reader will be prepared for this. It is important to make sure that the order of your topics, as set out in the introduction, is followed. You have told the reader to expect them in a specific order so keep to that sequence in following paragraphs.

Section 5 is your **conclusion** and will sum up key factors of the topics discussed and relate back to issues in your introduction. Never introduce new topics in this section.

This five-section structure is simply a model for the role of paragraphs/sections in an essay.

The paragraph structure

Students very often have difficulty understanding what a paragraph does, or how long it should be. Paragraphs are groups of sentences that express an idea.

You link paragraphs together in order to develop your ideas and your argument. As readers we use the paragraph as a guide to how the ideas are grouped and it gives us the flow of an argument as those ideas are developed (see 'Linking ideas' below). The paragraph itself has a structure: a beginning, a middle and an end. The first two sentences in a paragraph set up reader expectations as to what that paragraph will be about. You unconsciously know this when you read and it is a matter of being aware of it so you can make it part of your writing as well.

The first sentence (or two) in a paragraph lets you know what it is about, the next sentences develop the argument and the final sentence(s) leads on to another idea (or further develops the current idea), which then needs a new paragraph. You can use this knowledge to skim-read a document and get the gist before reading it in detail.

Linking ideas – writing coherently

Writing is all about making links – linking small pieces of information, bit by bit, in a linear way. If you don't get this right, your ideas won't hang together and your writing won't be coherent.

If your ideas don't hang together, it is hard for your tutor to estimate how much you know and how logical and scientific your thought processes are. Since your tutor will be a scientist, in the general sense of the term, it could be enough to tip the rage-O-meter to 8, regardless of what year you are in.

If you aren't linking your ideas properly, your tutor will comment that a piece of work is not coherent or that it doesn't make sense, but rarely tell you *how* to make it coherent. In this section we shall look at the mechanics of coherent writing, and it will need some concentration on your part, but once you have understood this, you should be able to improve your writing dramatically.

You can make your writing coherent by working *within* sentences (linking clauses) and *across* sentences (linking paragraphs).

Linking *within* sentences – working with clauses

Just as documents are made up of paragraphs, sentences are made up of clauses. A simple sentence has one clause: that is, a subject, a verb and some information about the subject. When you want to write about a more complex idea, you can join simple sentences using words like *and*, *or* and *yet*. This would give you a sentence with two independent clauses. For example:

The detailed data from this study indicate that students with a vocational school background used on average more time for their studies and achieved their target grades better than those with an upper secondary school background.

(Kolari *et al*., 2008).

See also examples 1 and 2 below.

You can also add clauses that are dependent on that simple sentence, using words like *if*, *although*, *whereas* and *since*, and if you do that, you have then added a dependent clause. All sentences have to have at least an independent clause, while compound sentences have a series of clauses that have a relationship to that independent clause. For example:

Second year Civil Engineering students on a health and safety course felt that advice given by their team-mates was better than that from post graduate students teaching them, even though they would expect them to be more knowledgeable than year two students.

(Petersen *et al*., 2008)

See also example 3 below.

In the sentence above 'even though' triggers the independent clause and once that is written it has to be either preceded or followed by a dependent clause in order to make a complete sentence.

Compound sentences will:

- link ideas of equal importance (coordinate clauses)
- link additional information to the main idea (add dependent clause(s) to add information)
- show a relationship between the main idea and other ideas (using, for example, which, that, who, whose).

Each of these links has trigger words that show how the clauses are linked. Let's look at some examples:

Example 1. A simple sentence (a single clause)
(a) *Volumetric analysis is a quantitative technique.*

Example 2. A compound sentence (two clauses)
Volumetric analysis is a quantitative technique and used to determine the concentration of a solution.

Notice that the two clauses could stand alone as two separate sentences; the second sentence being *it is used to determine the concentration of a solution*. These clauses are joined with the coordinating conjunction 'and'. (See the following table.)

Example 3. A compound sentence (two clauses)
(a) *European countries have their own standards for the remediation of brown field sites although there is a need for a unified Europe-wide set of standards.*

Notice that the second clause starting with 'although' could not stand alone because the 'although' triggers that it belongs to an independent clause. Words that trigger joining like this are called subordinating conjunctions. (See the following table).

(b) *Since bonds between specific atoms have particular vibration frequencies, IR spectroscopy provides a means of identifying the type of bonds in a molecule.*

Notice that the dependent clause is at the front of the sentence and triggered by the subordinating conjunction, 'since'. The independent clause begins with *IR spectroscopy provides*. Also note that if you start with a dependent clause you need a comma before the independent clause. You can also reverse the order of these clauses.

Example 4. Another compound sentence (two clauses)
(a) *The volume of standard solution that reacts with the substance in the test solution is accurately measured.*

Notice that the word 'that' refers back to 'the volume of standard solution'. It also triggers a clause that has pushed into the middle of the independent clause, *The volume of standard solution is accurately measured.*

The following table lists trigger words that show how clauses are linked together to form sentences.

Coordinating words	Subordinating words	Relative words	Function
and			Adds additional information or something similar.
but, yet	although even though unless		Shows a contrasting idea.
or, nor	while		Shows something different, an alternative.
for, so	if since because		Shows a cause and/or effect.
	since while when as after		Shows a time relationship.

Coordinating words	Subordinating words	Relative words	Function
□	△	○	
		who	Refers back to a person. For example: *Some researchers were already discussing the idea that time could be a fourth dimension, but it was Einstein who discovered it.*
		which, that	Refers back to a thing or the whole of the previous clause. For example, in this case 'the submitted paper': *He submitted a paper which contained the correct field equations for gravitation.*
		whose	Shows possession. For example: *Galton, whose work on heredity was based on novel statistical techniques, is seen as one of the first social scientists.* Main clause interrupted by relative clause. Main clause is: *Galton is seen as one of the first social scientists.*
		where	Refers back to a place. For example: *Niels Bohr studied at Copenhagen University, where, under the guidance of his professor, he gained his doctorate in 1909.*
		when	Refers to and expands on a time. For example: *The liquid droplet theory enabled the understanding of nuclear fission, when the splitting of uranium was discovered in 1939.*

Since some of you are visual learners, you may benefit from looking at this diagrammatically, and using symbols to illustrate the different trigger words that link clauses (See the next table below.)

Key	
————	An independent clause that stands alone as a sentence. For example: *Most networks are organised as a series of layers.*
☐	This is a word that joins independent clauses and allows you to add similar or show contrasting information. For example: *Most networks are organised as a series of layers <u>and</u> each layer is built upon its predecessor.* ——☐—— Note: you can use a coordinating conjunction to join two dependent clauses as well.
▪-▪-▪-▪	A dependent clause. This means that it can't stand alone as a sentence. For example: *... <u>because</u> this helps to reduce the design complexity.*
△	This is a word that allows you to link a dependent clause to an independent clause. For example: *Most networks are organised as a series of layers <u>because</u> this helps to reduce the design complexity.* ——△-----
◯	Examples of these words are: who, whom, where, which, that. Like subordinated clauses, they cannot stand alone. For example: *Most networks are organised as a series of layers <u>which</u> are dependent on their predecessor.* ——◯---

All sentences must have at least a main, independent clause and you can build them up to be more complex. See if you can use this to build your own.

ACTIVITY 4 Linking <u>within</u> sentences – working with clauses

Using the key above, take the patterns of the sentences below and write your own sentence below. You may want to look at the feedback section first to get some ideas before you try your own.

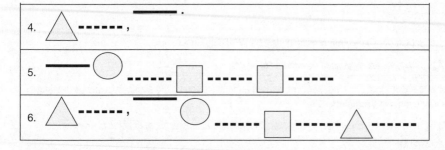

As you can see, the more clauses you link, the more difficult it can become to read. A classic error that many students make is around pattern 6 above. Students often start a sentence with a subordinator, e.g. *although*, and then start linking other ideas at that level and forget to finish the sentence off with an independent main clause. Remember that good technical writing is characterised by clarity, so don't make long compound sentences that are difficult to process.

Linking <u>across</u> sentences – working with paragraphs

In the previous section we looked at linking clauses together to form compound sentences that express an idea coherently. We now look at how to link across sentences in a coherent way to form a paragraph. It is useful to think of a sentence as having two packets of information, the **subject** (i.e. what/who it is about) and the **point** (i.e. what you are saying about the subject). The follow-on sentence can either tell you more about the subject or expand on the point you're making. Usually there is a mixture of both. You can imagine that if you continued to expand on the subject alone, your writing would appear to be a list of information, which would not attract a good mark. If you expanded on the 'point' then you could see how you to develop your argument. As usual, we need a mixture of techniques. For a visual representation see Figure 14.3.

Subject/what   Point/why

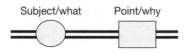

Figure 14.3 Sentence as a beam of information

Now let's look at a few examples.

Example Pattern 1

Pollution prevention and control is a regime for controlling pollution from certain industrial activities. The regime introduces the concept of Best Available Techniques (BAT) to environmental regulations.

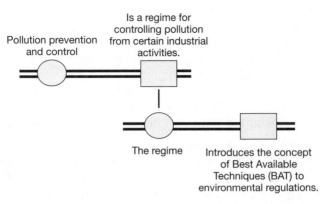

Figure 14.4 Linking sentences using a nesting pattern, i.e. expanding the 'point'

So, you take forward the 'point' of the sentence (Figure 14.4) into the subject of the next sentence. This allows you to develop a theme and you can see that it follows a 'nesting' pattern. As an experienced reader you can now anticipate what the next sentence could start with. As readers we could anticipate that the writer may go on to talk about BAT and further develop that. The writer may be able to discuss this all in one paragraph or spread it across various paragraphs if he or she wants to expand on it.

Example Pattern 2

The aim of BAT is to prevent and reduce pollution to air, land and water from industrial activities to an acceptable level. It also aims to balance the cost to the operator against benefits to the environment.

In this example the sentence development is through adding more information to the subject and it follows a 'listing' pattern (Figure 14.5).

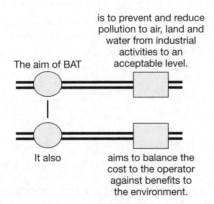

Figure 14.5 Linking sentences using a listing pattern, i.e. developing the 'subject'

These 'listing' and 'nesting' patterns of development are a fairly simple way that can help you write coherently once you have planned what you want to say. As you can see, you need a mixture of 'nesting' and 'listing' to take things forward. Some problems with students' writing are that they tend to write predominantly with a 'listing' pattern, and as you can imagine this then just sounds like a list of items that never develop. If you have a tendency to write many very short paragraphs you are probably just using the 'listing' pattern. Take a look at the text in Activity 6.

Each sentence sets up your expectations as a reader and you predict the direction the next sentence will go in. This is why we can read so efficiently. If it does not, you have a break in coherence and you often find yourself having to reread the previous sentence as you think you may have missed something. The reader can accommodate the occasional 'bad link', but if you do it consistently, then you can see how difficult it is for the reader, and in the case of your coursework, your tutor. Understanding how to 'list' and 'nest' paragraph development will enable you to write text that hangs together, is easy to read and has clarity.

ACTIVITY 5 What comes next?

Look at the following sentences and estimate what you think the writer will discuss next; you don't have to write the sentence, just give the gist of what could come next. As an experienced reader you should be able to do this without understanding the topic. The sentences below are all from different student writers.

1. Detecting and monitoring structural damage for aerospace, civil and any mechanical engineering structure is referred to as Structural Health Monitoring (SHM).

2. When it comes to damage detection several methods can be used to assess the amount of sustained damage.

3. With the development of material technology, it has been found that physical properties of some specially synthesized polymers can change when the external field changes. As a result of this 'smart' property, these materials have promising futures for practical applications in many fields.

See the feedback section.

ACTIVITY 6 Paragraph coherence

The following sentences are from a student essay on 'Nature of vegetation cover' and they make up one full paragraph. Take each sentence and analyse it as in the diagrammatic patterns 1 and 2 above. Also, give your comments on the coherence of the text from a reader's viewpoint. See the feedback section when you have finished.

Student text to analyse:

Vegetation acts as a protective barrier to the increased effects of the natural influences of erosion i.e. wind and rain. In decay, it also provides richness and protection in the form of a sticky substance (Humus) (Peak District National Park Authority 2008). A mosquito gauze raindrop experiment into the reduction of soil erosion by plant cover (Hudson & Jackson 1959; Zanchi 1983; in Morgan 1995), measuring two clay soil plots, one fully exposed, the other covered by a suspended fine wire gauze. Results from the gauzed plot showed a reduced velocity to raindrops hitting the ground by absorption of impact and allowing water to fall from a lower height as a fine spray. Vegetation intercepting raindrops at and close to the surface is thus considered a more efficient means to controlling soil erosion levels (Institute of Pedology 1987).

Now look back over this paragraph and, in a couple of key words, identify its message.

Using your own work, with a friend read the first two sentences of a paragraph and ask him or her to tell you what (a) the paragraph is about, and (b) what he or she thinks your next sentence will be. Then reveal what you have written and ask if it is OK. This way you can detect how well you structure a paragraph and how well your sentences can list and nest information.

Diagrams, equations and lists

In addition to text, your technical writing will include diagrams, equations and a list of things you may need to put as a bulleted list.

Working with diagrams

Diagrams represent your ideas visually and if you have a complicated system or process, it is very often better for you and the reader to see it visually. The visuals in this book have similarly been used to display information in a shorthand way which gives you an overview at a glance (Figure 14.6).

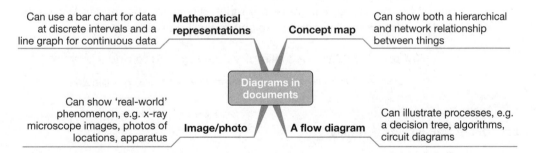

Figure 14.6 Thinking about diagrams in your document

Whenever you have diagrams in your text you must ensure:

- The diagram has a title, a key to explain the symbols, a suitable size for your page and is readable and has a number.
- The graphs must have a title, a key (legend) clarifying the data and labelled axes, and a number so you can refer to it in the text.
- The diagrams are referred to and discussed in the text.
- Your diagrams are correctly referenced, if you take them from a website or a book.

Working with equations

You can create equations using Microsoft Equation Editor, although for more complex equations this may not be sufficient. If you are writing a lot of equations, your institution may suggest you use LaTeX. As with diagrams, ensure your equations are numbered and symbols used explained (where necessary). If you are writing a sequence of equations to support your argument, then number the equations in your sequence so that you can refer to any part of that sequence in your subsequent text.

Working with lists

There will be times when you find yourself writing a list of things and you may not know if you are allowed to write bulleted lists in your document. If you feel uncertain, always check with your tutor.

Lists in a text can be difficult to manage if they are too long. Lists of about three or four items quite easily sit within a sentence. When you are making a list in a sentence you can also use a colon (:) before the list, commas between items and 'and' or 'or' before the final item. In addition, remember to make sure you write parallel structures when producing lists so that the reader can scan it better.

Writing lists

When you write lists, the grammatical construction between the items should be the same. This makes it much easier for the reader. When you read the 'not parallel' examples below, you will probably agree:

> *Not parallel:* Mary likes hik*ing*, swimm*ing*, and *to ride* a bicycle.

> *Parallel:* Mary likes hik*ing*, swimm*ing*, and rid*ing* a bicycle.

ACTIVITY 7 Writing lists that flow

1. **Not parallel**: The manager was asked to write his report quick*ly*, accurate*ly*, and *in a detailed manner*.

2. **Not parallel**: The lecturer said that she was a poor student because she wait*ed* until the last minute before studying for the exam, complet*ed* her lab problems in a careless manner, and *her motivation was* low.

3. Not parallel: The agency lists several areas for sustainable development: tighter licensing laws for abstraction, greater links between suppliers, infrastructure improvements and reducing 'lost water' through maintenance and repairs.

Hot Tip Parallel structures for lists also extend to headings and sub-headings. This is especially pertinent if you are writing a contents list as there you can really see if items aren't parallel.

Bulleted lists

If you use a bulleted list then make sure that the construction of the list follows the lead-in sentence above. See the bulleted list above. Each item flows with the lead-in sentence.

3 On reflection

This chapter has looked more at the mechanics of writing that should enable you to address some of the feedback given to you by your tutors. The most important aspects for graduate and hence professional writing is your ability to work with all the writing systems. With practice, it will be a seamless mesh of skills, that culminates in good technical writing.

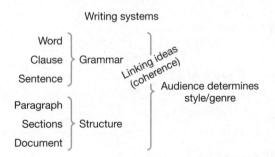

Summary of this chapter

Take a quick look at Figure 14.7 and assess if you are now familiar with these areas.

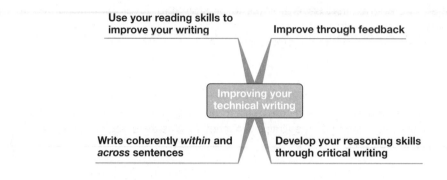

Figure 14.7 Summary of the chapter

ACTIVITY 8 Update your personal development planner

Now reflect on your current abilities and consider what you need to do to improve. You may want to transfer this information to your own institution's personal development planner scheme.

Grade your confidence on a scale of 1–5 where 1 = poor and 5 = good.

Developing my skills	Confidence level 1–5	Plans to improve
I know the kind of feedback I want and what to do with it.		
I understand the importance of critical evaluation in writing.		
I know how to develop my ideas coherently.		

Date: _____

Getting extra help

■ If you want to learn more about giving and receiving feedback, check out this BBC online (very) short course. Type 'feedback' into the search box. It is available at: **http://www.bbctraining.com/** [last accessed August 2008].

■ There are many online writing centres and you only need to put in a search term such as 'online writing laboratory' (OWL) to get a good sample. The most famous one is Purdue University. If you add scientific or technical writing you can also narrow it down.

- Your institution may have help facilities if you are having writing difficulties. It is worth checking this out with your student services office.
- You may also be able to get some information from your Students Union office.

Feedback on activities

ACTIVITY 2 Understanding your grade

If you answer 'yes' to 1 and 2:

This means you have not analysed the question(s) carefully enough. Look at the section 'Crack the code' in Chapter 12.

If you answered 'yes' to 3, 4 and 5:

This means you need to develop your critical writing skills. Check out 'Critical writing' in this chapter.

If you answered 'yes' to 6, 7 and 8:

This means you that you don't fully understand how to structure your work. You need to identify the sections if writing a report and structure your thoughts within each section. Similarly, with an essay, you need to structure your argument and develop a clear structure that takes the reader through logically. One basic problem is in not understanding the function of paragraphs. The paragraph is an element that discusses an idea and how you link these ideas becomes a logical and coherent argument. Also, you may use a difficult and complex sentence structure, if so, look at the section 'Linking ideas' in this chapter.

If you answered 'yes' to 9, 10 and 11:

This usually means that you have failed to proofread your work. Look at Chapter 12, Section 3, for guidance on checking your work.

If you answered 'yes' to 12–16:

You are well on your way to becoming a critical writer.

ACTIVITY 3 Focus on precision

The following sentences are examples of vague writing around the use of frequency and quantity. How would you make them more precise?

The measurements were recorded at frequent intervals.	The measurements were recorded at 15-second intervals.
The apparatus was stable, so it was rarely checked.	The apparatus was stable, so it was checked every two hours.
A substantial amount of reagent was applied.	7.25 ml of reagent was applied.
An appropriate amount of sulphur was added.	1.25 g of sulphur was added.

The degree of accuracy will depend on your experiment.

ACTIVITY 4 Linking within sentences

1. ━━━

Carbon dioxide is the dominant contributor to current climate change.

2. ━━━ ▢ ━━━

Carbon dioxide is the dominant contributor to current climate change <u>and</u> its atmospheric concentration has increased from a pre-industrial value of 278 ppm to 379 in 2005.

3. ━━━ △ ------

There are a variety of renewable sources of energy <u>although</u> most of them still require more technological or commercial development.

4. △ ------ , ━━━

<u>Unless</u> *we make significant efforts to reduce our emissions of greenhouse gases, **the global climate will continue to warm rapidly over the coming decades and beyond**.*

Notice the comma if you start a sentence with a subordinate clause.

If you start a sentence with a subordinate clause, notice the comma.

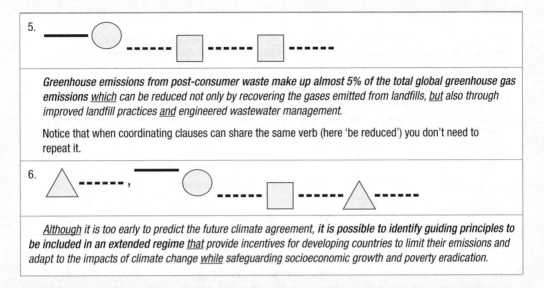

Greenhouse emissions from post-consumer waste make up almost 5% of the total global greenhouse gas emissions _which_ can be reduced not only by recovering the gases emitted from landfills, _but_ also through improved landfill practices _and_ engineered wastewater management.

Notice that when coordinating clauses can share the same verb (here 'be reduced') you don't need to repeat it.

Although it is too early to predict the future climate agreement, **it is possible to identify guiding principles to be included in an extended regime** _that_ provide incentives for developing countries to limit their emissions and adapt to the impacts of climate change _while_ safeguarding socioeconomic growth and poverty eradication.

You can see that, as a reader, the more clause links you have, the more complex they are to process.

ACTIVITY 5 What comes next?

Look at the following sentences and estimate what you think the writer will discuss next; you don't have to write a sentence, just give the gist of what could come next. These are all student writers and show some problems with coherence.

1. Detecting and monitoring structural damage for aerospace, civil and any mechanical engineering structure is referred to as Structural Health Monitoring (SHM).

What did come next

As defined by Farrar [1], damage can be considered as 'Changes to the material and/or geometric properties of the system'. Farrar also extends the definition of damage to the changes of the boundary conditions and system connectivity, 'which adversely affect the system's performance'. Motivations for developing accurate and reliable SHM process are numerous in the aerospace and civil engineering field. One of the most motivating factors here is the 'failure' factor due to structural damage resulting in loss of life and Mission failure or structural destruction [2].

Comment

We would have expected something about SHM, but the writer has not followed the listing or the nesting pattern correctly so there is a slight mismatch with the next sentence. We would move that first sentence to the end of the paragraph and then discuss SHM.

2. When it comes to damage detection several methods can be used to assess the amount of sustained damage.

What did come next

Damage can be defined as the change between two different states of system, which affects the current and future performance of it. Geometric and material properties of the structure can be modified as well as changes in boundary conditions and connections between members. Rytter in [1] defines four stages of damage identification: a) determination that damage is present in the structure, b) the geometric location of damage, c) quantification of the severity of the damage, d) prediction of the remaining service life of the structure.

Comment

We would have expected to read something about the several methods of damage detection, but the reader went on to define 'damage'. If you are defining something, it is better to place it at the beginning as this lets the reader know your position on the topic. We are sure you, as a reader can feel the mismatch between the first sentence and the following ones.

3. With the development of material technology, it has been found that physical properties of some specially synthesised polymers can change when the external field changes. As a result of this 'smart' property, these materials have a promising future for practical applications in many fields.

What did come next

When comes to the vibration control problem, a tunable vibration absorber is a widely used approach. This method requires a tunable springs system to maintain optimal performance in the face of changing vibration environment. Considering both, it is not hard to imagine using smart materials as components of a tunable vibration absorber system.

Comment

We would expect the writer to discuss some of the practical applications. The author has done this in some way, but it takes the reader to the second sentence to realise he or she is talking about a specific application (vibration control) and even then you have to 'work at' understanding it. We think you need to prepare the reader by first expanding on the particular aspect of the 'smart' properties and then say you will only look at one application. Always prepare your readers so they know what to expect.

ACTIVITY 6 Paragraph coherence

Analysis of student text

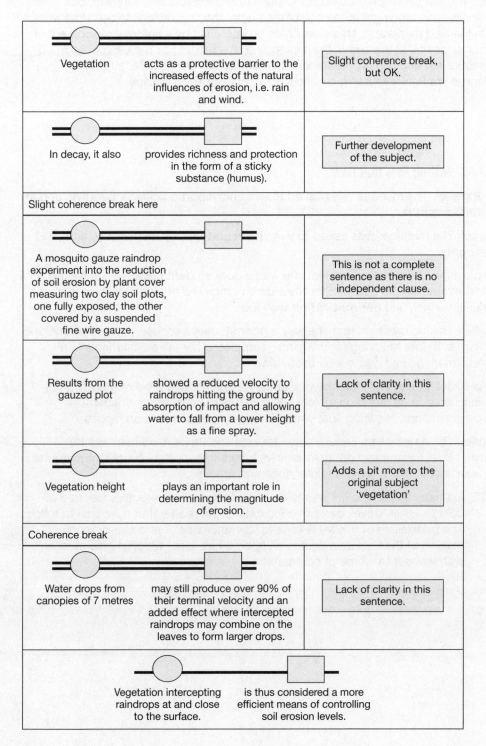

Vegetation	acts as a protective barrier to the increased effects of the natural influences of erosion, i.e. rain and wind.	Slight coherence break, but OK.
In decay, it also	provides richness and protection in the form of a sticky substance (humus).	Further development of the subject.

Slight coherence break here

A mosquito gauze raindrop experiment into the reduction of soil erosion by plant cover measuring two clay soil plots, one fully exposed, the other covered by a suspended fine wire gauze.		This is not a complete sentence as there is no independent clause.
Results from the gauzed plot	showed a reduced velocity to raindrops hitting the ground by absorption of impact and allowing water to fall from a lower height as a fine spray.	Lack of clarity in this sentence.
Vegetation height	plays an important role in determining the magnitude of erosion.	Adds a bit more to the original subject 'vegetation'

Coherence break

Water drops from canopies of 7 metres	may still produce over 90% of their terminal velocity and an added effect where intercepted raindrops may combine on the leaves to form larger drops.	Lack of clarity in this sentence.
Vegetation intercepting raindrops at and close to the surface.	is thus considered a more efficient means of controlling soil erosion levels.	

343

Generally this sample of text shows more of a listing character, which means that the reader has the feeling that the subject and hence the argument is not being developed sufficiently. There are some coherence breaks between the sentences, which the reader 'repairs'. The last sentence showed some signs of nesting and development, but because this has come right at the end of the paragraph, it is difficult to see what would follow in the next paragraph. This work could be improved by a tighter development of some of the 'points' at the end of the sentence so the reader has more information on the impact of soil and rain on vegetation in relation to soil erosion. Because the paragraph is not tightly written it is difficult to identify its key message.

ACTIVITY 7 Writing lists that flow

4. **Not Parallel**: The manager was asked to write his report quick*ly*, accurate*ly*, and *in a detailed manner*.

   Parallel: The manager was asked to write his report quick*ly*, accurate*ly*, and *thoroughly*.

5. **Not parallel**: The lecturer said that she was a poor student because she wait*ed* until the last minute before studying for the exam, complet*ed* her lab problems in a careless manner, and *her motivation was* low.

   Parallel: The lecturer said that she was a poor student because she waited until the last minute before studying for the exam, complet*ed* her lab assignments in a careless manner, and *was poorly* **motivated**.

6. **Not parallel**: The agency lists several areas for sustainable development: tighter licensing laws for abstraction, great*er* links between suppliers, infrastructure improvements and reducing 'lost water' through maintenance and repairs.

   Parallel: The agency lists several areas for sustainable development: tight*er* licensing laws for abstraction, great*er* links between suppliers, **better** infrastructure and *less* 'lost water' through maintenance and repairs.

   NOTE In this example, the list was fairly complicated and the author inserted a colon (:) after 'development' to indicate to the reader that a list was to follow. The parallelism of this list relates to 'comparisons', i.e. better or worse. Instead of the final item ending with 'er' it has 'less' which is also parallel with respect to words of comparison.

References

- Kolari, S., Savander-Ranne, C. and Viskari, E. L. (2008) 'Learning needs time and effort: a time-use study of engineering students', *European Journal of Engineering Education*, 33(5–6), 483–498.

- Petersen, A. K., Reynolds, J. J. and Ng, L. W. T. (2008) 'The attitude of civil engineering students towards health and safety risk management: a case study', *European Journal of Engineering Education*, 33(5–6), 499–510.

15 Writing a technical report

As a student of science, engineering or technology, you will need to understand how to write a technical report. This is not a skill that is confined to your student days, but will follow you into all your graduate-level jobs. These reports will be some of the longest and most complex documents you will have written and you may feel daunted by it. However, once you know the objectives of your report and how to break it down into sections, you can treat it as a series of smaller, but linked activities. You may be expected to write various reports: for example, a laboratory report, an individual project report, a group project report or a technical report from a work placement. The writing style for all these reports is similar and is easily learnt.

In this chapter you will:

1. work through the writing process for technical report writing
2. know what to put in each section of your report
3. start to write clear and accurate statements to get you started.

USING THIS CHAPTER

If you want to dip into the sections	Page	If you want to try the activities	Page
1 Developing a process for a technical report	347	1 Improve the titles	352
		2 Simplify your language	353
2 Working with sections in your report	352	3 Write your own thesis statement	355
3 On reflection	358	4 Update your personal development planner	359

Estimate your current levels of confidence. At the end of the chapter you will have the chance to reassess these levels and incorporate this into your personal development planner (PDP). Mark between 1 (poor) and 5 (good) for the following:

I know how to work through the writing process for a technical report.	I know what to put in each section of the report.	I write clear and accurate statements in my work.

Date: _____

1 Developing a process for a technical report

Good writing is the ability not only to string sentences together, but also how to manage the whole process and get your research right. Once you are comfortable with the process, you will feel a lot more confident and understand how to dip into sections that you can easily work on and gradually build up. When you understand the process, you will know that you don't have to start at the beginning and work to the end.

Document your practical work: using a lab log

As a student in this area, you will be carrying out work in the laboratory, and like any good professional scientist or engineer, you will be expected to keep a lab log or lab notebook. In this lab log you will record, in note form, details of each lab session. You should complete your lab log during your laboratory session, recording observations and any key data as they occur. Make sure you come to a conclusion at the end of every experiment. Your lab log should be a hard-backed book that will serve as a diary for all your lab sessions. You may find you are only assessed on your lab log, but if you have to write a full laboratory report, then you will need the information here to work from. Remember to record all your observations accurately.

NOTE If you are carrying out fieldwork, you may have a field log or notebook. It has the same function.

Headings for your lab log

This can vary between institutions, so check with your lecturer the format required. Some examples of headings are given below:

Contents page	Keep a few pages free at the front to enter experiments as you go.
Description	Briefly state in a few sentences what the experiment is about.
The experiment	Give a title, the question you are trying to answer and your hypothesis or what you are testing.
Apparatus	List everything you need to carry out this experiment/testing.
Methodology	Say what you did, add hand-drawn diagrams.
Data/results	Prepare data tables beforehand and explain what the data represent.
Brief discussion	Did you have appropriate evidence for your hypothesis? Say what you have learned and how you could improve the experiment.
Date your work	Always date your entries. As an employee in a company this is important in checking when something was done or discovered.

Checklist for your lab log

- Write with a **pen** not a pencil.
- Date and title your lab session.
- Write simply and clearly so that someone else could repeat your experiment from your notes.
- Prepare a data table beforehand and complete during the experiment.
- Put a line through mistakes and make clear corrections. Explain what changed and why.
- Keep your log tidy.
- Make drawings where necessary.
- Record your results carefully, make conclusions, offer suggestions and evaluate any errors.
- Use a hard-backed book

NOTE In commercial research laboratories, the lab log is a quasi-legal document that can be consulted if there is a dispute. It is important to have dated entries to retain a sequence of events. It is an important document.

Think, plan and start writing

Chapter 12, 'Taking control of the writing process', shows the importance of understanding the whole writing task before, during and after you actually write. In this section we are going to 'walk through' this process in relation to the technical report. The stages range from thinking through to editing and proofreading.

| **THINK** | PLAN | WRITE | EDIT | PROOFREAD |

What does your reader want to know and what do you want to say?

Think about scoping your report

Using the questions in Figure 15.1, take a report you will be working on and ask yourself those questions. It doesn't matter what order you do this in.

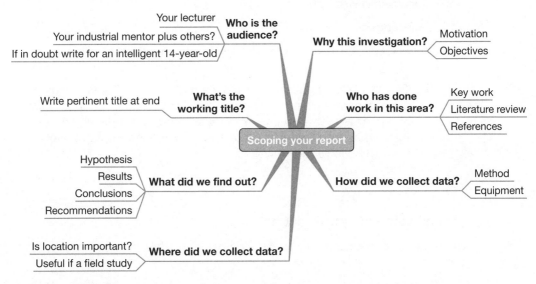

Figure 15.1 Scoping your report

These are all the *why, what, how, where, who* types of questions **the reader** will want answered when reading your report. You don't need to give complete answers at this stage, but you do need to be able to give outline answers.

| THINK | **PLAN** | WRITE | EDIT | PROOFREAD |

Plan the structure of your report sections

You will need to know the structure of the report you are writing. Check with your tutors as they may have a particular structure for you to use.

Sometimes institutions expect you to write your reports as experimental papers that follow the format of a particular journal. Your tutors will tell you if that is the case.

A typical structure for a report is:

1. **Title**

2. **Author(s)**

3. Summary (abstract)

4. Table of contents (advised)

5. **Introduction** (what the report is about, can include a literature review)

6. **Method** (procedure, equipment, or **Design** including testing for engineering)

7. **Results**

8. **Discussion**

9. **Conclusion**/Recommendations

10. **References**

11. Appendices (e.g. raw data, programming code, mathematical derivations).

NOTE The structure of your report may be a lot simpler. These headings are a general guide for most scientific/engineering reports. There is no set template to use. You must, therefore, check with your tutor what is expected of you. Those sections in bold above are likely to be included.

Planning tips

Detail some of your sections

Some of your sections can be detailed early on while with others you need wait.

- **Method section**. Plan how you are going to report this. Is it a complex experiment? Will you need sub-sections? If you use sub-sections within a section, then make sure you have at least two. If you only have one sub-section, then you don't need sub-sections at all. This is probably the easiest section to plan.
- **Introduction** (possibly including a literature review/synopsis of the area). This is probably the most difficult section to plan as it is similar to a small essay. You need to carry out your research, take notes and then plan how to structure what you've read. See Chapter 12, Section 2. You may want to consider several sub-sections here to structure your argument and help the reader.
- **Results section**. This is a fairly easy section to structure. It is important that you make sure that you present your data logically and

in the order you carried out your study. You need to give some context for the data to help the reader interpret what you know so well.

- **Discussion section**. It is best to wait a little and then plan this section once you are confident with the literature review (as your discussion should link back to your introduction and literature review) and your results. Once again, this is like a mini-essay where you critically evaluate your results. This is one of the most important sections.
- **Summary/abstract**. This will be the last section you write. It should be approximately 200 words and outline what you have done, what you have found and your conclusion.

| THINK | PLAN | **WRITE** | EDIT | PROOFREAD |

Start where you feel most comfortable

Look at your notes from the **THINK** and **PLAN** sections above as these are your starting blocks and you can get started with a few sentences where you feel most comfortable. When you feel you *have to* start 'at the beginning', there is a tendency to get writers' block or the 'white page syndrome'. Writing is an organic process so start with a few sentences and paragraphs where you feel most comfortable and then start to populate the section plans.

At this stage you have thought about the general scope of your report based around these key questions and you have started to plan how you might structure some sections. You are now ready to get a few sentences down on paper and in the correct section, even if you have to move them around, or even delete them later. See your response to the sentences in Figure 15.1 and your planning notes as your 'starter kit' and a skeletal start for some of your sections.

You may want to look at Chapter 14 in order to understand some of the mechanics of writing to ensure your style is correct and that you can write coherently,

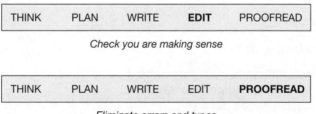

| THINK | PLAN | WRITE | **EDIT** | PROOFREAD |

Check you are making sense

| THINK | PLAN | WRITE | EDIT | **PROOFREAD** |

Eliminate errors and typos

For both of these activities see Chapter 12, Section 3.

2 Working with sections in your report

Although we have discussed a number of the sections in a report above, it must be remembered that this is just a guideline and that report sections need to be guided by the purpose of the document rather than some rigid template. Engineering reports, for example, may be more practical and reporting on a solution to a problem rather than a scientific enquiry. Engineering students therefore may have to discuss how they designed, tested and analysed various iterations of a solution and then recommend how best to implement it. Technical writing may also be as a result of a design project, the implementation of your design, your work placement, proposals and the scientific essay. The example discussed here concentrates on the laboratory report.

Despite those caveats, there are general principles that cover the spectrum of 'technical/scientific reports' that we can consider, and we shall be looking at these in the following sections.

Title and contents page

Start with a working title (unless given one by your tutor) that enables you to stay focused while writing. However, once you have finished you need to select a title that *succinctly* reflects what your report is about. Some titles tend to be either too vague or too long. Look at the examples below.

ACTIVITY 1 Improve the titles

1. Studies on the Electrodeposition of Lead on Copper

2. Hampshire and Isle of Wight New Forest Catchment Rivers Avon, Beaulie, Blackwater, Cadnam, Darkwater and Lymington Fish Survey Report 2001

See the feedback section.

Your titles should be:

- accurate (reflects the document contents/findings)
- specific (avoid general terms)
- succinct (you want an informative title in as few words as possible).

Contents page

As a general rule, use a contents page if your report is longer than four pages. The contents page gives the reader a quick overview of the structure of your report and it is easy to locate sections.

Summary/abstract

In research papers this is a 'standalone' section. It is possible to search online for abstracts, which is why this section must be able to sum up your whole report succinctly in its own right. You are usually expected to work within a 150–200-word limit. Your abstract or summary should include:

- **Why**: Why you carried out this study, your motivation, (the problem to solve) and objectives or hypothesis. This gives context.
- **How**: How did you go about collecting the data or evidence? Write a sentence or two on your chosen method.
- **What**: What were your results? Write a sentence on your major finding(s).
- **What**: What was your conclusion, recommendation? The reader will want to know how successful you were in meeting your objectives.

You will write this at the very end. Best practice is to try and keep, as near as possible, to one sentence per area. At first simply write your abstract and then go back and refine. You can do this by cutting out words that don't add information, such as: *might, appears to, may fulfil, by means of, in the position of being able to*. Write very simply and be precise.

One of the classic mistakes of novice writers is to use wordy, redundant phrases in an attempt to write more formally. Try to avoid this.

ACTIVITY 2 Simplify your language

Look at the following phrases and see how you can simplify and use them in less words. There are many more examples and it would be a useful exercise to summarise a book section or article in 200 words to see how you can simplify your language while retaining the gist of the original text.

Wordy/redundant phrase	Simplified equivalent
adequate supply of …	
already prepared	
arrived at the conclusion that …	
absolutely vital	
as a consequence of …	
because of the fact that	
assuming that	
with regard to the	

See the feedback section.

Introduction section

This section identifies the purpose or objective of your work and lets the reader know why you are interested. It can include the wider context of your subject, the theoretical background and a short review of what other people have done in the field. This section gives you the opportunity to show your lecturer what you know about this subject.

The clearest way to tell the reader what the objective of your project is through the **thesis statement**. This is a sentence (or two) that captures what your project is all about. During the **THINK** phase you were asked to jot down some answers to these questions, see Figure 15.1, 'Why this investigation?' Go back and look at what you wrote and make a note of it below; it doesn't have to be a well-crafted sentence, ideas are enough. This will form the basis of your thesis statement later.

What is a thesis statement?

This is a sentence or two that tells the reader, specifically and clearly, what your report (or essay) is about. Your thesis statement should be near the beginning of your report (or essay), usually in the introduction and ideally at the end of the first paragraph. It should not be tucked away in the middle of a paragraph in the middle of your report. Your thesis statement also needs to express some controversy or something around which you can discuss or evaluate.

Your thesis statement should :

- be clear
- be specific
- be strong
- express the main idea of your work.

Poor thesis statement	Better
I hope to discover how human behaviour affects wildlife.	This study determines those human activities that negatively and positively impact on wildlife in urban areas.

Comment

The initial statement is neither clear nor specific; it is far too general. Is this referring to human behaviour in towns, the countryside or in national parks? It is rather weak as it starts with 'I hope'. A thesis statement needs to be assertive, reflecting your competency in the area. Because it is unclear and too general the reader has only a vague idea of what the work is about and feels unsure of your competence.

	Better
The experiment lets us estimate Young's modulus of elasticity using a static and a dynamic method.	A. The experiment was designed to estimate Young's modulus of elasticity using static and dynamic methods. B. Using static and dynamic experimental methods, Young's modulus of elasticity was estimated using … Both methods were then evaluated with respect to …

Comment

It is best not to use 'The experiment lets us' as this can sound a little weak. Remember: you want a bold statement. Also, for the reader it is not clear why two methods have been chosen. There is the assumption that both of these methods will be evaluated for their accuracy. Is the material you are going to use important? If so, say what it is.

Hot Tip

Never use phrases like 'I hope to show' as this shows a tentative rather than a strong approach to your study. Make a bold and confident statement. If you search the Web using the search term 'thesis statement', you will discover many sites that can help you take this further.

Once you have written your thesis statement it is easier for you to structure the remainder of your introduction, as this becomes the 'blueprint' for it.

ACTIVITY 3 Write your own thesis statement

Look at your notes above, taken from the **THINK** section. Write a thesis statement that is clear, specific and bold. Ensure that the reader knows what your report will be about. ▶

Give your statement to some friends as ask them:

1. Does the statement sound clear and confident?

2. Do you know how the report will develop?

Writing a brief literature review or synopsis of your area

In the introduction you need to discuss the background or theoretical position of the subject area within your study. This may mean you can go to textbooks and summarise the main issues, or if you are carrying out some of your own research in a project, then you will access a few journal articles. Whichever way you do it, you need to read, take notes, summarise and write a coherent introduction – see Chapter 12, Section 2.

It is very important in this section that you reference your work correctly. You will be referring to the work of others so make sure you have the full reference and put it in your references at the end. When you make a statement about another person's work you need to cite it in your text, directly after you have mentioned this person's work, so it is firmly linked to that person.

The following examples use the Harvard in-text citation format

---

What does an in-text citation look like?

At the end of a sentence – (Name, date)
An interesting development was the Microcosm system developed at the University of Southampton (Hall, 1993). This provided a ...

Within a sentence – Name (date)
Jones (1999) states that 'essays encourage students to write in the academic discourse of their discipline'.

Smith (2004) has shown how students' understanding and confidence of their own discipline improves when they are asked to write. He assessed this through ...

What do I do with these citations?

These in-text citations will be fully referenced in your References section. Every citation must have a full reference at the end of your work. For example:

Hall, W. (1993) 'Hypermedia tools for multimedia information management', Proceedings of '*Multimedia Systems and Applications*', *Leeds, December*.

Results section

This section is the presentation of your results from, for example, observation, experimentation, testing. You need to present this information clearly, logically and in an order that may have been discussed in the report earlier. If you have a series of studies, iterations or testing, then maintain their order of presentation.

In this section you need to:

- Present your data in table or graph format.
- Include only key results and data. Other findings can go into the appendix.
- Number every table or graph. An easy way is to refer to them all as 'Figure' and then number them consecutively together with a caption (heading).
- Ensure your graphs are readable. Large data sets should go into the appendix.
- Label the units on the graphs and tables
- Interpret the results for your readers, don't allow them to try and work it out for themselves: for example, 'Figure 1 shows the relationship between temperature and stress in the steel bar'. However, don't go into a lengthy discussion as that is for the next section.

Discussion section

This is a very important part of your report and the section with the most intellectual challenge. You need to evaluate critically the work you've done.

- **Method**. Show you are alert to where errors in your results could have crept in – don't see this as a failing, report it. Indicate how the method/approach could be improved, even if it was set up for the class by your tutor.
- **Results**. Have your results supported or refuted your hypothesis? Look at your results objectively; are they what you expected?
- **Analysis**. Critically evaluate your results given the method you used.
- **Conclusion**. What has come out of your report; what knowledge have you gained? You need to refer back to the theory/literature discussed in the introduction. Critically evaluate how your results conform (or not) to the literature.
- **Recommendations**. This can be a separate section if it is that type of report and could also include implementation. Recommendations can also be a sentence or two at the end of the discussion section.

Appendices

The appendices will contain all those parts of your study that are too detailed or too clumsy to put in the main body of the text. They could comprise, for example, mathematical derivations, raw data, illustrations, maps. Make sure your appendices are numbered and when you refer to an appendix in your text ensure that it is in numeric order. So, as the reader goes through your text, Appendix 1 will be referred to first.

References

If you do not include in-text citations and then full references at the end of your document, you may find yourself accused of plagiarism. You need to check with your tutor the referencing style to use. Generally, scientists use the Harvard system and engineers the IEEE system, or something similar. The IEEE system uses numbers for in-text citations and then links to a numbered reference in the References section. See Chapter 13 for more information.

Practical work and assessment

It is worth noting that you will not have to write a full report each time you carry out some practical work. The sections here give you as near to the full picture of a technical report as is necessary for this book. You may find that only your lab log is assessed, or you are only expected to write up your results and write a short interpretation. In some cases you may only be expected to write the summary. It will vary considerably. However, knowing where your assessment fits into the larger picture of a technical report is important and the style of writing you are expected to use will be just the same. If you feel you want to look more carefully at the mechanics of technical writing then go to Chapter 14.

3 On reflection

This chapter has in essence been a 'walkthrough' of the technical report writing process. You should realise that it is an iterative process with a vague start, a series of loops in the middle and a clear end. If you are expected to write a full report, and this will be the case if you are doing your individual project or a group project, then you now know that you will have to get on top of the process and manage these chunks of work effectively.

Summary of this chapter

Take a quick look at Figure 15.2 and assess if you are now familiar with these areas.

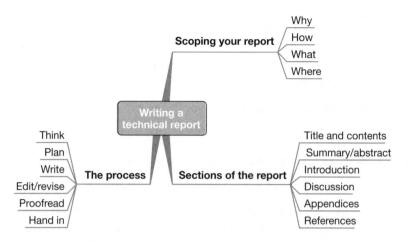

Figure 15.2 Summary of the chapter

ACTIVITY 4 Update your personal development planner

Now reflect on your current abilities and consider what you need to do to improve. You may want to transfer this information to your own institution's personal development planner scheme.

Grade your confidence on a scale of 1–5 where 1 = poor and 5 = good.

My developing skills	Confidence level 1–5	Plans to improve
I know how to work through the writing process for a technical report.		
I know what to put in each section of the report.		
I write clear and accurate statements in my work.		

Date: _____

Getting extra help

- Check with your institution or department as they may have a standard template or format for document writing.
- If you are having problems with the writing, check with your institution as it may have writing workshops that you can attend.

Feedback on activities

ACTIVITY 1 Improve the titles

1. Studies on the Electrodeposition of Lead on Copper

Comment

This title is rather vague. A more precise version could be:

The effects of Rhodamine-B on the Electrodeposition of Lead on Copper

2. Hampshire and Isle of Wight New Forest Catchment Rivers Avon, Beaulie, Blackwater, Cadnam, Darkwater and Lymington Fish Survey Report 2001

Comment

This title is rather long and since these are rivers from the New Forest a more succinct title could be:

New Forest Rivers' Fish Survey Report 2001

ACTIVITY 2 Simplify your language

Look at the following phrases and see how you can simplify and use them in less words. There are many more examples and it would be a useful exercise to summarise a book section or article in 200 words to see how you can simplify your language while retaining the gist of the original text.

Wordy/redundant phrase	Simplified equivalent
adequate supply of …	*Sufficient supply of*
already prepared	*prepared*
arrived at the conclusion that …	*concluded that*
absolutely vital	*vital*
as a consequence of …	*therefore, so*
because of the fact that	*because*
assuming that	*if*
with regard to the	*regarding*

5 Solve mathematical problems

In order to be efficient at mathematical problem solving you need to spend time developing your skills. The way you tackle a problem will depend on the level of expertise you currently have and of course the type of problem. You obviously need to have some mathematical literacy in order to be successful but you also need a structured approach. These chapters, 'Preparing to solve mathematical problems', 'Solving the problem' and 'Getting help, and helping yourself', serve to talk you through the intellectual process you need to adopt. If you can master this, you should be able to: (a) answer the questions set, (b) identify the level of mathematical reasoning needed and plan a solution strategy, (c) know how you can check your answers and (d) know when and how to ask for help.

16 Preparing to solve mathematical problems

In most science, engineering and technology subjects, you will be asked to solve mathematical problems both as part of your coursework and in exams. Many lecturers will provide sheets of examples for you to work through and it is tempting to rush straight into trying to find a solution. Students who are attracted to science, engineering and technology subjects are often people who like to learn by doing things, but a little time spent preparing yourself to tackle a set of problems, and a little time after to record what you did, can help you to develop efficient and effective problem-solving skills.

In this chapter you will:

1. define what you find hard about solving maths problems
2. think about how the kinds of maths questions you meet will change as you progress through your studies
3. consider how to improve your study skills for maths
4. learn the key words that can tell you about the type of problem.

Estimate your current levels of confidence. At the end of the chapter you will have the chance to reassess these levels where you can incorporate this into your personal development planner (PDP). Mark between 1 (poor) and 5 (good) for the following:

I am aware of how I currently think about and approach maths problems.	I am aware of how the kind of maths problem I might meet will change as I progress through my studies.	I know how the language used in maths problems indicates what I must do to solve them.	When I revise a topic I remember what I learnt the first time I worked through it.

Date: _____

1 Thinking about problems

Many people are attracted to science, engineering and technology subjects because they find solving practical and logical problems very satisfying. Perhaps this was one of the things you considered when you chose your course? You will find that your lecturers and tutors often give you a worksheet with a set of example problems so you can check your understanding of a new topic. These can provide you with useful formative feedback about how well you have understood the new material you are learning. However, many of you will be familiar with that feeling when you look at a problem on a worksheet and you just can't think how to begin. This can be very frustrating and demotivating. You think you understood the lecture but you can't see how to apply your knowledge to get to a solution. Understanding why this can happen may help you to avoid many hours staring at your worksheets with little or no progress.

ACTIVITY 1 Problems with problems

Think about a worksheet or problem set you have found difficult during your course so far. What happened? Tick any of the statements below that describe how you felt. Do you want to add any further scenarios to the table?

	✓
1. I looked at the problems and I just didn't know how to begin to tackle them.	
2. I knew how to do the problems, but I made errors in the algebra and/or arithmetic as I worked, so I never got the right answer at the end.	
3. I knew what I was trying to find but I didn't know how to go about it.	
4. I could do the problem sheet when it was set, but when I came to revise for my exam I had forgotten how I did it.	
5.	
6.	

See the feedback section.

Spending hours staring at the same problem and not getting anywhere or else doing all the problems on a worksheet but getting them all wrong are not efficient ways for you to learn. Getting everything right but then forgetting how you did it later is also frustrating. So how do these problems arise, and what can you do about them?

In the next two sections you will consider the levels of difficulty of different kinds of problems and the language used to tell you what you are supposed to do.

How problems change as you progress

One change you will notice as you progress through your course is that the problems you are set get harder to solve. This might sound obvious, but often students expect techniques they have learnt as beginners at problem solving to continue to see them through as the depth of their studies increases. To improve your problem-solving skills, a good first step is to understand how the kinds of problems you are given change, and how things that are difficult now become routine as they become more familiar to you.

Problems to develop numeracy and memorise relationships: basic maths skills

Your early school maths will have concentrated on numeracy and arithmetic. The idea was to teach you relationships between different numbers, such as their products and sums. The problem sets you were given most likely consisted of a lot of very similar examples and the aim was to embed these relationships between different numbers in your memory for later use.

There are many things in maths that are useful to remember. You need to be able to recall them instantly while you are trying to solve harder problems. An example from your primary school is your multiplication tables. To begin with you need to learn them, and later you need to have them at your fingertips so you can multiply numbers easily without a calculator. Learning this kind of information often involves a lot of repetition, which some people find tedious, but it is worth it in the long run because when you are solving harder problems, the arithmetic is second nature and you don't need to think about it much. You are free to concentrate on the more complex aspects of your problem without getting bogged down.

Hot Tip

Trying to do maths without good numeracy is like trying to read without knowing the sounds of the alphabet. As you work, always try to find factors, add numbers, work out products, etc., in your head before you reach for a calculator. You can use the calculator afterwards to confirm your answer.

Problems to make new skills become routine: algebraic and geometric skills

The next stage in studying maths usually involves learning some simple algebraic skills such as rearranging formulae, solving simple equations, learning about the geometry of simple shapes and so forth. Again, these problem sets are designed to give you lots of practice at using the skill and can also be very repetitive. You need this basic toolkit of algebraic skills to be as much second nature as the numeracy skills if you are to tackle harder problems. For instance, if you are trying to solve an equation and you need to add some fractions as part of the process you want the fraction-adding to be pretty slick so you can focus on the new stuff. However, it isn't possible to give you a list of the numeracy and algebraic skills that fall into the categories discussed above because it is an ever-changing set. When you are learning something new you have to think hard about how to do it, but in time and with sufficient practice it becomes part of your established skill set.

Let's look at differentiation as an example

When you first meet differentiation you solve problems where the aim is simply to find the differential. After a while you have grasped how to do this for a set of standard differentials and that task becomes routine. Your next challenge is to apply your knowledge. The task of finding a standard differential becomes merely a small, routine step within the bigger solution.

As you study further, not only the standard differentials but also, for example, the way to find maxima and minima become routine to you and you can consider them as tools to solve problems which are even more complex. The process is summarised in Figure 16.1.

Time step	Example skill			
	Differentiation	Integration as the reverse of differentiation	Integration by substitution	Solving differential equations
1	New skill			
2	Routine skill now used to understand and carry out new skill	New skill		
3	Second nature – hardly need to think about how to do it	Routine skill now used to understand and carry out new skill	New skill	
4	Second nature – hardly need to think about how to do it	Second nature – hardly need to think about how to do it	Routine skill now used to understand and carry out new skill	New skill

Figure 16.1 How new skills become routine over time

Problems that bring different known skills together: applying your skills

Once you have a good maths toolkit, you solve problems by applying your known skills, facts and theory in the right way. You may be told what method to use in the problem statement. In doing this you are bringing together things you have memorised, things you have practised and some recently learned theory to get a feel for how the new theory works or how it may be applied.

These problems are frequently expressed in words rather than just symbols and expressions, and you need to be able to convert from the words to the equivalent mathematical statements before you can solve them. A systematic approach to problem solving as described in Chapter 17 will help you learn to do this efficiently.

You will probably have started to solve this kind of problem more frequently during your pre-degree studies and you will be expected to develop your ability further to solve similar problems during the early stages of your degree programme.

Problems that require application of known skills to new situations: extending the application of your skills

Even harder problems involve the application of your existing skills and theory to unfamiliar situations. You know the necessary facts and you have the necessary skills and concepts, but you need to learn about the situation before you can proceed.

Once you have understood how your existing knowledge applies to the new circumstances, you need to develop a strategy to solve the problem. In these problems you are not expected to be able to find a solution straight away. These are advanced problems. You need to consider how the unfamiliar situation might resemble a situation you are more familiar with and learn to ask yourself relevant questions to work towards a solution:

- Can you make any valid assumptions about the situation described in the problem statement?
- Which of the theories that you already know about might apply?

This may be unknown territory for you, but perhaps someone has published the information you need to make the link? You need to work out how to track it down.

Solving these less well-specified problems takes persistence and patience, but once you have found a solution to any given problem you are well on your way to also considering this type of problem as routine.

Problems that require research into new methods: developing an advanced toolkit

Finally, we come to problems where you need to extend the range of facts, skills or theory you know before you can apply them to an unfamiliar situation. Here you may know some of what you need, but your first task is to identify what you don't know. Then you need to acquire new skills, facts or theory to help you. Finally, you need to apply it all to the new situation.

At their most complex, these are the kinds of problems academic researchers consider. You might face a challenge like this in an extended project towards the end of your degree programme.

> **Hot Tip**
>
> To tackle the kinds of extended problems that require you to teach yourself a new method it is frequently helpful to try to break them down into smaller problems and to deal with each one separately to begin with.

How things will change

Before you started your degree course, it is likely that you mainly worked on the more routine kinds of problems to build up your numeracy, your toolkit of mathematical methods and your ability to apply the theory you were taught.

As you progress through your course you will be expected to tackle gradually more ambitious problems requiring greater creativity and thought to reach a solution. These more complicated problems usually require you to use a multi-step approach, and may involve several different mathematical skills and techniques to be combined with logical thought. You will build towards these more complex problems as the range of solution techniques you have acquired grows.

> **Hot Tip**
>
> If you find you need additional practice with the more routine problems to consolidate what you know or with the new topics you are learning, have a look at **www.mathcentre.ac.uk** which offers a range of leaflets, videos and other resources to help you with your maths.

Cracking the code (specialist language of problems)

In engineering, science and technology there are lot of specialist words that are used to indicate the type of solution to a problem that is expected. There are also many words that look like everyday words, but which have a special meaning in a technical or scientific context. Understanding what these jargon words mean is vital to being able to decide on the approach you will take to solving a given problem. You may find it helpful to write a glossary of new words and their meanings as you meet them, which you can keep on your computer and search through on future occasions.

The language chosen to express maths-based problems often gives you a big clue as to the kind of solution you are looking for and this helps to get you thinking along the right lines about how you will get to that solution.

ACTIVITY 2 Specialist language

Look at the words in the table below. All these can be used in maths problems to tell you about the thing you are trying to find. Can you find an example where each is used in the problems you have been asked to solve during your course so far?

	Common meaning	An example problem from your own subject
Find ...	Work out an algebraic or numerical expression.	
Evaluate ...	Find a numerical value from a formula.	
Solve ...	Find numerical values for any unknown variables.	
Find a value for ...	Same as 'evaluate'.	
Prove ...	By logical reasoning show that something is true.	
Derive...	Show how a particular formula or rule is obtained from other rules or laws.	
Show that ...	Same as 'prove'.	
Simplify ...	Use algebraic manipulation to make an expression less complicated (e.g. by cancelling common factors).	
Express in terms of ...	Describe one parameter in terms of a particular other parameter.	
Express in the form ...	Rearrange an expression to a specified form.	
Expand ...	Make an expression more complicated by, for example, using a series or multiplying out brackets.	
Rearrange ...	Change to give an expression or equation in a different form.	
Transpose ...	Change the subject of an equation.	

2 Preparing yourself to solve ...

Most lecturers in maths-based courses provide example questions, either from worksheets or from a recommended textbook. These will be based on the kinds of questions you are expected to solve for the assessment. Tackling these problems during the course will help you to judge how you are progressing. Your solutions may also be marked to give you some credit towards your final grade.

The temptation for many students is to rush into an attempt at solving the problems as soon as they are given the sheet. Students in engineering, science and technology often prefer to learn by doing, so a hands-on approach really suits their style. However, you can't solve the problems if you haven't got to grips with the basics of the theory you need to do the job. To get the most from a set of example questions you need to prepare, so it's worth taking a bit of time to do some groundwork before you dive into the worksheet. It will pay off in the long run.

1. Read through the printed notes and your own notes from the lecture. You don't need to try to understand everything at this stage – just get a feel for the main points of the topic.

2. Work through the worked examples in the notes. Don't just read them – try to do the examples yourself using the notes as a guide. Can you see how and why each step is taken?

3. If you have difficulty following the steps and ideas in the example problems, are they to do with the new material or missing background knowledge (e.g. basic algebra or arithmetic skills)?

4. Can you find a textbook or a friend to help you with any difficulties? Even if your example problems are to be assessed it is fine to ask a friend to help you understand the underlying theory or to explain the examples given in the lecture. (Make sure, however, that the final solutions you submit for assessment are your own individual work. See Chapter 13, Section 1, on academic integrity.)

5. Make a list of the questions you need to ask at a tutorial. Try to be specific about what you don't understand. Mark the step in the worked example where you got stuck. Attend the tutorial and ask the questions. (See Chapter 18, Section 2, for a discussion of useful questioning techniques.)

6. Once you feel you have understood the topic reasonably well, you are ready to start on the worksheet.

7. Finally, after you complete the worksheet, read the lecture notes again. This time you are making sure you have grasped the detail. Solving the problems should have helped you to gain a more in-depth understanding of the topic.

ACTIVITY 3 Steps to success

Consider the questions below. Are you taking every possible step to help yourself to success? If you give yourself a low score on any of the questions, what might you do about it?

▶

Do you ...	Mark along the line where you feel you are				
	Never				Always
	1	2	3	4	5
Attend all your lectures and tutorials every day?					
Make notes in lectures about worked examples even when you are given printed notes?					
Study regularly, sorting out problems as they arise?					
Work through notes and worked examples noting what you do and don't understand?					
Go prepared to tutorials and ask questions?					
Attempt all the problems on the worksheets?					
Find extra examples in textbooks from the library?					

See the feedback section.

3 Keeping a useful record

You may find that you can do a problem when the topic is new, but when you go back a few weeks later, you can't make sense of it anymore. Solving problems is very satisfying in its own right, but you are studying for a qualification, and eventually you will probably need to complete an assessment. You can help yourself prepare for an assessment if you take a little extra time to think about your solutions after they are completed and to make notes. You may be so excited to find a good method that you are tempted to scribble down the minimum amount needed to check your solution will work before hurrying on to the next problem. When you revise your work, this is often very hard to decipher. In the future, when you are in the workplace, a clear record of what you did and why is a vital part of professional practice, so get into good habits now.

Make sure you write down what you are doing at each step of your solution. This doesn't have to mean a lot of writing – just a quick note will do.

Consider the two solutions to the same problem below. Which will be better to revise from?

Solve for x and y:

$2x + 3y = 1$
$x - 4y = 17$

Solution 1	Solution 2
$2x + 3y = 1$ $x - 4y = 17$ $x = 17 + 4y$ $2(17 + 4y) + 3y = 1$ $34 + 11y = 1$ $11y = -33$ $y = -3$ $x = 5$	$2x + 3y = 1$ (1) $x - 4y = 17$ (2) Rearranging (2) gives $x = 17 + 4y$ (3) Substituting (3) into (1) gives $2(17 + 4y) + 3y = 1$ Then simplifying and rearranging gives $34 + 11y = 1$ $11y = -33$ $y = -3$ Substituting the value for y back into (3) gives $x = 5$ So the solution is $x = 5$ and $y = -3$.

It doesn't take much extra time to make the notes and in the long run it saves you time trying to puzzle out what you meant when you come back to the problem in the future.

Once you have solved a problem, take a moment to reflect on the solution. You can help yourself even more by making extra notes next to your solution to remind you:

- Whether it was hard or easy. Why?
- If you had to look anything up or get help. With which bit? What did you find out?
- Whether there were any particular tricky bits? Did they relate to new material or gaps in your basic skills (e.g. arithmetic or algebraic manipulation)?
- How it was different to the previous example. Or to the next example?

Jotting these things down next to your solution can really help when it comes to revision. The solution you write is there for you to learn from in the future. Don't be scared to write notes on it in any way that helps you.

Would you find the extra notes on the solution in Figure 16.2 useful for revision?

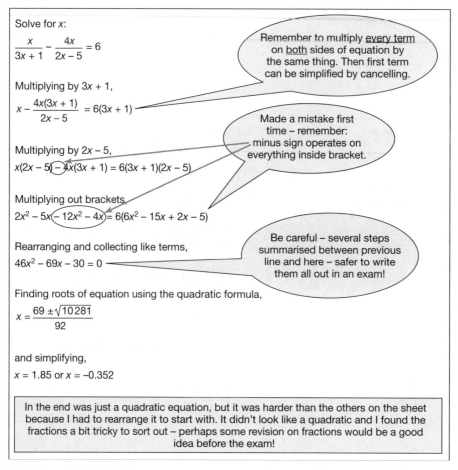

Figure 16.2 An annotated solution

4 On reflection

This chapter has asked you to consider the approach you currently have to problem solving and has discussed the different levels of problem you might meet. The kinds of problems you are presented with become gradually less well defined and rely more on your own creativity the deeper you go into your chosen area of study. It's no use just diving into a problem set and expecting to be able to work out how to do it; you need to prepare yourself first by understanding the topic from the notes. Once you have gone to the trouble and hard work of sorting out how to do your problems, you can make it easier to revise by writing down what you got wrong or found hard.

Summary of this chapter

Have a look at Figure 16.3 and make sure you are familiar with the concepts.

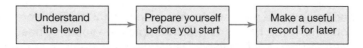

Figure 16.3 Summary of how to prepare for and record your problem-solving activities

ACTIVITY 4 Update your personal development planner

Reflect on your current abilities and consider what needs to improve. You may want to transfer this information to your institution's personal development planner scheme.

Grade your confidence on a scale of 1– 5 where 1 = poor and 5 = good.

My developing skills	Confidence level 1–5	Plans to improve
I know the strengths and weaknesses in my approach to problem solving.		
I understand that problems will get harder as I progress through my course. I am doing Ok with the problems that should be more routine to me.		
I know what I need to do before I start on a set of problems		
I make a useful record of how I solved each problem.		

Date: _____

Getting extra help

■ Make sure you know when your timetabled tutorials are and attend them regularly.

■ Is there a study centre or a system of drop in tutorials for maths that you can access when you need extra advice?

Feedback on activities

ACTIVITY 1 Problems with problems

1. You may need to do some more work understanding the topic before you start to solve the problems. If you have grasped the topic then you may need to do more work to understand the problem itself. Developing a systematic approach to problem solving will help with this.

2. You can lose a lot of marks through poor accuracy with numbers or algebra. You need to work on accuracy just as much as you work on new topics.

3. You need to develop some tools to help you find solution strategies. There are some standard approaches that are often worth trying when you can't see a way forward.

4. You need to work on the way you record your progress and the challenges you meet as you practise solving problems.

Activity 3 Steps to success

Do you ...	Feedback ...
Attend all your lectures and tutorials every day?	In maths-based courses, each section builds on your previous knowledge. It is important to keep up steady progress with your work. If you miss a lot of sessions, through illness for instance, make sure your tutor knows in case you struggle to catch up.
Make notes in lectures about worked examples even when you are given printed notes?	If the printed notes aren't clear about a complete method or approach, write additional comments on them during the lecture.
Study regularly, sorting out problems as they arise?	This makes it much easier to prepare for exams at the end of the term or semester – revision really is re-vision then.
Work through notes and worked examples noting what you do and don't understand?	You will be actively helping yourself by sorting out problems as they arise, not leaving them until later in the course.
Go prepared to tutorials and ask questions?	There are almost always other students wanting to know the answers to the same questions you have. If you are in a big group you may feel more comfortable asking the lecturer face to face at the end of the session.
Attempt all the problems on the worksheets?	Maths-based subjects are learned by **doing** problems. The problems help you learn the formulae and techniques you need to know, as well as improving your problem-solving prowess.
Find extra examples in textbooks from the library?	In maths-based subjects, practice in using new methods, theories and techniques is the only way to really grasp them. The more, the better.

Reference

■ Mathcentre, **www.mathcentre.ac.uk** [last accessed 14 August 2008].

17 Solving the problem

Experienced problem solvers like your lecturers often seem to look at a problem and just know how to solve it as if by magic. Going from the statement of a problem to a chosen method of solution is one of the things students find hardest in engineering, science and technology courses. Nobody can give you a foolproof method that solves every problem every time but a combination of experience, gained from tackling lots of problems, and a systematic approach to planning your strategy will take you a long way.

In this chapter you will:

1. see how to analyse a problem initially
2. get an overview of strategies for solution
3. investigate the benefits of working in symbols
4. consider ways to tell if your solution is working.

USING THIS CHAPTER

Estimate your current levels of confidence. At the end of the chapter you will have the chance to reassess these levels where you can incorporate this into your personal development planner (PDP). Mark between 1 (poor) and 5 (good) for the following:

Getting started on a problem.	Choosing a method for solution.	Working with symbols.	Knowing if you are heading the right way.

Date: _____

1 The problem-solving process

In this chapter we shall look at how you go from a statement of a problem to a solution. Problems come in all different shapes and sizes and the problems you meet during your studies will of course be very dependent on your subject. Nobody can give you a magic method that you can just apply without thinking to get the answer to any problem, but you can develop a systematic approach to problems that makes the process easier to manage. You are aiming to produce a toolkit of methods, not a recipe book of solutions, so taking time to understand the theory on which your problem is based is crucial (see Chapter 16, Section 2).

Learning a to use a process works just the same way as learning new facts; proficiency comes with practice and experience, so you need to take the solution methods described in this chapter and get in the habit of applying them each time you have a problem to solve. Improving your techniques and strategies for solving maths-based problems will help you to gain better marks and to learn more effectively and efficiently.

The problem-solving process can be divided into two parts: thinking and doing. Within each part you can systematically carry out a number of different tasks for each problem you try to solve.

Thinking and doing

For successful problem solving you need to:

1. **Understand the problem** by working out what information you have been given in the problem statement and what other information you will need.

2. **Devise a strategy** for solving the problem.

This is the ***thinking*** part of the process.

Then you need to:

3. **Carry out the strategy** for solving the problem.

4. **Write down the steps** for the solution.

5. **Check your answer**.

This is the ***doing*** part of the process.

Have a look at Figure 17.1 which summarises the steps to take in each part of the process.

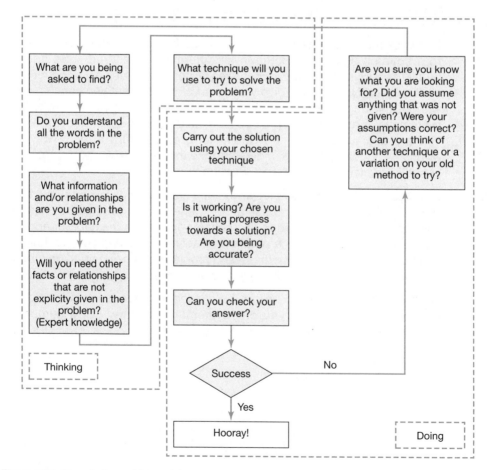

Figure 17.1 Steps in the problem-solving process

As you can see from the figure, the process contains a loop that you only leave when the problem is solved. One of the biggest problems for the novice problem solver is having the stamina to go round the loop again and again until the problem is solved and the experience to try a slightly different method each time. The other big problem for the beginner is knowing when to give up and get help. The methods described here can help with these judgements, but again there is no substitute for practice and experience. It's a bit like running a marathon: you can read about the best tactics, but the only way to achieve your goal is by actually going out and running. In the same way that you would gradually increase your training distances, you need to increase slowly the complexity of the problems you tackle.

2 Understanding the problem

It is never wise to start by trying to apply a solution method. First you need to think about your problem and really try to understand what you are dealing with. This might seem unnecessary with problems where you can see how to do them straight away, but you need to train your brain on these easier questions to approach the harder ones the right way. Get into good habits early and you will have an easier time as the difficulty of the problems you meet increases.

Closed and open problems

We can think of two broad classes of problems:

- **Closed problems**: where all the data you need to get to a solution is in the problem statement. You may have to come up with a method or choose which physical laws to apply but you don't expect to have to make estimates of, for example, the numerical values to use for different quantities. These are the kinds of problems you normally meet in a traditional exam.
- **Open problems**: where you may have to research some information or where some of the facts or values you need may not be known at all. These are more like the problems that researchers try to solve. You might come across this kind of problem in lab work or in an extended project.

ACTIVITY 1 Closed or open?

Are the following problems closed or open?

	Closed or open?
Two dustcarts collected bags of rubbish. One collected 47 bags and one collected 56 bags. How many bags of rubbish were collected all together?	Closed
What would be the best type of dam to use to dam the River Thames?	Open
Solve $2x + 3y = 1$ $x - 4y = 17$	
Estimate the distance from the earth to the sun.	
If Tom has three times as many apples as Susan and Susan has a quarter as many as Joe, who has four, how many does Mary have if Mary has two more than Tom?	
A round wheel with a radius of 37 cm rolls at a constant speed of 3 revolutions per second. How far does the axle of the wheel move in 8 seconds?	
Is it better for you to walk or cycle to university?	

See the feedback section.

What are you trying to achieve?

Whether the problem is closed or open, the first step towards solution is to define what you are trying to find. In some problems you will find a sentence that makes this clear. In other problems it is harder to work out what is needed, and in some very complicated problems, working out what will count as a valid solution is a whole problem in itself. Make sure you really understand your problem. This is the first part of the thinking stage.

You need:

■ First, to make sure you know what all the words in the problem mean. If you find one you don't understand then look it up in a dictionary. Is it an everyday word or a specialist or technical word? (See 'Cracking the code' in Chapter 16.)

■ Next, to identify the required result. You might like to underline it or rewrite it in your own words. What will it look like? Will it be a number; a conclusion in words, a proof, a diagram or something else? (For some further hints on how to identify parts of a question see the BUG technique in Chapter 12.)

For more open problems, the first attempt to define what you are looking for may be very vague, but thinking about why it is vague can be a valuable way to start to make the problem definition more precise.

You must always keep your goal in mind as you work through a problem.

Hot Tip

If you are looking for something, you will never find it if you don't know what it is!

Example: Identifying what you are trying to achieve

In the problem below, the part of the statement that tells you about the solution has been underlined.

Two pickup trucks collected bags of rubbish. One collected 56 bags of rubbish and the other collected 47 bags of rubbish. <u>How many bags of rubbish were collected all together?</u>

The solution you are looking for will be a number.

ACTIVITY 2 What are you looking for?

What about the problems below? Simply identify what you are trying to find and what form the solution will take.

	The solution will be ...
If Tom has three times as many apples as Susan and Susan has a quarter as many as Joe, who has four, how many does Mary have if Mary has two more than Tom?	
Design an efficient tin opener.	
Solve: $2x + 3y = 1$ $x - 4y = 17$	

See the feedback section.

> **Hot Tip**
>
> If you can't get started on a problem at all, the most likely reason is that you haven't properly identified what you are looking for. Once you know what you are after, it is easier to see ways you might try to get to it.

What are you given?

The next step in solving a problem is to work out what information you have been given in the problem statement.

You can write a list or underline parts of the question as you prefer. (See the BUG technique in Chapter 12.)

You need to be very clear about what you do and don't know. It is very easy to make assumptions without really knowing you have made them. It may help to get in the habit of writing down what you are given in your own words.

Example: Identifying what you have been given

Let's return to the problem we considered before:

Two pickup trucks collected bags of rubbish. One collected 56 bags of rubbish and the other collected 47 bags of rubbish. How many bags of rubbish were collected all together?

You are given two pieces of information in the question:

Truck 1 collected 56 bags
Truck 2 collected 47 bags

In this simple example you may feel that what you have been given is obvious, but it is worth getting into the habit of asking yourself this question explicitly even for simple problems. Once it is second nature, you will be able to use the same framework to deal with more complicated problems.

ACTIVITY 3 Identifying givens

For the problems below, identify the information you have been given to help you solve the problem:

	I have been given ...
If Tom has three times as many apples as Susan and Susan has a quarter as many as Joe, who has four, how many does Mary have if Mary has two more than Tom?	
Design an efficient tin opener.	
Solve $2x + 3y = 1$ $x - 4y = 17$	

See the feedback section.

What else do you know?

The information you are given in a problem statement is often not the only information you need to solve the problem. Frequently you are assumed to know something else as well. This is especially true in open problems, but even in closed problems you are not always told which method to use and must decide for yourself.

The extra knowledge may be common sense or well-known information or it may be specialist knowledge you have obtained from studying your course. All these additional pieces of knowledge you bring to a problem are part of your own **expert knowledge**.

This can be summarised by the diagram in Figure 17.2.

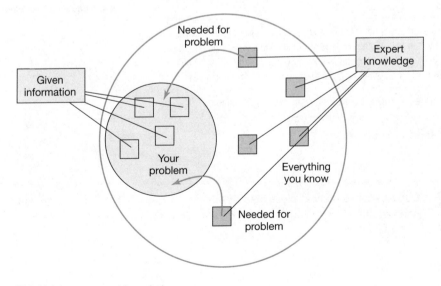

Figure 17.2 Using your expert knowledge

Expert knowledge might be a physical law, a piece of common knowledge, a piece of specialist language or something you have learnt from experience. For example, in the problem below we can see that there is some common knowledge needed and also some understanding of simple technical terms.

Problem	Expert knowledge needed
A round wheel with a radius of 37 cm rolls at a constant speed of 3 revolutions per second. How far does the axle of the wheel move in 8 seconds?	The writer of this problem is assuming you know what is meant by the common terms *round*, *wheel*, *rolls* and also by the more technical terms *radius*, *revolutions per second* and *axle*. You also need to know a physical law: the relationship between the radius of a circle and its circumference. None of this information is given to you by the problem statement.

ACTIVITY 4 Using your expert knowledge

What assumptions is the problem setter making about what you know in these next two problems?

Problem	Expert knowledge needed
1. Mary looked out of her window and saw some chickens and cows passing by. She counted all the legs of the chickens and cows and found that the total number of legs added up to 66. How many of each kind of animal passed by her window if the total number of animals is 24?	
2. A car travels at 60 mph. How far does it travel in 30 minutes?	

See the feedback section.

Hot Tip

Don't forget to make a clear note of the expert knowledge you decide you may need as this will help you to decide on a strategy for solution.

3 Strategies for solution

Once you have really analysed your problem thoroughly you will know what you are looking for and what you know already. You will also have identified the expert knowledge you think you might need. Now you are ready to think about solution strategies.

In routine problems (see Chapter 16), which test memory and your ability to apply basic skills, you may be told in the problem statement which method to use.

Examples

1. By using Simpson's rule with six intervals, determine

$$\int_0^{\pi/2} \sqrt{(2\cdot5 - 1.5 \cos 2\theta)}\,d\theta$$

2. Put the following equations into matrix form $Ax = b$:

$$2x + 3y = 1$$
$$x - 4y = 17$$

then find the inverse matrix A^{-1} and hence solve the set of equations for x and y.

You may need to learn or revise the methods, but there is no mystery here about what you are expected to do: use Simpson's rule in the first example and use matrix methods in the second.

In more complex problems, you are more often left to work out what method to use for yourself.

Examples

1. Integrate $\displaystyle\int \frac{\sin\theta}{\cos\theta}\,d\theta$

2. If 150 m of fencing is required to enclose three sides of a rectangular field, while the remaining side is bordered by a river, determine the lengths of the sides such that the area enclosed will be a maximum.

In the first example you know you need to use integration, but you will need to bring your expert knowledge gained from lectures and textbooks into play to decide which of the various methods of integration will be the right one here to get you to the answer. In the second example there is more than one possible method. If you have studied differentiation the word 'maximum' might start you thinking in a profitable way; if not, you might try a geometric method perhaps or a drawing.

Generally, students find selecting a method for solution one of the hardest skills to develop, especially when the problem is expressed in words rather than in mathematical symbols. In Section 2 you have already thought about how to analyse a problem when you first meet it, and this certainly helps you to make a start. Look at all the things you know about the problem and all the expert knowledge you feel might be related to it. Can you think of strategies you might try? If you can think of more than one strategy for your problem, write yourself a list so you don't forget your other ideas while you try out your first one.

Once you have an idea about how to start, you need to be very systematic. The process you need is shown in Figure 17.3.

DEVISE	CARRY OUT	REFLECT	CARRY OUT	REFLECT	
Select your solution strategy	Start using it to solve the problem	Is it going OK? YES	Finish it off	How did it go? Was it a good method? YES	STOP
	Go back and try another method	NO		NO	

Figure 17.3 The problem-solving process

Hot Tip

Remember: you have only failed to solve the problem when you have run out of strategies to try!

But what if you can't begin to think of a strategy at all?

George Pólya was a mathematician, born in Budapest in 1887, who noticed that his students often had trouble solving problems even though they knew a lot of maths. To help them he tried to write a methodology for problem solving. In the end he found that, while there were no hard and fast rules, there were a number of strategies that all worked well at least some of the time. He couldn't find a rule to tell you which strategy to use in any particular case, but he said that all the methods listed below (and some others) were worth considering (Pólya, 1990). You just pick the one that looks most promising for your particular problem and give it a try.

As your experience grows you should be aiming to develop a toolkit of solution methods based on a deep understanding of how the underlying maths works, not a recipe book where you just follow a set of steps to get the answer. This level of skill takes time and effort to develop but by doing all the examples you are set you are going in the right direction.

Making a picture

This tactic is so fundamental to problem solving in science, engineering and technology it should be second nature to you; as soon as you see a problem statement you start to think how you might represent it as a picture. Drawing a diagram helps you to analyse the problem and can sometimes lead directly to a solution. Diagrams, graphs and drawings for problem solving don't need to be beautiful works of art, but they do need to be informative to you, the user.

You can draw any diagram that helps **you** to understand the problem you are considering. It may be a sketch of equipment, a map, a graph or bar chart, a pie chart, a calendar, a Venn diagram, a picture, a spider diagram, a mind map or something else.

Example

A metal block of mass 100 kg rests on a plane surface inclined at $\theta = 20°$ to the horizontal. The coefficient of friction, μ, is 0.75. A force is applied to the block with a rope parallel to the slope of the plane. What is the smallest force required to move the block up the plane? The acceleration due to gravity may be approximated as 9.8 kg m s^{-2}.

Problem analysis

What are you trying to find?

The force required to pull the block up the plane.

The answer will be a number of Newtons.

What are you given?

Mass of block m = 100 N

Angle of block to horizontal $\theta = 20°$

Coefficient of friction $\mu = 0.75$

What expert knowledge might you need? (This will come from your lectures or from reading a mechanics textbook.)

■ The weight of the block $W = mg$, which acts vertically downwards.

■ When the force is just enough for the block to start to move the system is in limiting equilibrium. The sum of forces acting parallel to the plane is zero. The sum of the forces acting perpendicular to the plane is zero.

▶

- The friction force, F, acts in the opposite direction to the direction of motion.

- A normal reaction, N, acts perpendicular to the plane.

- F and N are related by the relation $F = \mu N$, where μ is the coefficient of friction.

At this point a diagram with the forces indicated by arrows should help you to visualise the situation.

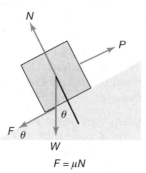

$$F = \mu N$$

Your diagram may look something like this where W is the weight of the block and P is the force pulling up the slope. Note the reminder of the relationship between F and N jotted down next to the diagram.

ACTIVITY 5 Drawing a diagram

What kind of diagram would you draw to help with each of the problems below?

Problem	Diagram
1. John is going to cook a big meal for his friends. He wants to serve the main course at 12:30 and the dessert approximately 30 minutes later. He will cook roast lamb, which takes 10 minutes to prepare, 2 hours to cook and 15 minutes to rest and carve. Also, roast potatoes, which take 10 minutes to prepare and 90 minutes to cook; sprouts, which take 8 minutes to prepare and 20 minutes to cook; and gravy, which takes 10 minutes to prepare and is finished with the contents of the roasting tin after the lamb is removed. For dessert he will make apple pie, which takes 30 minutes to prepare and 40 minutes to cook. He needs to find time to whip some cream (10 minutes) to serve it with. There can be a gap between preparing an item and cooking it. Can you help John to plan how to get the food to the table?	

Problem	Diagram
2. A uniform ladder, of length L, rests against a smooth wall at an angle of θ to the floor. The coefficient of friction between the ladder and the floor is μ_s. Show that the shallowest angle at which the ladder is stable is given by the equation $$\theta = \tan^{-1}\left(\frac{1}{2\mu_s}\right)$$	
3. The professor invited all 40 of the students on his course to tea and provided them with jelly, ice cream and cake. The students who arrived early were hungry and soon all the food was gone. The students who arrived later were faced with an empty table! Fourteen students ate cake, 13 ate jelly and 16 ate ice cream. Three of them ate jelly and cake. Five had cake and ice cream. Eight had jelly and ice cream and two had a plate with all three desserts on. How many students got nothing to eat?	

See the feedback section.

Breaking the problem into parts

Many problems are easier to solve if you break them down into smaller parts, solve each part separately and then build a final answer from the solutions to the smaller parts. This works especially well for more complex problems. Breaking the problem down into parts makes it more manageable. Often you can solve the easier parts first and worry about the harder questions later. This helps you to build your confidence about the problem.

ACTIVITY 6 Breaking into parts

1. You wish to build a dam across a river. How will you design your dam?

The solution to this problem is made up from the solutions to a whole set of related problems. First, consider some quite **broad questions** like those shown in the table below. Can you think of some more that might apply?

Broad initial questions
What is the budget?
What is the time scale for construction?

These then lead to more **specific questions** like those below. You can't answer these until you have answered at least some of the first set of questions Can you think of more of these questions?

More specific questions
Where will you put the dam?
What shape should it be?

You may have added questions about materials to use, number of workers required, equipment needed, etc.

Now pick one of your more specific questions from above and try to break it down further into detailed questions you will need to answer.

Detailed questions

2. Can you break this problem down into the steps you need to carry out to get to a solution?

A cubic polynomial is given as $P(x) = ax^3 + 7x^2 + 2x - b$. When $x = -1$, $P(x) = 0$ and when $x = 1$, $P(x) = 8$. Sketch the graph for P(x) showing clearly where it crosses both axes.

Step 1:
Step 2:
Step 3:
Step 4:
Step 5:

etc.

HINT: You will need to find the roots of the polynomial. See the feedback section.

Solving a simpler, related problem

Sometimes we are faced with a problem that looks too complicated to solve straight away. We can often make some progress by solving similar, but simpler problems until we can see a pattern emerging. Choosing a related problem that gives you insight into the original problem is something you can only learn with practice. Whenever you can use this method, however, it is likely to save you a substantial amount of time and also give you a great feeling of satisfaction.

Example

Find the value of

$$\frac{2 + 4 + 6 + 8 + 10 + 12 + 14 + 16 + 18 + 20 + 22 + 24 + 26 + 28 + 30 + 32 + 34 + 36 + 38}{3 + 6 + 9 + 12 + 15 + 18 + 21 + 24 + 27 + 30 + 33 + 36 + 39 + 42 + 45 + 48 + 51 + 54 + 57}$$

Why do you think this problem looks hard? Probably because there are a lot of numbers on the top and bottom of the fraction. It would be easy to make a mistake when you added them all up.

The most obvious way to simplify it is to reduce the size of the problem.

What do you get if you calculate:

$\frac{2}{3}$?	
$\frac{2 + 4}{3 + 6}$?	
$\frac{2 + 4 + 6}{3 + 6 + 9}$?	

Have you spotted a pattern yet? Do you need to try some more to convince yourself?

So what do you guess the solution to the first problem to be?

ACTIVITY 7 Simplify to find the pattern

1. The factors of 360 add up to 1170. What is the sum of the reciprocals of the factors?

Hint: Expert knowledge required: you need to know what a factor is and what a reciprocal is before you can make any progress. Don't forget to make sure you know what you are trying to find.

2. Find the sum of the first 25 odd numbers.

See the feedback section.

Getting a feel for the size of the answer

Often, when you can't see the answer to a problem straight away it helps to try to estimate the approximate size of the answer. For example, if you calculate the distance of the earth from the sun and get an answer of 22 km then you can be pretty sure your answer is wrong! If you make a point of thinking how big or small an answer might be before you start, then errors in order of magnitude are easier to spot and you can avoid mistakes.

ACTIVITY 8 How big and how small?

Estimate the approximate magnitude of the following:

Item	Approximate size
Wavelength of ultraviolet light	
Land area of Great Britain	
Thickness of a grain of salt	
Diameter of the earth	
Diameter of a golf ball	
Speed of an average person walking	
Distance from the earth to the sun	
Diameter of a human hair	

See the feedback section.

As well as being able to estimate realistic values for physical quantities it is useful to be able to estimate the answer to arithmetical problems. Again, if you estimate before you calculate you have a check on whether your answer is reasonable.

ACTIVITY 9 How big will the answer be?

Try to estimate an answer for these calculations without using a calculator. You are not trying to get the exact answer, just to get an idea of the size of number your answer should be. Instead of using the exact numbers you can use numbers that are easier to deal with to construct an estimator. The numbers you choose for your estimator need to be of the same size as the original ones. Using scientific notation can simplify the process further and often shows you where parts of the calculation cancel each other out. The first two rows give you examples.

Problem	Estimator	Approximate answer
$983 \times 256 \times 198$	$1000 \times 250 \times 200$ $= 1 \times 10^3 \times 25 \times 10 \times 2 \times 100$	50×10^6
$(2439 \times 1220 \times 56) \div 430$	$(2500 \times 1200 \times 50) \div 400$ $= (25 \times 100 \times 12 \times 100 \times 5 \times 10) \div (4 \times 100)$ $= (25 \times 3 \times 100 \times 5 \times 10) \div (1)$	375×10^3
$5236 \div 7805 + 2300 - 4534$		
$(34\,387 \times 54\,567) + 585\,734$		
$((385\,730 \times 348) - 57) \div 680$		

See the feedback section.

You can find out more about these problem-solving strategies and others that Pólya suggested by reading his book *How to solve it* or by looking at the book by Posamentier and Krulik (1998) *Problem Solving Strategies for Efficient and Elegant Solutions*, which gives lots of examples of how to apply Pólya's techniques to both mathematical and more everyday problems.

Above and beyond anything else, you need to practise problem solving using your structured approach. This is the best way to develop your skills. Remember, your lecturers probably aren't cleverer than you; they just have more problem-solving experience.

4 Putting the numbers in

In many problems you have a choice of whether to work with symbols to begin with and to put numbers in later or whether to work with numbers from the start.

Which of the two solutions below might be most useful when you come to revise the topic?

A hinged trapdoor of mass 15 kg and length 1 m is to be opened by applying a force F at $90°$ to the door surface at the opposite end to the hinge. Calculate the magnitude of the force F. Assume the acceleration due to gravity is $10\,\mathrm{m\,s^{-2}}$.

Using symbols first:	Using numbers first:
Let the mass of the door be m. Then the weight of the door is mg where g is the acceleration due to gravity and let l be the length of the beam.	If mass of door is 15 kg, weight of door can be taken as 150 N.

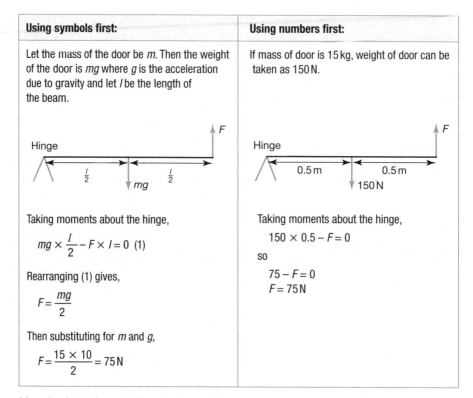

Taking moments about the hinge, $$mg \times \frac{l}{2} - F \times l = 0 \quad (1)$$ Rearranging (1) gives, $$F = \frac{mg}{2}$$ Then substituting for m and g, $$F = \frac{15 \times 10}{2} = 75\,\text{N}$$	Taking moments about the hinge, $$150 \times 0.5 - F = 0$$ so $$75 - F = 0$$ $$F = 75\,\text{N}$$

Now look at the problem below and compare it with the problem above. You should be able to see the similarities even if you haven't studied this topic before.

A uniform beam of length 2 m is attached to a wall at one end by a hinge. The mass of the beam is 10 kg. The beam is supported at the other end by a rope which is attached to the ceiling vertically above the end of the beam. Find the tension in the rope. Assume the acceleration due to gravity is $10\,\text{m}\,\text{s}^{-2}$

Using symbols first:	Using numbers first:
Let the mass of the beam be m, then the weight of the beam is mg. Let g be the acceleration due to gravity and let l be the length of the beam.	If mass of beam is 10 kg, weight of beam can be taken as 100 N.

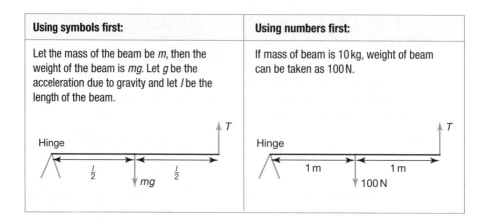

Using symbols first:	Using numbers first:
Taking moments about the hinge, $mg \times \dfrac{l}{2} - T \times l = 0$ (1) Rearranging (1) gives $T = \dfrac{mg}{2}$ Then substituting for m and g, $T = \dfrac{10 \times 10}{2} = 50\,\text{N}$	Taking moments about the hinge, $100 - T \times 2 = 0$ so $100 - 2T = 0$ $T = 50\,\text{N}$

Using the symbols until close to the end highlights the similarities between the two problems and allows you to see patterns easily. The more patterns you can spot, the less you need to memorise methods. You can see that it is often much harder to spot the similarities and patterns when you put the numbers in early in the solution process.

5 Carrying out your strategy

At this stage of your solution you should have worked out:

- what you are trying to find,
- what you have been told,
- what else might be useful,
- one or more ideas about how you could proceed.

You are now ready to try out a solution.

If you are lucky, the first method you try will work. If not, you need to know when to stop trying one way and to try another. Is it the wrong method or have you made a mistake along the way?

Knowing whether your solution is working

You may start out with one or more solution methods in mind. You pick the most likely one and start your solution. How do you know if it is working? At what point should you abandon it and try another way?

Unfortunately there is no hard and fast rule about this. Just like the ability to think of a variety of methods in the first place, knowing if your method is going to work comes with experience. However, there are some questions that you may ask yourself that can help:

Useful questions to check your progress	Comments
Are you confident that each step is correct as you take it?	See Chapter 18 for advice about spotting errors as you work.
Can you imagine what the next step will be? And the next? And the one after that?	You should be looking forward after each step. If you are heading in the right direction, things should be becoming clearer. You should be more aware after each step how you are going to proceed to your goal. The looking forward is like playing a strategy game. The best chess players know all the options for many moves ahead; a novice knows some moves for the next step. You can develop this skill with practice.
Have you used *all* the information you were given?	In textbook problems you are usually given no extraneous information, so if you have a use for it all, it's probably a good sign. In real-life problems this may not be true, so use this question with care.

6 On reflection

This chapter has taken you through the steps in solving a problem. First you really need to get to grips with what you are looking for and what information you have been given. Only then can you start to think about how you might solve your problem. Solving the problem itself is often an iterative process: you try a solution to see if it works and, if not, you adapt it a bit or try a different method until you get there. With plenty of practice you can build up your abilities and develop a systematic approach that gives you a sturdy framework for problem solving.

Summary of this chapter

Have look at Figure 17.4 and make sure you are familiar with the concepts.

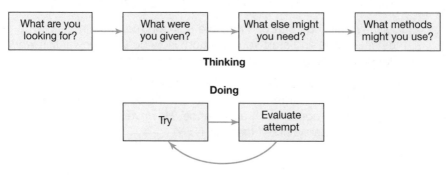

Figure 17.4 Summary of the problem-solving process

ACTIVITY 10 Update your personal development planner

Reflect on your current abilities and consider what needs to improve. You may want to transfer this information to your institution's personal development planner scheme.

Grade your confidence on a scale of 1–5 where 1 = poor and 5 = good.

My developing skills	Confidence level 1–5	Plans to improve
Getting started on a problem.		
Choosing a method for solution.		
Working with symbols.		
Knowing if you are heading the right way.		

Date: _____

Getting extra help

- Is there a skills centre or drop-in maths workshop you can attend?
- Is there a timetabled workshop or tutorial provided to help answer your questions?
- Does the tutor who set the problem sheet have 'office hours' where you can go and ask for help?

Feedback on activities

ACTIVITY 1 Closed or open?

	Closed or open?
Two dustcarts collected bags of rubbish. One collected 47 bags and one collected 56 bags. How many bags of rubbish were collected all together?	**Closed** – you need to come up with a method but no further data.
What would be the best type of dam to use to dam the River Thames?	**Open** – you need to know where it is to be dammed, what the dam is for, how wide the river is, etc.

	Closed or open?
Solve $2x + 3y = 1$ $x - 4y = 17$	**Closed** – you need to know a method to solve simultaneous equations but all the facts about x and y and their relationship are contained in the question.
Estimate the distance from the earth to the sun.	**Open** – you can just have a guess or you can try to improve your estimate by researching facts, but there is no information at all to help you in the question statement.
If Tom has three times as many apples as Susan and Susan has a quarter as many as Joe, who has four, how many does Mary have if Mary has two more than Tom?	**Closed** – the question statement may take a bit of deciphering, but all the information about the relationships is there.
A round wheel with a radius of 37 cm rolls at a constant speed of 3 revolutions per second. How far does the axle of the wheel move in 8 seconds?	**Closed** – you need to make sure you understand the more technical words and you need to know how speed, distance and time are related, but you don't need any extra data to get the answer.
Is it better for you to walk or cycle to university?	**Open** – for a start you need to define what 'better' might mean in this context.

ACTIVITY 2 What are you looking for?

	The solution will be …
If Tom has three times as many apples as Susan and Susan has a quarter as many as Joe, who has four, how many does Mary have if Mary has two more than Tom?	How many apples Mary has. The answer will be a number.
Design an efficient tin opener.	A diagram or description in words. To give a more precise description of the answer for this open problem you would need to work on the problem statement to define it more precisely. For instance, in what way should the tin opener be efficient?
Solve $2x + 3y = 1$ $x - 4y = 17$	Values for x and y. The answer will be two numbers.

ACTIVITY 3 Identifying givens

	I have been given …
If Tom has three times as many apples as Susan and Susan has a quarter as many as Joe, who has four, how many does Mary have if Mary has two more than Tom?	The number of apples Joe has ($J = 4$). The relationship between the number of apples Susan has and the number Joe has ($S = J/4$). The relationship between the number of apples Tom has and the number Susan has ($T = 3S$). The relationship between the number of apples Mary has and the number Tom has ($M = T + 2$).
Design an efficient tin opener	Very little – I know what function a tin opener has, but I will need to find a definition for *efficient*. This is a very open problem and open problems are characterised by having fewer 'givens' and therefore more that you must define yourself by research or thinking.
Solve $2x + 3y = 1$ $x - 4y = 17$	Two relationships between the value of x and the value of y.

ACTIVITY 4 Using your expert knowledge

Problem	Expert knowledge needed
1. Mary looked out of her window and saw some chickens and cows passing by. She counted all the legs of the chickens and cows and found that the total number of legs added up to 66. How many of each kind of animal passed by her window if the total number of animals is 24?	How many legs a chicken has. How many legs a cow has.
2. A car travels at 60 mph. How far does it travel in 30 minutes?	The meaning of mph. The relationship between speed, distance travelled and time.

ACTIVITY 5 Drawing a diagram

Problem	Diagram
1. Cooking the dinner	You might find a time line to be the best diagram for this one. You can put in the time for dinner and for dessert to be served and work backwards from there.
2. Leaning ladder	This is a more traditional type of diagram for a mechanics problem. You can start with the wall, the floor and the ladder. You may need some expert knowledge to put all the force arrows in.
3. Tea party	A Venn diagram with a circle for each type of food might help you to sort this one out.

ACTIVITY 6 Breaking into parts

1. You wish to build a dam across a river. How will you design your dam?

Broad initial questions
What is the budget?
What is the time scale for construction?
What is the dam for? It might be to control flooding, to generate hydroelectric power or it may have more than one purpose.

You might also have thought of the environmental impact, the geology and topology of the area, communications with the build site, availability of materials, annual rainfall, etc.

More specific questions
Where will you put the dam?
What shape should it be?
What dimensions should it have?

You may also have added questions about materials to use, number of workers required, equipment needed, etc.

Detailed questions
What constraints does the local topography place on the shape?
What load will be on the dam due to the water behind it?
Will it need to have a road on the top?

2. A cubic polynomial is given as $P(x) = ax^3 + 7x^2 + 2x - b$. When $x = -1$, $P(x) = 0$ and when $x = 1$, $P(x) = 8$. Sketch the graph for $P(x)$ showing clearly where it crosses both axes.

The steps could be:

Step 1: Use the remainder theorem to derive the system of equations that a and b must satisfy.
Step 2: Solve the equations from step 1 and by using the values of a and b, rewrite $P(x)$ with the values you find, replacing the symbols a and b.
Step 3: By using the remainder theorem show that $x + 3$ is a factor of $P(x)$.
Step 4: Factorise $P(x)$ into linear factors and solve $P(x) = 0$.
Step 5: Find the value of $P(x)$ when $x = 0$.

You now have everything you need to sketch the graph.

ACTIVITY 7 Simplify to find the pattern

1. The factors of 360 add up to 1170. What is the sum of the reciprocals of the factors?

You are trying to find a value for

$$\frac{1}{1} + \frac{1}{2} + \frac{1}{3} + \frac{1}{4} + \ldots + \frac{1}{120} + \frac{1}{180} + \frac{1}{360}$$

What about trying the same thing with the factors of 12 or of 15 and looking for a pattern?

The answer you are looking for is 1170/360.

2. Find the sum of the first 25 odd numbers.

Start with 1, then $1 + 3$, then $1 + 3 + 5$, etc. What is the pattern?

The answer you are looking for is 625.

ACTIVITY 8 How big and how small?

Estimate the approximate magnitude of the following:

Item	Approximate size
Wavelength of ultraviolet light	400 nm
Land area of Great Britain	241 590 km^2
Thickness of a grain of salt	1 mm
Diameter of the earth	10^7 m
Diameter of a golf ball	4 cm
Speed of an average person walking	4.5 kph
Distance from the earth to the sun	150×10^9 m
Diameter of a human hair	100×10^{-6} m

ACTIVITY 9 How big will the answer be?

Problem	Estimator	Approximate answer
$983 \times 256 \times 198$	$1000 \times 250 \times 200$ $= 1 \times 10^3 \times 25 \times 10 \times 2 \times 100$	50×10^6
$(2439 \times 1220 \times 56) \div 430$	$(2500 \times 1200 \times 50) \div 400$ $= (25 \times 100 \times 12 \times 100 \times 5 \times 10) \div (4 \times 100)$ $= (25 \times 3 \times 100 \times 5 \times 10) \div (1)$	375×10^3
$5236 + 7805 + 2300 - 4534$	$= 5000 + 7000 + 2000 - 4500$	10 500
$(34387 \times 54567) + 585734$	$= (34000 \times 54000) + 580000$	1.8×10^9. Note that adding the final value makes little difference to the estimate as it is four orders of magnitude smaller than the product of the first two terms so it has no effect on the first two figures.
$((385730 \times 348) - 57) \div 680$	$= ((380000 \times 350)) - 50 \div 700$	190×10^3. Again – not worth subtracting 50 from something of the order of 10^6 when only looking for an estimate.

References

- Pólya, G. (1990) *How to solve it*, 2nd edn. Harmondsworth, Penguin Books.
- Posamentier, A. S. and Krulik, S. (1998) *Problem Solving Strategies for Efficient and Elegant Solutions*, Thousand Oaks, CA, Corwin Press.

18 Getting help, and helping yourself

If you take a systematic approach to problem solving you will find it gets easier, but there will always be topics and ideas you find difficult. No matter how careful you are, you will make algebraic and numerical errors as well from time to time. If you can learn to find your own errors you will quickly see your marks improve and you will find the whole problem-solving process less frustrating; good ideas about how to solve won't be messed up by introducing avoidable errors along the way. In the long run, everyone needs help from time to time however good they are at maths, but if you can get targeted help that is aimed at the difficulties you have identified yourself, you will learn faster and improve more quickly. Employers particularly value the ability to reflect and appraise your own work so you will also be developing a transferable skill.

In this chapter you will:

1. find out about testing the answer you arrive at
2. learn how to spot errors in your work
3. think about the best way to define and get the help you need.

USING THIS CHAPTER

If you want to dip into the sections	Page	If you want to try the activities	Page
1 Checking your work	407	1 Is the answer right?	409
2 Getting useful help	418	2 Can you spot the errors in the calculations below?	410
3 On reflection	421	3 Check the dimensions	417
		4 Update your personal development planner	421

Estimate your current levels of confidence. At the end of the chapter you will have the chance to reassess these levels and incorporate this into your personal development planner (PDP). Mark between 1 (poor) and 5 (good) for the following:

Testing whether your answer is correct.	Finding numerical and algebraic mistakes in your own work.	Knowing how to check whether you have the right formula.	Asking for help that really helps you.

Date: _____

1 Checking your work

When you have finished working through a problem you will want to try to check if you have the right answer. While you are learning how to use a new method of solution or acquiring a new skill you will often be given at least the numerical parts of the answers to a problem set by your tutor. In the real world, we hardly ever know what the answer is, so it is a good idea to get used to checking whether your own answer is plausible before you look at any answers you have been given. If you develop this habit while you have the opportunity to check, you will carry it on into the situations where you can't check and it will help you to have confidence in the solutions you come up with.

Checking your solution has two aspects:

1. Testing your answer.
2. Spotting your errors.

Testing your answer

It isn't always easy to see how to check your answer independently. Sometimes it is almost as hard as finding a solution method in the first place. With practice, however, you can train yourself to be better at devising a good way. You should get into the habit of thinking of a check for every problem you solve and carrying it out. Some useful things that can work are:

- substituting your answer back into the first line of the problem – this is often good for numerical answers and solutions to equations;
- working backwards from the answer statement to the problem statement – try this for proofs;
- putting your solution away for an hour or two and then going back to try it again. Do you get the same answer? Getting the same answer the second time can increase your confidence in your answer. Getting different answers tells you at least one of them is wrong so it is then worth your while to take some time to consider why. If you can't find a mathematical way to test your answer then this is your best option.

Examples

1. Solve for x and y

$$2x + 3y = 1 \quad (1)$$

$$x - 4y = 17 \quad (2)$$

Answer:

$$x = 5, y = -3.$$

Check by substituting answers back into the left-hand side of equation (1):

$$2 \times 5 + 3 \times -3 = 10 - 9 = 1$$

which equals the right-hand side of equation (1) so the answer is likely to be right. As an extra check you can also substitute your answer into the left-hand side of equation (2) if you wish.

2. Split into partial fractions

$$\frac{3x + 5}{(x + 3)(x - 1)}$$

Answer:

$$\frac{3x + 5}{(x + 3)(x - 1)} = \frac{1}{x + 3} + \frac{2}{x - 1}$$

Check you have the right partial fractions by working backwards. Add the fractions in the answer to see if you get back to the initial expression:

$$\frac{1}{x + 3} + \frac{2}{x - 1} = \frac{1(x - 1) + 2(x + 3)}{(x + 3)(x - 1)} = \frac{x - 1 + 2x + 6}{(x + 3)(x - 1)} = \frac{3x + 5}{(x + 3)(x - 1)}$$

This is the initial expression so the answer seems to be correct.

ACTIVITY 1 Is the answer right?

Can you find a way to check if the given answers are correct?

1. Find the roots of the quadratic equation $6x^2 + 5x - 4$.

    Answer:

    $$x = \frac{1}{2} \text{ and } x = -\frac{4}{3}$$

    Can you check it?

2. Find the length of the unknown side using Pythagoras's theorem.

    Answer: 8 units.

    Was it correct?

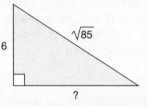

3. Solve for x and y

    $$x + 3y = 14$$
    $$2x - 3y = -8$$

    Answer:

    $$x = 2 \text{ and } y = 5$$

    Right or wrong?

4. Find $\int \cos 2x\, dx$.

    Answer: $\frac{1}{2} \sin 2x + C$

    How can you tell if this is right?

See the feedback section.

Spotting your errors

If you find your answer is wrong you need to go back and check your solution to find the error. In fact, even if your answer is right you may have made errors that cancel each other out, so checking your reasoning and your working are good habits to get into for every problem you solve.

Often students talk about 'going over' their solution, but this can be a very ineffective way to check your work if all you mean by it is: looking back at each line to see if it appears right. After all, if you made a mistake the first time, you are quite unlikely to spot it unless you take an active approach to tracking it down.

If you make errors in algebra or arithmetic, you will lose marks even if your overall solution follows a sound method. You may only be penalised a small amount for each error, but the lost marks can add up to a substantial penalty. Good accuracy saves these marks and makes it easier for you to check that your solution works.

If you think you know how to solve a problem it's easy to rush ahead at top speed writing down the answer. Taking a more measured pace will help you to maintain your accuracy. It might seem slower, but if you only have to do the problem once to get it right it will save you time in the long run. Think tortoise not hare!

A frequent cause of errors is miscopying from one line to another. Reading each line aloud and saying what you have done can help because you spot changes in numbers more readily. Of course, in an exam you won't be able to do this, but doing it during private study can train you not to make this kind of error very often.

Hot Tip Accurate working is a habit. Checking for errors as you work trains you to spot errors more readily.

ACTIVITY 2 Can you spot the errors in the calculations below?

The more you practise with your own work, the better you'll get at this.

Try talking to yourself aloud about what is happening at each stage. Does it help you to find the mistakes?

Can you spot the errors?	Say to yourself …	Answer
1. $3x + 1 = 25$ $\quad 2x = 24$ $\quad\quad x = 12$	Three x plus one equals 25. Taking the 1 to the other side and subtracting it from 25 leaves 24 on the right so then two x equals 24 and dividing by 2 to leave x on its own tells me that x equals 12.	(You should have found one error.)
2. $24x - 3y - 2(x+y) + 5 = 10x + 5y - 4$ $24x - 3y - 2x + 2y + 5 = 10x + 5y - 4$ $\quad\quad 22x - y = 10x + 5y + 1$ $\quad\quad\quad 12x = 6y + 1$		(You should have found two errors.)
3. $3(8x + 6) = 10$ $\quad 27x + 18 = 10$ $\quad\quad 27x = -8$ $\quad\quad\quad x = -8/27$		(You should have found one error.)

See the feedback section.

Common errors

It is impossible to list every error you might make and why, but if you can avoid the ones in the table below you will be doing well. They are all based on common misconceptions or errors that are found in many students' work.

	Wrong	RIGHT!	Comments
$3(2x + 1)$	$= 6x + 1$	$= 6x + 3$	The 3 outside the brackets multiplies **every term** inside the brackets.
$2x + 1 - (x + 2)$	$= x + 3$	$= x - 1$	The minus sign operates on **every term** inside the brackets.
$-\int x + 3\,dx$	$= -\dfrac{x^2}{2} + 3x + C$	$= -\dfrac{x^2}{2} - 3x + C$	The minus sign operates on **every term** inside the integral.
$\sin(x + y)$	$= \sin x + \sin y$	You can't simplify this without more information.	One of the first rules of maths you learn is $3(2x + 1) = 6x + 3$. It seems natural to assume it works in cases other than multiplication. Mostly **it doesn't!** Try it – let $x = 30°$ and $y = 60°$. Does $\sin 90° = \sin 30° + \sin 60°$?
$(x + y)^2$	$= x^2 + y^2$	You can't simplify this without more information.	As for the case above, squaring doesn't follow the same rules as multiplication. Try it – let $x = 2$ and $y = 3$. Find $x + y$, then square your answer and compare with the answer from squaring x, squaring y and then adding.
$\sqrt{x + y}$	$= \sqrt{x} + \sqrt{y}$	You can't simplify this without more information.	This is another similar case. Test it out using $x = 2$ and $y = 3$ again.
$\log(x + y)$	$= \log x + \log y$	You can't simplify this without more information.	And again. This is especially confusing because $\log(xy) = \log x + \log y$ is true. Make sure you have learnt your log rules really well.
$\dfrac{1}{x + y}$	$= \dfrac{1}{x} + \dfrac{1}{y}$	You can't simplify this without more information.	And another of the same type of confusion. Once more – try it with $x = 2$ and $y = 3$.
$\dfrac{d(uv)}{dx}$	$= \dfrac{du}{dx} + \dfrac{dv}{dx}$	$= v\dfrac{du}{dx} + u\dfrac{dv}{dx}$	Another case of the same. If it was as simple as the wrong answer – we wouldn't need the chain rule.

Study Skills for Science, Engineering and Technology Students

	Wrong	RIGHT!	Comments
$\int uvdx$	$= \int udx + \int vdx$	The right answer here depends on u and v. Maybe you need to substitute or to use the chain rule. You'll have think further about the form.	This is like the one above. We have lots of rules for integrating products depending on the form of the product, but it is rarely as simple as the wrong case shown here.
$\log \sqrt{x}$	$= \sqrt{\log x}$	You can't simplify this without more information.	This is a different type of confusion from above – but it also comes from working mainly with numbers in your early studies. For multiplication $2 \times 3 = 3 \times 2$. The order you do things doesn't matter. However, **mostly order matters**. You can't change the order of operations just because you feel like it. Evaluate the expression in both cases with $x = 2$. Same answer each time? No! So the two expressions can't mean the same thing.
$\sin 3x$	$= 3 \sin x$	You can't simplify this without more information.	As above – you can't just change the order. Convince yourself by considering $x = 30°$
$\dfrac{(3x+7)(2x-9)+(4x-1)}{(3x+7)(x^2+1)}$	$= \dfrac{(2x-9)+(4x-1)}{(x^2+1)}$	You can't simplify this without more information.	This is a confusion about cancelling. Think about numerical fractions. There we say that $\dfrac{2}{6} = \dfrac{1}{3}$. The top and bottom have a common factor. We can do the same for $\dfrac{5+10}{25} = \dfrac{5(1+2)}{25} = \dfrac{1+2}{5} = \dfrac{3}{5}$ Notice that the 5 multiplies **every term** on the top. In our algebraic example, if we are to cancel, the same must be true. There must be a factor which multiplies every term on the top and the same factor which multiplies every term on the bottom.

412

	Wrong	RIGHT!	Comments
$\dfrac{x}{3x+1} + \dfrac{4x}{2x-5} = 6$	$x + 4x$ $= 6(3x+1)(2x-5)$	$x(2x-5)$ $+ 4x(3x+1)$ $= 6(3x+1)(2x-5)$	The rule for equations is: whatever you do to the right-hand side you must also do to the left-hand side. If you multiply the right by $(3x+1)$ you must also multiply the left by $(3x+1)$. That means **every term** on the left and right gets multiplied by $(3x+1)$. For the first term then, the x is multiplied by $(3x+1)$ and divided by $(3x+1)$, a common factor so you can cancel.
$\sin^2 x$	$= \sin(x^2)$	$= (\sin x)^2$	Here the notation is meant to distinguish between 'take the sine of x and then square the answer' and 'take x, square it and find the sine of the answer'. Only the first is correct.
$\sin^{-1} x$	$= \dfrac{1}{\sin x} = \operatorname{cosec} x$	$= \arcsin x$	This notation is used to mean the inverse operation of taking the sine: the arcsine or inverse sine. It **does not** mean the reciprocal of the sine (known as the cosecant) even though in other cases the power -1 does mean 'one over'. This is really confusing and inconsistent – so watch out.

Checking the dimensions

In applied subjects where the equations you use describe real physical events and quantities, you can use the **dimensions** of your equations to help you check you are getting things right. The dimensions are the units that describe the quantities you are working with.

The fundamental dimensions are:

Dimension	SI unit
Mass	metre (m)
Length	kilogram (kg)
Time	second (s)
Electric current	ampere (A)
Thermodynamic temperature	kelvin (K)
Amount of substance	mole (m)
Luminous intensity	candela (cd)

413

If you are unfamiliar with SI units and their notation you can find a good reference at the National Physical Laboratory website (**http://www.npl.co.uk/server.php?show=nav.364**).

From these fundamental units you can build up derived units. Some of the more common derived units have been given a name of their own. Often they are called after a famous scientist, so for example the dimension of force is $kg\,m\,s^{-2}$ which is also known as the Newton (N). Some of the many derived units are shown in the table below:

Quantity	SI unit	Also known as ...
Frequency	s^{-1}	Hertz (Hz)
Force	$kg\,m\,s^{-2}$	Newton (N)
Energy	$m^2\,kg\,s^{-2}$	Joule (J)
Power	$m^2\,kg\,s^{-3}$	Watt (W)
Area	m^2	
Volume	m^3	
Speed	$m\,s^{-1}$	
Acceleration	$m\,s^{-2}$	
Density	$kg\,m^3$	
Voltage	$m^2\,kg\,s^{-3}\,A^{-1}$	volt (V)
Current density	$A\,m^{-2}$	
Electrical resistance	$m^2\,kg\,s^{-3}\,A^{-2}$	ohm (Ω)
Capacitance	$s^4\,A^2\,m^{-2}\,kg^{-1}$	Farad (F)
Magnetic field strength	$A\,m^{-1}$	
Molar heat capacity	$m^2\,kg\,s^{-2}\,mol^{-1}\,K^{-1}$	$J\,mol^{-1}\,J^{-1}$
Luminance	$cd\,m^{-2}$	

When you add physical quantities together they must have the same dimensions. You can't add a mass to a force because it has no real meaning – it's like adding apples and oranges. Also, when you say one quantity in an equation is equal to another they must have the same dimensions. You can't say a force equals a mass: again it has no real meaning and it's like saying a sheep equals a goat. These two facts give us a very useful way to check equations:

- When equations have terms that are added or subtracted they must have the same dimensions.
- When there is an equals sign (=) the terms on each side must have the same dimensions.

So when an equation is written down it is quite easy to see if something is wrong.

Example

1. Is the following equation written down correctly?

$$E = mgh + \frac{1}{2}mv^2$$

where E is the total energy of an object, m is its mass, g is the acceleration due to gravity, h is the distance of the object above the earth's surface and v is its current velocity.

Answer: The SI units of energy are Joules, which have the dimensions $[m^2\,kg\,s^{-2}]$.

The equals sign tells us that the right-hand side of the equation must also have the dimensions $[m^2\,kg\,s^{-2}]$. Also, since there are two terms added together on the right-hand side, they must each have the same dimensions, so each of those terms must have the units $[m^2\,kg\,s^{-2}]$. Notice that we usually put the dimensions in square brackets.

Consider the first term on the right:

  mgh is a mass × an acceleration × a distance

with dimensions

  $[kg] \times [m\,s^{-2}] \times [m] = [m^2\,kg\,s^{-2}]$

so this term has the same units as the energy on the left-hand side.

Now look at the second term on the right:

  $\frac{1}{2}mv^2$ is a pure number × a mass × a squared velocity

with dimensions

  $[1] \times [kg] \times [m^2\,s^{-2}] = [m^2\,kg\,s^{-2}]$

so this also has the same dimensions as the left-hand side.

We are able to conclude that our equation is likely to be correct because each term on the right has the same dimensions and both have the same dimensions as the term on the left.

Hot Tip

Numerical multiplying constants like the ½ in the second term have dimensions of [1].

You might be surprised that we are only saying our equation is likely to be right; after all, it passed both our tests. The terms we are adding have the same dimensions and the terms on either side of our equals sign have the same dimensions. What this method can't tell you, however, is whether the constants are correct. All multiplying constants have dimensions of [1] so we can't use this method to check whether we have the right values for them. The correct equation could equally well be

$$E = mgh + \frac{1}{25}mv^2$$

We wouldn't know. It wouldn't change the dimensions. (In fact the original version was correct.)

Dimensional analysis is a good test for whether something is wrong, but you are likely to need some expert knowledge to decide what is wrong and to fix it.

Example

2. Is this equation likely to be correct or incorrect?

$$h = ut + \frac{1}{2}gt^3$$

where g is the acceleration due to gravity, h is the distance of an object above the earth's surface, u was its initial velocity and t is the time elapsed since it started to move.

Answer: The right-hand side represents a height so the dimension is [m].

The first term on the left is ut which is

velocity × a time: $[m\,s^{-1}\,s] = [m]$

so that is the same as the right-hand side.

The second term on the left is $\frac{1}{2}gt^3$ which is

constant × an acceleration × a time cubed: $[1] \times [m\,s^{-2}] \times [s^3] = [m\,s]$

This is not the same as the right-hand side. it is also different to the first term on the left.

Something is wrong with the equation!

Since we have ended up with an extra factor of [s] in our dimensions we should suspect either the acceleration term because it has $[s^{-2}]$ in it or the time term which has $[s^3]$. A quick check in the table of derived units above tells us the dimensions of acceleration are correct, so it is likely we have the wrong power of t. In fact it should be t^2.

Some useful things to know for using this dimension-checking technique are:

- For differentiation the units of the denominator of the differential coefficient divide the units of the numerator, so if v is a velocity then the dimensions of dv/dt are

$$[\text{m s}^{-1}] \div [\text{s}] = [\text{m s}^{-2}].$$

Note that the expression turns out to have the dimensions of acceleration as you might have expected.

- In integration the variable of integration multiplies the units so, for example, if a is an acceleration the dimensions of $\equiv a dt$ are:

$$[\text{m s}^{-2}] \times [\text{s}] = [\text{m s}^{-1}].$$

Note that this integral therefore has the dimensions of velocity.

- Angles in radians are defined as a ratio of two lengths. They have units $[\text{m}] \div [\text{m}] = [1]$. So x radians has dimensions of $[1]$ like a constant.
- Some mathematical functions can only be applied to quantities with dimensions of $[1]$. For instance, you can take the sine, cosine or tangent of a number or an angle in radians but it makes no sense to talk about the sine of a mass or of a length. The same is true for $\log x$, $\ln x$ and e^x; the x must be a pure number with dimension $[1]$. If you are applying these functions and you find the expression you are applying them to has dimensions other than $[1]$, something is wrong with your formula.

ACTIVITY 3 Check the dimensions

Are the formulae given in the left-hand column of the table correct?

Formula	Working	Formula appears correct? (Yes/No)
$\Delta Q = mc\Delta T$ where ΔQ is heat gain in J, m a mass in kg, c is a specific heat capacity in $\text{J kg}^{-1}\,\text{K}^{-1}$ and ΔT is a change in temperature in K.		
$F = \dfrac{Gm_1 m_2}{r}$ where F is a force in N, G is the gravitational constant with dimensions $\text{N m}^2\,\text{kg}^{-2}$, m_1 and m_2 are masses in kg and r is a distance in m.		

Formula	Working	Formula appears correct? (Yes/No)
$\dfrac{dp}{dr} = \dfrac{\rho u^2}{r}$ where p is pressure in $kg\,m^{-1}\,s^{-2}$ (also known as Pascals, Pa), r is a distance in m, ρ is a density in $kg\,m^{-3}$ and u is a velocity with units of $m\,s^{-1}$		
$T = 2\pi\sqrt{\dfrac{l}{g}}$ where T is a period in seconds, l is a length in metres and g is the acceleration due to gravity in $m\,s^{-2}$.		
$y = A\sin(\omega t + kx)$ where y is a distance [m], A is a distance [m], ω is an angular velocity $[rad\,s^{-1}]$, t is a time [s], k has dimensions $[m^{-1}]$ and x is a distance [m].		
$V = V_0\left(1 - e^{\frac{-t}{RC}}\right)$ where V and V_0 are voltages, R is a resistance and C is a capacitance.		

See the feedback section.

Finally, what if your equation or expression is not given in SI units? It doesn't really matter from the point of view of dimension checking. You can express your force in $[g\,km\,h^{-1}]$ if you wish; it's unusual, but it won't affect your check for correctness.

2 Getting useful help

To be successful in studying maths-based subjects, you need to be **actively involved** in managing your learning process and your study time. The first time your tutors notice you're having trouble may be when you perform poorly on an assessment, and that may be too late to put things right.

If you can help yourself by reflecting on your progress and asking for help as soon as you need it, you will minimise any risk of failure. You need to be realistic; you mustn't give up on a topic or set of problems too soon, but on the other hand you shouldn't struggle on alone for ever. For some students, working with a friend is helpful; others feel too shy to say they don't understand when they are working with someone who seems to know it all. You need to think carefully and decide what suits you best.

In maths-based subjects, the new material builds on your previous studies, so anything you don't understand now will make future material more difficult to understand. If you don't sort out your problems as they arise you will be building on shaky foundations.

Get help as *soon* as you need it. Don't wait until a test is near.

Use the resources you have available

- **Ask questions in class**. That way you get help *and* stay actively involved in the class.
- **Attend the tutorials**. Lecturers like to help students who want to help themselves.
- **Ask friends**, members of your study group, or anyone else who can help. The classmate who explains something to you learns just as much as you do; he or she must think carefully about how to explain the particular concept or solution in a clear way. So don't be reluctant to ask, the classmate will probably find it as useful as you do.
- **All** students need help at some point, so be sure to get the help *you* need *when* you need it.

Don't be afraid to ask questions. *Any question* is better than no question at all (at least your lecturer/tutor will know you are confused), but a *good question* will allow your helper to quickly identify *exactly* what you don't understand.

Have a look at the questions in the table below and consider the likely outcomes:

Not very helpful comment:	Likely outcome
I don't understand this section.	The best you can expect in reply to such a remark is a brief review of the section, which may miss out the particular thing(s) which you don't understand.
Good comment:	**Likely outcome**
I don't understand why $f(x + h)$ doesn't equal $f(x) + f(h)$.	This is a very specific query that will get a very specific response and hopefully clear up your difficulty.
Okay question:	**Likely outcome**
How do you do question 17?	Someone may tell you how to do it, but then you will learn nothing about the problem-solving process. Alternatively they will give a brief hint that may solve your difficulties or may not.

Better question:	Likely outcome
Can you show me how to get started on question 17?	Someone can give you a targeted hint and then let you try to finish the problem on your own.
Good question:	**Likely outcome**
This is how I tried to do question 17. What went wrong?	The focus of attention and explanation is on your thought process and your misconceptions.

You need to recognise that sometimes you do need help to make progress in learning maths and it is up to you to seek out that help. As soon as you do get help with a problem, try to work through another similar problem by yourself. This reinforces your understanding so you will be more likely to remember the point in the future.

You must control the kind of help you get. Helpers should be coaches, they should encourage you, give you hints as you need them, and, very occasionally, show you how to do problems. They should not, nor should they be expected to, actually do the work you need to do for yourself. They are there to help you work out how to understand and learn the maths you need, but after all: your tutor can't take the exams for you.

Very often students ask to be provided with model answers. This means a complete solution to the problems that the tutor has written out for them. Although this seems an attractive idea because it will allow you to see how to do the problem with minimum effort on your part, a model answer can't teach you to develop the skill of problem solving. All the thinking part of the solution has happened by the time you write down the first line of the solution. You can only learn how to get started on a problem by practice through solving lots of problems and questioning how you do it as you go. If you look at a model answer too soon you will avoid doing the thinking for yourself. This doesn't help you to learn how to tackle the early stages of the process that students find hardest to master.

If model answers or worked examples are available then they can be useful for the third and fourth parts of the problem-solving process; the doing parts. You can always use them to check whether any final numerical answer you have obtained is correct. If they use the same methods and techniques that you have chosen, you can use them to check your method as well, but remember: there is usually more than one way to do a problem. If you have used another method then the model answer won't help you to know if it is valid or not. So use these model answers if they exist, but use them wisely and don't use them to bypass the work you need to do yourself if you are to improve.

3 On reflection

If you take an active approach to your studies by questioning, defining your difficulties as clearly as you can and reflecting on your progress from time to time, you will find that your problem-solving abilities grow. Being able to spot your own errors is a skill that develops the more you work at it and, in the long run, getting into good habits such as testing your solution whenever you can will be worthwhile in terms of both time and effort. Everybody gets stuck from time to time when they are learning a new subject, so preparing carefully before you ask for help will make sure you really get what you need from your tutorial sessions.

Summary of this chapter

Have a look at Figure 18.1 for a summary of the key points.

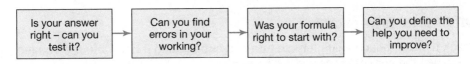

Figure 18.1 Checking your answers and getting help

ACTIVITY 4 Update your personal development planner

Reflect on your current abilities and consider what needs to improve. You may want to transfer this information to your institution's personal development planner scheme.

Grade your confidence on a scale of 1–5 where 1 = poor and 5 = good.

My developing skills	Confidence level 1–5	Plans to improve
Testing my answers.		
Finding my mistakes.		
Checking dimensions of formulae.		
Asking for useful help.		

Date: _____

Getting extra help

- Make sure you know when your timetabled tutorials are and attend them regularly.
- Is there a study centre or a system of drop-in tutorials for maths that you can access?
- Can you swap your work with a friend and check each other's? Sometimes you can't see your own errors but you can often develop your skills more quickly with another person's work.

Feedback on Activities

ACTIVITY 1 Is the answer right?

1. Check by taking each value for x in turn and substituting it back into the equation. If it's correct the sum of the terms will be zero.

   The answer was correct.

2. Take the answer and the length of one other side. If you apply Pythagoras's theorem to this do you get the same value as the remaining side?

   The answer was wrong.

3. This needed the same method as the example. The given answer was wrong, though.

4. Differentiation is the opposite of integration. Differentiate the answer to see if you get the initial expression that you were asked to integrate.

   This answer was correct.

ACTIVITY 2 Can you spot the errors in the calculations below?

Can you spot the errors?	Answer
1. $\;\;\textcircled{3x} + 1 = 25$ $\;\;\;\;\;\;\textcircled{2x} = 24$ $\;\;\;\;\;\;\;\;x = 12$	$3x$ became $2x$ – a transcription error.

Can you spot the errors?	Answer

2. $24x - 3y - 2(x + y) + 5 = 10x + 5y - 4$
    $24x - 3y - 2x \boxed{+\ 2y} + 5 = 10x + 5y - 4$
       $22x - y = 10x + 5y \boxed{+\ 1}$
         $12x = 6y + 1$
	The minus sign outside the bracket multiplies each of the terms inside so it should be $-2y$.
	
	 The 5 was taken to the other side of the equation but the sign wasn't changed. If you think of the operation 'subtract 5 from each side' rather than 'take 5 across and change the sign' you will make fewer errors when you rearrange equations.

3. $3(8x + 6) = 10$
    $\boxed{27x} + 18 = 10$
      $27x = -8$
        $x = -8/27$
	$3 x 8 = 24$ not 27

ACTIVITY 3 Check the dimensions

Formula	Working	Formula appears correct? (Yes/No)
$\Delta Q = mc\Delta T$ where ΔQ is heat gain in J, m a mass in kg, c is a specific heat capacity in $J\,kg^{-1}\,K^{-1}$ and ΔT is a change in temperature in K.	LHS: $Q\,[J] = [m^2\,kg\,s^{-2}]$ RHS: $mc\Delta T$ [kg] $\times$ [$J\,kg^{-1}\,K^{-1}$] $\times$ K $= J = [m^2\,kg\,s^{-2}]$	Yes
$F = \dfrac{Gm_1 m_2}{r}$ where F is a force in N, G is the gravitational constant with dimensions $N\,m^2\,kg^{-2}$, m_1 and m_2 are masses in kg and r is a distance in m.	LHS: $F\,[kg\,m\,s^{-2}] = [N]$ RHS $[N\,m^2\,kg^{-2}] \times$ [kg] $\times$ [kg] $\div$ [m] $= [N\,m^2] \div [m] = [N\,m]$.	No – there is an extra [m] from somewhere. In fact the bottom term r should be squared.
$\dfrac{dp}{dr} = \dfrac{\rho u^2}{r}$ where p is pressure in $kg\,m^{-1}\,s^{-2}$ (also known as Pascals, Pa), r is a distance in m, ρ is a density in $kg\,m^{-3}$ and u is a velocity with units $m\,s^{-1}$	LHS: $\dfrac{dp}{dr}$ $[kg\,m^{-1}\,s^{-2}] \div [m] = [kg\,m^{-2}\,s^{-2}]$ RHS: $\dfrac{\rho u^2}{r}$ [1] $\times$ [$kg\,m^{-3}$] [$m^2\,s^{-2}$] $\div$ [m] $= [kg\,m^{-1}\,s^{-2}] \div [m] = [kg\,m^{-2}\,s^{-2}]$	Yes

Formula	Working	Formula appears correct? (Yes/No)
$T = 2\pi \sqrt{\dfrac{l}{g}}$ where T is a period in seconds, l is a length in metres and g is the acceleration due to gravity in ms^{-2}.	LHS: T [s] RHS: $2\pi \sqrt{\dfrac{l}{g}}$ $[1] \times \left[\sqrt{\dfrac{[m]}{[ms^{-2}]}}\right] = \left[\sqrt{\dfrac{1}{s^{-2}}}\right] = \left[\sqrt{s^2}\right] = [s]$	Yes
$y = A\sin(\omega t + kx)$ where y is a distance [m], A is a distance [m], ω is an angular velocity [rad s^{-1}], t is a time [s], k has dimensions [m^{-1}] and x is a distance [m].	RHS: ωt [s^{-1}] $\times$ [s] = [1] $\qquad kx$ [m^{-1}] $\times$ [m] = [1] so same dimensions means OK to add terms and both terms dimensionless means OK to take sine of that sum – and answer will also be dimensionless. Therefore RHS has dimensions [m] $\times$ [1] = [m] LHS: y [m]	Yes
$V = V_0 (1 - e^{-\frac{1}{RC}})$ where V and V_0 are voltages, R is a resistance and C is a capacitance.	RHS: RC [m^2 kg s^{-3} A^{-2}] $\times$ [s^4 A^2 m^{-2} kg^{-1}] = [s] and $-\dfrac{1}{RC}$ = [s^{-1}] So something is wrong already, because we can't raise e to a power that has dimensions. In fact the correct formula is $V = V_0 (1 - e^{-\frac{t}{RC}})$ so then $\dfrac{-t}{RC}$ has dimensions [s] $\div$ [s] = [1] and it is then valid to find $e^{-\frac{t}{RC}}$. The answer to that part has dimensions of [1] so it can be subtracted from a number (again dimensions of [1]) and multiplied by a voltage to give dimensions of volts. The RHS and LHS have dimensions of [V].	No

Reference

- National Physical Laboratory website: http://www.npl.co.uk/server.php?show=nav.364 [last accessed 16 September 2008].

Index

Index

Index

Index